ANGLES OF VISION

ANGLES
OF
VISION

A MEMOIR OF MY LIVES

PHILIP M.
KLUTZNICK

WITH SIDNEY HYMAN

Chicago • Ivan R. Dee • 1991

Library of Congress Cataloging-in-Publication Data:
Klutznick, Philip M., 1907–
Angles of Vision : a memoir of my lives / Philip M. Klutznick with
Sidney Hyman.
p.   cm.
Includes index.
ISBN 0-929587-64-2 (acid-free paper)
1. Klutznick, Philip M., 1907–   . 2. Jews—United States—
Biography. 3. Statesmen—United States—Biography. 4. Real estate
developers—United States—Biography. 5. Jews—United States—
Politics and government. 6. B'nai B'rith International—Biography.
I. Hyman, Sidney. II. Title.
E184.J5K58 1991
973'.0492402—dc20
[B]   91-6633

To Ethel, My Wife

Her children arise up, and call her blessed,
her husband also, and he praiseth her.
—Proverbs 31:28

Foreword

Goethe once remarked that "three things are to be looked for in a new building: that it stand in the right place, that it be securely founded, and that it be successfully executed." Without pressing the analogy too far, something like these three elements may be looked for in this memoir. They are: whether it has a respectable place among books about specific Jewish concerns and those of the larger American society; whether it deals with issues whose roots run deep in common experiences; and whether the public meaning of the personal episodes comes through loud and clear, like sound compressed in the narrow passage of a trumpet.

In the course of a long life, I have been in the thick of contests on private and public fronts. A summing up of their results would show some successes along with compromises, frustrations, and failures. More than a few times, in the heat of conflict, my private mood, if given voice, would be like that of the French polemicist who warned a rival, "I will argue with you as long as I can, and I will then plunge my rapier into you as far as I can." Nonetheless, it would be false to my afterthoughts if this memoir took shape as a weapon fashioned to strike back at my adversaries in years past, to even the score.

I am not prepared to scatter goodwill—amoral and apolitical—in all directions. I believe with the prophets that there are proper objects of anger as there are of love. Yet in treating individuals with whom I was in personal contention, I hope the picture drawn, while not lacking in passion, will be a fair one. In particular, at points where I take the reader behind the scenes of major conflicts and lay bare what would not be known to him simply from a reading of the newspapers, I hope I have respected the right of my adversaries to their own humanity, to judge cases and controversies from their own perspective, and to press their cause in a forthright manner.

Portions of this memoir cover more than eight decades in which the existence of Jewish communities in different lands was put at risk—fatally so in some places. Midway in those decades, the rebirth of the state of Israel and its trials profoundly altered the tone and focus of Jewish life in other lands. Then, starting in early 1991, the fallout from the war in the Persian Gulf enveloped the state of Israel, to test its capacity to be the author of its own destiny. Long before that new test became clear, I joined others in advocating proposals which I believed would promote the long-range security and development of Israel among its Arab neighbors in the Middle East. Alternative proposals no doubt will be forthcoming in the aftermath of the fighting. But I fervently hope that the peace that follows will not be like the one which in earlier years recalled the anguished cry of Isaiah, "In peace is my bitterest bitterness."

My association with Sidney Hyman in the preparation of this memoir has been not an "as-told-to" relationship but an authentic collaboration. Sidney is a noted scholar, author, and editor whose books about aspects of power have been widely published in both the academic and popular press. He has been able to fill in gaps in my own knowledge by drawing on the biographies he has written of some men who figure in my memoir, as well as his intimate work with them in a government context. Of equal importance, his formative years as the first-generation child of an Orthodox Jewish family in a small town in the Midwest, and the stages of his Americanization process, were strikingly similar to my own. At times he would literally draw on his own experiences to reconstruct what happened to me.

It was understood from the start that Sidney would have full access to all documents in my files. But in addition, in our many conversations there was a shared sense of purpose and interest in discovering the mainsprings behind particular actions, a common willingness to face up to hard questions, and a recognition that the answers to some of these questions would determine the credibility of the memoir as a whole. Commenting on the nature of our collaboration, Sidney remarked that it corresponded to the sense of three terms familiar to Jewish tradition. "We passed," he said, "from *diaspora* (a wide wandering over the possible terrain of the memoir) to *kibbutz* (a gathering of themes and materials) to *aliyah* (a going up in quest for meaning)."

We have both incurred debts to individuals who have been especially helpful in the preparation of this memoir. My two secretaries, Rita Svetlik and Patricia Kelly, always knew where things were buried and were traffic managers for the flow of documents, appointments, and manuscript drafts. Max Baer read and corrected successive drafts of the manuscript, and Bernard Simon and Michael Neiditch offered pointed editorial suggestions. Sidney Hyman's friend, Harold Grinspoon, drew timely attention to certain critical gaps while Newton Minow was the source of indispensable information about various events touched on in the text. Not least of all, we are in debt to Ivan Dee, whose personal attention to the manuscript was something rare among present-day publishers. His judgment helped us to winnow the wheat from the chaff in the editing of the text.

P.M.K.

Chicago
January 1991

Contents

ANGLES OF VISION

1 □ The Turning Point

The passing years have revealed the meaning of things hidden by the days. In times past I meant to retrace the steps that led me into the practice of law in Omaha and from there into other work—in peacetime public housing, as U.S. commissioner of defense public housing, as a private builder of new towns and regional shopping centers, as president of the International B'nai B'rith, as United States Ambassador to the United Nations Economic and Social Council, as president of the World Jewish Congress, as Secretary of Commerce under President Jimmy Carter, and as an appointee of seven U.S. presidents in all, beginning with Franklin D. Roosevelt. I also meant to retrieve what I thought as I moved between tasks centered in the American Jewish community and those centered in the larger American society. "When I am in Jerusalem," said Josephus, the Jewish historian, military commander, Roman citizen, and friend of the emperor Vespasian, "I long for Rome, and when I am in Rome, I long for Jerusalem." Perhaps some such ambivalence was true in my case as well.

My intentions, however, produced nothing more than a slender book entitled *No Easy Answers*—an essay about Jewish voluntary organizations in the United States. The text, as published in 1961, was a third less than what I had read in galley proofs on the eve of my appointment to the U.S. permanent mission at the United Nations and ambassador to its Economic and Social Council. The parts cut at the insistence of the State Department contained references to the Middle East, and it was feared that their publication would complicate my dealings with Arab and other delegations at the U.N.

I continued to believe that aspects of my personal experience might be of interest and perhaps instructive to assorted readers. There were, however, two reasons why I settled for *No Easy Answers*: it was still too early to try to "memorialize" myself, and I was still too close to events which I had witnessed from the "inside." Sometime in the future would be a better time.

That sometime is now.

This does not mean that I am as detached from the cross-currents of life as an anthropologist studying primitives. But at my present age, when competitive personal ambitions are a thing of the past, I am better placed to pay a decent respect to the integrity of words, to call things by their right names, to admit to gross errors of judgment I have made in the past, to render to others the honors that are due them, to trace the links between causes and effects, and to distinguish, as the Talmud recommends, between arguments worth having for the "sake of heaven" and those which have no purpose except as expressions of bombast and bluster. I also believe I am better armed to wrestle with questions that haunt any reflective memoir—questions of fate and freedom, determinism and chance, God's will and man's choice.

[II]

Of the many turning points in my life, some were due more to the accident of having been in the right place at the right time than to any calculated plans. Yet it seems right to start this memoir not with the phrase "I was born" but with a meeting I attended in the White House in June 1945. I was thirty-eight years old, happily married for fifteen years to Ethel Riekes, and the father of three children.

The meeting was a kind of continental divide in my experience. On the one side of the divide, the governmental post I held at the time capped the formative events of my life. On the other side, the consequences of that meeting eventually led to my roles in mounting large-scale private building projects—a new town, followed by many regional shopping centers, mini-towns, and towns within towns. Further, the income from these projects enabled me in midlife sharply to reduce the attention I had to give to purely business matters. Aside from an aversion to ostentatious displays, I now had sufficient assets to provide for my family, and was secure for having enough. I was spared the need to make what Winston Churchill, in his profile of Lord Balfour, called "the kinds of compromises, increasing under modern conditions, between an entirely dispassionate outlook upon affairs, and daily bread." I could devote the greater part of my time to actions in the public realm—to government service, to the concerns of private associations such as the Committee for Economic Development, to the interests of the American Jewish community, and to the complex economic needs and political problems of the state of Israel.

[III]

The June 1945 meeting in the White House, which fell two months after President Roosevelt's death, was on an issue important to the shape of the postwar world. In Europe at the time, what had been Nazi Germany was digging its way out of rubble. In the Pacific, U.S. and Allied forces still faced bitter fighting, but it seemed only a matter of time before Japan would be forced to surrender. The prospective end of the war also outlined a domestic need whose urgency explained the identity of the sixteen men whom President Truman had called to the White House. All were directly or indirectly involved in the federal government's housing programs. I was one of these, being the commissioner of the Federal Public Housing Authority, a wartime post to which I had been appointed by President Roosevelt.

Starting the meeting, President Truman repeated what some of us had heard him stress before. There were, he said, twelve million veterans who had been away from their families, whether overseas or still in training camps in the United States. He meant to release them as quickly as possible from the armed forces once the military victory in sight was secured. Housing must be available for those with families, for those who wanted to go to work, and for those who would take advantage of the educational provisions of the new GI Bill of Rights proposed by Franklin Roosevelt in his 1944 State of the Union Message.

President Truman then recalled what he and many other veterans with families had experienced when they were demobilized after the end of World War I. The veterans were marched down boulevards and main streets in victory parades and were given their discharge papers—but after that very little was done to ease their transition to civilian life. In his own case, he had difficulty finding a home for his wife Bess and their infant daughter Margaret. Countless veterans were left to shift for themselves in an economy in which rampant inflation was followed by an economic collapse more precipitate than the one at the start of the 1930s. The cynicism born of the contrast between the wartime vision of a promised better world and the distress which many veterans experienced personally in 1919–1920 prompted many Americans to reject Woodrow Wilson's vision of a League of Nations as the cornerstone for a peaceful world order.

The president stressed his resolve to prevent the onset of any such cynicism that might shatter the hope that the United States would take the lead in the creation of the United Nations. He agreed with the accent President Roosevelt had placed on the connection between "security at home" and a secure world order. Most immediately, housing was central to any movement by veterans back into channels of peacetime life. Everywhere in the nation, however, there were acute housing shortages whose causes were layered one on another. During the depression of the 1930s few people could afford to build homes, though New Deal measures such as the FHA and the Federal Home Loan Insurance program for savings and loan associations were meant to spur private home construction. Subsequent defense and war needs drew massive amounts of material and labor away from ordinary home construction. The resources available for housing—built either by private developers or by government public housing authorities—were confined mainly to the housing of war workers in defense-impacted areas. Yet in the fifteen years between 1930 and 1945, the U.S. population grew from 123 million to 145 million—a net increase of 22 million people who thus exerted added pressures on the housing supply.

After sketching this familiar picture in broad strokes, President Truman made the rounds of the men grouped before him and asked what the government agency of each could do to help meet the urgent need for postwar housing when building materials would again be available. The administrator of the FHA noted that his agencies did not build houses. All they did was to insure housing finance. It would take developers from twelve months to two years to plan and secure the financing necessary to generate significant housing under the FHA program. The chairman of the Home Loan Bank Board, when asked the same question, made a similar projection. "Well, Phil," the president said when he got around to me, "what can the Federal Public Housing Authority do that would be helpful?"

[IV]

My personal relationship with Harry S Truman started in Kansas City, Missouri, my birthplace, where the first political speech I ever made was in support of his 1922 candidacy for county judge of Jackson County, an administrative post. I was fifteen years old at the time, and the meeting where I exhorted the audience to vote for Truman had been organized by my father who was working to elect him.

Truman, of course, had more substantial support than that of a Jewish youth, a "star" debater bent on exhibiting his forensic talents before a captive audience. He had the backing of the Pendergast machine in Kansas City. Despite this connection, Truman's personal honesty was never questioned, though some local people repeated a gossipy story about how he was later chosen as the Democratic nominee for U.S. Senator from Missouri. In 1934, he supposedly had asked Pendergast for a local office that paid about ten thousand dollars annually in fees, but the Missouri boss protested that Truman lacked the qualifications for that lucrative post. Instead he offered to make him the candidate for U.S. senator, which carried a salary of ten thousand dollars a year. The version I favor, though lacking in charm, is that after Truman was urged by his friends to file for the senatorship, Pendergast agreed to support him because he needed a respectable candidate to defeat the Republican candidate hand-picked by Senator Champ Clark. In 1940 Truman emerged untouched by the scandals that broke the back of the Pendergast machine, and won reelection to the Senate on his merits.

In the mid-1920s I shifted my venue from Kansas City to Lincoln, Nebraska, for a short stay at the University of Nebraska, and then to Omaha where I settled after my graduation from the law school at Creighton University and my marriage to Ethel Reikes. I did not, however, lose contact with Truman. Whenever we were in Kansas City at the same time, I arranged to see him for a talk about "general conditions." In later years, and especially after the spring of 1941 when I moved to Washington because I had been drawn into the defense housing program—while Truman was drawn deeper into his work as the Senate's watchdog of the defense production effort—I was counted among the Kansas City intimates with whom he could relax. Whenever a certain mutual friend came to town who had been in his artillery company during World War I, I was invited to join a poker party in which Truman would also be a player. The pattern extended from his Senate days to his brief tenure as vice president.

As it happened, before the 1945 White House meeting I had asked some of my associates in the Federal Public Housing Authority to conduct experiments on housing conversion. The authority had housed almost a million people nationwide at the height of the war effort, and the experiments I had in view entailed a search for the best methods to reduce temporary houses and barracks so that their material could be used in building temporary housing on new sites such as college campuses. The findings lay behind my response to the president at the White House meeting.

"What my agency could do to help," I said, "is contingent on whether we are free from the constraints of the surplus property act. If we are at liberty to dismantle, crate, ship, and reconstruct the housing without having to get bids on each phase of the work—if we could proceed on a straightforward 'cost-plus' contract basis—I believe we can substantially reduce the elapsed time required by normal private development."

"Give me a definite time," the president insisted.

"I can let you know by tomorrow morning once I consult my staff and make some estimates."

On returning to my office I went to work on the problem with key members of my staff. We knew the location of existing war defense housing and the portions that were soon likely to be surplus. So we proceeded to make "worst-case" estimates of the elapsed time to "deconstruct" a defense housing project, crate its parts, and transport them a hypothetical thousand miles where they would be rebuilt on a new site. One set of estimates assumed that each step of the process would be subject to the usual need for bids. A second set assumed that all stages would be unified and entrusted to a contractor under a cost-plus contract. In the first case, the elapsed time appeared to be at least as twice as long as the second.

The next morning, when I saw President Truman, I explained how the two sets of figures I gave him had been computed. "Well," said the president, "let's go with the cost-plus arrangement." "Mr. President," I said, "I don't want to go to jail." "What do you mean?" he asked.

I explained that the defense public housing contractors we had dealt with were generally honest, as were the men and women who held key posts in my organization of 25,000. But in a program involving hundreds of millions of dollars in public funds, I could not guarantee the top-to-bottom cleanliness of a cost-plus operation. Temptations for tainted deals would always be there. Audits held a year or two after I and my associates had left the government at war's end might bring such deals to light, and I, as the responsible wartime head of the FPHA, could be charged with wrongdoing.

I then suggested a way to reduce such possibilities. The General Accounting Office, instead of waiting a year or so after our job and internal audit were completed, should conduct its audit concurrently with our own. President Truman, on hearing this, at once placed a call to the director of the GAO. Technically, the president was violating the GAO's independent authority. Nonetheless, I heard him say, "I have a young fellow sitting next to me in my office and he doesn't want to go to jail. Please talk to him and see if the GAO can conduct an audit at the same time his agency conducts its internal audit." The director said, "Send the young man over to me now."

When I met the director, I explained the anticipated gains from a program for converting defense public housing to peacetime use on a cost-plus basis for the contractors, but also noted the risk from the standpoint of accountability. The director agreed to conduct a GAO audit simultaneously with ours. The arrangement made possible the speed with which surplus wartime public housing was converted to peacetime use with the maximum cooperation of private contractors.

[V]

The government's $450 million Veterans Temporary Housing program was fully launched by the eve of VJ Day, when I was visited in Washington by Carroll Sweet of Chicago. I had come to know and respect him through his wartime work in the Chicago regional office that issued private housing priorities; Sweet had lately joined Nathan Manilow's construction company in Chicago. Manilow was also someone I had come to know well and favorably as a builder of private defense housing projects in the area. The purpose of Sweet's visit was to ask if private developers could buy demounted sections of defense public housing which my agency was converting into temporary dwellings for veterans. If so, the Manilow Company would use such sections to build homes for GIs on a suitable site—in essence, a GI town.

I noted that our policy prohibited sale of the material to private developers; besides, I would personally oppose using that material to build anything resembling a "GI town." I had visited veterans' villages springing up on college campuses and elsewhere. The housing they provided was better than foxholes and pup tents, but that standard did not fit my idea of what returning veterans deserved. A "GI town"—an excellent idea in itself—ought to be properly conceived, planned, and located. The homes should be built with quality materials and not confined to the reuse of those in the hands of the FPHA. Structures using inferior material should be scrapped as soon as possible. "I would be ashamed," I said to Sweet, "to build a permanent GI village or anything else that way. If you and Nate Manilow want to build a GI town, make it one worthy of the men who served the country so well." That was that.

Like other heads of wartime agencies, I thought I would be free to return to civilian life immediately after VJ Day. But this was not to be. I was approached by an emissary from President Truman with a message to the following effect: The president was grateful that I had stayed at my post in contrast to some executives who left the government soon after FDR died, or immediately after VE Day. He had no right to "impose" on me, but he hoped that as a "personal favor" to him I would continue a while longer to serve as commissioner of the FPHA, to oversee the program for converting wartime to peacetime public housing. I was also needed in that role because of the close working relationship I had developed with Senator Robert Taft, whose legislative support was central to the government's postwar public housing program.

All this led to the "bite." The president, said the messenger, was under fierce pressure to appoint someone he didn't want as commissioner of the FPHA. If I stayed on, there would be no vacancy to fill, and a distasteful appointment could be avoided. The request, couched in some such terms on behalf of a friend who happened to be the president of the United States, was one I could not readily refuse. I agreed to stay on as commissioner, but only for a limited period.

[VI]

Soon I was visited again in Washington by Carroll Sweet, and this time Nathan Manilow was with him. The pair said they wished to build a new veterans' town from the ground up out of quality material as it became available. My wartime role in the creation of defense-related communities or of entire towns could be put to peacetime use. Would I join them in the town-building venture they had in mind?

Like other administrators of wartime agencies, I had already received attractive offers from the private sector. One entailed a partnership in a major New York law firm. Another offered the presidency and a stock interest in a firm that would manufacture prefabricated housing. The salary alone was attractive after five years of family life on a fixed government income and a drain on my private resources—while my children had increased from two to three. There was also the prospect of returning to my Omaha law firm in which I still had a partner-ownership interest.

I told Manilow and Sweet that I might be interested in joining them if what they meant to build was a *town,* not just another housing project or suburban development. I recognized that building a town would be like building defense-related communities. In addition to the construction of houses, it would require utilities, roads, a sewage system, water supply, schools, shopping facilities, churches, and recreational facilities. Yet building a town as a private venture posed problems fundamentally different from those encountered in government-built towns—problems, for example, regarding land acquisition, financing, cost overruns, marketing, and timing. Another key difference was not to be overlooked. People who lived in towns built and operated by the government during the war might be consulted by town managers on matters of common interest. But a privately built town could become a vital *community*—not just a collection of houses—only if the inhabitants fully participated in the decisions affecting their common lives. This meant two things. First, the town must be incorporated at the earliest possible hour. Second, and more explicitly, the inhabitants, through their right of suffrage, must form and control local governing units such as a village or city council, school board, police and fire departments, and taxing agencies. The alternative would be for the new town to be annexed to an existing small town. Apart from these cautionary notes, I said I was convinced that if a new town were wisely planned (and much could be learned from the "Greenbelt towns" built during the prewar years of the Roosevelt presidency), the returns would not be limited to the pleasures of altruism. The returns would be fair profits to the private builders.

None of this comprised a personal commitment to Manilow and Sweet, but the chance that I might join their venture induced them to scour the Chicago metropolitan area for a site on which to build a new veterans' town. They soon called me from Chicago to ask if I would be coming their way in the near future. They had narrowed their search to two possible town sites and wanted me to assess their merits. I was due to make a short trip to Omaha, so I agreed to stop off in Chicago to look at what had drawn their interest.

When I joined the pair in Chicago, the first site they took me to was twenty-eight miles south of the city. It consisted of an abandoned golf course, some farmland, and a sizable swamp. Manilow had an option on part of the land but believed he could secure options on additional acreage. If a new town were built on the site, the necessary land could be assembled at the relatively low cost (at that time) of $500 an acre. Of equal importance was nearby public transportation, the Illinois Central railroad. This would give commuters fairly swift access to places of work along the north-south axis of the railroad—steel mills, manufacturing plants, wharves, warehouses, and the University of Chicago as well as the offices, stores, museums, theaters, and governmental centers in Chicago's Loop.

The second site was in a pleasant setting near Wheaton in DuPage County to the west of Chicago. The area, however, had two physical drawbacks. For one thing, the estimated cost of assembling the land was approximately $2,500 an acre; the capital used merely to buy the land would increase both the price of homes or of rental property, and would also increase the amount of capital needed for the actual construction of the new town. Also, the site lacked adequate public transportation, and super-highways linking employment centers in a major city such as Chicago and its outlying residential districts had not yet been built. As between the two sites, my own preference was for the one south of Chicago.

"Phil," Manilow now said to me, "if I were to buy enough of this land, would you serve as president of a company that would organize and manage the construction of a GI town on it?" He would advance the first seed money for the enterprise. But for my work as president I would be offered half the common stock of the company plus an annual salary of $25,000—a sum well below the salary I was offered to accept the presidency of the firm that was to manufacture prefabricated housing. I repeated my interest in his proposal but mentioned my promise to President Truman to remain in my government post for a set period. When I was free to return to private life, I would give Manilow a definite yes or no.

In the spring of 1946, when I was ready to leave government service, I met in Chicago with my brother-in-law Sam Beber, who had been my law partner in Omaha. Also present was Sam's brother David, my contemporary and now a partner in the same law firm. After two days of weighing the pros and cons of my future, I finally said to the pair, "I've now been away from Omaha for six years, and I don't think I can go back to practicing law in that city. I want to do this town thing."

"Well then," Sam said, "you can keep your name with the law firm in Omaha, and David can open up and be in charge of a branch office in Chicago. You can practice law part time out of the Chicago office while you give the remainder of your time to the town-building project."

After more talk back and forth, I agreed to devote "part time" to the Chicago branch of the law office. That's how the die was cast. When the law office was eventually opened, it was located near the offices of American Community Builders, the corporation formed to build the new town. At that turning point in my life, the foresight of all the biblical prophets combined could not have envisioned what lay ahead for me—except for the fact that from early youth I had had a genetic urge to "shine," to make the most of split-second opportunities, to challenge the conventional wisdom of "authorities," to have a taste for the risks of innovation, and to act on my own responsibility.

2 □ On Coming into the World

A memoir provides a man with a "sense of otherwise"—with a sense of how different the course of his life might have been but for some stroke of chance or luck, or the impact of an unexpected encounter. I have often wondered what my life—if any—would have been like subject to three "ifs." If my parents, as Zionists, had been spurred by the 1905 Kishinoff pogrom to join the *aliyah* from eastern Europe to Palestine which would then have been my birthplace. If my parents, and I with them, were like the millions of Jews who had stayed frozen in place in eastern Europe because they preferred the known physical hardships of their setting, and their ties to the graves of their forebears, to the uncertainties of a migration into the unknown. Or if my parents, as part of the mass migration of two million eastern European Jews who came to the United States between 1880 and the start of World War I, had settled in the ghetto of New York City which would then have been my birthplace.

All things weave themselves into a single whole, but the life I knew was spun from the strands of different chance factors.

[II]

My parents did not spend their formative years in a *shtetl*—the generic name for the villages of eastern Europe where Jews comprised virtually the total population. Both were reared in factory towns located on the main railroad line that ran from Warsaw to Saint Petersburg (now Leningrad). In the case of my father, Morris, the place was Grodno, a trading center for the nearby breeders of livestock as well as a site for distilleries and factories producing woolen cloth, leather goods, and tobacco. Access to leather may have had something to do with my father's early vocation as a cobbler. My mother, Minnie, was originally from a *forfort* (suburb) of Bialystock, the capital city of the province by the same name. Like Grodno, but on a larger scale, Bialystock was an agricultural center and factory town, besides being a leading center for Jewish culture.

The *shtetl* Jew, surrounded on all sides by specifically Jewish concerns, did not worry at length about the world's realities that had agitated the realm of the tsar since the 1830s. The *shtetl* Jew's public politics were pinned on the hope that the Messiah—the only diplomat Jews had until the creation of the state of Israel—might some day arrive and lead all Jews back to their point of origin in Eretz Yisrael. Meanwhile, what engaged his attention was the intense internal politics of the *shul* (synagogue), or his bread-and-butter relationships with Isel the timber merchant, Berl the flour and iron dealer, Herschel the carpenter and furniture maker, David the cobbler, Moti the furrier, Yacob-Schmuel the *shochet* (ritual slaughterer), Yudle the tax collector, Zalman the matchmaker, Jossel the mystic, and Hava and Hunda the lunatics—the saying being that "a *shtetl* without a lunatic is not much of a *shtetl*."

Jews, such as my parents, who lived in a factory town could neither know the all-encompassing Jewish reality associated with *shtetl* life nor escape daily reminders of their minority status amid a non-Jewish minority. They must learn at an early age how to come to terms with the non-Jewish majority—a point which anticipated the differences between Jewish immigrants who settled in the ghetto of New York City and those who settled in communities such as Kansas City, Omaha, Des Moines, and South Bend, spread over the hinterland of the United States. Moreover, to a significant number of Jews who lived in the factory towns of eastern Europe, the politics of the tsarist realm *did* matter and were hotly debated within the Jewish community. They led to ideologies and political alignments which immigrant Jewish artisans would duplicate on American soil—as was true of an uncle of mine, a carpenter by trade, who was an ardent social democrat and remained one in Kansas City even when he was the successful owner of a furniture store.

Most Jews such as my parents who lived in the factory towns, however, shared with the *shtetl* Jew an attachment to an idealized version of Zionism, without too much thought about the political means by which a Jewish homeland could actually be attained in Eretz Yisrael. It would have been hard for any of them to imagine a future time when contemporary Israelis would tell a bittersweet fable about a pious Jew who raised his voice in a prayer in a Tel Aviv synagogue, to say, "For two thousand years, O Lord, we have prayed to Thee for the return of Thy people to Eretz Yisrael, but why did it have to happen in my day? All we have now are *big problems!*"

In addition to their attachment to an idealized version of Zionism, most Jews in the factory towns shared with the *shtetl* Jew the various tenets and practices of orthodoxy. They believed in one God who was transcendent, who *had* to be, and who was the source of all created things. They knew what to expect in their earthly life and were equally certain of what awaited them in *Olem Habah* (the world to come). Fortified by such certainties, they could never feel like outcasts despite the hardships of their Diaspora situation. Because they had only limited opportunities to earn a living, they were not likely to get ulcers worrying if they had made the right career choice. That was something for the emancipated Jews of Vienna to experience.

[III]

I don't know how my parents met. Was theirs an arranged marriage as was common in their day? Was it a case of romantic love fulfilled? Children of my generation never asked such questions, nor was information volunteered.

My father was undersized in physical stature. When I was of an age to understand something about him, I realized that he was not a master of classical Jewish learning. He could read Hebrew, could read and write Yiddish, could recite by heart some passages from the Bible as well as the sayings of Jewish sages. But he never had the makings of a *yeshiva bucher*, a full-time student whose promise in mastering talmudic tracts warranted an investment by the Jewish community in his upkeep so that he might continue his studies without being distracted by the mundane need to earn a living. Like other eastern European Jews of his generation, my father stood in respectful awe of yeshiva talmudic learning, and he counted it a duty even when he was in the United States to contribute to the upkeep of the famous Slabodka Yeshiva in Russ-Poland. But like other Jewish artisans, he was more at home at the folk level of Yiddish culture, with its stories, plays, music, ironic laughter, and fantasies, where man equalizes the distance between himself and God, and corrects God on the error of *His* ways.

In other respects I came to know my father as a man with a sunlit personality who was concerned with the well-being of others. He could have been a significant entrepreneur because he was alive to opportunities as they presented themselves, but he was not satisfied merely to make a living. Among other things, he led a group of Orthodox Jews in Kansas City in a health benefit society whose members could mutually aid one another. The synagogue was at the core of his life, and if it had not been for the fact that he had to provide for his family, he would probably have spent all of his time there. In later years, when his children were grown, he not only lived in and for the synagogue but actually died there of a heart attack. Even in his strained English he could stir me when he spoke from a public platform in support of a "cause," and in Yiddish he was in many ways incomparable. All this, in time, would leave a deep imprint on my own psyche.

My mother suffered from the educational limitations common among Jewish women in eastern Europe. In contrast to men, the schooling of women seldom went beyond the acquisition of functional literacy—though in this respect they were at least emancipated from the darkness in which the mass of Christian women in eastern Europe lived out their unlettered lives. My mother could read Yiddish but could only recite from memory some of the Hebrew liturgical prayers. In the United States she never learned how to read or write English.

This fact, however, did not obscure a larger reality which was also common among Orthodox Jewish women from eastern Europe. There must have been many instances when a wife, glancing over at the sleeping head of the husband on the pillow next to her own, knew she could think rings around that head but dare not reveal her natural superiority in public. What happened in the privacy of the home—and it was the real-life source of jokes about the domineering "Jewish mother"—was another matter. In the privacy of the home, Mama ruled by guile, by strategies, by forward planning, by the exercise of natural authority, or by the fact that Papa was often "on the road."

When I was old enough to understand such matters, I realized that my mother was the organizing brains and managerial head of the family—just as my wife Ethel would be when we were parents of a family of five children. It was my mother who gave the

definitive commands—Do This, Do That, Don't Do This or That.
It was my mother who pulled her family of four dependent
children safely through some very hard times. She set the tone for
a warm, intimate family life and extended her embrace beyond her
family to help people in want. There is no question in my own
mind that I absorbed something of my father's love of communal
work and my mother's practical sense regarding close-in material
needs, which must be attended to as well.

[IV]

Among eastern European Jews the *landsmanschaft* ranked alongside the synagogue as the first unit of community organization in
the life of the immigrant. A particular *landsmanschaft* society was
comprised of people who had lived in the immigrant's *shtetl*, town,
or *gebernia* (province) and who were the first to provide the new
arrival with companionship and material assistance.

When the bite of poverty and the trauma of the Kishinoff
pogrom in 1905 induced my parents to migrate to the United
States, the letters they received from blood relatives, personal
friends, and from other landsmen from the Grodno and Bialystock
areas fixed their thoughts on Kansas City, Missouri, as the place to
which they would immigrate. I have often wondered what it was
like for a young couple such as my father and mother, with a very
young daughter on their hands, to conclude that they must leave
their native setting and embark on a journey into the unknown.
Would the embrace at leave-taking be the last time members of the
same family would physically see and touch one another? I can only
imagine that the dead-end physical aspects of Jewish life in eastern
Europe made the pain of immigration the preferred alternative.

Many national Jewish philanthropies, underwritten in some
cases by German Jews who had "made it" in the United States,
actively helped Jewish immigrants bound for America. Perhaps the
best known was the Hebrew Immigration Aid Society (HIAS), a
philanthropy always featured in writings about Jewish immigration
and immigrant life in the United States which focus mainly on
Jews in large cities. Other philanthropies were often overlooked,
perhaps because they worked outside the line of vision of
metropolitan-based Jewish writers. Among these was the Baron de
Hirsch Fund, whose specific object, shared by the Jewish Agricultural Society, was to settle immigrant Jews from eastern Europe on

farmlands in the United States. Another national philanthropy, the Industrial Removal Society, tried to divert immigrant Jews from metropolitan centers into the interior of the country. Within a few years after the start of the 1900s, for example, it helped settle six thousand Jews from eastern Europe—many of whom were artisans in all the trades—in fifty-one Missouri towns alone. It was the Industrial Removal Society that aided the immigration of my parents and their first child, Helen, on their voyage to Kansas City, not by way of Ellis Island but by way of an offbeat landing in Galveston, Texas.

My parents and Helen settled in Kansas City in an enclave of other eastern European Jews comprised of artisans, small merchants, peddlers, and junk dealers. Their common lives were a world apart from the eminent German Jewish families who had settled in Kansas City and St. Louis before the Civil War and had played a significant role in the economic, political, and cultural life of the state as a whole.

[V]

By 1907, the year of my birth—which coincided with the onset of a severe nationwide money panic and depression—my father had somehow managed literally to lift himself by his bootstraps. He was no longer a cobbler. He was an entrepreneur, an owner of a shoe store where he also repaired shoes—though he would later move on to own a furniture store and then a grocery store. A small flat above the shoe store, the first home I can recall, was located in a neighborhood where black and white families met along the lines of a common frontier they seldom crossed. A second family home, a modest cottage, dated from the time when my father's small business grew and the children in the family increased to three with the birth of a second daughter, Esther. A second son, Arthur, came later.

The location of that first home was almost always referred to on occasions in later life when I received some sort of award. The person charged with presenting the award would observe—as Senator Charles Percy did when he introduced me to the Senate committee that considered my appointment by President Carter to be the Secretary of Commerce—that I was "still living above the store." The reference was to my seventy-second-floor apartment on top of the Water Tower complex which my company planned and built in the 1970s, with consequences that changed the character of a substantial part of Chicago.

3 □ Shul and School

I was an undersized and chubby child with a prominent birthmark on my forehead. The birthmark was later partially reduced by surgery, but my weight in proportion to my height was another matter. I ballooned in girth to a point where I weighed 212 pounds by the time I was ready for my first year in college, though lifesaving relief came soon afterward.

Being fat, I was so slow of foot that I could never hope to make a team in a competitive sport. I played tennis but could not run fast enough to return a ball when it was lobbed over my head or landed some distance from my feet. Sports were neither encouraged nor understood by immigrant parents from eastern Europe. My own parents were no exception to this general rule. Sports to them was a waste of time. A child studied. A child helped out in a store. A child helped with household chores. But sports for the sake of the body or simply for the joy of play had little place in their scheme of things.

My parents' idea of outdoor recreation, which I also favored as a child, was to go to Swope Park in Kansas City with their children, their kinsmen and friends, and then spend the afternoon eating and talking. They never insisted that I slim down. My mother's constant refrain, like that of most Jewish mothers of eastern European background, was "Ess, ess, my kinde" (Eat, eat, my child). I did more than stoke food into my stomach with the blessings of my mother. I was vaguely aware that only the righteous need not fear thunderbolts, but when I had a few pennies to spare, I would sneak into a bakery shop near my father's store and buy the sweet rolls I favored—though they were made with lard, an ingredient banned by Jewish dietary laws. In addition, I was powerfully drawn to the nonkosher hot dogs sold in Electric Park. These I also stealthily consumed when I had the purchase price.

In a retrospect of later years, I told myself that I felt no special pain as a child because I was fat. I certainly was not denied parental love on that account, nor devoted attention by my teachers. The fact is, however, that as a child I simply lacked the self-discipline necessary to eat less. When I eventually slimmed down, I must have been disgusted by memories of the time when I was full of waddle; I am told by my brother Arthur that I tried to collect and destroy all the photographs of how I appeared as a youth.

[II]

The glowing memories of my formative years are largely drawn from two overlapping realms of experience. The first was the Orthodox *shul* to which my parents and some of my relatives belonged, including those who arrived in Kansas City after my father had saved enough from his slim income to help pay for their passage. The second realm was comprised of the public schools I attended—Woodland Grammar School, Morse Grammar School, and Manual High School.

The spacious name of the *shul,* Beth Hamedrosh Hagodol (the large house of learning), did not match its physical aspects. The place probably seated no more than a few hundred worshipers. Yet the importance which the *shul* later gained in my own thoughts transcended its size. I came to see that Beth Hamedrosh Hagodol was a vital school where one could learn much about "authority" in voluntary organizations and about "participatory democracy" —matters of concern to me in later years when I was the head of voluntary organizations that were national or international in scope.

In the United States these days it is common for a synagogue or temple to contain secular as well as religious features. Almost all, for example, have a "hall" for "lectures" with an attached kitchen where meals can be prepared for social gatherings. Almost all have a library, and some have a gymnasium and swimming pool. Many are managed by a full-time "administrator," as part of a broader trend in which the direction of national Jewish organizations in the United States has passed from lay leaders to a professional staff. Classes in schools attached to a synagogue or temple are often taught by academically trained teachers, and the tools they use, say, for the teaching of Hebrew, may include computers. In fact, when I was president of the Memorial Foundation for Jewish

Culture, one of the worldwide programs we introduced was the use of modern technology in the Jewish learning process.

None of this was even remotely true of Beth Hamedrosh Hagodol. The place during my formative years had no facilities for "secular" use. The separation of the women from the men, mandated by Orthodoxy, was achieved with a movable lattice which divided the floor of the sanctuary; later, in a different structure, there was a balcony for the women and for those boys who had not yet been bar mitzvah. No literature was in sight except for biblical texts and prayer books which were the common property of the members. The prayer books themselves, through extended use, were often held together only by a thread, their pages brittle with age.

The *heder* (elementary school) was located in the dimly lit basement of the *shul*. Classes, which began soon after public school hours ended, were held throughout the workweek except on Friday, though they were resumed on Sunday morning. The *melamed* (teacher) was a Russian Jew who had lost an arm as a conscripted soldier in some irrelevant war for the tsar. Untrained in pedagogy, he taught by rote. A teacher by courtesy title only, he did not hesitate to use the switch which he held in his one good arm to drive students "onward" when they faltered.

Small congregations such as Beth Hamedrosh Hagodol could not afford to maintain a *rov* (rabbi) full time. Moreover, because each Jewish congregation was equal to all others in authority, each, like Beth Hamedrosh Hagodol, was very much on its own. In the absence of a hierarchy, as in many Christian denominations, the congregation governed itself according to its own taste and temper. When incumbent officers incurred the displeasure of the members, which was not a hard thing to do, the way they were removed from office had none of the face-saving devices common among present-day organizations. Officers could be "shouted out" and "thrown out." *Roberts Rules of Order* were never invented in a *shul*. If my own father was not similarly assailed when he served as treasurer of the *shul* for many years, no doubt the reason was because no one in the congregation coveted his thankless job.

When our family went to the Beth Hamedrosh Hagodol for a service, I sat next to my father. My sister Helen sat next to my mother in the "women's section." There was no such thing as "children's services" based on a simplified version of the liturgy. In Beth Hamedrosh Hagodol in those days there was only one liturgy, and children as well as adults were expected to follow it.

On High Holy Days, when the service droned its way through the extended liturgy, adult members of the congregation could be as restless and noisy as the children. They were too full of the raw surge of life to freeze themselves into attitudes of stained-glass piety. They wandered from seat to seat to gossip, to show off their children or grandchildren, exchange jokes, or discuss the latest installment of a political treatise published in translation in *Der Tageblat* (the conservative Yiddish daily) or *Der Forvertz* (the Yiddish daily favored by social democrats).

An officer of the *shul* might slap down hard on a prayer book in an attempt to restore order, or angrily cry out, "Shaa, shaa, Schtil." On a remembered occasion when this occurred, someone in the free-wheeling congregation who resented the censorship cried back in Yiddish "Shaa yourself! Do you want to turn this *shul* into a church, like a Reform temple?"

My first introduction to *tzedakah* (righteous action) was the blue-and-white *pushke* (alms box) that hung from a wall in our home. Pennies, nickels, dimes, quarters, and sometimes the immense sum of a silver half-dollar would be dropped through a slot into the *pushke* by my parents or by others in the family. There were assorted *pushkes* in the home, but the blue one with the white Star of David on it was earmarked for the Keren Kayemuth, which bought and held in perpetuity the land in Palestine for Jewish settlement.

There was a public as well as a private side to the practice of *tzedakah*. On the eve of any of the High Holy Days, for example, before the services began and it was still permissible for an Orthodox Jew to carry money in his pockets, collection plates were laid out on a table in the foyer of Beth Hamedrosh Hagodol. Each was marked with signs identifying worthy causes, from the purchase of land or the planting of trees in Palestine, to support for the Slabodkah Yeshiva in Poland, to orphanages and hospitals and old people's homes in the United States. I remember my childhood sense of heady munificence when I placed all my pennies in a plate which I chose, or distributed them among a few plates. But I always started with Keren Kayemuth, for even then I was stirred by the vision of a Jewish state. Those pennies in a *tzedakah* plate in the foyer of Beth Hamedrosh Hagodol may have been the remote source of my involvement in assorted fund-raising campaigns where the goals set—especially after the birth of the modern state of Israel—were awesome.

In my Yiddish-speaking home—I learned how to speak Yiddish before I learned how to read my ABC's in English—I was vaguely aware that somewhere "out there" in Kansas City was a breed of Jews different from those in my Orthodox enclave. As the entrenched descendants of the German Jewish immigrants who had settled in Kansas City and elsewhere in Missouri between the 1840s and 1880s, they had embraced "classical" Reform Judaism with its calculated rejection of Zionism and of most of the things which made Orthodox Judaism orthodox.

In my youth I knew nothing about the history of the Reform movement in the United States, and did not as much as step into a Reform temple until I was in high school. At an early age, however, I was made aware of the German Jewish domination of B'nai B'rith, a Jewish fraternal organization begun in 1843 in a café in New York City. The B'nai B'rith lodge in Kansas City did not readily admit eastern European Jews to its membership, though exceptions were made for Jewish doctors and lawyers. Merchants of eastern European origins, such as my father, were virtually barred from membership until a second lodge was formed in Kansas City.

I later learned that the lines drawn between the firmly established German Jews and the eastern European Jews struggling to take root were not unique to Kansas City. Similar divisions in communities elsewhere were often expressed in terms of neighborhoods, though in time local and national leadership roles in Jewish communal affairs passed in large measure from German Jews to eastern European Jews. The things which made for a "Jewish renaissance" in the United States—in scholarship, the natural sciences, belle lettres, the fine arts, the performing arts, and labor relations—would be in large measure the work of the children and grandchildren of eastern European immigrant Jews.

In time also, the American-born sons of parents who belonged to an Orthodox *shul* such as Beth Hamedrosh Hagodol took over the pulpits of Reform temples previously held by the sons of the German Jews. The members they faced in the pews were to an increasing degree the sons and daughters of Orthodox families from eastern Europe who had a mystical homesickness for the remembered "warmth" of the *shul*. Together they would help lead the temples away from the cold touch of "classical" Reform Judaism and toward some of the intimacies associated with features of the Orthodox synagogue. Today Reform and Conservative

Judaism alike are striving to rekindle the warmth associated with the Jewish faith.

[III]

The grammar school I attended was a different place of learning. The headiest of all facts for my parents, as for other immigrant Jews from eastern Europe, was that their children could attend free of charge a state-supported public school. Not only could but *had* to attend in order to stay on the right side of the law. It was far different in the world they left behind with its system of parochial schools, and where access to state-supported public schools, insofar as they existed at all, was a privilege reserved primarily for gentiles; the exceptions made for a handful of Jewish youth generally involved parents who could afford to grease the palm of officials.

There were few dropouts among the Jewish schoolchildren of my own generation and family background in Kansas City. When any of us came home and announced, "Teacher said," the house shook. The teacher was God's vice regent on earth. We would disgrace our parents if we were unruly in class, if we did not turn in our homework on time, if we played hooky or dressed in a slipshod way. We must be freshly scrubbed, and even if the clothes were hand-me-downs with patches, they must be spotlessly clean.

My sister Helen had some difficulty with her schoolwork, but I found my own to be easy. I became a "teacher's pet." A teacher I adored, a Miss Richards, made me a "monitor" in her third-grade class. When I asked what being a monitor implied, she said, "I expect you to help me in my duties during the class and to keep a general eye on what is happening among your fellow students and keep me informed." I was immensely proud of my responsibilities, though I soon learned the price one can pay for being a "monitor" of what other people are doing.

The place of learning was the playground on the day the United States formally entered World War I. A bullying boy, twice my size, was declaiming to my classmates how the United States declaration of war against Germany was a great day for the world. I thought it my duty as a monitor to know all that was going on, so I interrupted his paen to war. What, I asked, was so glorious about war in preference to peace? My question angered him, and he called me a "German lover." This in turn angered me, and with my little fists I went after him. Even at this distance from the event, I wish I could report that I emerged the victor in the fray, but the outcome was hardly in my favor. With his big fists he laid me low with one blow. I may have concluded that in future disputes I had better rely on lawyerlike talking than on a test of physical strength.

I am not certain when I decided I actually wanted to be a lawyer, though it may have been around this time when I joined my father for a visit to his own lawyer. The controversy that prompted the visit may have had something to do with the operation that was supposed to remove the birthmark on my forehead, or it may have been due to a dispute over an automobile accident. My father had managed to buy an automobile, but because he was quite short he had chronic difficulty in seeing clearly what was coming at him or where he was going. Accidents regularly occurred, and there was substantial truth to the time he vehemently protested his innocence, saying, "I tell you I was not at fault! I tell you that because I am an expert on accidents!"

In any event, in the lawyer's office I clearly remember the highly excited way my father inveighed against an injustice, and how the lawyer urbanely placed a cooling hand to my father's overheated manner and calmed him down. None of us at home could have handled my father so deftly when he was agitated. The magic of what I saw in the lawyer's office perhaps convinced me that I must master the secrets of the law.

[IV]

The public school had its painful moments for me as it did for other Jewish children. These occurred primarily as Christmas drew near, when the schools were festooned with Christmas artifacts and the songs sung in assemblies were Christmas carols. But these moments of isolation were far offset by the secular features of the educational process which shaped children of immigrants to be American citizens—or perhaps more accurately, to adhere to America's civil religion on a plane apart from conventional religious sects. They included the pledge of allegiance to the flag at the start of the day and a stand to attention at the end of the day when the flag was being lowered. They included studies focused on the lives of national heroes, and on the background of national holidays such as Thanksgiving, the Fourth of July, and Memorial Day, as well as committing to memory passages from the "American Testament"

—the preamble to the Declaration of Independence, the preamble to the Constitution of the United States, and the Gettysburg Address.

"Auditorium" or "assembly" was a vital aspect of the way the public school trained us for citizenship in a democracy. There we practiced public speaking before an audience of classmates. We were encouraged to state our arguments when we nominated and elected officers to preside over the "auditorium" for a set number of sessions. We were introduced to the elements of *Roberts Rules of Order*—about motions, seconds, amendments, debates, "calling the question," votes—and to other aspects of orderly parliamentary procedure. What we learned in "auditorium" directly influenced the way we managed the various clubs to which we belonged.

The effect, within the sphere of our youthful concerns, attached many of us, as a habit of the heart, to "procedures," to a "rule of law," to the devices of debate as a means for arriving not at absolute truth but at tolerable decisions that made group life possible. The praise I heard for being "quite a talker" after speaking in "auditorium," fed my confidence at an early hour that I *could* communicate *myself* to an audience whenever I was called on to "say something." Here is the dim origin of a reality that recently struck my eye when I reviewed a batch of photographs which amounted to a chronicle of my adult life. Many of the pictures show me standing open-mouthed behind a lectern in the full tilt of a speech.

4 □ A Crisis in My Jewishness

World War I speeded up the process of change in virtually all aspects of American life, including the enfranchisement of women. The physical hazards of ocean travel during the war had reduced to a trickle the flow of America-bound immigrant ships, and the trickle was further reduced when the 1920 immigration act took effect. But there had been major shifts of population within the country as migrant workers, white as well as black, left their roots in the rural South and came north to work in the defense industries. There were now more factories than ever before—along with more slums, greater tensions between the races, and an increase in organized crime when immense profits were discovered in the liquor trade that violated the new Volstead Act. The omnipresent smell of horses was displaced by the smell of gasoline fumes from an ever-increasing number of automobiles in common use—the same automobiles that began to end the age of remoteness in the United States.

To many "nativist" Americans—rural, white, Anglo-Saxon, Protestant—the changes associated with urbanization seemed to threaten an idealized past. Someone was messing up *their* America. The unities of blood, race, religion, language, common memories and experiences—the unities of all the things which were deemed essential behind the word "American"—seemed splintered. It was hard for rural "nativists" to understand that what was going on all around them was not the end of a dream but the beginning of a new synthesis of peoples who had been changing the demographic face of America. The work of synthesis in the *common* interest continued around the clock, day in and day out, like the flow of a river quietly passing, always passing, never the same.

My bar mitzvah, marking my coming of age as a moral agent, coincided with the postwar depression of 1919–1920. Its causes were beyond my grasp, but its effects were clear enough. They could be seen in idle factories, bankruptcies, unemployed veterans, bank failures particularly in rural areas (at a time when there was no depositor insurance), and the flaming crosses of a resurgent Ku Klux Klan. More immediately, I saw how the depression hit my father and some of my Kansas City kinsmen. As my father's small business suffered, there was belt-tightening in the family, and my mother was in firm charge of scarce resources.

Bar mitzvah marked the end of my afterschool Jewish education in the *heder* of Beth Hamedrosh Hagodol. To tell the truth, I felt at the time as though I had been liberated from a Babylonian captivity. At least I felt light-headed when I found I now had free hours after the end of the regular school day.

I could read Hebrew, but I would eventually lose whatever command of the spoken tongue I had gained when I studied under the *melamed* with the switch. As was true of most Jewish boys of my generation, bar mitzvah was the cutoff point in my Jewish education, though what passed as "education" seldom went beyond what a boy needed to know to read a portion of the Pentateuch and the prophets that were part of the bar mitzvah ceremony. Even within the narrow orbit of what comprised the texts we read in *heder*, we were denied access to the kind of scholarship that could have given luminous meanings to various books of the Bible. The conflicts between different versions of the same events, and the reasons for the conflicts, were never touched upon. The political subtleties, for example, of the Book of Ruth, the religious subtleties of a seemingly nonreligious book such as Esther, the complex moral significance of a book like Jonah, and the haunting mysteries of a book like Daniel—all of which are the subject of dazzling analyses by notable contemporary Christian scholars such as Andre La Cocque—were left far outside our range of vision.

I was left with the vague notion that Judaism and the "Jewish religion"—which consisted of articles of faith—were mutually inclusive terms. It never occurred to me that while the Jewish religion was the vital center of Judaism, it was not the whole of it. Indeed, until the publication in the mid-1930s of Mordecai Kaplan's *Judaism as a Civilization*, I would not be aware of anyone who showed systematically how Judaism included "that nexus of a history, literature, language, social organization, folk sanctions, standards of conduct, social and spiritual ideals, and esthetic values, which in their totality form a civilization."

[II]

In common with most first-generation American Jewish youth, my aim was to become thoroughly Americanized. I was increasingly aware that I belonged to two worlds and must find bridges between them. I was also aware that anti-Semitism was in the air, though for a long while I knew of its manifestations only second hand through readings or through the stories my parents used to tell. In the presence of my parents and their kinsmen, I adhered to their Orthodox practices in a kind of mechanical way where familiar stimuli were followed by familiar responses. Outside their presence, other stimuli were at work.

My roaming area expanded sharply after I entered high school. The sites of Kansas City high schools corresponded to economic,

social, and religious enclaves in the city as a whole. "Our people"
—meaning, in part, the children of striving east European Jewish
families—attended either Manual High School, as I did, or Northeast High School. "Their people"—meaning the children of "old
line" gentile families and of well-established German Jewish families—
attended either Central or Westport.

Manual High School, as its name suggests, was vocational in
emphasis and functioned in considerable measure as the intended
end of the academic road for the greater number of students. Few
among them went on to college. But its vocational aspects included—
well in advance of the case elsewhere—a concern with the performing arts. It had an excellent music department, for example, and
this fact explained the presence in the school of Marion Talley, a
classmate who later won celebrity as a *diva* with the New York
Metropolitan Opera. A year ahead of me was Rose Kaplan who
became a shining Broadway star under the stage name of Rose
Kean and who married the producer Howard Shumlin. I liked
drama and appeared in several plays with Rose in which, due to
my girth, I was quite literally cast as a "heavy," generally in the role
of a grandfather.

My consuming interest, however, lay elsewhere. As a Jewish
youth in a school setting that was overwhelmingly non-Jewish, I
was driven to excel by the belief that only by quick reflexes of the
mind—given the fact that I had no quick muscular reflexes—could
I attain the status of an "insider" among my non-Jewish classmates. Manual High School had a print shop in which the school
paper, the *Manualite,* was published. I joined its staff and in
time became its editor. I also won a place on Manual's varsity
debating team. Interschool debates in those days were major
citywide events held in large halls before packed audiences. As
a member of Manual's varsity team, I savored the heady taste
of victory in intense competition with other schools in the
city—something which foretold my reactions in later years where
I enjoyed being in the thick of controversies as much as I enjoyed applause. In fact, my habits of sustained talk on or off
a public platform led someone to say of me in later years that
my "occasional flashes of silence" were among the more appealing
aspects of my conversation.

The debating activity led to cherished lifelong friendships. The
first among these was my Manual teammate Abraham Margolin.
Through interschool debates Abe and I met debaters from Central

and Northwest, leading to the formation of our intimate friend-ships with Lewis Sutin and William Horowitz.* By the time I was sixteen, my high school was quite literally my second home. There was so much to do within its precincts—whether in connection with the school newspaper or the debating team—that during the school week I seldom returned to my own home until dusk.

Where our teachers were concerned, neither Abe Margolin nor I nor any other youth in our circle of Jewish friends was ever the object of a discriminatory gesture. To the contrary, they devoted extra hours of their own time to our various bids for success. They drilled us, held us to a high standard, prodded and encouraged us in our studies and in our extracurricular activities, and made clear their immense pride in our young triumphs. They seemed fulfilled in themselves as teachers by such successes as they helped us attain. We worked hard to gain their approval because they seemed to us to be the bridge over which we could more readily pass into the non-Jewish world. In the elegiac moments of later life, we might agree with Thoreau's mournful generalization that the same mate-rials "youth gets together to build a bridge to the moon, or perchance a palace or temple on earth," are applied to a dif-ferent end by the middle-aged man. "He concludes to build a woodshed with them." Yet the happy excitement shared by my circle of intimate friends during my youth in Kansas City sprang from a sense that we were being prepared for "a mighty purpose."

My favorite teacher was Helen Naismith, daughter of Dr. James Naismith, the originator of basketball. A Canadian by birth, Dr. Naismith had held various posts in physical education but had settled at the University of Kansas in 1898. When he came to Kansas City to visit his daughter, she would assign me to be his guide around the city; I, in turn, recruited my father to be our chauffeur. Dr. Naismith was the man who saved my life when I was drowning in obesity.

Manual High School's Greek-letter fraternities had never admit-ted a Jew until Abe Margolin and I were elected to one of them. A

---

*Abe Margolin became an honored leader of the Missouri bar and of many civic causes in Kansas City and throughout the state. Lewis Sutin capped a private practice in law by being elevated to the New Mexico appellate court. William Horowitz distinguished himself in business and financial enterprises in New Haven and became the first non-Protestant to serve as a trustee of Yale, his alma mater.

third Jewish youth, Max Wolf, wanted to join us. He had all the qualifications but was blackballed apparently because three Jews in the fraternity would be too many. Perhaps it was feared we would combine to fill the first vacancy in the Trinity. In any case, the fraternity was presently left with no Jews because Abe and I resigned.

This generalized slight merged with a personal one. The public library in Kansas City, a source of the research material for debaters, was near the Kansas City Young Men's Christian Association (YMCA). Whenever I took a break from research I would drop in for a swim or a game of pool. In this way I happened by chance to join the HI-Y Boys Club of the YMCA and was later elected its vice president. When new elections were scheduled not long afterward, the youth worker called me into his office to say that though I had served well as vice president of the club, and though it was customary to advance the vice president to president, it would be misunderstood if a Jewish boy became president of a youth club sponsored by the YMCA, a Christian organization.

It had never before occurred to me that I or my Jewish friends might be denied coveted leadership posts in our boyhood world on grounds other than merit. I could not understand how ordinary, decent, kindly human beings—the Christian members of the Greek-letter fraternity and the youth worker at the YMCA—could each in his own way say no to a Jewish youth solely because he was Jewish. My immediate reaction was to grit my teeth and silently address those who were huddled behind their exclusionary walls: "Just you wait. Draw all the satisfaction you can get out of your present status. Later on, when we compete for the stakes in the real world, I'll show you a thing or two." At the height of my inner turmoil I wondered whether vengeance did indeed belong solely to the Lord!

Mine was not a case where a storm clears a foul sky. Long after my double encounter with social anti-Semitism, I continued to wonder why Jews clung to their Jewishness. Why didn't they undergo mass assimilation when this was possible? Why, in particular, should I cling to my own Jewishness when it made me vulnerable to hurts? Besides, in what did Jewishness consist? Rituals? Dietary laws? Some sort of messianic vision of the Jewish role in human history? The ready answers seemed too weak to explain why many Jews remained over the millennia—as Moses noticed in his own time—a "stiff-necked people," set in their ways. It did not explain why so many accepted death rather than live with a sense of treason if they forsook their Judaism in favor of a loss of identity.

I might have broken psychologically with Judaism but for the providential return of a young man to his home in Kansas City after a brief stay in Omaha. The young man was Nathan Mnookin, born in Kansas City of Orthodox Jewish immigrants, and a recent honor graduate in chemical engineering from the University of Kansas. His name may be unknown to most readers. It is enough to say that he presently established the Industrial Testing Laboratories with Dr. J. C. Patrick, and that their joint efforts led to sixteen important advances in chemical engineering, including thiokol. Products derived from thiokol would be put to many industrial uses besides being the source of the rocket fuel that powered the astronauts to the moon.

Upon his return to Kansas City, Mnookin contacted William Horowitz, whom he knew, and described the nature of a Jewish youth group which had been formed in Omaha and for which he had served as an adviser. He asked Bill to assemble some of his friends in Kansas City so that he could talk with them. Bill soon tapped Lew Sutin, Abe Margolin, and me. What Mnookin had to say to us when we met concerned the creation in Omaha of Aleph Zadik Aleph (AZA). Would we be interested in forming the second chapter of this organization? We were and we did.

[III]

AZA, as the "junior B'nai B'rith," eventually grew into the largest organization of Jewish youth in the United States. More important, it was a "nursery" for successive generations of leaders in American Jewish affairs and of Jewish leaders in American society at large. A kind of law of natural selection drew a particular kind of Jewish youth into the organization. Once a member, he received unique training in the skills of communication and ample opportunities to use them. The seedtime years of the organization, therefore, merit more than a passing word.

AZA began in June 1922 when in Omaha, Nebraska, fourteen boys—all sons of eastern European Jewish Orthodox immigrants and all between the ages of fifteen and seventeen—met to form a fraternal club which might fit comfortably into their American and Jewish environments.

The exemplary Jewish community in Omaha, which numbered almost ten thousand, owed its origin to an influx of German Jews after 1856, when the Kansas-Nebraska Bill opened Nebraska for settlement. But the tone of the community had been altered—more substantially than was the case in Kansas City—when the Industrial Removal Society in the early 1900s settled two thousand east European Jews in Omaha. By the early 1920s Jews of eastern European background were beginning to move into leadership posts in the Omaha lodge of B'nai B'rith.

East European Jews in Omaha, like many of their counterparts elsewhere, were Zionists by inheritance from the Old World. It was natural that a Zionist youth club called the Maccabees surfaced among them. But when a divisive issue within the club could not be resolved, the discontented members split off to form the nucleus of the first chapter of Aleph Zadik Aleph. Complex interpretations were initially advanced to explain what the three Hebrew letters symbolized. In fact, the organizers simply wanted the Hebrew name of the new club to sound like a Greek-letter fraternity. When Aleph Zadik Aleph for Young Men later became Aleph Zadik Aleph of B'nai B'rith, the name was formally reinterpreted to match the motto of B'nai B'rith's "Benevolence, Brotherly Love, and Harmony." Thus the first Aleph was construed to stand for *Ahovoh* (brotherly love); the Zadik for *T'Sdakah* (benevolence); and the final Aleph for *Achdoos* (harmony).

It is significant that AZA began in relatively small Omaha and not in New York, Philadelphia, or Chicago. It is equally significant that fifteen of the first twenty chapters would be located in small Jewish communities in the Midwest, with the other five in mid-sized Jewish communities also in the Midwest.

Why? Jews concentrated in places such as New York, Philadelphia, and Chicago were sufficiently numerous to live in and by themselves, after the fashion of the east European *shtetl*. Their numbers alone enabled them to maintain and preserve causes, institutions, dogmas, and ideological disputes they brought with them from abroad. But Jewish communities such as those in Omaha or Kansas City lacked many of the opportunities for Jewish expression and the luxuries of self-centered advocacy found in large Jewish centers. Circumstances forced them to make a rapid and effective adjustment to the American environment—to fashion institutions that would serve specific needs at the grass roots of

American Jewish life, and yet fit into a setting that was over-whelmingly *not* Jewish.*

When Nathan Mnookin returned to Kansas City, the AZA boys in Omaha found another adviser in twenty-three-year-old Sam Beber. Like the youth who looked to him for guidance, Beber was the son of east European immigrants who toiled to establish themselves in their new land. He himself had been born in Minsk, Russia, and with his immigrant parents settled in Omaha with the help of the Industrial Removal Society. He aspired to be a doctor, but the costs of the long regimen of training were beyond his reach. As an alternative, he entered the law school of Creighton University in Omaha—a Jesuit institution devoted from the moment of its origin to "equal opportunity"—and was graduated magna cum laude.

Beber, when approached by the AZA boys in Omaha to take Mnookin's place, said he had no desire to be the adviser of just another club. But would the boys be interested in forming Chapter No. 1 of a national fraternity that would entail serious work and would also be enjoyable? They would. Perhaps they were intrigued by the romantic aspects of a proposal to form a national (and international) Jewish youth movement, starting with a handful of boys who lived off the main highways of the United States.

After consulting with leading Omaha Jews who were among his friends, Beber called an organization meeting on May 3, 1924, in the home of Harry H. Lapidus, president of the Omaha Fixture and Supply Company. Lapidus, a major leader in the Jewish community and in the business and civic life of Omaha as a whole, was long at the forefront of campaigns to rid the city of corrupt officials. The effort later cost him his life and had a direct bearing on my own.

Although the AZA chapter in Omaha was the only one waiting to be formally chartered, with the Kansas City chapter next in line, the men brought together by Sam Beber constituted themselves the *Supreme* Advisory Council. Sam Beber became grand president, Nathan Mnookin grand vice president, and Nathan Bernstein, a

*For the same reason, one of the most important areas of B'nai B'rith, District No. 6, embraced medium-sized or small Jewish communities in the states of Michigan, Nebraska, Iowa, the Dakotas, Illinois, Wisconsin, and Minnesota, and (until 1981) the Canadian provinces of Alberta, Manitoba, and Saskatchewan. The district was the birth-place of what are now the three major international agencies of B'nai B'rith—the Anti-Defamation League and the Hillel Foundations as well as Aleph Zadik Aleph.

real estate man, grand treasurer. Harry H. Lapidus filled another office as did Harry Trustin, an engineer who later became and served for some years as a city commissioner of Omaha. The Omaha group was now formally chartered as the Mother Chapter No. 1 of Aleph Zadik Aleph for Young Men. It was also decided that once other chapters were chartered, a "national" convention would be held in Omaha before the end of summer.

Those of us who met with Mnookin in Kansas City to form an AZA club modeled after the one in Omaha, added something distinctive on the initiative of Bill Horowitz. He knew that in Jewish mysticism the first letter *Aleph* derives its importance from the fact that it embraces all the letters of the alphabet; the rest draw their energy from it. To satisfy the tastes of our members who had a strong liking for rituals and passwords, Bill proposed and the rest of us agreed that every member would be known as Aleph. Being the oldest of the four founding members—he was seventeen at the time—Bill was elected Aleph Godol (president); Abe Margolin, Lew Sutin, and I were elected to the other principal offices. Mnookin served as our adviser, and it was understood that the B'nai B'rith lodge in Kansas City would be approached in the hope that it would agree to be our sponsor. We were chartered on May 10, as AZA Chapter No. 2, and we were followed in quick succession by chapters chartered in Lincoln, Nebraska, and in Des Moines, Iowa. The Supreme Advisory Council was now in a position to set in motion the arrangement for the first "national" convention of the four chapters to be held in Omaha.

[IV]

Aside from my involvement in these new activities associated with AZA, my senior year at Manual High School sped by in a torrential rush of happy activities. Abe Margolin and another student and I won the citywide debating contest. As editor of the *Manualite* I was often courted by teachers who were not indifferent to favorable printed references to their work. The *Manualite* itself was judged that year to be the best high school newspaper published in Missouri. As its editor, I was elected president of the state's Interscholastic Press Association which met at the University of Missouri at Columbia. That is where I was introduced to Dean Walter Williams of the university's school of journalism, one of the great pioneers in the teaching of journalism.

These heady successes momentarily drew me toward journalism as a career and away from my resolve since early boyhood to be a lawyer. But the pull in that direction stopped when I was briefly assigned by the *Kansas City Star*, while still in high school, to help cover a national convention of the Shrine. I was struck by the scruffy aspects of work as a cub reporter and decided that I wanted no part of that life. My choice of law as a future career remained firm, and in the process many other things fell into place.

Though students were not ranked according to grades in the 1924 graduating class of Manual High, individual students were singled out for special awards. Mine was a gold medal won in the school's oratorical contest. The manner of my delivery owed much to the training I received from Herbert Drake, the drama teacher in our school. He reminded me repeatedly not to think of myself when talking but to look in the eye of the audience. More generally, he also preached the wisdom of not tying oneself down to a written page in public speaking if it could be avoided—a lesson I respected in future years. With due allowances for inflated diction, the heart of my winning oration was close to what I said in later life from many formal platforms, including the rostrum of the United Nations when I was Ambassador to the Economic and Social Council. The title of the oration was "War, Creed, and Color," and the extract reproduced below is taken from the text as published in the high school annual *The Nautilus*:

> When you enter into a worldly existence, life is not imposed upon you as a privilege to abuse. You are not born to scorn those of opposite creeds, to oppose those of another color. No. This privilege is given to you to build up in this world of ours some achievement by which you will be remembered after your worldly work is done. But when you turn from that which is wonderful to a life in which war and fight are dominant, you have abused nature's greatest gift, the right of life. We are taught, but we forget. It seems we have already forgotten the horrors of that last world struggle—a war of race against race and creed against creed. God grant that such a struggle be never repeated.

After graduation, I joined my friends in preparing for the first AZA convention in Omaha, which was to have lifelong consequences.

5 □ Chance and Its Chain Reactions

I had reason to believe I could get a scholarship to Washington University in St. Louis, the leading private institution of higher learning in the state. But I was in no position to meet the costs of living in St. Louis, or for that matter, anywhere else. Upon graduating from high school I went to work in my uncle's furniture store, saving what I was paid except when I dipped into my earnings to cover part of the costs of attending the AZA convention in Omaha in July 1924.

Present at that convention, held in the Jewish Community Center, were two-thirds of the combined membership of the four chapters, a total of ninety-four boys in all. On the grand scale of human history, a convention of teen-age Jewish boys from four midwestern cities merits little attention. For its bearing on my *personal* history, however, what transpired at that convention set the stage where one chance event led to a second, the second to a third, and so on—all of which, taken together, opened onto the main actions of my life. To cite just one chance detail, it was at that first AZA convention that I met Ethel Riekes, my future wife— who has often reminded me in what is now more than sixty years of marriage, that initially she couldn't stand anything about me, least of all my corpulence.

[II]

Although most if not all the boys present at the first AZA convention were the sons of Orthodox Jewish immigrants from eastern Europe, the conduct of the convention attested to the speed with which we had been "Americanized" in our Midwestern communities. The convention was organized along the lines of the national nominating conventions of the Democratic and Republican parties, with committees on credentials, resolutions, platform, and so on. The actual conduct of the convention, moreover, was subject to a scrupulous respect for the parliamentary procedures taught us in our public schools. Anyone who had not mastered those procedures could be tied up in legalistic knots by other AZA youths who bore themselves in the grand manner of leaders of the bar and bench.

The high point of the convention—the election of the Grand Aleph Godol (supreme president)—featured a contest between Charles Shane, Aleph Godol of the Des Moines chapter, and Bill Horowitz, past Aleph Godol of the Kansas City chapter. After a deadlock in several delegate votes, the convention referred the contest to the Supreme Advisory Council. There Sam Beber observed that because Charles Shane was twenty years old and would not be eligible for office the next year, it might be best to choose him over seventeen-year-old Bill Horowitz. Bill could be elected Grand Aleph Godol when the next convention was held in Kansas City. The convention endorsed this line of reasoning, and Shane was elected Grand Aleph Godol. But what was reasonable did not work out as planned.

My experience at the convention, where I managed Bill's candidacy, gave me a taste for life's excitement on a great stage for action far beyond anything I had previously known in Kansas City. But there were more immediate bread-and-butter needs to attend to. I continued to work through the summer and fall months in my uncle's furniture store. By January 1925, or the middle of the regular academic year, I had saved enough money to enroll in Kansas University at Lawrence, a forty-minute bus trip from Kansas City.

Bill Horowitz was one of my two roommates at K.U. The other, Henry Brown, was part of our AZA circle in Kansas City. His strength lay in science and technology, and he later emerged as a top-ranking engineer at General Motors. When the three of us decided to be roommates at Kansas University, the immediate engineering problem to be solved, however, did not involve engines, but how to allocate our sleeping space. There was a double bed, but I was too fat to be a comfortable bedmate. So Bill Horowitz and Henry Brown shared it, and I was consigned to a single bed.

A physical examination, required of all entering students at Kansas University, brought me before Dr. James Naismith, then director of the physical education department. He remembered me as his guide when he visited his daughter in Kansas City. "Young man," said Naismith, pointing to my excess weight in proportion to my height, "I am going to save your life." His regimen combined a strict diet with a rigorous program of day-in and day-out exercise. I reported to him at set intervals to assure him that I was adhering to his rules. No doubt I was spurred by the fact that getting a girl to go out with me often exceeded my powers of persuasion.

Naismith's regimen seemed at times to be the equivalent of a continual Yom Kippur fast, but I stuck to it, and the promises he held out were fulfilled. When I dropped from 212 pounds to 150, Naismith and I were both satisfied. I shifted to a "maintenance" regimen with regular exercise which I have continued to the present. I have seldom exceeded what I weighed after Naismith released me from redemptive care. In later life, when for a while I shared an ownership interest in the Chicago Bulls professional basketball team, I remained more grateful to Dr. Naismith for what he did for me personally than for the fact that he invented basketball. My release from his care came on the eve of my eighteenth birthday, and I eagerly looked forward to the second national convention of the AZA in my own town of Kansas City, Missouri.

Meanwhile, the Atlantic City convention of the Constitution Grand Lodge of B'nai B'rith had officially endorsed the AZA as the "junior auxiliary" of the B'nai B'rith. Within my own ambitious little world during this same period, Bill Horowitz and I had won a "national" AZA debating contest held in 1925. With this added ground for celebrity, Bill had reason to believe he would be elected Grand Aleph Godol of AZA at the second annual convention. So he simply bided his time. He was always a prodigious worker, and it was entirely out of character for him passively to await a promised distinction.

[III]

In the undoing of Bill's trust in the inevitability of his election, I, his confidante, roommate, teammate, and campaign manager at the 1924 convention, emerged as the devil of the piece. What happened was this. AZA's total income in the two years of its existence had not exceeded $800, and we had a hard time in

Kansas City raising the funds needed to pay for the second convention. We meant for it to be a splendid affair, suited to AZA's new status as the officially designated junior auxiliary of B'nai B'rith, with fifteen chapters in existence and with many pending applications for charters.

On returning to Kansas City from a semester at Kansas University, I resumed my job in my uncle's furniture business, but at free moments I joined several local AZA boys in raising funds for the convention. Bill did not join us in doing so, and because his inactivity piqued some of the AZA fund-raisers, they urged me to seek election as Grand Aleph Godol. I might have said no but for the fact that Abe Margolin who, like me, was one of Bill's closest friends, volunteered to be my campaign manager. Abe's intervention soothed my conscience, troubled, as it should have been, by intimations of disloyalty to Bill.

The second annual convention of Aleph Zadik Aleph opened on July 17, 1925, at the Jewish Community Center in Kansas City. On the first ballot of the voting for the office of Grand Aleph Godol, with fourteen chapters voting under the unit rule, I received eleven votes and Bill Horowitz three. The results strained our personal relationship to the point where Bill did not return to Kansas University when school resumed in the fall. To put as much distance as was possible between himself and his subversive young friends in Kansas City, he transferred to Yale University, which had been a dream of his for a long time.

The pattern of his life owed much to that change of venue. At Yale he supported himself by teaching Hebrew, and he remained in New Haven after his graduation where he married a sister of the Botwinik Brothers. In time he became president of General Bank and Trust Company in New Haven, vice president of Botwinik Brothers, vice president of a radio station, vice president of Baker Industries of New Jersey, president of the National Friends of Yale B'nai B'rith Hillel Foundation, and chairman of the Connecticut State Board of Education. In 1987 he was awarded the Yale Medal, the highest honor Yale bestows on an individual for work on behalf of the institution.*

The outcome of the election for Grand Aleph Godol set my life

---

*Before the Israeli war for independence, Bill Horowitz and two colleagues managed to get to the Haganah, the Jewish self-defense force in Palestine, large quantities of machinery which were critically important in the production of guns—this at a time when there was a U.S. embargo on the shipment of arms to the Middle East.

on a new course, but neither Bill nor I ever forgot that 1925 contest for Grand Aleph Godol. The strain in our friendship was transient in nature; we remained close friends. Yet at our reunions it became almost a required ritual—like the reading of the *Haggadah* during a Passover meal—for both of us to allude, even in our eighties, to an event that occurred when we were eighteen. On the occasion of the fiftieth anniversary celebrating the founding of AZA, Bill addressed the generations of AZA members before him, and said, "Anyone present who was a candidate for Grand Aleph Godol and failed to be elected, please come up here and stand by my side. Let the world see that we nonetheless amounted to something."

With my election as Grand Aleph Godol, I transferred from Kansas to the University of Nebraska in Lincoln in order to be close to AZA headquarters in Omaha. I had spent only one semester at Kansas, and my leaving it seemed to prefigure a future pattern where I never retrod the same patch of ground but was repeatedly drawn to new challenges. My critics, and there were to be many of them in the years ahead, faulted me on that count.

During vacation periods in the 1925–1926 school year, I traveled the country on behalf of AZA, explaining its purposes before countless groups, advising local youth leaders on how to organize new chapters, and installing chapters when they were ready. Since AZA had no headquarters for the first two years or more, Sam Beber's law office in Omaha was the only AZA office. In the nature of the case, we had to work together; he was to be my future brother-in-law, law partner, and, still later, business associate. I also came to know Dr. Boris D. Bogan, the new executive secretary of B'nai B'rith, who became my mentor in the management of volunteer organizations.

At AZA's third annual convention, held July 1926 in St. Paul, Minnesota, I proudly reported that the new chapters organized during my tenure as Grand Aleph Godol had made AZA an authentic national movement. We had twenty-three chapters in all. More than that, a Canadian chapter in Calgary, and another soon to be installed in Winnipeg, enabled us to claim that we were "international." Yet at the third convention I felt lost turning over to the newly elected Grand Aleph Godol the two-by-four board that had served me as a gavel. At the age of 19, the greater part of my advanced education still lay ahead, but the prospect seemed dull compared with the flush of excitement I had experienced in my year as Grand Aleph Godol.

The letdown I felt did not last long. While still in St. Paul, Dr. Bogan and Sam Beber called me aside to ask if I would be willing to take on the new part-time job of assistant secretary to the Supreme Advisory Council. I would be paid fifty dollars a month. I was interested, but it meant a move from Lincoln to Omaha, a sticking point because my academic track as an undergraduate at the University of Nebraska pointed toward an eventual entry into its law school.

Sam Beber switched my direction. In arguing for the superior quality of the law school at Creighton University in Omaha, he pointed to himself and to Henry Monsky, a leader of the Omaha bar and a rising star in the International B'nai B'rith, as products of that school. I accepted the offer and changed my venue from Lincoln to Omaha. That meant I was enrolled in three different universities in three different cities all within three academic semesters. The fifty-dollar-a-month pay as assistant secretary was a welcome addition to my slender pocketbook, though I also received some financial help from my father and "invested" in stocks the monetary gifts I received from relatives on gift-giving occasions.

[IV]

My work as assistant secretary—later to be known as executive secretary of the Supreme Advisory Council of AZA—drew me into the orbit of the dominant figures in B'nai B'rith. I studied them carefully and came to recognize at a relatively early age that every man pays some price in weakness for his elements of strength— that the greater his strength, the more conspicuous his points of weakness. I also began to formulate some provisional notions of how leaders sustain the morale of their followers. I began to see, if only in silhouette, that two seemingly contradictory elements lay at the heart of the process. The first was the leader's own positive attitude toward the future and toward what he could accomplish through his own intentional acts. The second was the leader's recognition that life was filled with ambiguities, that nothing can be taken for granted, that those who strive may stray, yet in striving find the right way to attainable goals.

The president of B'nai B'rith was Alfred M. Cohen, who was also chairman of the Hebrew Union College board and its Reform Seminary in Cincinnati. In the course of working with Cohen, my encounters in Cincinnati with leaders of the mature German

Jewish community, and with the key institutions of Reform Judaism they helped build, forced me to fill in the gaps in my own knowledge of American Jewish history. I came to understand why some things, from an organizational standpoint, were possible while others were bound to be resisted—and that any pressure to attain them in the face of long-standing opposition could split an organization down the middle.

German Jewish laymen who were part of the great migration to America had worked hard after the 1840s to mold their local communities into proud, active, and productive entities. A high proportion of them had been on the "winning" abolitionist and pro-Union side in the Civil War, but they failed to produce an able lay leadership comprised of men of vision such as Britain's Sir Moses Montefiore. Leadership among German Jews was provided by its forceful immigrant rabbis, particularly by two outsized figures who were the theorists and field marshals of rival wings of the Reform movement in American Judaism, Rabbi Isaac M. Wise, a conservative, and Rabbi David Einhorn, a radical.

In the contest between the factions of the Reform movement, the Easterners led by Einhorn possessed what Wise lacked—formal training in the classics and in European philosophy as well as exposure to the "higher biblical criticism" being advanced in German universities. In the end, though Wise was the institution builder, it was Einhorn's radical version of Reform that carried the day on points of doctrine, ritual, the rabbinate, the sermon and music. In fact, Wise eventually sided with the radicals when he presided over the Pittsburgh conference they had called in 1885, and enthusiastically approved its platform. The platform described itself as a "declaration of independence" from traditional concepts and practices. Its key passage read:

> We recognize, in the modern era of universal culture of heart and intellect, the approaching of the realization of Israel's great Messianic hope or the establishment of the kingdom of truth, justice, and peace among all men. We consider ourselves no longer a nation but a religious community, and therefore expect neither a return to Palestine, nor a sacrificial worship under the sons of Aaron, nor the restoration of any of the laws concerning the Jewish State.

B'nai B'rith, formed on October 13, 1843, in a café on Essex Street in New York's lower East Side, had spread throughout the Midwest and elsewhere under the successive leadership of German Jews. It thus tended to be natural for the organization to reflect the attitude of Reform Judaism—until it was challenged by new leaders who emerged from the body of east European Jews. The latter, as time went by and the assimilation process continued, accepted the views and practices of Reform regarding dietary laws and rituals. They did not reject Zionism and the establishment of a Jewish state, as did "classical" Reform Judaism.

[V]

In the idiom of football, my work as assistant secretary of the Supreme Advisory Council of AZA entailed "broken-field" running between gaps of time in my undergraduate studies at Creighton University. Most of my courses faded from my memory once an examination was over. But I clearly recall a course in scholastic philosophy centered on the work of Saint Thomas Aquinas. At Kansas University I had taken a course in comparative religion. The one in scholastic philosophy offered at Creighton was not a prerequisite for an undergraduate degree, yet I enrolled in the course because it seemed a sensible way to get a better understanding of Catholicism with an eye to a future hour when I might be in a position to cooperate with Catholics in matters of common concern.

Before my introduction to the work of Saint Thomas Aquinas, the very term "saint" placed before a name usually conjured up in my mind images of plaster-cast figures that were the objects of devotions resembling pagan idol worship. I was also inclined to believe that Catholic thought was confined to mechanically repeated words of a catechism, which in turn could spark engines of persecution. Some such preperceptions accounted for my surprise when I encountered in Saint Thomas Aquinas a mind of extraordinary range, one which consistently mustered reason into the service of "faith seeking enlightenment." I was all the more surprised to discover how often Aquinas drew on Moses Maimonides (1135–1204), the great Jewish philosopher, as an authoritative source of support for his own views regarding Old Testament issues.

The gentle father who taught the class in scholastic philosophy was a Jesuit, Creighton itself being, as indicated already, a Jesuit institution. I still recall how on the first day of the class, he walked to the blackboard and drew two circles. "This one," he said, pointing to it, "encompasses things that are knowable by men, and these we will discuss." Then he pointed to a second circle: "This one encompasses the things known to God alone, and these we will not discuss." In the unfolding days of the course, I sensed that the father was treating me with kid gloves. During classroom discussions I was only a bystander to the treatment of issues lying in the realm of "ecclesiastical Christianity"—the meaning of the Trinity, the Immaculate Conception, the Virgin Birth, the relationship between original sin and the Crucifixion. I was, however, an active participant in discussions whose focus was on Aquinas' powerful treatment of jurisprudential issues such as the nature of men and the purposes of the state; the varieties of law, including "natural law"; the relationship between law and justice; the grounds on which the lawfulness of the law itself could be judged; and the right of and limits to civil disobedience. In other words, I was actively involved in discussions whose great sounding echoes were heard in the 1950s and 1960s when Martin Luther King attacked segregation ordinances as not being laws at all.

While I was engrossed in all such matters, I was also in a hurry to get on with my "career." I called on the dean of the Undergraduate College to say, first, that by the end of the semester I would have the requisite credits to qualify for admission to the Creighton law school. Would I be permitted to enroll in January 1927—though this would mark the start of the second semester in the first year of law school studies? After a conversation with law school Dean Louis J. TePoel, I was granted permission to do so. I would face problems entering in mid-year, Dean TePoel cautioned, and I should not be disappointed if I flunked out.

6 □ Coming of Age

I entered Creighton Law School in January 1927 and at once learned that Dean TePoel had not understated the difficulties I would face. While courses elsewhere had been easy for me, they were not so now. Merely to keep up with the rest of the class I had to study harder than at any other time in my formal education. Though I was the "new boy" in the class, I was expected to be as prepared to answer questions asked without forewarning as any of the "seasoned veterans" among my classmates.

Besides the demands of classes, I had to organize my time to carry on with my work as AZA assistant secretary and to court Ethel Riekes with whom, fortunately, I had been brought in contact once again. Although she had been repelled earlier by my roly-poly appearance, the sixty pounds I had shed under the care of Dr. Naismith had made me more acceptable in her eyes. My coming together with Ethel owed something to the ways of Jewish *mishpochology* (the science of family ties). Sam Beber, my senior by about five years but with whom I was working very closely, had married Helen Riekes, one of Ethel's older sisters. Ethel's brother Max and Sam's brother David, both of whom were my age and fellow members in AZA, had become my close friends after my move to Omaha. Max would have David and me over to the Riekes' home for a Shabbes meal with the family, and Sam and Helen would sometimes be there for the occasion.

My own home in Kansas City took its tone from the firm managerial style of my mother and from my father's good nature. The Riekes' home reflected the dominant influence of the remarkable father of the family, Samuel, after whom I later named one of my own sons. As an immigrant from eastern Europe, Samuel Riekes had started a small bottle supply company that became in the hands of his sons a substantial enterprise. But the real source of his authority within the family—and among the community of eastern European Jews in Omaha—was his status as a former *yeshiva bucher*, wise and learned in the fine points of talmudic *halacha* (law). Yiddish was as likely to be spoken as English in the Riekes home, while the respect paid to *kashrut* (the dietary laws) gained its own special kind of public acknowledgment. When Rabbi Kook, then the chief rabbi of Palestine, visited Omaha, he was lodged in the Riekes home in the confident assurance that among Orthodox Jewish homes in the city, it would pass his inspection regarding every detail in the code for *kashrut*.

My work with AZA was wedged in between everything else. On weekends and holidays I traveled around the country to consult with local AZA chapters on their activities or to help organize or install new chapters. This kind of work was extended to Canada. There, as in the United States, AZA became a magnet for many Jewish youth who were destined to make their mark in the arts and sciences, in the legal profession, in business, and in government.

When, for example, I was Ambassador to the Economic and Social Council of the United Nations, it was hard to keep my feelings hidden behind an impersonal diplomatic mask once I discovered that a Canadian representative to the council was also a former AZA boy.

The steady growth in the size of AZA—it would reach seventy-two chapters between 1927 and 1929—was gratifying on its own terms. But debates, oratorical contests, basketball tournaments, and dances were not enough. Dr. Bogan stressed the need for more emphasis on the specific Jewish content of an AZA program. Sam Beber and I agreed, and we worked with him to develop a comprehensive educational agenda that set the course AZA has followed to the present day.

[II]

All the while I kept my eye on the law school timetable to determine when Dean TePoel would offer either of the two courses he regularly taught, in municipal law and in constitutional law. Ultimately I took both, and they later had a pervasive effect on my career as a lawyer.

To sit in TePoel's class was to undergo a rigorous intellectual exercise and to be treated to an aesthetic delight. A difference between TePoel and other law professors was the way he tried to inculcate in us, through the force of his own example, a concern for a precise reading of texts. He would listen carefully when a student ventured to reconstruct the facts of the case. But what was the principle of law at issue? If a student tried to duck the question or began to stammer, TePoel, without glancing at the casebook, would say, "Mr. X, if you will turn to page 223 and look at the first paragraph in the middle of the page, you will find that the principle of law is stated as follows...." We would discover that the principle cited from memory was right *there,* word for word.

In July 1928 I observed my twenty-first birthday. I continued as AZA assistant secretary, but under the bylaws I could no longer be a member of AZA. I was, however, old enough to join B'nai B'rith, which I promptly did. Two years later I became president of the Omaha lodge.

Now that I had reached my majority, I also increased my activities on other fronts in Omaha, to the extent that my law school studies and status as a young man permitted. Almost as a matter of inheritance, I began to move in the footsteps of my father in Jewish charitable and not-for-profit organizations. But I was also prodded by the reminder that keen as were the Jewish sages on the study of law, they taught that study without moral practice was absurd—that the *mitzvah* (righteous deed) of aiding one's neighbor took precedence over the *mitzvah* of loving God, because mortals were more in need of love and sympathy than was God.

I became secretary of the Conservative congregation of which Sam Beber was president. I was involved in the creation of the Federation of Jewish Services and the Bureau of Jewish Education, the source of a united, citywide Jewish education program. The cause of Zionism and Palestine were not on the agenda of the so-called prestige organizations in Jewish life, either nationally or in Omaha. In fact, to be a professed Zionist was often taken to be a confession that one was not a member of the Jewish "upper crust." Nonetheless, because I believed in the objectives of Zionism, I added them to my personal commitments while still in my early twenties. The cause of Zionism became all the more urgent in my eyes when Jews in Palestine were slaughtered by Arab rioters and when emergency meetings were called in Jewish communities nationwide to raise relief funds to help the Yishuv.

With various activities piled on top of one another, and all collectively piled on top of my work in law school, a point was reached where I could not, unaided, attend to the affairs of AZA as its chapters continued to multiply. Sam Beber agreed that I needed an assistant. Julius Bisno, an eighteen-year-old high school graduate, was my choice. Julie had been Aleph Mazkir (secretary) of AZA's Memphis Chapter 71, which in 1929 had been judged "the best all-around chapter." His pay would be fifty dollars a month, but he could be my roommate and would have to absorb only one-third of the rent.

In January 1930 I was graduated from Creighton Law School, a certified J.D., and accepted by the Nebraska State Bar, which qualified me to practice law. I would soon have an intimate professional working relationship with Dean TePoel, and the memory of the man and my gratitude to Creighton University generally, and to the law school in particular, accounted for the pleasure I found in later years when I was in a position to do something for the institution. In the early 1960s, when a new law school building was being planned at Creighton, I helped acquire a substantial gift for its construction and provided $250,000—as much as I could then afford—for the library portion.

The law school building contains a private apartment for use by a visiting guest of the school. I once spent a happy week living there as an invited lecturer. When I opened the door of the refrigerator in the apartment's kitchen, I saw that the thoughtful Jesuit fathers had stocked the shelves with an ample supply of kosher dill pickles, corned beef, salami, rye bread, and bagels. This was a real touch of delicatesse on their part.

Father Morrison and the dean of the law school visited me one day in Chicago in the early 1980s and asked me to consider endowing a chair in constitutional law at the school. I countered with a proposal of my own. I was prepared to endow a professional chair for the teaching of Jewish civilization, something along the lines of what I had earlier contributed to Brandeis University. I had made the same offer to Dr. Arnold Weber, president of Northwestern University, a private institution founded by Methodists. (A parallel offer I had made to the University of Chicago was rejected by its acting president John Wilson on the ground that Judaism was not a civilization.)

Both Creighton and Northwestern accepted my proposal, but I particularly recall Father Morrison's gleeful response. When I asked why he was so happy to be offered an endowed chair in Jewish civilization and not one in constitutional law, he replied, "Jewish civilization helps to authenticate the birth of Catholicism." The million dollars which Ethel and I assured for each endowed chair—both were created at about the same time—were among the most personally satisfying benefactions I've ever made. The terms I set for the endowment vested in each university the sole right to select the professor who would be appointed, and to ensure for that person all the benefits associated with academic freedom. Holders of the chair were to be respected scholars and not apologists for any special Jewish interest. As it happened, the holder of the chair at Creighton became a beloved figure on the university faculty and in Omaha's Jewish community, and by his very nature served as a kind of intellectual grappling hook drawing Creighton and Omaha Jews closer together.

7 □ My Start in Law

My license as a lawyer was at the outset little more than an invitation carefully to sort out my strengths and weaknesses. Time would show that my strength did not lie in litigation before juries. I never handled a criminal case or a divorce case, nor was I ever a lawyer for a case involving a claim against an insurance company or in defense of one. My strength and interest lay in negotiations between parties, in preparing and arguing briefs before appellate courts, and in the interpretation and application of public law. More immediately, while I continued to work part-time for AZA at a salary of fifty dollars a month, I was engaged at a monthly salary of seventy-five dollars to work part time in the Omaha law firm of Fradenberg, Stalmaster, and Beber. This was intoxicating stuff, and I suspect that I strutted even when I was seated.

Sixty years ago the vast majority of lawyers in private practice were either sole practitioners or persons who practiced in small firms with no more than two or three partners and perhaps a young man who was reading for the bar. As Shirley M. Hufstedler, later to be my colleague in the Carter cabinet, has written:

> The lawyers performed the functions of a family solicitor, took care of small businessmen's problems, handled a modest amount of tort litigation and occasionally handled a criminal case for a respectable client, whose peccadillos could be expected to be forgiven by a jury of his peers. A few large law firms existed in places like Chicago and New York, with as many as 20 or even 30 lawyers, catering to the more specialized tastes of railroads, banks, and utilities. But the average lawyer was a generalist who had little overhead.

His paraprofessional was a devoted secretary who typed wills and pleadings and talked to the telephone operator to place his calls. Lawyers could and did handle the few needs of their middle-class clients for prices within their clients' reach. They saw very few poor clients; the poor were chiefly visible as uncounseled defendants in criminal cases.

Today, Mrs. Hufstedler went on to say:

The cozy little office of the past is not equipped to undertake the complex legal problems besetting private individuals and businesses. Huge law firms have been and are being built in every major metropolitan area of the country. They are staffed by batteries of specialists who are prepared to cope with international legal problems confronted by their transnational corporate clients, to negotiate for or against labor unions in complicated collective bargaining packs, to acquire and shed corporate subsidiaries, to fight antitrust actions, to undertake sophisticated real estate developments, and to negotiate with and to fend off the bureaucratic hand of government.

These major metropolitan law firms are not designed to deal with the legal problems of just plain folks, and the economic facts of life are that the average person cannot possibly afford to pay the overhead attached to the square feet upon which a big-firm lawyer has planted his desk. Although I have used their services, I have often wondered if I would ever be at home practicing law today in a major law firm with its specialized subdivisions and its battalions of lawyers whose personal aptitudes are often judged mainly by their ability to "bill" more hours for their clients. In retrospect, I believe the firm of Fradenberg, Stalmaster, and Beber was a cut above most firms in Omaha at the time, and that its generalized practice made it an excellent schoolroom in which I could acquire a thorough training in the law crafts.

At first, though, my work amounted to an apprenticeship in handling the waves of paper in which the law swims. Things that did not interest the partners were passed on to me—collections, simple contracts, simple wills, examination of deeds, filing of motions. I attended to these matters in between the legal business I attracted from my acquaintances in the Omaha community, including young men of my age who were embarking on their own full-time careers in different fields.

Soon after I was employed in the firm I was called into the office of Stalmaster, who was a part-time assistant attorney general under Nebraska's legal system. There I was introduced to Nebraska's Attorney General Sorensen, whose son Theodore, then but a toddler, later became President Kennedy's close aide.

Attorney General Sorensen, a stickler for the law, faced a problem involving an Omaha institution, Ak-Sar-Ben (Nebraska spelled backward), which was comprised of Omaha's elite in society and business. Among other things, Ak-Sar-Ben owned and operated a track where horse races and pari-mutuel betting took place. Attorney General Sorensen believed this was in violation of the state constitution, and he threatened to close the track. If the members of the social organization wanted to change the constitution, let them try to do so. But as long as the constitution barred gambling, he was going to enforce the law. The Ak-Sar-Ben people, for their part, hired Arthur Mullen as their legal counsel; Mullen, a key Democratic political leader in Nebraska, was later FDR's floor manager when he was nominated for the presidency in 1932.

Under Nebraska state law, an attorney general facing a major constitutional issue could skip over the lower trial courts and institute an original action in the supreme court. The assistant attorney general, backstopped by the attorney general, explained to me the need for an affidavit to the effect that betting was going on at the Ak-Sar-Ben track. Also, the person signing the affidavit must be someone who could be trusted to stand up under pressure. I was chosen to be that someone. When I said I had never been to a track in my life, they said, "Don't worry." I merely had to go to the track, bet, and then make the affidavit.

As it happened, I knew that several of my friends were going to the races on a certain day. I went with them, and they explained parimutuels to me while we rode out to the track. I scanned the entries for the first race. When I ran my finger down the racing form I saw a horse named "Bill Henry" whose odds were 60 to 1. I placed a two-dollar bet on that horse, partly because I wanted to lose so that my affidavit could show that I had bet and lost. But my main reason for picking the horse was that my roommates at Kansas University had been William Horowitz and Henry Brown— "Bill Henry." My seemingly hopeless horse won, and I collected $122. It was the most cash I had had in my hands in a long time, and I applied it to a down payment for a used Chevrolet coupe. I placed another two-dollar bet, but this time I lost. My affidavit was among the factors which enabled Attorney General Sorensen to win his case. The race track was closed but only temporarily. Ak-Sar-Ben, through the use of its organizational strength and civic popularity, got the Nebraska electorate to adopt a constitutional amendment which legalized parimutuel race track operations.

Despite my modest means I had somehow managed in preceding years—with the aid of a booming stock market—to accumulate stock valued at around sixteen thousand dollars on paper. This, coupled with confidence in my own future as a lawyer, made the ring of wedding bells more attractive in my ears. I had been seeing Ethel Riekes fairly regularly during the period before and after she graduated from the University of Omaha (now the Omaha branch of the University of Nebraska), and was drawn to her to the exclusion of other young women in our circle of friends. Sometime in the spring of 1930, while we were on a golf course in Omaha, I plucked an engagement ring out of my pocket and she accepted it. A golf course as a place for one of the primary decisions of adult life was as far removed as one could imagine from the setting for a *shiddach* (matchmaking) and *ketuba* (negotiated marriage contract) such as our respective parents had known in eastern Europe.

We were married on Sunday afternoon, June 8, 1930, by two rabbis, one Orthodox, the other Conservative. The time was the lingering aftermath of the stock market crash in late October of the previous year. Alternating declines and partial recoveries had been the rule in the intervening months. "Wall Street may sell stock," intoned the *Saturday Evening Post*, "but Main Street is buying goods." Others grinned at the billboards which announced, as if in retrospect of an event in the dimming past, "Wasn't the depression terrible?" If the man on Main Street thought all would be well again once the wave of panic selling was checked, his amateur opinion was shared by the certified "experts" comprising the nation's business and intellectual leadership.

In my own case, I had some fairly clear views about how an individual business enterprise was or should be run. I was also attuned to "conditions" in and around Omaha. But I had not stopped to educate myself about the forces that affect the performance of the national economy. In later life I had the privilege of acquiring a postgraduate education in *political* economy when I became a trustee and vice chairman of the Committee on Economic Development and chairman of its research and policy committee. That education was extended further when I served in the federal government and particularly as Secretary of Commerce in the cabinet of President Jimmy Carter. But in 1930, as a young man of twenty-three, I had no reason to question the belief, common among bankers, business leaders, and economists, that nothing was out of the ordinary despite the thunderous noise of the Great Crash on the exchanges. The decline in prices, production, and employment—and their associated process of forced liquidation of debts—conformed to the traditional pattern of a downturn in the business cycle after an expansionist upside phase.

On the evidence of several precedents, the downturn would last a relatively short time before the redeeming forces of "natural correctives" would again set things right.

In June 1930, when Ethel and I were married, I needed $2,500 to cover the costs of our planned honeymoon to the West Coast, and I intended to get the money by selling some of the stock I held. But my new brother-in-law Sam Beber, who had heavily invested in the market, advised me against the sale when stock prices were depressed. I should hold the stock in anticipation of the hour when, as all the experts predicted, there would be jubilant recovery. Sam gave me more than advice. He generously offered to loan me the $2,500 in question. I accepted the loan and went off with Ethel on our honeymoon.

By the time we returned to Omaha four weeks later, the value of my stocks, far from returning to the level of my original investment, had fallen to so low a point that I was wiped out. The shock was due only in part to the loss of all my capital. More important, the event marked the first time in my life when I did not feel in control of my destiny. "Well, Sam," I could only say to my brother-in-law in a salute to his advice and generosity, "you are going to have to wait a little while before I can repay you the $2,500."

Ethel and I started our family in 1932 when our only daughter Bettylu was born. In time we were the parents of four more living children, all sons; a child, Richard, who died at three; and a stillbirth. The living sons were Tom, born in 1939, followed by Jim in 1943, Bob in 1947, and Sam in 1948.

Three of my four independent-minded sons would eventually be my business partners until I retired from an active role in business and it seemed wise for each to go his own way. Bob had gone his own way at an early hour when his interest in teaching and school administration drew him to Boulder, Colorado, where he made his home. Throughout the intervening years, however, it never occurred to me to think of my daughter Bettylu as a prospective business associate. This would not be strange if she were passive, or lacked the zest for the rough-and-tumble aspects of life in a large business setup. But she was very much of an "activist," wished to be included in the conduct of business enterprises, and had impressive managerial talents as evidenced by the part she played in many civic enterprises. I can only plead guilty to cultural lag—to the fact that my attitudes about family roles jelled in the era before the women's liberation movement opened the eyes of fathers (as well as those of employers) to their own kind of sex discrimination against their daughters.

A detail of my early married life which remains lodged in my memory involved my first approach to a bank for a loan. I had never borrowed money from a bank before my marriage, and I had no line of credit. But at one point Ethel wanted to buy something for which I would need $250, which I did not have. As it happened, the Omaha National Bank, of which Dale Clark was the president, was on the ground floor of the same building in which my law firm had its offices. The partners of the firm were favorably known to Clark. I had apparently caught his eye as well, for when I talked with one of the bank's officers about a $250 loan, I received a return call from Dale Clark. He reached me in my law office and asked me to drop down to see him.

When I sat opposite Clark in his private office, he eyed me in long silence. After an eternity he began to speak. "I understand," he said, "that you are doing well and are going to do well in the practice of law. As for the loan you want, lending money is good for us. That is our business. Borrowing money, however, is not good for a young man who is practicing law. Think through what you want to do with the money. Is it the right thing to do?" His continued talk in this vein triggered the flash point in my temper. In a blaze of anger, I told him I would not have come to the bank for a loan if I didn't need it. I could do without his lecture. Nonetheless, he continued to sermonize for forty-five minutes. My anger had not subsided several hours after I left his office and returned home. When I told Ethel what had transpired, she calmed me down, and after some even-tempered talk it was decided between us that I might borrow the $250 from my law firm against my salary.

In future years I thought it ironic that when I went to a financial intermediary such as a bank or insurance company and asked for a loan in the tens of millions, *I* did most of the talking and was respectfully heard. But when I wanted to borrow $250 as a young lawyer and family man, I was subject to the long harangue about the evils of borrowing.

Dale Clark, a good soul who remained my personal friend as long as I lived in Omaha, was fairly typical of bankers of the day. Most banks in the first decades of the 1900s, like those in the previous century, were managed by men with little formal education beyond high school. They had often begun their careers as messengers, starting young and rising to successive posts of teller, bookkeeper, cashier (the key executive in country banks), vice president, and president. They grew up with an institution and seldom left it for a rival institution, an action thought "treasonable." They held their cards very close to their chest and were subject to only casual demands for "public disclosure" of how they played them. They thoroughly understood the technical operations of their bank but gave little thought to the interaction between it and the surrounding society.

In a time of drastic deflation, individual bankers such as Clark did what they felt compelled to do in order to "keep liquid." They forced the liquidation of loans and securities to meet the demands of depositors, thus helping to drive down prices and make it more difficult for debtors to pay back what they had borrowed. By their policies of credit stringency—even in connection with a loan as small as $250—they threw a double loop around the throat of an economy that was already gasping for breath. In a time of drastic deflation, a rational policy should have been one of monetary ease. But individual bankers, in seeking their own salvation—by "keeping liquid"—contributed to the general ruin. It would take the collapse of the entire banking system, led by the Federal Reserve Board, to force into being new concepts and institutional relationships, subject to law.

[II]

Aside from voting, I did not actively participate in the 1932 presidential election, but I was soon heavily drawn into the work of an Omaha reform movement. Omaha for some time had been politically dominated by what was known as the Dennison machine, which allegedly had tie-ins with the criminal syndicates that lived off of gambling and the bootleg liquor traffic. Harry Lapidus was among the leaders in the local Republican party who fought to cleanse the city from the practices of the Dennison machine. In fact, he and others of his persuasion went to Washington to seek help from the Department of Justice during the Hoover administration. It was rumored that knowledge of this trip and its purposes enraged some local politicians in command of the Dennison setup.

My initial AZA association with Harry Lapidus was followed by later associations with him in B'nai B'rith, the Zionist organization, the Jewish Community Center, and the board of the city Talmud Torah. One night we met in the Jewish Community Center to deal with matters pertaining to the city Talmud Torah. When the meeting adjourned, Lapidus volunteered to drop me at my apartment which was on his way home. I thanked him for the offer but added that I had my own car with me. Later that night, someone called me to say that en route home Harry had been murdered. No one to this day has identified the assassin or figured out why anyone should want to kill him. The only plausible explanation is that his reformist efforts frightened those who profited from political corruption and racketeering in the Omaha area.

I was torn between horror over the murder of my friend, a civic leader, and the unnerving thought of what might have happened to me if I had not driven my own car to the meeting—the same car I had bought with earnings from my long-shot race track bet on "Bill Henry." This was not a time, however, for elegiac thoughts about how the long-shot difference between life and death is always in precarious balance and how the most prosaic decisions of the moment can have immense consequences. It was a time for mourning, for rage, and for a measured response to cruelty.

The murder occurred when the lines were being drawn for an election in the city of Omaha. Omaha had a mayor-commissioner form of government, and seven commissioners were periodically elected in a nonpartisan election. Those of us who were outraged by the murder of Lapidus were joined by people who on other counts were eager to turn out the Dennison machine. Together we organized the Independent Voters League in anticipation of the primaries and election scheduled for April and May 1933. No one gave us a chance to win, though many hoped we would. We fielded a candidate list headed by Roy N. Towl, an engineer whose family was highly regarded; his mother was a leader in Nebraska's temperance movement.

Few of the other candidates on the list were well known. Yet to control the administration under a mayor-commissioner form of government, we had to win four seats in the city council. That was not easy under conditions where the same people who denounce corruption in the abstract, and enjoy its fruits in the concrete, tend to be full of excuses about how things really "aren't so bad." Yet to virtually universal surprise, four of the six candidates on our list were elected. In addition to Roy Towl, two of these in particular were to figure in the work I would soon be doing. One was Harry Trustin, a Legionnaire, engineer, and Jewish leader in Omaha who, like Lapidus, had been a founding member of AZA's Supreme Advisory Council. The other was Dan Butler, a leading "independent" in Omaha politics.

Once Roy Towl was installed as mayor and got a close look at the city's financial picture, he saw that his administration was in deep trouble. His predecessors had already spent virtually all the budget income for the whole year of 1933, even as tax revenue had shrunk drastically because of the depression. Towl had nothing in common with reformers who know they are going to heaven and want the place all to themselves. He was the genuine article, an authentic agent of change. He needed help to reorganize the city's legal department and bring the city government to a point where it would function in an atmosphere of responsible power.

What he needed he found when he persuaded Dean TePoel to take a leave of absence from the Creighton University Law School to become corporation counsel. At the same time Seymour Smith, a lawyer with extensive experience in both law and in practical politics, became the city attorney. I was asked by the mayor and Dean TePoel to join the staff at city hall as an assistant to TePoel in his capacity as corporation counsel and to Smith in his capacity as city attorney. I had just begun to make a living in the actual practice of law, but I believed—and Ethel agreed—that this was an invitation I could not reject. I took a leave of absence from the law firm—and from a prospective partnership in it—to enter on my first official public payroll job in May 1933.

Dean TePoel was the person responsible for my appointment as an assistant in the office of corporation counsel—and the reason he gave became the most cherished compliment of my life. He noticed, he said, that when I was a student in his classes, I regularly analyzed problems from every angle. My tendency to recognize that there were at least two sides to a controversy was of critical importance in the approach to issues lying in the public realm—issues that could seldom be resolved by dogmatism. My attempts in later years to take my bearing from that same perspective did not always make me popular in inflamed contests.

My salary as an assistant wearing two legal hats was meant to be six thousand dollars a year, but the sum was like a beautiful plate with only half an entree on it. The barren city treasury forced the new administration drastically to cut all salaries. Mine was slashed in a stroke to three thousand dollars at a time when I had an infant child to provide for. Ethel, as usual, calmly accepted what was done. She knew that if I had been sheared, at least I had not yet been skinned. She never suggested, not even by a sour look, that I made a bad choice when I went to work for the city. As in all other turns of what would be our long life together, she backed what I wanted to do, even though it might impose new burdens on her. To get on with my work in the city administration, I resigned as executive secretary of the AZA Supreme Advisory Council. My replacement in the post was my assistant Julius Bisno.

[III]

Soon after I moved into my office in Omaha's city hall, I participated in a meeting with Mayor Towl, Dean TePoel, Commissioner of Public Improvements Harry Trustin, and Commissioner of Finance Dan Butler. The question before us was as plain as a pikestaff. How could the bankrupt city of Omaha benefit from the new public laws Congress was enacting on the initiative of the Roosevelt administration?

After much talk back and forth, I was given my first major assignment: study the new laws and report on those related to the urgent question under discussion. In this way I became (and remained) an avid reader of the *New York Times*. Though its reports on New Deal legislation reached me several days late, it would be weeks before the texts of the same law were available in Omaha following a written request to the U.S. Government Printing Office. In fact, until the creation of the Federal Register during the early New Deal, there was no one place which listed all the new laws enacted by Congress as well as the administrative rulings pouring out of executive departments and agencies.

I soon found that Congress had approved a work-relief program entailing the use of federal funds to improve roads and highways. Locally, a strong case could be made for widening Dodge Street, an arterial highway in Omaha (which happened to run past the apartment building where Ethel and I were living). To qualify for the program, however, state and local authorities had to match the federal funds allocated to a project, something neither Nebraska nor Omaha were in a position to do.

The only possible source of revenue for the purpose was a

gasoline tax which Nebraska's unicameral legislature had approved at the start of the 1930s, as had other revenue-starved states. Checking on how funds from that source were being used elsewhere, and following the Michigan example in particular, I developed a program whereby gasoline tax revenues were pledged to cover the city's matching share of the costs for improving Dodge Street. The program was widely approved, and in the mirror of my mind I may have appeared to be one of the great builders in universal history back to the time of the Romans, if not the Egyptian pharaohs. Some other projects, significant in my own mind but actually piddling when judged by other criteria, were mounted with funds teased out of their hiding places, or which were allocated to Omaha on a prorated basis by the state of Nebraska.

Our situation changed remarkably when Congress on June 13, 1933, approved the National Industrial Recovery Act (NIRA). It is beyond my need to dwell on the aim of the act, its dubious logic, its flawed administrative structure, and its doomed fate as a recovery measure. What counts here is a seemingly offhand provision in the act which struck my eye in Omaha when I read the text of NIRA as reported in the *New York Times*. For the first time ever, the federal government was authorized to initiate a slum clearance and public housing program with an initial appropriation of $100 million. The need for matching funds by city and state governments was not mentioned. The Department of the Interior, headed by Secretary Harold Ickes, would be in overall charge of the program, though operational responsibility was subcontracted to the Housing Division of the new Public Works Administration, also under the command of Secretary Ickes.

Few cities at the time had "housing authorities" or any kind of locally planned and financed public housing programs. New York, Chicago, and Cleveland were among the exceptions. It could be expected that they and several other large communities would actively bid to slice up the $100 million in federal funds earmarked for slum clearance and public housing. On the other hand, it was part of a conceit common among most cities and towns in the 1920s and 1930s that they had no slums. One might believe they all were located in the suburbs of Utopia.

Minutes after I read the NIRA slum clearance and public housing provisions, I outlined the details for Mayor Roy Towl, saying that they offered Omaha a chance to get some federal funds that could put some local people to work. Mayor Towl, who agreed, at once called in Commissioner of Finance Dan Butler who also agreed. By now I was very much in a "take-charge" frame of mind, bent on seeing the end of the matter from the very beginning. So I suggested that Edward Burke, a Democrat who had previously represented the Omaha district in the U.S. House of Representatives, and was now a senator, should be asked to lend a hand. Burke, when contacted, was ready to help. He was in Omaha at the time, and we made the train trip to Washington together.

[IV]

Among the alternative traditions of biblical leadership, the one I never fit was that of the leader as a "suffering servant"—initially a passive figure minding his own dull business who receives "a call," resists it at first, but then accepts it after a long struggle with himself. I was never reluctant to assume responsibilities for actions in a public sphere—including actions at the level of local government—and I never "suffered" from the burdens that went with that role.

In later years, when I could figuratively step outside my own skin and take a long look at myself, I seemed to fit the tradition of biblical leadership spelled out in stories which biblical scholars group under the heading of "Clever Acts and Words." Such stories tell of a person of humble extraction who is summoned by a kingly person to solve a problem that is beyond the wit of his viziers. The person who is called seemingly out of nowhere solves the problem and is rewarded in ample measure.

My trip to Washington with Senator Burke marked the onset of some such story in my own case. To the principal beneficiaries of the Old Order which collapsed in the early 1930s, the whole of the physical world seemed to have been wrenched from the socket in which it turned. To them, history itself exuded the odor of death. To those of us, however, who had never been certified members of the Old Order—though our economic losses in the 1929–1932 collapse might have been proportionally as great or relatively greater than theirs—history exuded the odor of springtime life. This was all the more true of those of us who were young. To be in Washington in the "constituent months" of the New Deal, to be young and in the company of other young people who were converging on the place with heads filled with ideas, was to have a sense of being chosen to receive a gift straight from heaven. The very disorder in the country at large and in Washington itself invited the young to join in transforming the chaos into an orderly cosmos.

Escorted by Senator Burke I quickly discovered the confusion prevailing within the division of the Department of the Interior that was to handle the housing and slum clearance program. It was clear that the division had not yet been organized, though we were told it soon would be. Something else was also clear. Because Omaha lacked a housing authority comparable to those in New York, Chicago, or Cleveland, it might be handicapped when it tried to qualify for the new housing and slum clearance program.

On returning to Omaha I suggested to Mayor Towl that we form a citizens' committee on housing. The members should not be confined to known advocates of public housing; they should include those who might initially oppose it because of imperfect knowledge. They should also include construction men, real estate interests, architects, bankers, building and loan representatives, and public-spirited citizens. That advice left its imprint on the actual composition of the mayor's housing committee. When the members came together for their initial meeting, I suggested that we apply for slum clearance and public housing projects before any federal regulations were issued which would restrict our options. I argued that if administration is nine points of the law, timing is the tenth. The committee agreed.

To the best of my recollection, I was never shy about acting the part of a "take-charge" type. By temperament, I seemed instinctively to agree with the sense of Napoleon's remark that "the tools belong to the man who can use them." Even so, I was surprised to discover that though I was still learning the ABC's of public housing, I was suddenly viewed as an "expert"—perhaps because other people nearby knew even less than I did about the subject.

Robert Kahn, a distinguished architect who was the first director of the division of housing in the Department of the Interior, visited Omaha in an official capacity, and I met with him to refine the details of the plan drafted by our committee. When I asked if there was a "form" we could use in applying for funds, he said that Washington was still working on the matter. He had something helpful to add. Because government procedures required many clearances, especially for allotments of credits or funds, we should prepare an application predicated on the general spirit of the act. The sooner we did this, the better Omaha's chances would be.

Soon afterward I suggested to Mayor Towl and to the leaders of the Omaha housing committee that we apply for two projects on political grounds and as a safety measure. One was for north Omaha where slum conditions struck the naked eye and where the population was predominantly white with a large component of Jewish families. The other was for south Omaha which had been absorbed by the city and whose population was primarily black. When I was asked what chances Omaha had to get two projects out of sixty that were to be funded by the federal government for the nation as a whole, my reply was drawn from my experiences in fund-raising for Jewish organizations: If you wanted one thing, you asked for two, and the worst that could happen was that you got both, one, or none. Besides, the politics of the case would make it difficult for administrators in Washington to favor one Omaha constituency over another.

There were no funds to take the photographs that had to go with the application. I imposed on my friend "Doc" Cook, a photographer for the *Omaha Bee News*, to join me on a walking tour of areas in north and south Omaha where he could photograph their depressing housing conditions.

Armed with these photographs and a set of applications prepared with the help of the architects and other knowledgeable people on our housing committee, I headed for Washington. By now the office of Robert Kahn and a small staff was open in the Department of the Interior for the housing division, and a man named Packard was handling applications. Senator Burke arranged for me to see him on my arrival in town. Packard's desk and nearby office furniture were covered by a mantle of paper documents, but he did not appear to be very busy. Upon handing him Omaha's two applications, I asked if they were acceptable, to which he replied with a question of his own. How long did I expect to stay in Washington? I told him I expected to stay through the next day. "Well," said he, "come back later this afternoon and I will tell you whether they are acceptable or not."

By the time of my return, Packard had read the applications and pronounced them "splendid in form" except for one detail. Our plans did not indicate the kinds of houses we intended to build. I agreed that the application was defective in that respect, but not because of a mindless oversight. We simply didn't know what kind of federally financed houses his division wanted us to build. Packard confessed that he too was uncertain on the point. Regulations, however, required that plans for houses be attached to applications.

With that I called Alan McDonald in Omaha, one of two architects in our housing group, and told him I needed some plans for houses. "What kind?" he asked. "Any kind," I replied. "And I need them by tomorrow to qualify in advance of other possible applicants." McDonald said that somewhere in the office they had some plans for small houses. If I stayed over in Washington he would get a man to bring them by train. I stayed over. The plans put in my hands the next day were for neat little cottages which no one would ever think of building in connection with a slum clearance and multiple public housing program. But I attached them to the applications and in this way complied with the general rules.

When the first sixty projects were announced, Omaha was awarded two, one for the north and the other for the south side, while the Housing Authority Act on which I had been working was moving through the unicameral Nebraska legislature.

My introduction to public housing gave me a brief but heady taste of public law and legislation. The sense of usefulness to the community as a whole which went with the taste, spoiled me for anything else, even after I returned to my law office in 1934. The partners needed me there, and I was offered and accepted a junior partnership in the firm.

Here one day I got a call from the Omaha Chief of Police Robert Samardick. "Phil," he said, "have you done anything wrong? The FBI is here checking on you." "Well," I said, "if I have done something wrong, I guess I will find out soon enough." An hour later District Judge Thompson called me to repeat what I had heard from the Omaha chief of police. I began to worry that something strange was afoot until a Mr. Maguire visited my law office and introduced himself as an FBI agent. He told me not to be alarmed. I was merely being considered for a federal appointment. He asked me some questions, and with each answer I felt more relaxed. A few weeks later I was offered and accepted the post of special assistant to the U.S. Attorney General for Public Lands in connection with slum clearance matters in Nebraska. It was part-time employment at a salary of five thousand dollars a year, with no need to leave Omaha, Nebraska. It allowed me to continue in the private practice of law when I was not otherwise involved in governmental matters.

8 □ Dark Winds

While I was getting on with my personal life and professional life, events overseas were seldom far removed from my thoughts. I had heard with growing concern the strident tone of Nazi anti-Semitism on the streets of Germany and in Nazi appeals to the electorate. In common with most other American Jews, however, I did not envision even in my nightmares its monstrous consequences. I shared a general tendency to analogize the attacks on German Jews to the pogroms in tsarist Russia, a dreadful tool of politics but mainly localized, something that stopped short of a plan to annihilate the whole of European Jewry.

Newspaper and newsreel pictures out of Germany focused on the physical aspects of Nazism—immense parades and rallies of brownshirts, along with bands of Nazi thugs on the prowl. But what of the German universities? I clung to the hope that these retained enough of their moral and political authority in German affairs to check the Nazis before they overwhelmed the whole of German life. That hope was sustained by an inexplicable ignorance of the different elements that were drawn into the Nazi movement.

I did not know, for example, that Nazi student organizations captured control of the universities before the thugs captured control of the streets—that many university professors, along with many intellectuals, acclaimed Hitler as the model for the New German, and also justified a suspension of moral restraint on action as a precondition for what they said would be Germany's moral regeneration. When I belatedly learned of the appeal of Nazism within circles of German learning, I could say with the Jewish sages that knowledge divorced from justice must be called cunning rather than wisdom. But the maxim did not explain why so many German university students, professors, and intellectuals sanctioned the use of brute force when it served their particular version of a social ideal or their careerist ambitions.

As a young president of the Omaha lodge of B'nai B'rith, I was not a policy-maker for the Order, but through my previous work in the AZA I knew most members of the executive committee under the leadership of President Alfred Cohen and other prominent figures nationwide. From periodic talks with them, and from the reports I received through B'nai B'rith's national headquarters, it was clear to me from the early 1930s onward that B'nai B'rith's official response to Nazi atrocities against Jews was complicated by the Order's relationship to its 22,000 members in Germany.

Those members included some of the most distinguished personalities of German Jewry. Rabbi Leo Baeck, the president of the German district grand lodge and a noted Jewish scholar, was the epitome of the university-trained, cultured German Jew and a major figure within Germany as a whole. In an utterance characteristic of his humanistic outlook he once wrote: "Judaism speaks of the good *man*; the words 'a good Jew' are foreign to both the Bible and to the oral law. It is *man* who is set before God." Alfred Cohen, as president of the international B'nai B'rith, naturally turned to the German rabbi for advice regarding what American Jews might do to help their brethren in Germany during the years before Hitler gained the chancellorship. To benefit from their counsel first hand, he had gone to Germany with his son-in-law, a noted rabbi, for meetings with leaders of B'nai B'rith. Baeck, who viewed events of the time from the perspective of a German Jew committed to Jewish life in Germany, advised the B'nai B'rith president to act with restraint—meaning, do nothing at all.

Cohen, out of respect for Baeck's authority, generally followed his lead regarding appropriate actions by American Jews. In September 1931, for example, reports of Nazi assaults on Jews in Berlin prompted Cohen to cable Baeck: "Deeply concerned Berlin events. Is any action by B'nai B'rith or American Jewry desirable to arouse public opinion here?" Baeck immediately cabled back: "Hearty thanks. At present nothing." In this way the eminent German-Jewish rabbi influenced all of B'nai B'rith on urgent issues posed by Nazi anti-Semitism. Was there any alternative except to hew to the line of Baeck's advice? The question, like much else in the period, continues to haunt me almost six decades later. The harsh reality was that in the late twenties and thirties an international organization headquartered in Cincinnati did not have ready access to news and communication facilities we now take for granted.

Judgmental failures about issues of fact followed. Thus, on January 29, 1933, the day before Hitler assumed the chancellorship of Germany, President Cohen reported to a meeting of the executive committee of B'nai B'rith: "Happily, it seems that Hitlerism is on the wane." In support of this conclusion he cited an extract from a recent letter from Baeck. "The strong wave of anti-Semitism is already beginning to ebb off," the German rabbi wrote. "One cannot speak of an imminent National Socialist danger in the same terms as one had spoken half a year ago." Even after the Nazis disrupted American contacts with the German B'nai B'rith in 1933, Cohen continued to resist any initiative that he thought would endanger the members of the Order in Germany.

The menace of Nazism, subject to many conflicting interpretations, seemed only to increase the divisions among American Jewish organizations. Rabbi Stephen Wise, head of the American Jewish Congress, for example, called for the creation of an international World Jewish Congress. Based upon the concept of the Jewish people as a unified organism, it would be empowered "to deal with all questions affecting Jewish life, and to represent the Jewish people to the outside world in its struggle for civil and national rights." The official representatives of other organizations that were approached—the American Jewish Committee, the World Zionist Organization, and B'nai B'rith—expressed their abhorrence of any such idea.

Another attempt at unity was initiated in February 1933 when B'nai B'rith convened a meeting of representatives of the American Jewish Congress and the American Jewish Committee, two other national organizations committed to the battle against anti-Semitism and to the defense of Jewish rights, to try to develop a plan for cooperation or at least the coordination of activities. The three organizations agreed that "for the present, public agitation would not serve the cause of Reich Jewry," and instead established a joint conference committee "to keep a close watch on conditions in Germany." The life of this agreement lasted less than a month; it was shattered on the rocks of tactics. The Congress favored mass protest meetings; B'nai B'rith and the American Jewish Committee, for their part, rejected noisy displays.

When American Jews at last grasped the fact that Nazi Germany was embarked on a ruthless official policy of anti-Semitism, the immediacy of the threat led to a call in the spring of 1933 by the Jewish War Veterans, the Yiddish-speaking *landsmanschaft* federation, and the pro-Zionist American Jewish Congress for a boycott of German goods as a "moral obligation" and an "action of self-defense and for the defense of the interests of humanity." B'nai B'rith was invited to join the boycott movement, but its executive committee "after painful soul searching" refused, citing as its reason the Order's large membership in Germany. The Order, in an antiboycott statement of its own, "recognized the ethical basis for the justice of a spontaneous boycott," but considered "an organized boycott unnecessary." It had "faith that Americans, both Jews and non-Jews, as individuals, would deal with the situation justly and effectively." The American Jewish Committee took substantially the same antiboycott position.

Alfred Cohen ceaselessly urged the State Department to assist German Jews in all ways possible, and he claimed special consideration for B'nai B'rith in Germany on the grounds that it was a branch of an American organization. State Department pressure, in turn, may have secured for B'nai B'rith a longer life in Germany than any allowed to other fraternal organizations. For in 1933 the Nazis ordered all German branches of international organizations to disband, but Baeck refused to disband B'nai B'rith, which was allowed to function for four more years. The "privileged" position of the Order during that period may have contributed in part to the reluctance of the executive committee of B'nai B'rith to participate in the boycott movement.

[II]

Zionist organizations initially grew more than did B'nai B'rith because of the rising menace of Nazism. The Zionist Organization itself, however, was badly split in the opening years of the 1930s, as I learned first hand after I became president in 1931 of the Omaha District of the Zionist Organization of America (ZOA), and served as a delegate to the ZOA convention in Atlantic City. This was the first meeting held in the United States after the stormy convention of the World Zionist Organization (WZO) where Chaim Weizmann had been forced to step down from its presidency. Rabbis Stephen Wise, Louis Newman, and Abba Hillel Silver were among the American Jewish critics who criticized his policy of negotiating with the British mandatory power to secure

Zionist objectives in Palestine in contrast to the "direct action" they favored.

In Atlantic City, the ZOA meeting seemed to be devoted mainly to lofty speeches for the edification of any hearkening angels, and to political maneuverings for office. Still, some ZOA heavyweights on the scene, who included a number of my B'nai B'rith friends, pushed my name forward as a prospective future leader. That is how I found myself on the resolutions committee which, among other things, considered a series of draft pro forma greetings.

One of the draft resolutions of greetings was addressed to Chaim Weizmann. I considered it an appropriate salute to a man who had served the cause of Zionism with great distinction, including his crucial role in securing from the British government the Balfour Declaration recognizing the Jewish right to a home-land in Palestine. To my astonishment, Rabbi Lewis Newman mounted a stinging attack on the resolution—at attack really designed to vindicate his own policy position in opposition to Weizmann's. The proposed resolution of greetings to Weizmann was withdrawn. I was depressed by the proceedings, which were totally devoid of the "sportsmanship" associated with American political mores, where even defeated candidates for the presidency send congratulatory messages to their victorious rivals.

In my unhappy frame of mind I packed my bags, left the convention, and went on to New York City for other work. I remained a firm supporter of the Zionist concept of a Jewish state in Palestine, but I never again attended a Zionist convention as a delegate. I was, however, present at some of them as a participant on convention programs, and I worked with leading Zionists in connection with community matters. I always maintained my local Zionist affiliation.

[III]

Before Hitler's assumption of power in Germany, the need for sustained immigration to Palestine was of secondary importance to many of the official world leaders of the Zionist movement. They labored for *political* recognition by the major powers of the Jewish title of right to a homeland, but they did not dwell on the question of how the homeland was to be settled. Ben-Gurion from the start saw matters differently. As early as 1917, at the height of enthusi-asm for the prospects opened up by the Balfour Declaration, he argued that "the Declaration was not the culmination of Zionism but its beginning." What needed to be done now was to bring back the people of Israel to the land of Israel. "History," he continued, "will not wait. We must create a Jewish majority in the land of Israel in the next twenty years. We must connect the creation of a Homeland with the fate of the Jewish masses."

In 1933, coincident with Hitler's triumph in Germany, Ben-Gurion defined the tasks of the Zionist executive in ways bordering on authentic prophecy:

> The tragedy that has struck the Jews of Germany has not struck them alone. Hitler's regime endangers Jews everywhere....Nor is Hitler's Germany threatening the Jewish people alone. It cannot exist for very long without embarking upon a war of revenge against France, Poland, and Czechoslovakia and other neighboring countries where Germans live, or against the vast Soviet Union. Germany will not go to war today because she is not prepared. However, she is preparing. It appears that the danger of war today is as great as it was in 1914. And if havoc breaks out again, it will cause greater havoc than the last one.
>
> The Jewish people are not important enough in the world to prevent a war or even to limit its impact. But there is one corner of the world where they are a very important factor, if not yet the decisive one. It is on this corner of the world that our future as a people will depend. What will be our strength and importance here when disaster strikes the world? Who knows, this terrible day may be only four or five years away (if less). In the meantime, we must double our numbers, for the size of the Yishuv on the day of decision may well determine its future. That is one of the reasons the question of immigration is the most important one facing us.

After 1933 the Nazis used every kind of economic and social pressure to force Jews to emigrate from Germany, but in the next four years only 25 percent actually left. A fundamental change for the worse dates from April 9, 1937, when the Nazis seized all B'nai B'rith property in Germany and arrested Leo Baeck and other Jewish leaders of the Order in Germany and carted them off handcuffed to a concentration camp. Next, the Nazi march into Austria in the spring of 1938 was followed at once by the persecution of 180,000 Austrian Jews. In the fall, the Munich conference, which added the Sudentenland area of Czechoslovakia to Germany, led to the swift imposition of the Nazi pattern of terror and persecution on resident Jews. Then came *Kristallnacht*, November 9, 1938, marked by the most lethal violence against

Jews in prewar Germany. Thousands of Jewish businesses were burned, synagogues of every description were destroyed, hundreds of Jews were killed, and thousands were sent to camps.

Under the existing German quota provided for by the U.S. immigration law, 27,000 refugees *could* have been *annually* granted visas, for a four-year total of around 110,000. In actual practice, no more than 30,000 to 35,000 emigrants from Nazi Germany came to the United States in the *full four years* between 1933 and 1937. The U.S. consuls who handed out visas vigorously followed the stringent guidelines first approved by President Herbert Hoover in response to the depression, and later modified slightly by President Franklin Roosevelt.

B'nai B'rith did not openly ally itself with efforts to liberalize restrictive immigration laws and administrative practices when the U.S. economy was depressed. Nor did the desperate plight of German Jews and those threatened elsewhere in central Europe draw the Order away from its traditional neutrality to the Zionist concept of a Jewish national state. It continued to keep that concept at arm's length, as did the American Jewish Committee (AJC).

This seems a good place to say that the composition and work of the AJC that exist today are different from what I encountered as a young man. I believed at the time that the AJC could have evolved into the greatest Jewish organization in the United States. Most American Jews viewed it as a potential powerhouse whose lines of communication ran to concentrations of Jewish wealth and to sources of political authority at the summit of American life. Jewish organizations of the day were deeply suspicious of one another, and their mutual enmities were often drawn along pro- and anti-Zionist lines. So it was in the case of the AJC. Its failure to emerge as *the* preeminent Jewish organization in the United States was due in no small measure to its ideological opposition to Zionism, and its fear of being associated in any venture in which Zionism would be a constituent element. As more American Jews gravitated to the cause of Zionism in consequence of the events in Europe, the AJC lost its likely constituency in the decades between the 1930s and 1950s—though it came to purposeful life again in connection with other vital matters.

Even the B'nai B'rith's cautious response to the idea of Palestine as a place of refuge for imperiled German Jews was initially cast in philanthropic terms alone. In 1934, for example, the Order opened a shelter home in Jerusalem for refugees. Later it made a substantial donation to the Jewish National Fund toward the establishment of the settlement of Moledeth (Homeland) B'nai B'rith, also known as Alfred M. Cohen Moledeth in honor of the B'nai B'rith president. Somewhat later the Order repeated the contribution and another colony, known as Ramat Zvi (Heights of Henry), was established in honor of then President Henry Monsky.

[IV]

In May 1938, Alfred Cohen, who was then seventy-eight, refused another term as president of the Order, and Henry Monsky was elected in his place. Monsky was the first man of eastern European background to serve as president of the Order, and his election was emblematic of demographic changes within the American Jewish community.

The 1940 census would soon reveal that more than 80 percent of American Jews were of eastern European origin while 70 percent were already native born. It would also show that Jews now were found in increasing numbers in the ranks of shopkeepers and white-collar workers. They had secured bridgeheads in the professions of medicine and law but were still markedly under-represented in engineering and architecture. They could be found in posts of high visibility on teaching and research faculties for the biological and physical sciences. Yet certain departments in major universities were virtually off limits to Jewish graduate students who aspired to careers as university professors. This was notoriously true in areas of study such as American history, political science, and English literature.

The same convention of B'nai B'rith which elected Monsky president of the Order also voted an end to the arrangement whereby the location of B'nai B'rith's headquarters depended on where the president lived. The convention debated the question whether the permanent headquarters should be in New York or in Washington, D.C. The latter won out, partly because delegates from the medium and smaller towns around the nation feared that in a New York location B'nai B'rith would be caught up in the maelstrom of other Jewish organizations centered in New York and lose its distinctive voice. At first, however, what passed as the "permanent" headquarters of the Order in Washington amounted to little more than some space rented in an office building on K Street N.W.

During Monsky's first year as president, B'nai B'rith added twenty thousand members to its rolls, most of them of eastern European background. In his approach to leadership, Monsky tried to avoid ideological conflicts. He was personally dedicated to Zionism, but until the early 1940s—when the nature of the Holocaust passed from the realm of rumors to the realm of shattering proof—he carefully avoided any move that would formally commit B'nai B'rith to the creation of a Jewish state in Palestine. He would have B'nai B'rith concentrate primarily on efforts to increase the number of Jewish refugees who were permitted to enter Palestine by the British Mandatory power. He played a major role in the creation of the General Jewish Council, composed of the American Jewish Committee, the Jewish Labor Committee, the American Jewish Congress, and B'nai B'rith, which nonetheless failed to create a position on anti-Semitism that unified American Jews. Despite desperate pressures on communal organizations for cooperation, their respective institutional values took priority in shaping their behavior, and the General Jewish Council ultimately collapsed.

[V]

Meanwhile, there had been a growth in the absorptive capacity of the Yishuv in Palestine. In 1931, 4,000 immigrants arrived; in 1932 the number rose to 10,000, followed by 30,377 in 1933; 42,259 in 1934; and 61,854 in 1935—exclusive of tourists who settled in the country. These were the peak years of "legal" immigration during the British mandate. What followed has been told so many times as to become a monologue which most students of modern Jewish history know by heart.

A royal commission appointed to investigate the causes of Arab riots in which many Jews were murdered, concluded that the British mandate over Palestine was no longer workable. Its recommendations for a partition of Palestine west of the Jordan—between a Jewish state and an Arab state—were debated within the British government but without effect. A successor government, however, formally approved the recommendation of a later royal commission which called for a reduction of Jewish immigration to twelve thousand a year, and to the retention of British control over the entire country rather than part of it set aside for the Arabs.

Zionist circles realized that it was imperative for immigration to Palestine to continue even without the permission of the British government. Small groups of illegal immigrants had previously arrived by boat with the help of the governments of the countries whose ports served as points of departure. In 1938, however, when the British began to impose restrictions on immigration, illegal immigration began on a much larger scale. Some 105,000 of the total 115,000 illegal immigrants until the eve of World War II were brought into the country by Aliya Bet, the code name for the operation.

[VI]

It was during this period of growing darkness and confusion that I was first introduced to a book whose thrust was to have a decisive impact on my understanding of Judaism, its needs, and my response to them. I refer to the 1935 printing of Mordecai Kaplan's *Judaism as a Civilization*.

Kaplan, unlike the leading Jewish orators of the day such as Rabbis Stephen Wise, Lewis Newman, and Abba Hillel Silver, was no "thunderer." Ordained as an Orthodox rabbi, he had held the pulpit of an influential Orthodox congregation in New York but soon found himself drifting away from the traditional interpretation of Judaism. When he could no longer conscientiously preach and teach within the limited frame of Orthodox doctrine, he left the rabbinate in favor of work on the broad fronts of Jewish education, social concerns, and community organization. *Judaism as a Civilization* gave voice to his reflections on how to square the meaning of Judaism with some of the problems of inner conflict that beseiged the minds of the students and the laity whom he was trying to teach—conflicts such as I had known since my high school days.

Kaplan was profoundly concerned with the physical disasters that had already struck or threatened Jews in Germany and in central Europe. Yet the focus of his text was on the crisis in the spiritual side of Jewish life in the United States.

In measured words, he advanced the thesis that each of the three groups of Jews in America—Reform, neo-Orthodox, and Conservative—conceived of Judaism in exclusively religious terms. Because each assumed that Jews differed from non-Jews primarily in matters of religious belief, each envisioned Jewish survival as a problem of so adapting religious tenets to the exigencies of the time as to hold at bay the prospect that Jews would be absorbed by the environment. Yet a Judaism conceived of only as a religion could not unaided withstand the forces of dissolution at work all around it—the obsolescence of the traditional concept of salvation as the exclusive privilege of the Jewish people, the enjoyment of civil rights, the exigencies of the modern economic order, and the intellectual appeal of the humanistic outlook which substituted reason and experiment for the authority of tradition.

Kaplan remarked that when a person is about to abandon a house for fear that it might fall on his head at any moment, it is folly to try to convince him that he ought to remain in it because of the beautiful frescoes on its walls. Jewish life was becoming uninhabitable because it was in danger of collapse. The problem was how to reconstruct the house in order to make it more habitable. In Kaplan's terms, this meant that "apart from the life which, as a citizen, the Jew shares with the non-Jew, his life should consist of certain social relationships to maintain, cultural interests to foster, activities to engage in, organizations to belong to, amenities to conform to, moral and social standards to live up to as a Jew." Kaplan did not hide behind that sweeping generalization. He detailed in concrete terms what each of these constituent elements of Judaism as a civilization called for.

The theoretical and practical aspects of Kaplan's book, taken as a single whole, gave me a feel for something I had been groping for all along—a synthesis between Judaism as a religion and Judaism as a culture, both in harmony with my aspirations as an American citizen. I underlined in pencil many paragraphs in my copy of his book—all by way of saying "Amen." Fifty-five years after I first read what Kaplan wrote, I had occasion to leaf through my copy. I found that the ideas in the paragraphs I had underlined prefigured those which sounded through many of my own utterances in later life.

9 □ New Directions

A candle which lights up a small side chapel in a cathedral sinks into a spark when carried into the great vault of the nave. The image suggests the limits of my involvement in the response of American Jewish organizations to the plight of German Jews in the 1930s. In that decade I served as a leader at different times of the Omaha Lodge of both B'nai B'rith and the Omaha District of the Zionist Organization of America. I had, however, only a limited influence among the men who made official policies in B'nai B'rith and the ZOA.

I could buttonhole acquaintances among them. I could question the facts on which they based their judgments. I could reflect on how they bore themselves at the head of their respective organizations. I could talk, write, argue, implore, direct membership and fund-raising drives. In these and other ways I tried to be "useful." But it would take World War II to accelerate by half a generation the time by which men of my age normally attained places of national leadership in their organizations. Beforehand, in the forums to which I had access, I argued that B'nai B'rith must emancipate itself from the chain which tied it to the Pittsburgh platform adopted in the late nineteenth century by the Germanic leaders of Reform Jewry in America who rejected the concept of political Zionism. Emancipation would come, but only after the unspeakable disaster that destroyed European Jewry.

Meanwhile, I had work to do in my dual role as special assistant to the U.S. Attorney General for Public Lands and in my private law practice in Omaha. The work as a special assistant, which continued until the fall of 1936, entailed frequent trips to Washington to gain new information about the developing housing program and how Omaha could benefit from it. To the same end I became a member of the National Association of Housing Officials, the predecessor of the National Association for Housing and Redevelopment. In this way I came to know and be known to leaders in the field of housing, and I welcomed a chance to move among them.

I was not so starry-eyed as to assume that all were fit for the company of saints, if not angels. Some, no doubt, were driven by ambitions no more lofty than those of common humanity. But I believed then, and I still believe, that most of the people with whom I worked on housing and slum-clearance projects were animated by a vision of what a good society should be like and how an adequate housing program could serve it. We shared with other men and women who were drawn into other rapidly evolving fields of public policy a sense of having been entrusted with an historical enterprise calculated to change the face of the United States. The idea of assuming responsibility for the welfare of the entire community carried with it a sense of awe. I felt then, and still feel, that the government of a free country is no less holy than the service in a synagogue.

Slum clearance and public housing were only one of the dimensions of the federal government's housing program. There were others as well, and in my work as a special assistant I learned their fine points of detail. So it was with the program set in motion by the Federal Housing Act of 1934. The act not only revolutionized the nature of home mortgages, backed by the FHA's celebrated insurance principle, but extended the revolution in two further directions. First, the creation of the Federal Savings and Loan Insurance Corporation (FSLIC), under the Home Loan Bank Board, provided member savings and loan associations with insurance coverage along the lines of the Federal Deposit Insurance Corporation (FDIC), whose coverage applied only to commercial banks. Second, the FHA act authorized the creation of Federal Mortgage Associations which could buy up mortgages, large and small, and issue bonds against them in denominations that could be purchased by investors anywhere. In this way, mortgage investment funds could flow from areas where they were in surplus to those where they were in short supply.

The radical concept of mortgage financing at the heart of the FHA measure should have made large headlines. Ironically, its proponents were forced to mute that aspect of the FHA bill and to stress instead how the bill would spur new construction. They would not openly justify the reform on what was in fact its strongest ground—that it would end the restrictive mortgage loan practices of creditor agencies with harmful consequences to the economy as a whole. Most banks and many insurance companies were opposed to the FHA's mortgage market reforms, just as most banks, with the major ones in the lead, had historically opposed everything of benefit to the banks themselves, such as the creation of the Federal Reserve System and the Federal Deposit Insurance Corporation. Bankers as a group commonly believed that the commercial banking system should not be encouraged to engage in long-term mortgage financing. Some assumed that if private financial institutions did not take advantage of the measure which authorized the creation of Federal National Mortgage Associations, the FHA system as a whole would collapse, and mortgages would again advert to the old basis of high down payments, high closing costs, high interest rates, and short maturity dates. That assumption, like much else that issued from some narrow-gauge bankers, was undercut when the Reconstruction Finance Corporation promoted the rise of a secondary market for mortgages by creating what came to be known as Fanny Mae.

The FHA new-home construction program did not suddenly fulfill the high hopes that rode on it as a recovery measure. It was not easy to formulate and win assent to workable nation-wide rules for appraising homes. What the University of Chicago's President Robert M. Hutchins once had to say about education—that it is as difficult to change a curriculum as it is to move a cemetery—had a matching piece in the difficulty of altering airy-fairy but hallowed rules for property appraisals. In fact, the new rules at first were so restrictive that virtually the only people who qualified for FHA-insured mortgages were those who did not need them. The picture here would eventually change for the better when legislative amendments revised the rules and liberalized operation. So, too, the financial institutions that had bitterly opposed the FHA measure, or refused to participate in the program, or didn't understand how it worked, eventually awoke to the fact that the insured FHA mortgage was a profitable credit instrument for *themselves*. With that, the stage was at last set for an historical process wherein the FHA mortgage enabled tens of millions of American families to acquire homes. In the aggregate, that changed the American landscape.

Long before that time, however, I gained an increasing number of clients in need of a guide through the mass of legislation pouring out of Washington. Prospective builders and developers, for example, came to my office for advice on how the new instruments of action would enable them to be multiple builders.

Tract development, after a hesitant start, became common in America solely because programs like FHA and others broadened the market enormously by making credit available over a long period of time for repayment.

My law practice also grew on other fronts. It is enough to mention a key case. The Nebraska legislature had enacted a tax law which treated intangible property such as notes and accounts as if they were real property. The object of the law was to escape the limits courts had set on how much personal property could be taxed, though there were no limits on the level of real property taxes. I was retained by the Merchants Association to challenge the constitutionality of the tax; in the absence of that challenge, the rate on intangible property would have been several times what it had been before.

Here, as always, I followed Dean TePoel's classroom injunction to look for the kernel in the nutshell—and found it in an opinion by Supreme Court Justice Benjamin Cardozo. He remarked that while the power of the legislature is enormous, it does not extend to calling black white and white black—or, in translation, to calling intangible property real property. My legal brief, based on a single sentence in Justice Cardozo's opinion, was one of the shortest I ever wrote. The tax legislation at issue was held unconstitutional, and the victory before the Nebraska Supreme Court brought more merchants as clients to my law office.

[II]

The character of public housing and slum clearance in the United States was fundamentally recast by the Housing Act of 1937. As noted, the first New Deal program for public housing entailed direct grants to the states and principalities through the Federal Housing Division within the Department of the Interior. Between 1933 and 1937, 21,600 dwellings were constructed in sixty public law rental housing projects in thirty-seven cities. But this was a drop in the bucket compared with need.*

Under the Housing Act of 1937, states henceforth could create

*The first comprehensive national survey of housing was made in connection with the 1940 census. It showed that of the nation's 21,616,000 urban dwelling units, 5,350,000 lacked inside baths or toilets, lacked running water, and were in need of major repairs. Of the 6,060,000 rural nonfarm units, 4,892,000 were also deficient in these respects, while three-fourths of farm units out of 7,625,000 were similarly deficient.

local housing authorities which in turn were required to study the low-income housing needs of their communities. Local authorities could then apply to the federal government for contracts and loans to finance project construction and for subsidy aids so that housing projects could operate at appropriate rentals for low-income families. The rents themselves were calculated to pay for maintenance and improvement of the project, and local authorities under state laws could issue tax-exempt bonds to be paid off over a period of up to forty years. Further, the U.S. Housing Authority— as a source of loans and as the ultimate guarantor of the bonds issued by local authorities to finance their operation—could take control of local housing projects if local authorities failed to adhere to standards set for tenant selection, maintenance, budgeting, policy, sanitation, fire protection, and so on.*

Omaha city officials speedily created a local housing authority as required by the Housing Act, because Nebraska statute books already contained a law, which I had drafted, authorizing the creation of such an authority. When the enabling legislation was challenged before the state supreme court, I was retained to defend the constitutionality of the measure. The court was dominated by "conservatives," but the legislation was unanimously upheld. In fact, during this period I was retained as a lawyer in four of the eight important constitutional cases that came before the Nebraska Supreme Court.

In the country at large, the Housing Act helped *eventually* to strengthen the financial underpinnings of state and local housing authorities. I say *eventually* because private financial institutions were slow to buy the new tax-exempt notes and bonds which local housing authorities issued to supplement the direct financial aid they received from the federal government. Aside from being put off by the novelty of the financial instruments, some banks no doubt were deeply suspicious of the prospective "landlord" role of the United States government. Even in the case of privately financed housing, a landlord's role was shot through with uncomfortable ambiguities. Why should the federal government's be any better?

I encountered a case of the "slows" in connection with the new financial instrument when I contacted Dale Clark, the president of my own bank in Omaha, in the hope that he would buy notes

---

*After VJ Day in 1945, it was my duty to call this legal point to the attention of the Chicago Housing Authority and to city officials, led by Mayor Ed Kelly, because of deteriorating conditions in the Chicago Housing Authority.

issued by the Omaha Housing Authority. Although he had once warned me that I was endangering my future because I wanted to borrow $250 from his bank, I thought he would see the merit of buying tax-exempt fully secured notes which paid between 5 and 6 percent—a high yield in a depression context. Clark, however, was put off by the novelty of the financial instrument. "Don't rely on us for your market," he said to me. "You had better go East in your search for buyers." Later on, when bankers became familiar with the notes issued by local housing authorities, the tax-exempt features of the notes and bonds, even at interest rates far below the initial offering, made them attractive as investments.

As often happens when federal, state, and local agencies must work in tandem, differences surfaced soon after the Housing Act went into effect—starting with the administrator's duty to see that local housing authorities properly spent the funds and subsidies they received from the federal government. In particular, strains arose at the point where policing functions merged with policy issues. Local housing authorities therefore needed spokesmen who could represent them in dealings with the U.S. Housing Authority at the highest level. Two members of the National Association of Housing Officials—Dr. Bryn Hovde, director of the Pittsburgh Housing Authority, and I, as representative of the Omaha Housing Authority—were chosen by the administrator of the U.S. Housing Authority in Washington to speak to matters of common concern to local housing administrators. The work broadened my perspective on both public and private housing as a single whole.

Actual operations under the Housing Act began amid a recession which started at the end of August and led to an economic contraction more precipitous than the one that began in 1929. My surprise at the onset of the recession could not have been greater than if I saw mice suddenly chasing cats. The event forced President Roosevelt to abjure his loyalty to Treasury Secretary Henry Morgenthau's conviction that a balanced budget was the guarantor of economic recovery. On April 14, 1938, the president sent Congress a program for a resumption of large-scale government spending—for WPA, Farm Security, the National Youth Administration, the Civilian Conservation Corps, federal highways, federal buildings, and flood control. In addition—and the matter was of special interest to me in view of my involvement in public housing—the new spending program also increased funds available for slum clearance and low-cost public housing beyond the levels previously set in the Housing Act.

The administration's antirecession moves helped return the economy to its level on the eve of the 1937–1938 contraction, but the revival was too late to help many administration-backed candidates during the 1938 congressional election. The Democrats retained control of Congress, but the fabulous majorities which they had won in 1936 were reduced from 244 to 93 in the House, and from 58 to 46 in the Senate. On paper these were still formidable margins, but a newly formed coalition of conservative Republicans and Southern Democrats served notice that Capitol Hill might revolt. The mere existence of the coalition made Roosevelt reluctant to battle over domestic issues. He must conserve his political strength for use in seeking increased appropriations for a military preparedness program in the face of the threat of war abroad. The 1938 congressional elections in effect marked the cutoff date for action on the domestic agenda of the New Deal.

What had been accomplished since 1933?

The great and durable works of the New Deal are now so much a part of the air we breathe that it is sometimes hard to recall when they were not in being; I believe this will also be the case with the achievements of President Johnson's program under the Great Society. The New Deal's achievements included the creation of major regulatory institutions such as the National Labor Relations Board, the Securities Exchange Commission, the Federal Communications Commission, and the major restructuring of the Federal Reserve Board under the Banking Act of 1935. They included insurance systems for banks and for savings and loan institutions. They included innovations in the housing field—the Home Owners Loan Corporation, the Federal Home Loan Bank, the FHA-insured mortgage, a start on slum clearance and low-income public housing. They included rural electrification, assistance to farmers, advances in the generation of electrical power, and a major start on an extensive social security program.

States and municipalities were to a large extent subsidized by federal outlays for public works. Land-grant colleges, which received federal funds under various New Deal programs, built major physical facilities which later enabled them to meet an intense postwar demand for higher education. Vast numbers of young men and women were rescued from enforced idleness. Some were put back to work on socially valuable projects under the auspices of the Civilian Conservation Corps; others were trained in useful crafts or were kept in school through programs offered by the National Youth Administration. The much maligned WPA, along with the PWA (which rescued military installations from obsolescence), built an extensive infrastructure of "public goods"—roads, sewers, airports, water works—which were to be of incalculable importance to the national defense effort between 1939 and 1945 and to the postwar nationwide development of new communities. Finally, the national income had been raised from forty billion dollars annually in the trough of the depression to approximately seventy billion dollars at the start of 1939—or only ten billion dollars below where it had been in 1929.

The New Deal, however, did not "solve" the problem of mass unemployment. Despite substantial increases in production, along with impressive earnings by industry, unemployment never fell below eight million, or one-sixth of the total available labor force. While approximately ten million workers who were unemployed in March 1933 found jobs between 1933 and 1939, the high level of continued unemployment was partly due to a demographic factor— to the entry into the labor market of a half-million new workers each year without any commensurate increase in job openings.* One could say of Roosevelt what an intense competitor like Vince Lombardi said of his Green Gay Packers: "We did not lose, but time ran out on us."

As of 1939, various opinion leaders claimed that the army of unemployed could be fixed at eight or ten million—a view that would gain fresh currency after VJ Day when eminent professional economists predicted that the nation would experience mass unemployment of ten to twelve million. All calculations concerning the future, however, were radically altered once the U.S. defense preparedness program got under way in earnest. The same event had a fundamental impact on my own life.

---

*Today the economy must annually generate jobs for more than two million new workers, including women and minorities.

10 □ Housing for Armageddon

In the months immediately before the outbreak of World War II, Congress grudgingly approved small increases in appropriations for the U.S. armed forces. So things went even after the Nazis, by the end of September 1939, absorbed the part of Poland that figured in their strange pact with the Soviet Union. Although Roosevelt called Congress into extraordinary session, the immediate purpose was not to spur the U.S. defense program but to repeal the arms embargo clause in the U.S. neutrality law so that war materiel could be sold to the Allies on a cash-and-carry basis.

It was during this period that I first came to know Eleanor Roosevelt and to lay the ground for a friendship with this remarkable woman which would mature over the years and endure until the hour of her death.

She was deeply involved in projects designed to help young people, and, because of my own work with B'nai B'rith youth programs, I was appointed to one of her committees. She had invited a few of us on that committee to lunch with her in the White House. When I glanced at the table silverware that flanked my plate, individual pieces were etched with the words "The White House" and "The President's House." But then came another: "The YMCA." I turned to the priest sitting next to me and said, "Look at this! The etched words must reflect the history of changes in the names of the President's residence." He replied: "You don't yet know Mrs. Roosevelt well enough. If you go into one of the nearby restrooms, you will probably find some Pullman towels. She is as plain as an old shoe and doesn't worry about being elegant."

I was to learn much about Mrs. Roosevelt in later years, especially when we served together in the United Nations. She was in the most precise sense of the term a gentlewoman, but she could also show a steely trait when she believed certain notions had to be set straight. In this connection I once heard Mrs. Roosevelt politely but firmly remind a high U.S. official who had invited her to ride in *his* limousine that the vehicle was not *his*; it was the property of the American people.

[II]

During the so-called phony war I continued to make short trips to Washington upon call from U.S. housing officials. The trips grew more frequent and the time spent in Washington grew longer after Germany invaded Norway and Denmark on April 9, 1940, followed a month later by the invasions of Holland, Belgium, Luxembourg, and France.

The horrible confusion of the civilians in the Low Countries—driven to panicked flight along narrow roads and machine-gunned and bombed as they fled under skies dominated by Stuka dive bombers—shook people far from the scenes of combat. Hearts were lifted by the British success in evacuating 335,585 men from the beaches of Dunkirk, France, but anyone with a sense of military reality knew that this remarkable human achievement had a grim underside. The men evacuated had been forced to abandon all their heavy equipment, and there were pitifully few replacements in Great Britain. When Winston Churchill, who succeeded Neville Chamberlain as prime minister, proclaimed in Parliament that "we will fight them on the beaches," Anthony Eden, his foreign minister, reportedly whispered to a colleague, "Fight them with what? Broken bottles?" America would provide the answer by way of the protracted process that eventually made the United States the decisive strategic factor in the war.

When President Roosevelt asked Congress to enact the first peacetime draft in American history, I marveled at the shrewd way he evoked golden metaphors of the past to form his defense in historical depth. The draft, he explained, was simply a call to the youth of the nation to answer "the militia muster," as in former times when America was still in its childhood. World politics thereupon shrank to the size of an Indian uprising on the American frontier; aircraft became watchtowers, battleships became canoes, and tanks became squirrel rifles used in defense of log cabins. Once the selective service law was enacted in the spring of 1940, I was among millions of American men who registered for the draft, not knowing when my number might be called for what was initially the one-year life of the law.

The president also asked Congress to provide funds for an immediate expansion of military supplies, including the production of fifty thousand aircraft, a goal that seemed no more than a propaganda stunt, or perhaps a summons to strive for an unattainable objective. As the event proved, the U.S. would eventually produce more than 200,000 aircraft. Then again, Roosevelt created what was known as the National Defense Advisory Commission (NDAC), the parent of all the war production, food production, defense housing, priority, and price-control organization—and the predecessor of the War Production Board. This marked the start of the mobilization of manpower for civilian purposes, as selective service was for the military. The twin leaders of the NDAC were William S. Knudsen, president of General Motors, who was in charge of industrial production, and Sidney Hillman, president of the Amalgamated Garment Workers Union, who was in charge of the labor front. The NDAC was placed in an amorphous institutional setting known as the Office of Emergency Management, with links to the Office of the President.

A radical speedup in the pace and scope of defense production soon underlined the need for adequate housing in defense-impacted areas to which workmen and their families were migrating in large numbers. The government's initial response was to convert peacetime housing aids to defense housing purposes. But to chart a course that went beyond that initial response, Roosevelt created a Division of Defense Housing Coordination in the Office of Emergency Management. To administer the division he appointed Charles F. Palmer of Atlanta, a man who combined the diction of an English patrician with the bearing of an Atlanta gentleman of *Gone with the Wind* vintage. Palmer had been head of Atlanta's public housing authority and a former president of the National Association of Housing Officials—and, not unimportant, he was a close friend of Eleanor Roosevelt. Jacob Crane of Highland Park, Illinois, a respected city planner, was appointed his deputy, and Ferd Kramer of Chicago also held a key position in the setup. Kramer and I were closely associated after the war, either in mounting creative private housing ventures or as advisers to public bodies.

Some of us who had previously worked closely with Palmer were called by him to Washington—on a six-dollar per diem basis—to advise on policy questions. Where, for example, should low-rent housing under construction or not yet started be diverted to defense housing? Where should housing be built with funds derived from War and Navy Department appropriations specially earmarked for defense housing? Other questions sprang directly from the terms of the Lanham Act, the basic congressional measure governing the way federal funds were used for the construction of federally owned defense and wartime housing.

Among the various policy questions we considered, one in particular stands out in my mind, mainly because of its future consequences. The discussion centered on a draft legislative proposal whose aim was to help convert the Federal Housing Administration's preoccupation with peacetime housing to private defense housing. The standard FHA loan was then 20 percent down with a twenty-five-year amortization. But it was correctly argued that the terms should be further liberalized to make more private housing available at reasonable rates for essential workers in defense-impacted areas. To that end a Title VI would be added to the FHA act, applicable to areas certified as being in need of defense housing. By its terms, the initial down payment on homes up to a limit of six thousand dollars for sale or rent would be reduced to 10 percent, with the amortization period lengthened from twenty-five to thirty years. Of equal if not greater importance, the mortgage should cover "90 percent of value."

At an early point in the discussion, I said that I generally favored private financing of home construction to direct public expenditures, but if we were to approve the draft of Title VI we should understand its implications. A reduction to a 10 percent down payment, coupled with a total mortgage based on "90 percent of value," was a formula which would enable developers of large-scale housing projects to put up little cash, if any, of their own. Why? Because depending on the land appraisal, added value was created simply by taking a piece of raw land and placing a cluster of new houses on it. Some of the other people at the meeting disagreed with me, but having said my piece, I returned to Omaha and marked time until Title VI was added by Congress to the FHA law.

After a discussion with my law partners, they agreed to test the possibility under Title VI of constructing a cluster of houses and investing little, if any, private funds. Our law office, as noted, represented realtors and architects as well as an insurance company that was an FHA-approved lender. Through one of the realtors, we located a site for twenty-eight houses. He also gave us an option on the land, subject to payment only if and when we developed a plan whereby the FHA would approve loans to build the twenty-eight homes.

We then arranged for an architect friend to prepare preliminary blueprints for the houses; it was understood he would get the job only if the plans were approved for an FHA loan. We used our own legal services to incorporate a company, then applied through the corporation to the insurance company for insured loans under Title VI of the FHA law. When the loans were approved and opened, we paid the realtor for the land in the defense impact area, and we paid the architect to complete the plans. Construction began at once. The houses, when built and sold, netted our little corporation what was then a tidy profit of $28,000.

This test did not prove my point to the exact letter as to what could be done with virtually no money. A fee of $26.50 was paid for filing the incorporation. But the test showed that under the 10 percent loan provision and redefinition of a mortgage based on "value," a developer could profit handsomely from a major housing project by putting only his expert knowledge, "sweat equity," and a little capital at risk.

At the time, no one could have foreseen how Title VI would be a mainspring for the emergence of great tracts of defense-related housing built during the war years, and for the even larger projects that followed the end of the war. It would also be central to my own work, undertaken with Nathan Manilow and Carroll Sweet, in developing Park Forest on the outskirts of Chicago—one of the first planned towns built in the United States immediately after World War II, for veterans' preference and occupancy.

[III]

In 1940, when I was periodically commuting between Omaha and Washington as a consultant to the defense housing coordinator, I was elected president of B'nai B'rith District No. 6, a fertile area for so many institutional innovations in the Order. I was thirty-three years old at the time, the first product of AZA ever to hold the presidency of a district of the Order. The next year, after my election to succeed Sam Beber as president of AZA's Supreme Advisory Council, I came to the second annual meeting of the Women's Supreme Council of B'nai B'rith, where questions were asked about the institutional relationship between AZA and the young women's group that had been formed. Anita Perlman of Chicago, who was a leader of the B'nai B'rith Women, argued for fair treatment of the girls.

I envisioned a Jewish youth movement of the future wherein the boys and girls would retain their separate organizational identities but B'nai B'rith would provide a roof structure for them. In later conversations with Henry Monsky, president of the Order and with Maurice Bisgyer, executive secretary, I stressed that the growing strength of B'nai B'rith Women would generate sufficient financial support to serve chapters of girls as well as boys. The B'nai B'rith Youth Organization, which brought boys and girls together along the lines I had envisioned, ultimately materialized in late 1944. The men and women who constituted the backbone of the organization administered a single set of programs for both boys and girls.

[IV]

In early 1941 I was asked to spend more time in Washington in the office of the Coordinator of Defense Housing, starting with a tour of duty set at around sixty days. My family remained in Omaha during this period so as not to disrupt the schooling of the children; I regularly commuted from Washington to be with Ethel and my two children, Bettylu and Tom. But I was increasingly drawn to Washington-based tasks, especially after Congress, on March 11, 1941, approved the Lend-Lease Act. The act empowered the president of the United States "in the interests of national defense" to make available to governments whose defense he deemed vital to the defense of the United States a widely defined range of "defense articles," not excluding essential civilian needs. Though eligibility for lend-lease aid was determined in the light of overall strategy, Great Britain was the country to be helped at once.

The drive to step up the production of supplies for both the U.S. armed forces and Great Britain carried with it an urgent need for more housing in defense-impacted areas. So now I was among those who were asked to spend still more time in Washington.

In a Washington newspaper one day, I read a statement by Sidney Hillman, co-director with William Knudsen of the Defense Production Board, to the effect that a new defense city should be built in the Detroit area. Although I had been working closely with one of Hillman's aides, I had been told nothing about the proposed defense city. It seemed to me that here was a clear breakdown in communication between the Office of Defense Housing Coordinator and the Defense Production Board. I telephoned my chief, Charles Palmer, to ask what he knew about the matter. Palmer had seen the same announcement and was jarred by it. "Housing and new cities," he said to me, "is our business, not Hillman's, and I will tell him so when I see him." Did he want me to come along for the meeting? "Yes," Palmer said emphatically, "you make the appointment so that Hillman and Knudsen are both present."

At the meeting I was a bystander to a wonderful made-in-America encounter between two conscientious, patriotic Americans of radically different pedigrees. One was Charles F. Palmer, a courtly Atlanta gentleman who spoke in a clipped English accent. The other was Sidney Hillman, a man who rose from the ranks of immigrant Jewish tailors to be a national labor leader, who spoke in sing-song style with a Yiddish ring, and who was a trusted political associate of President Roosevelt.

Palmer said, "Your planned new city in the Detroit area invades the territory of *my* organization! We have not decided how much housing should be built in that area, who should build it and where!"

Hillman, who answered for Knudsen, was experienced in dealing with even more inflamed men—the heads of garment companies who regularly took their stand in labor negotiations on the high ground of "principle and justice." "Mr. Palmer," he began soothingly, "don't get angry. Do you want to build the city? That's all right. It can be worked out. But listen. I must first tell you why I told the papers what I did. I was at the White House when President Roosevelt said to me, 'Sidney, those sons-of-bitches in Detroit are continuing to build passenger cars. That's not what we need. We want them to build tanks. We've got to bring more workers to Detroit for defense work. But we can't get them to come unless we get houses for them. Get houses.' Now, Mr. Palmer, when the president of the United States gives me an order like that in plain English, it could only mean that I should go ahead and do what he says. Look, Mr. Palmer, I make mistakes. You make mistakes. Isn't the president of the United States entitled to make a mistake also? He is at least entitled to a writ of *rachmones* [compassion]."

When we were outside Hillman's office after reaching a procedural agreement on the point at issue, Palmer turned to me and said with relish, "We sure goosed him, didn't we?" I managed not to answer the question.

I later went with Palmer to Detroit for an on-site study of defense-related housing needs. En route back to Washington, Palmer suggested that the U.S. would "inevitably" be drawn into the European war as a belligerent. He urged me to lay aside my status as a consultant to the Division of Defense Housing and to join its regular Washington staff. I agreed.

My decision demanded some changes in my private life. I had previously shared an apartment in Washington with Congressman Samuel Weiss of Pennsylvania, and Max Baer. But to avoid long separations from Ethel and our two children—Ethel was pregnant at the time—I rented a home in Bethesda, Maryland, on the northern rim of Washington, in the hope that we could live a normal family life. I also took a leave of absence from my law partnership.

At the time, no head of a bureau in the executive branch of government could be paid a salary higher than that of a U.S. senator. That meant a maximum of ten thousand dollars annually. People in my position, with two homes to maintain—and frequent official travel and entertainment to be covered only by a fixed six dollars per diem—needed a second source of income beyond their government salary to avoid going into debt. My share of the fees of what had been my law business, forwarded to me after I left the law firm, enabled me to pursue government work.

[V]

The pressure for increased production grew even more acute after the Nazis invaded the Soviet Union in July 1941, followed by a U.S. commitment to ship war materiel to the Soviets under the Lend-Lease Act. As usual, the call for stepped-up production carried with it a demand for more housing in defense-impacted areas. At the same time the air crackled with rumors about how various aspects of the defense preparedness program, which were either in disarray or were not keeping pace with needs, would be reorganized. Charles Palmer was called to the White House for a meeting with President Roosevelt. Later that same day, glancing out of my office window, I saw Palmer walking back to our headquarters, his lips moving as he talked to himself. I had no way of knowing whether he was bringing good or bad news back from the White House.

Roosevelt, who always found it hard to fire anyone, found it doubly hard in Palmer's case. He was a close friend of Mrs. Roosevelt and a dedicated public servant. But the president's new plans for the housing program required someone with more experience in the top reaches of government. John Blandford, a deputy administrator of TVA and a man in whom Roosevelt had a great deal of confidence, was appointed in Palmer's place. There were shakeups at subordinate levels too, though I continued to work out of the Washington headquarters of the Division of Defense Housing.

All plans were suddenly reshuffled on Sunday, December 7, 1941. My wife, our two children, and the nurse we had brought from Omaha to Washington had spent the morning and early afternoon at Mount Vernon. When we returned home the phone was ringing as I opened the door. I picked it up and learned that Pearl Harbor had been attacked. I immediately left Ethel and the children and sped to my office at 1600 I Street, N.W., not knowing what I meant to do. I was simply driven by the conviction that I must be on hand to do something, if only to get into a "make-war" frame of mind. My associates were also drawn to the place by the same conviction. They converged one by one on the headquarters of the Defense Housing Division, not in response to a command but through the force of a shared social discipline.

The devastating Japanese attack on Pearl Harbor in a single stroke freed President Roosevelt from the acute tensions caused by his knowledge of what must be done to prevent a Nazi victory and the isolationist political constraints on what he could in fact do. On Monday, December 8, Roosevelt addressed a joint session of Congress, and Congress in response to his request declared war on all the Axis powers—Germany, Italy, and Japan.

Fantastic rumors gained transcontinental currency because of the shock of the Japanese attack. The fears that gripped Washington pierced the frame of the school system as it did much else. In response to rumors of an imminent Japanese attack on the city, school administrators announced over the radio that classes were being dismissed so that children could return to the safety of their homes. Bettylu, then nine, was in a grammar school; Ethel, who was then only a few months away from the delivery of a third child (or fourth, since the second one born between Bettylu and Tom had died), rushed out of our home to look for her. She had no difficulty finding her, but Ethel's fright in a sea of confused excitement may have precipitated the miscarriage of the child she was carrying.

Jack Blandford asked that I stay on in Washington as one of his top aides. I agreed, subject to my draft status. I explained that I had told my draft board in Omaha that if my draft number came up, I would not claim an exemption on the ground that I was engaged in essential war work. Unless I had already accepted a prospective commission in the air force, I would report to an induction center just as millions of other men were doing. Blandford said he understood my intentions, and he accepted me on those terms.

Housing lacked the drama associated with the construction of ships and the production of aircraft and armaments. It was too closely associated with the normal needs of life in peacetime. Yet unless war workers and their families were to sleep under pup tents, provisions for adequate shelter were indispensable to an all-out defense production effort.

As one of Blandford's principal aides, I moved a step closer to important levers of power in Washington. That, as usual, was to my liking. I was not so vain, however, as to suffer from the illusion of central position. I was aware that had I suddenly vanished from the Washington scene, few people would have noticed. The sobering thought that the government of the United States somehow moves with the momentum of its own mass, served to remind me that I must always have outlets for work in fields alternative to government service.

Like tens of thousands of other people involved in what was now the war production program, I was at my office from early morning till late at night. New areas of housing activity must be programmed. The operating agencies in the housing field must be pushed to generate more housing, even with trailers or whatever else could shelter workers being assembled to intensify war production. The time I could spend with Ethel and the children seemed to be limited to the length of a kiss. Under the circumstances, it was best for them to return to our home in Omaha where they would have the companionship of a wide circle of relatives and friends. I moved into bachelor quarters in Washington which I shared with my friends Max Baer and Congressman Samuel Weiss.

At the time, many people were both impressed and depressed by the monolithic character of the Nazi regime. It seemed to offer unnerving proof of what a totalitarian state could accomplish through brutal coercion. Postwar studies, such as those of Alan Bullock, reversed the picture. The studies showed a system honeycombed with corruption, permeated by conflicts of authority and clashing vanities, and riddled with muddle and incompetence. On the American side of the picture, there was relatively little corruption, but there were conflicts of authority, clashing vanities, some muddle and' some incompetence. Yet postwar comparative studies showed that the American mobilization for war, once under way, was more thorough and far-reaching than was ever the case in Nazi Germany.

Major segments of the economy, including housing, were swiftly brought under complete mobilization for war purposes. Price and rent controls for new and existing housing were instituted at the end of January 1942, and the National Housing Agency (NHA), under the direction of John Blandford, set up as an emergency operation, embraced nearly all the nonfarm housing functions of the government. That included the FHA, the Federal Home Loan Bank Board, the U.S. Public Housing Authority, and the Home Owners Loan Corporation.

I have heard many eloquent speeches in my long life, but the short speech Donald Nelson gave in March on taking over the leadership of the War Production Board (WPB), when he addressed the assembled representatives of the wartime agencies, is among the few whose echoes still ring in my ears. He simply admonished us to remember that we were a *democracy* at war. In administering wartime programs, we should bear ourselves in ways which would find American democracy strengthened instead of weakened at the end of the war by the very manner in which its defense was conducted.

Meanwhile, at Blandford's request I agreed to establish myself in Chicago for a limited time—just long enough to organize a "model" regional defense housing coordination setup that could be replicated elsewhere in the nation. The region for which Chicago was the command post ran on an east-west line from Hampton Roads, Virginia, to Michigan. A small dot on the map in this region—Oak Ridge, Tennessee, was the site where the atomic bomb was eventually produced. My stay in Chicago shortened the distance I had to travel in order to visit my family in Omaha. It was here too that I first came into close contact with Carroll

Sweet, Sr., and Nathan Manilow, the pair with whom I would later collaborate in building Park Forest.

Sweet, a banker by profession, had tried to enlist in the U.S. armed forces when it looked like the U.S. would become a belligerent in the European war, but he was rejected for service because he was over sixty years of age. He had known Charles Palmer, and while the latter was still the head of the Division of Defense Housing, had applied to him for a defense-related job. That is how he came to be appointed senior priorities examiner in the Chicago regional office of the division. Every builder in the area who wanted priorities necessary for access to scarce building materials had to come to Sweet. He was a man of rock-ribbed integrity but with a crusty temperament. Even before the United States became a belligerent, he was intolerant of requests for priorities that did not plainly contribute directly to the defense effort. This attitude was further fueled by his increased zeal after Pearl Harbor: he had a son who was serving as a naval officer in the Pacific fleet.

As to Nathan Manilow, long before he started to build houses in Jeffery Manor—a war housing project of more than two thousand units on the south side of Chicago—he enjoyed an excellent reputation for cooperation with the priorities office of the National Housing Agency. Most builders of the time resisted renting the tract houses they built. They preferred a quick in-and-out policy— to get their six-thousand-dollar sales price which normally gave them a good profit on five-thousand-dollar Title VI FHA mortgages. Manilow was one of the few Chicago builders who was willing to build rental housing for the defense effort and agree to retain the structures for the duration. The few who held on, as did Manilow, found that what was considered a disadvantage became a higher profit when the war was over and ceilings on sales prices, previously set at six thousand dollars per unit, were lifted.

My stay in Chicago was terminated when Blandford called me back to Washington for another short-term assignment, the "home use" program. The country was dotted with half-finished or empty buildings which were generally casualties of the depression. If these were converted to use for defense housing—subject to help from the Home Owners Loan Corporation—they could be completed and then leased or acquired by the government at much lower cost than other houses and with less use of critical material. Completed but empty buildings could be similarly acquired.

It occurred to me, first, that just as advertising was used to help sell war bonds, it could help publicize the existence of the home use program to interested property owners. Second, it was necessary to change the outlook of key people in the HOLC's field offices. They seemed peculiarly blind to the realities of the wartime need for defense housing, and so tried to strike too good a deal on behalf of the government with property owners who might have something to offer to the home use program. Even a good deal for the owner still saved the government money as against new construction, and it also avoided upsetting residents in communities where new and temporary housing disrupted existing neighborhoods.

This advertising and educational program succeeded, and the home use program materially contributed to the supply of urgently needed defense housing at less cost and with a saving of scarce materials.

[VI]

After the home use operation was on a course that ensured its success, I was drawn yet another step closer to key levers of power with my appointment as assistant administrator in charge of programming for wartime housing. This job went to the heart of both the private and public realms of housing during the war. "Programming," for example, meant decisions about where defense housing was needed, how much, whether private or public sources should do the building, and the formulation of rules regarding the kinds of materials that could be used for building purposes. While private builders were encouraged to build as much as possible of the required new housing (two-thirds of the war housing program was accomplished through them), direct federal financing was used under two general conditions: The first occurred when housing could not be suitably provided by private builders within a set time, or when it was programmed as temporary. The second occurred when entire towns were built by the government under security wraps as was true of Oak Ridge and Vanport.

Private builders sometimes complained that the government was building too great a portion of the wartime defense housing. In their view, they could provide all that was needed. To their credit, many produced a great sweep of houses for rental or for purchase at a modest price. Many also became wealthy in the process.

As the assistant administrator in charge of programming for wartime housing, I represented Blandford at meetings of the War Production Board Requirements Committee. The committee, chaired by Julius A. Krug, allocated to different sectors of the U.S. defense effort and to our allies material in short supply. At the time, this meant virtually everything. The sixteen members of the committee, each the representative of a claimant agency, included James Forrestal, Undersecretary and later Secretary of the Navy; Admiral Williams of the Navy; General Lucius Clay of the War Department and later the first postwar commander of American forces in occupied Germany; War Manpower Administrator Paul McNutt; and Charles Taft, head of the wartime transportation agency. I was the youngest member of the committee and had reason to be thankful for my earlier formative experiences—in "running things" —which had caused me to age very quickly.

Each member of the committee sought what his agency needed, and the National Housing Agency was no exception. We were claimants for lumber and metals, particularly iron and steel—the same commodities needed to produce, crate, and ship weapons and munitions overseas.

Out of the blur of episodes related to the Requirements Committee, one in particular is etched in my memory as an example of how bigness itself in an organization can lead to broken connections between its parts. The incident occurred at a time when it was necessary quickly to produce more rocket powder for the military. Because the powder could only be manufactured at a safe distance from existing cities, workers had to be imported to out-of-the-way places and housed there. So the National Housing Agency formally asked the Requirements Committee for a substantial allotment of building materials. When the committee discussed the request, General Clay and Admiral Williams led the charge against it. Citing the urgent need for lumber and metal on vital production fronts, they insisted that it would be wrong to allow the material to go to the housing agency.

I was dumbfounded by their line of attack. When I found my tongue, I made a very short speech. I noted that the army and navy had assigned us the funds to provide the very housing which the general and admiral opposed. All I was claiming on behalf of the National Housing Agency was expressly confined to contracts which the military itself said must be urgently executed, given the pressing need for rocket powder which could only be manufactured in isolated areas. The immediate reaction, in which an embarrassed General Clay and Admiral Williams joined, was a committee vote to approve the request of the National Housing Agency.

11 □ The Search for Jewish Unity

As in the 1930s, I was more of a bystander than an actor in events related to world Jewry between 1940 and 1943. But I want to touch on them here because their aftereffects cast up problems I had to face in the postwar years when I held presidential posts in national and international Jewish organizations.

I start with David Ben-Gurion's perception that "once the war was over, the United States and not Great Britain would call the tune in Palestine." That is why Ben-Gurion, as chairman of the Jewish Agency executive, came to the United States in late 1939 and again in 1942 for a longer stay. His purpose was to enlist American Jews in support of two indivisible goals—to cancel the 1939 British White Paper which in effect nullified the Balfour Declaration, and to establish a Jewish state after the war.

The same objectives were pursued by Chaim Weizmann, then in his late sixties, who had returned to his role as president of the World Zionist Organization. The British government, after the Japanese attack on Pearl Harbor, had encouraged Weizmann to go to the United States to work on problems in chemistry related to the war effort. Once in the United States, however, Weizmann devoted himself, as he later recalled, "almost equally between science and Zionism." It was at this time that I first met him.

Weizmann's diplomatic tactics were not to the taste of Abba Hillel Silver and David Ben-Gurion. To Silver, Weizmann was "out of touch with American Jewry's temper." To Ben-Gurion he was "autocratic toward his colleagues, toward the *Yishuv* and was far too conciliatory towards the British." Ben-Gurion also presently publicly charged Weizmann with a major sin of omission, namely, that he failed to raise a public storm over the British Foreign Office opposition to the formation of an army of Jewish volunteers in Palestine.

In May 1942, for the first time ever, the different Zionist parties and organizations in the United States were brought together in a conference held in New York's Biltmore Hotel, and it was in consultation with Weizmann that they were able to agree on what became known as the "Biltmore Program." The program itself denounced the 1939 British White Paper and demanded a return to the Balfour doctrine on the ground that "the new world order that will follow victory cannot be established on a foundation of peace, justice, and equality unless the problem of Jewish homelessness is finally solved." It urged that the "gates of Palestine be opened to Jewish immigration" and that the Jewish Agency be authorized "to direct and regulate immigration into Palestine, and to develop the agricultural and industrial possibilities and the natural resources of the country." Finally and crucially, the platform urged that "Palestine be established as a Jewish commonwealth integrated into the structure of the new democratic world." Although the Biltmore Program was a product only of American Zionism, it soon became the official platform of the world Zionist movement.

When the Biltmore conference convened in May 1942, the extent of the holocaust which was overtaking European Jewry was not fully known. Weizmann, in his own address to the conference, however, put matters in prophetic perspective when he remarked:

> In a time of worldwide calamity, when it is impossible to turn the eye in any direction without being met by the spectacle of suffering and bloodshed, it may seem invidious to award to a single people the special crown of martyrdom. But a cold evaluation—if such a thing is possible— of the horrors visited upon humanity, lifts into tragic preeminence one people, the Jewish, as the most consistent and helpless target of a malignant fate.

On June 30, 1942, the British press and the Jewish Telegraphic Agency both carried the first public reports about the mass murders of Jewish civilian populations by the Nazis. Figures cited as of that date indicated that more than a million Jews had already been killed, but the public at large initially dismissed the reports as farfetched, a rewritten version of the atrocity stories about the "Huns" which were a propaganda staple during World War I. American Jews, however, soon accepted the reports as reliable.

A delegation of Jewish leaders now called on Roosevelt to urge "action by the United States in concert with the other countries at war with the Axis, to save what remained of European Jewry." Roosevelt, for his part, "assured the delegation that the Nazi criminals would be held strictly accountable," that together with its allies, the United States "would make every effort to save the Jews who could be saved; and that consideration would be given to the appointment of a joint commission to deal with the issue." By the time of this particular White House meeting, the use of gas chambers and ovens—in contrast to the previous labor-intensive system of extermination by gunfire—had increased the arithmetic of the slaughter to two million Jews.

What was to be done?

Henry Monsky in January 1943 invited thirty-four major national Jewish organizations to a preliminary conference in Pittsburgh to develop united proposals for future action on behalf of European Jews. The immediate goal was to save as many lives as possible. The long-range goal was to establish the postwar status of the Jews and the building of a Jewish Palestine. The American Jewish Committee (AJC) and the Jewish Labor Committee (JLC), however, refused to attend the Pittsburgh meeting. Both, for different reasons, still opposed the establishment of a Jewish commonwealth in Palestine. Both still meant to distance themselves from Zionists who predictably would be present in Pittsburgh.

The Pittsburgh meeting reached an agreement to hold what was called an "American Jewish Assembly" later in the year to "establish a common program in connection with postwar problems." A temporary Emergency Committee for European Jewish Affairs was also established to deal with rescue issues until the formation of a steering committee or central organization. Within a month, extensive publicity of the mass murder of Jews generated substantial public support for rescue efforts, especially after the arrival in the United States from Palestine of an emissary of the Irgun who went by the name of Peter Bergson, an alias assumed by Hillel Kook. Public agitation peaked in a massive rally at Madison Square Garden on March 1, 1943, the largest of its kind ever held by American Jews. Its dominant note was orchestrated by successive

speakers who attacked Roosevelt and the State Department's policy of "rescue through victory."

Several days later, American Jews received word of the plight of
the remaining Jews in the Warsaw ghetto: "Liquidation of Warsaw
remnants planned. Alarm the world. We suffer terribly. Remaining
Jews threatened with annihilation. Only you can rescue us." The
anguished cry momentarily broke the grip of the doctrines, tenets,
and dogmas that had held the AJC and JLC in thrall. The two
organizations on March 13, 1943, joined what now became
known as the Joint Emergency Committee for European Jewish
Affairs, which was to devote itself exclusively to rescue operations.
The recommendations which the committee prepared for a Bermu-
da conference on refugees, called by President Roosevelt, were
comprised of tears and desperation. They spoke of a will "to do
something" despite intractable difficulties. The committee, for
example, proposed that the United States deal with Germany and
other Axis governments in ways calculated to secure "the release of
their Jewish victims." It suggested that sanctuaries in Allied or
neutral nations be set up to receive the refugees, and that efforts be
made to find temporary havens in Latin America and Africa. The
program also included a recommendation to "open the doors of
Palestine for Jewish immigration," and to establish "an appropriate
intergovernmental agency" to implement the rescue program. The
committee recognized that to "relegate the rescue of the Jews of
Europe, the only people marked for total extermination, to the day
of victory is . . . virtually to doom them to the fate which Hitler has
marked out for them."

Some people believed that the success of the joint emergency
committee in uniting Zionists and anti-Zionists, socialists and
Orthodox Jews, presaged a new and unified future for American
Jews. To further that prospect, Monsky changed the name of the
pending American Jewish Assembly to the American Jewish Conference; the use of the term "conference" stemmed from a desire to
avoid any impression that an independent Jewish political entity
was being formed.

The conference, to be cochaired by Monsky and Rabbi Stephen
Wise—two strong-minded men—was set for late August. In the
interval, more than a million American Jews cast votes to elect
375 conference delegates apportioned among Jewish communities
according to their size, and an added 125 delegates divided among
64 national organizations. The General Zionists led the lists with

116 elected delegates, followed by the pro-Zionist American Jewish Congress. B'nai B'rith emerged in third place with 63 delegates, though 200 of the total number of those registered were B'nai B'rith members. I was a candidate to be a delegate from Omaha but was defeated by a local rabbi who stressed the fact that I was spending all of my time on official war-related work in Washington and would not be available when needed.

The five hundred delegates met in New York on August 29, 1943, "to create a new basis for unity," the theme developed by Monsky in his keynote address. The conference proceeded to concentrate on aspects of rescue operations until Rabbi Abba Hillel Silver, a delegate but not a scheduled speaker, took the floor to deliver a fiery speech in which he set forth the militant Zionist position. "We cannot," he cried,

> truly rescue the Jews of Europe unless we have free immigration into Palestine. We cannot have free immigration into Palestine unless our political rights are recognized there. Our political rights cannot be recognized unless our historic connection with the country is acknowledged and our right to rebuild our national home is reaffirmed. These are inseparable links in the chain. The whole chain breaks if one of the links is missing.

The Zionist majority, in the belief that "American Jewry had granted them a mandate," saw no point in relinquishing the leadership to which their numbers entitled them. In their eyes, any proposal for rescue that did not include the goal of a Jewish commonwealth was tantamount to betrayal. They placed the mass killing of Jews in "the perspective of history," and reasoned that if there had been a Jewish state, the murder of European Jews need not have happened. They rejected compromise and insisted on a commonwealth resolution without regard to its effect on the American Jewish Committee and the Jewish Labor Committee.

The American Jewish Committee, for its part, was jarred by the way the conference—as if in obedience to the will of Abba Hillel Silver—gave a higher priority to the problems of Jewish rights in the postwar world than to the immediate rescue issue. It was jarred again when the Zionists used the weight of their numbers to win approval for the commonwealth resolution. Two months later, in October 1943, the American Jewish Committee withdrew altogether from the conference, citing as its reason "the attempt to make the Commonwealth resolution morally binding on all Jewish organizations." The Jewish Labor Committee followed the AJC lead.

What it came down to was this: In a dire hour unprecedented in Jewish history, American Jewry's chief organizations could not unite in a search for ways to save those European Jews who, even in desperate circumstances, might still have been saved.

In July 1943 Chaim Weizmann returned to England still the nominal leader of the Zionist movement but deeply disturbed by even its disunity. On the eve of his departure from New York, he remarked in a letter to Rabbi Stephen Wise, "As we have seen it with governments and peoples far more powerful than we, disunity in foreign policy spells doom for that people. . . . It is infinitely more simple to indulge in high sounding but nevertheless sterile phrases than to counsel moderation, hard work and solid achievement." He concluded on a cautionary note: "I recall that I once remarked that I never wanted to use the phrase 'Jewish state' prematurely. . . . It must not be used in vain."

12 □ Commissioner

While these great events were on the move, my personal status in wartime Washington was undergoing a change. The circumstances were these:

In early May 1944, Herbert Emmerich, formerly of the Public Administration Clearing House in Chicago, resigned the twin posts he held in Washington. He had been wartime commissioner of the Federal Public Housing Authority and simultaneously the administrator of the U.S. Housing Authority. The two agencies were components of the National Housing Agency and were largely responsible for the use of public funds appropriated for the war housing program. Even when funds were allocated directly to the armed forces for housing purposes, they were transferred in the main, via interagency arrangements, to the Federal Public Housing Authority for expenditure.

The authority was nationwide in reach but was subdivided into seven regional offices which employed more than 25,000. Of these, one thousand worked in the Washington headquarters of the authority lodged in a building shared with an early version of the United Nations Relief Organization. The commissioner of the authority was accorded junior cabinet status.

John Blandford, head of the National Housing Agency, called me to his office one day to say that a number of men were eager to take Emmerich's place as commissioner of the authority, but that he was going to urge President Roosevelt to appoint me to the post. I thanked him for his expression of trust but said I doubted if I was even eligible to be considered for the appointment. Blandford knew what lay behind the doubt.

Although I was originally classified 1-A in the draft, unknown to me I had been reclassified by my Omaha draft board on the ground that the government post I held in Washington was essential to the war effort. When I learned of that action, I asked one of my former law partners in Omaha to advise the draft board to restore my status to 1-A without regard to my Washington work. This met with raised eyebrows in Omaha until the draft board was convinced that the request actually conformed to my wishes. The board then sent a message to the selective service office in Washington asking that my papers be returned to Omaha for reclassification to 1-A.

When Blandford spoke with me about being Emmerich's successor, I told him I would accept such an appointment on condition that if and when I was restored to 1-A status and called for service, neither I nor the government would seek an exemption.

What happened next I learned from Judge Samuel Rosenman, the president's counsel, who was present when Blandford recommended me to Roosevelt for the appointment. The president at the time was doing a great deal of work while he was still in bed. On the morning when my name came up for consideration along with other possibilities, Blandford summarized my services in the National Housing Agency. He added that I wanted to respond to the draft if I were called up, and that this might disqualify me from further consideration.

When the president heard of my attitude, he said, "Well, that is rather unique. It is usually the reverse. It would be a good thing to have a fellow who is eager to go into the military instead of working in the civilian branch. Also, what did you say this man's name was? Klutznick? Klutznick? We don't have a Klutznick in the government. We need one."

When I learned that my appointment would be forthcoming, I told Blandford that since the whole of the matter was still subject to Senate approval, I would have to discuss the prospect with Nebraska's two senators, both of whom were Republicans. One was Senator Paul Butler; the other was Senator Kenneth Wherry who had defeated George Norris but was known in Washington as "Wherry the Merry Undertaker" on other grounds. He was in fact an undertaker by vocation. I called Senator Butler first because he was senior, and he arranged a joint meeting with Senator Wherry. When I explained what was in prospect, the immediate response from both men was, "You must take the job!" Both explained that Roosevelt had not given Nebraska many appointments, though they had asked on several occasions for certain posts. They did not want to lose my appointment by default. Senator Wherry added, "Roosevelt is a very smart and able man. You will find it interesting to work for him."

When he sensed my surprise over this praise from an unlikely source, Wherry went on to explain the grounds for his judgment. "When I was sworn in with the new class of senators in January 1943," he said,

> Roosevelt had us all over to the White House for a party, which consisted of nothing more than sandwiches, soft drinks and beer. I went up to him when I had a bottle of beer and a sandwich in my hands and I said, "Mr. President, I would like to ask you a question. Is it true that you are planning on running for a fourth term?" The President looked at me, smiled and asked, "Senator, how many sandwiches and beers have you had?" I shamefacedly told him two of each. He said, "You go back there to the table and take a third sandwich and a third bottle of beer and a fourth sandwich and a fourth bottle of beer and then come back and ask me that question." He was smiling a big smile, and he left me speechless.

Senator Wherry then drew the moral of the story. "That's what makes Roosevelt so smart. He knows how not to answer a question as well as to answer it."

[II]

With my appointment and confirmation, my father back in Kansas City now regularly boasted to his cronies in the Beth

Hamedrosh Hagodol that his son "worked for the great President Roosevelt." I had no more been installed in office when the Lanham Committee, named after its chairman, Congressman Lanham of Texas, called me up for a review of the condition of the Federal Public Housing Authority. The committee was particularly interested in certain financial questions. It rightly suspected that some people around the country were "milking the cow behind the barn"—meaning that they were diverting into their own pockets certain funds and resources of the authority.

I had pored over the accounts given me by Herbert Wooten, the able controller of the authority, and was just getting into my car for the trip to Capitol Hill when Wooten ran after me to say, "I am sorry but some of those figures are not completely confirmed." Why? He explained breathlessly that because of a presidential order freezing manpower, the agency was short of at least fifty bookkeepers. Many transactions had not yet been recorded in the ledgers, nor had the associated documentation been brought together in book form. When he added that he had also found certain errors, I asked that he get into the car with me and we would both go to the Hill for the appearance before the Lanham Committee.

It was awkward to be a new boy on the Hill without being certain of my facts. Many officials in Washington masqueraded behind a false face, but on the assumption that the truth would serve me best, in my introductory statement I made a clean breast of the errors that had so far been discovered. I also asked the committee to excuse the condition of the records. Under the pressures of wartime movements of people in and out of agencies—and not least of all, pressures to get defense housing built in a rush—the records of my agency were not up to date.

Congressmen and senators do in fact respect candor, as I was to learn over and again in later posts in the executive branch. But in this baptismal experience I was bluntly asked by Chairman Lanham how I proposed to set right what was out of joint. I said that as soon as the hearing was over I would call on Harold Smith, director of the Bureau of the Budget, and ask for additional bookkeeping help, even if this exceeded our manpower quota. This I did, and the additional bookkeepers I got saved me trouble after the war when I returned to civilian life.

In addition, I set out to get closer to the people who controlled the work of our agency. I visited the seven regional offices whose respective staffs were spending a great deal of money to provide housing and other accommodations for more than a million people. In Washington I instituted monthly meetings, reporting to the staff on events in our area of responsibility and about our future plans. The staff members in turn were at liberty to ask challenging questions or to offer critical comments on what was in motion or in prospect. I would later adopt a version of this form of "networking" in my work as president of major Jewish organizations in postwar years, and to my last governmental position as Secretary of Commerce with some 45,000 employees.

In one instance, however, I had a special problem of communication with principal staff in the agency. One day an army colonel appeared in my office to say that fifteen hundred expandable trailers were needed for housing at a place called Oak Ridge, Tennessee. When I asked who would use the trailers at that location, the colonel replied that he was not at liberty to say. But if I was in doubt about the merit of his request, I could call the White House for reassurance. I said that *I* didn't call the White House. My chief, John Blandford, did such calling. Well, said the colonel, let *him* do it then. And so he did when I informed Blandford of the request for trailers. He came back to me and said, "Yes, the White House believes that the trailers are needed urgently for the Oak Ridge site."

The constant flow of expandable trailers toward Oak Ridge was accounted for in the weekly reports of the activities of the authority. They thus attracted the attention of our regional directors who had their own interest in securing scarce trailers to meet needs in their respective regions. There followed the same questions they customarily asked. Why so many? Why to *that* place? What for? By this time I had been given enough information on a "must know" basis to understand that something very much out of the ordinary was afoot at Oak Ridge, but I was plainly not at liberty to broadcast what I knew. Something, however, had to be said to quiet the regional directors. So at the next staff meeting in Washington I arranged to have all the regional directors addressed by the one whose jurisdiction included Oak Ridge. His manner of speaking was as imposing as his voice was sepulchral. After I called on him to address the meeting, he began a long narrative leading up to the climactic revelation. "All right," he said, "here it comes in the utmost confidence. The top secret things being produced at Oak

Ridge are fourth-term campaign buttons for President Roosevelt." Everyone then knew they could not be expected to share in the secret about Oak Ridge—namely the work on the atomic bomb.

Immediately after the Normandy invasion I was drawn into early congressional attention to postwar housing problems. Congress enacted the Serviceman's Readjustment Act, including home loan guarantees for veterans up to $4,000 or 50 percent of the loan, whichever was less. The figure here would later be increased to $7,500 or 60 percent of the loan. In working closely on housing matters with Senator Robert A. Taft and his wife Martha, I came to develop an affection for both. Martha Taft was in a very real sense the "third Senator from Ohio." She was deeply involved in her husband's concerns, especially in social areas such as housing, and was a steady source of sensible advice. I doubt if the extensive postwar program of veterans housing would have survived the legislative and political battle but for Taft's determined leadership.

The new demands on defense production that followed the D-Day landing in Europe, coinciding with the stepped-up pace of island-hopping in the Pacific theater, created ever-changing needs for war housing. In addition, essential support facilities had to be provided—an experience in "town building" and "shopping center building" that would prepare me for my as yet unforeseen postwar work. With so much war production established in out-of-the-way places, war workers brought in to work in the plants were in need of more than shelter. They also needed the infrastructure that makes a community—schools, places of worship, grocery stores, clothing stores, motion picture theaters, beauty parlors for "Rosie the Riveter," playgrounds, bowling alleys, and other recreational facilities. Authorizations for all this fell within the province of my wartime agency.

[III]

Equitable decisions often had to be made in a race against time and in the face of strong arguments from opposite sides. In matters where my authority to act was clear, I accepted personal responsibility for the decisions. In matters where ambiguities haunted my authority, I tried to resolve them before irrevocable choices were made.

Two episodes illustrate this, though the first occurred while I was still assistant administrator for programming in the National Housing Agency. After we acted to reduce priorities available to home builders in and around Peoria, Illinois, I was visited in my office by Everett Dirksen, then a member of the U.S. House of Representatives, whose congressional district included the Peoria area. He told me that local builders had pressured him to use his influence to reverse our decision.

In his later career as a Republican leader in the Senate, Dirksen's oratorical style led some of the Washington press corps to bestow on him the honorific title of "The Wizard of Ooze." When I met him face to face, however, I found he was direct, open to persuasion, and free of any verbal snake oil. I explained that priorities for private home building in and around Peoria had not been made available simply because there was little real defense production in the area. Peoria, to be sure, continued to be a major center for the production of liquor, but as workers in the distilleries were not deemed essential to the war effort, local builders did not qualify for priorities under the terms of War Production Board guidelines.

I added that I was about to leave for a survey of defense housing needs around the Hawkeye Ordinance Plant in Iowa. If Dirksen thought it helpful, I would stop off in Peoria, meet with the local builders, and explain the basis for the priorities decision. Dirksen seemed to be taken by surprise, perhaps because rank-and-file congressmen do not ordinarily command sympathetic attention from Washington bureaucrats. "Would you do *that* for me?" he asked. "Of course I would," I said. "*We* and not *you* made the decision that distresses the builders. They are entitled to an explanation directly from me."

Matters worked out that way, and Everett Dirksen became a good friend. The postwar public consequences of our friendship, as will be seen, were not small.

A problem which came to a boil in and around Detroit while I was commissioner of wartime public housing required handling of a different kind. A vast factory for the production of military aircraft had been built in Ypsilanti, near Detroit. Immense tracts of defense public housing had also been built in and around Ypsilanti to house the influx of aircraft factory workers, many of whom were Southern whites. Meanwhile, in Detroit itself, with the conversion of the automobile industry to war production, pressures on housing increased from one day to the next. Blacks who were drawn to

the Detroit area by defense work opportunities suffered particularly from the acute housing shortage.

With seeming suddenness, however, aircraft production at Ypsilanti was stabilized, and cutbacks in the labor force led to substantial vacancies in nearby public housing. When this fact became
known there was an understandable demand to make the vacancies
available to defense workers among the black families in Detroit
crowded cheek-to-jowl in squalid dwellings. Detroit had recently
been shaken by a race riot, and the makings of more trouble still
seethed beneath a surface calm. If black families in Detroit were
denied access to existing vacancies in Ypsilanti's public housing,
the event might spark another racial explosion. If, on the other
hand, black families were moved without careful preparation into
the Ypsilanti setup, they might be violently confronted by existing
residents.

Irrevocable decisions in this case could not be made at a
distance. Although the Federal Public Housing Authority had an
able regional representative in Detroit, I flew there for an on-site
discussion of the alternatives to be faced. We concluded that as a
matter of simple justice, black families must be accorded the right
of access to vacancies in the Ypsilanti area's war housing. To defuse
any will for trouble by whites or blacks, we set in place a
"peacekeeping" security organization involving the county sheriff
and local police as well as our own limited cadre of security
personnel who were confined to the public housing area. At the
same time the regional representative began face-to-face meetings
with tenant representatives to explain why they might find themselves with black neighbors, and to secure their cooperation for a
peaceful adjustment. Still, we could not be sure of what might
happen. If the prospective move triggered another race riot like the
earlier one in Detroit, the effect would seriously disrupt the flow of
urgently needed production.

When I returned to Washington, I thought the stakes in the
Detroit-Ypsilanti area were high enough to warrant a conversation with President Roosevelt. Aside from seeing the president on
ceremonial occasions, I had never met with him for a policy
discussion. Nor did I ever receive a note from the White House
directing me to find a place in my organization for "deserving
Democrats."

I called General Pat Nash, a fellow Nebraskan who was on the
president's key staff at the time. I explained what was afoot in the

Detroit area and why it was important for me to see the president. Nash replied that Roosevelt was so immersed in strategic military and political problems that the earliest open slot on his calendar was twenty or thirty days hence. "Thirty days!" I exclaimed. "Black families must be moved quickly into public housing in Ypsilanti. If the president wants me to countermand the move, I need his decision within twenty-four hours." "Well," said Nash, "you just go right ahead and do it. You've given me your report, and I'm certain the president will back you no matter what happens."

What was I to do if I had no access to the only man who could formally authorize me to act in ways I believed were necessary? My thoughts turned to Mrs. Roosevelt, with whom I had worked in connection with public housing for low-income and disadvantaged people, and in youth activities. I telephoned her to say that I needed her advice about a very serious matter. It was typical of her to answer, "Come right over."

I met her in the Red Room of the White House, explained the situation that was developing along the Detroit-Ypsilanti axis, and bluntly asked if she thought I was overcautious in not starting the move of black families into Ypsilanti public housing without the president's approval. She assured me that my precautions were warranted, and then asked, "When do you need to know what Franklin thinks?" I said the time had to be by 9:30 the next morning. "Well," said Mrs. Roosevelt, "fortunately Franklin will be home tonight, and I will discuss the matter with him. I'll call you at your office early tomorrow morning."

The call came through exactly as she said it would. "Franklin," she reported, "told me to tell you that he not only approves of your approach to the housing needs in the Detroit-Ypsilanti area but commends you for willingness to follow through on it." The signal was flashed to Detroit, and the movement of black families into Ypsilanti public housing projects went forward. If I managed to give the appearance of majestic calm, what I actually felt recalled the remark of a garment manufacturer who returned to New York with a Florida tan. To friends who spoke admiringly of his appearance, he said: "Don't let this tan deceive you. Beneath it I am really very pale." The integration of blacks into what had been an all-white public housing project turned out to be a peaceful operation. I would remember the experience in later years in connection with housing for blacks in the new town of Park Forest, Illinois.

13 □ Winding Up in Washington

The challenges in my work as commissioner of the FPHA changed from one day to the next, often in consequence of strategic decisions made in other quarters. A point was reached, for example, when the naval war against Japan posed an urgent need for small aircraft carriers. Henry Kaiser, who had been mass-producing cargo-carrying "liberty ships," was given a contract to provide a supply of mini-carriers. Kaiser proposed to carry it out "up north," near Vancouver. His plans were approved, and the currents set in motion converged on the FPHA, because workers drawn to the shipyard would need housing. Presently, therefore, on behalf of the FPHA we negotiated a contract with Kaiser to build Vanport, whose place name was derived from the fact that it was located between Vancouver, Washington, and Portland, Oregon. The arrangement was approved in Congress, subject to the understanding that Vanport, built to temporary housing standards, would be dismantled down to the ground once the war was over. The town that emerged was not noted for its beauty, but it served its utilitarian purpose for a population of around eighty thousand. Henry Kaiser himself, as a great impresario, did an extraordinary job in overseeing the production of a fleet of small aircraft carriers in record time.

As an aspect of its work, the FPHA, which housed 850,000 persons during the time I was commissioner, was one of the largest feeders of people in the United States. In other respects, the program for wartime public housing brought home to me anew a lesson I had learned in the prewar years. It was that building dwellings for low-income people was not just a matter of providing human beings with "filing cabinets" into which they could fit. There was often a social need to help new residents in the housing projects to adjust themselves to a new urban style of life.

In wartime public housing, as in peacetime versions, some families who had come from the rural South were literally unprepared to live in houses with assorted facilities. Their innocence cast up odd problems. Gas ovens, for example, would burst because Mama didn't know how to use one for cooking and baking. Complaints would be received about broken and leaking bathroom plumbing; but on investigation it would turn out that children in the family didn't know how to use the toilet, and so had relieved their kidneys on the floor. Contrary to well-intentioned dogma, decent housing alone did not solve all social problems, though without it some problems were clearly unsolvable.

In the course of my work as commissioner of FPHA, I was fortunate in having access to the advice of some of the wisest figures in the field of public housing. On the other hand, my wartime dealings with major figures in the world of architecture, engineering, and mechanics were memorable because the experience pointed up the way in which famous men of authentic genius can sometimes take leave of good judgment in their approach to practical problems. My dealings with Frank Lloyd Wright are a case in point.

During the New Deal years of the depression, it was possible to commission even the finest architects to work on federal projects. During the war, however, that outlet for their talents was practically shut down because most of the publicly financed dwellings were temporary housing for defense workers. When the war effort was at its peak, I received word from an architect on the FPHA staff in Washington that the great Frank Lloyd Wright was without adequate income to support a minimally decent standard of life.

The FPHA was assigning qualified personnel to jobs across the nation, so I did not hesitate to call John Kervick, head of the regional office in New York, to say, "Locate Frank Lloyd Wright and give him a job." Kervick established contact with Wright and secured his services, subject to strict provisions governing the amount of lumber and metal that could be used in each house, whose dimensions would be specified in advance. Wright was supposed to fit what we were able to provide under wartime regulations to a site that had been selected.

After an interval, Kervick called me to say, "Wright has come in with his plans. We couldn't use them to build public housing before the war. We certainly can't use them now. We have an allowance of two thousand board feet of lumber per house, and he has eleven thousand in the house. He drastically increased our allowances on other points of detail. What's more, the site we had chosen was too small for his plans, so he reduced the number of houses." Hearing this, I said, "John, didn't you explain to him that there is a limit to what we can do in times of war?" "Commissioner," Kervick replied, "I've done that a number of times, but as far as Wright is concerned, you either build according to his plans or you don't build at all." I said, "I think you'd best pay him for the work he's done and forget about the whole business." He agreed to try to do that.

Sometime later Kervick called me back. He reported that Wright refused payment and suggested that either his plans were accepted or he would appeal to a higher authority. The problem was shot through with more tension than Kervick cared to handle, so I told him to contact Wright again and have him come in to see me when he was in Washington.

My meeting with Wright lasted longer than I had anticipated because Wright insisted on rehearsing his stand down to the last detail. When he paused for breath, I cut in to say, "Mr. Wright, I fully sympathize with your sensitivity to what has transpired. Maybe when the war is over we'll find a site for public housing on which to build the attractive structures you have designed. But you have been misled. We didn't retain your creative talents to design something outstanding. We retained your mechanical talents, and you've given us much more than we asked for. We will pay you for what you were supposed to give us. That is what we want to do, and that is the most we can do." I told him that there was no appeal to the president, and that he should take a check made out in an amount roughly equal to what the FPHA ordinarily paid for such work. I had a check drawn already and offered it to him to purchase his plans for later use. He was in urgent need of funds and took the check.

[II]

One of the operating rules in my office as commissioner was that no staff conference should be interrupted by telephone calls—except from the White House or from my wife. On a day in April 1945, I was in a staff conference when my secretary, Mrs. Kelly, buzzed me to say that my wife was on the phone. "Phil," Ethel said, gasping for breath between her sobs, "the president died."

That's how I got the news that Roosevelt had died at Warm Springs. I passed the news on to members of my staff.

Roosevelt had so often bounced back from various reported illnesses—and more than that, had seemed so central to the course of American life—that it was hard to accept the possibility that he might be carried off by death. Yet there it was. "I have a fierce headache!" he had cried at Warm Springs. Then he slumped over, and his life was spent. After I ordered the members of my staff to return to their regular work, I called the White House for instructions. We were simply told to stand by. The next call I made was to Ed McKim, a friend from Omaha, who had been in Company D, the artillery unit commanded in World War I by Captain Harry S Truman of Kansas City, Missouri. We had scheduled a poker game for that night, which we normally did when Ed came to town. There would be no poker game. It was strange to realize that all of a sudden Harry S Truman, the former county judge in Kansas City for whom I, as a boy, made enthusiastic electioneering speeches, was now president of the United States.

During Roosevelt's long presidency the American Jewish community had committed itself to a love affair with the man. He had arrived on the national stage at the time Hitler was consolidating his grip in Germany. It appeared to most American Jews that Roosevelt, by his fidelity to democratic norms of conduct and by his policies in support of social justice, was a form of national insurance against the rise of Nazism on American soil. Not all Jews formed a chorus in praise of Roosevelt. Even during FDR's lifetime, before the historical revisionists began to indict him for failing to rescue European Jews from Hitlerism before the Nazis' "final solution," some eminent Jewish leaders assailed him on that same count. Once, at a Zionist meeting during the war, I was cornered by Rabbi Abba Hillel Silver. In his despair over the liquidation of European Jewry, he hurled an accusatory question at me. "Phil," he said, "how can you in clear conscience work for *that* man in the White House?" It was as if Roosevelt, unaided, had the means to save European Jews but failed to use them out of some sort of moral depravity.

A few days after Truman succeeded to the presidency, I received a call from his secretary, Matt Connoly. "The president," he said, "is mad as hell at you. You had better come over to the White House right away." The moment I walked into Truman's office he said to me, "Phil! What is this?" He handed me a piece of paper. It was my letter of resignation. "Mr. President," I explained, "that letter was dictated after a discussion with protocol. When a new president takes office it is appropriate to submit a letter of resignation, so as to free his hand to appoint officers of his own choice." "Phil!" Truman said as he tore up the letter, "you are not an appointee. You are my friend. Now get yourself back to your office and go to work. Quit bothering me with such nonsensical things."

There was plenty of work to do even as the war was winding down. In particular there was the problem of providing adequate housing for veterans, including those destined to converge en masse on the nation's campuses under the terms of the new GI Bill of Rights. I had ready access to President Truman regarding such matters, but he also told me that if I ever ran into difficulties on the public housing front, I should go to Senator Robert Taft for help. Truman and Taft, despite their different political loyalties and views on the role of government, were good friends. In fact, though the Senate was still controlled by Democrats, meaning that the Democrats would normally control all committee and major subcommittee chairmanships, Truman supported the arrangement which made Taft, a true-blue Republican, chairman of the Senate subcommittee on housing.

[III]

The various provisions of the GI Bill related to education and housing reflected the lessons of World War I about how *not* to treat returning veterans. President Truman, who never forgot his own shattering experiences when he reentered the economic world after he was demobilized in 1918, was exceptionally sensitive to veterans' immediate need for housing. After meetings with the president in June 1945, I was authorized to make cost-plus arrangements with individual contractors whereby they would saw down and reassemble surplus defense housing and military barracks for use as emergency housing for veterans.

The scenes with which I began this memoir concluded with an account of how and why I agreed to stay in my government post for almost a year after VJ Day, and the circumstances under which I finally accepted Nathan Manilow's proposal to serve as president of a corporation formed to build a new town on a site south of Chicago.

One more item remains to be added.

As commissioner, my weekly record-keeping and my lawyerlike precautions regarding a running audit of the cost-plus arrangement with contractors had fortunate postwar consequences. Briefly, Senator Joseph McCarthy of Wisconsin, who had won the Senate seat held by Senator Robert La Follette, Jr., first ventured to call national attention to himself by charging corruption in public housing and war housing. In response to his charges, a subcommittee of the Senate Banking and Currency Committee, under the chairmanship of Senator George Aiken of Vermont, arranged a hearing. Along with my immediate predecessor and others in the wartime housing setup, I was invited to present written testimony to the committee and was also told to be prepared to come to Washington to appear before the committee in person.

I retrieved all the weekly work papers that were part of my administration as commissioner as well as reports on the whole of the wartime public housing effort under my direction. I sent all this to Senator Aiken along with an overview statement. I was presently informed that I had received a clean bill of health for the period while I was in charge of the program, and would not be called to testify.

14 □ Life Begins Anew

At times in my life I was a party to matters that led to White House meetings with an incumbent president, but the experiences never became humdrum through repetition. Each time I walked into the president's office I was stirred anew by the atmosphere of the place, by the immediate "presentness" of the American past, by the sense of a mystic bond between successive presidents and advisers whose decisions reached in *this* room affected the lives of millions of people.

I felt all this with particular poignancy on a day in early July 1946 when Ethel and I, and our three children—Bettylu, Tom, and Jim—were invited to the White House to say farewell to President Truman on the eve of our departure for Chicago.

Truman at the time was beset on all sides by rising storms. On the domestic front there were crippling labor strikes, personal conflicts with major labor leaders, attacks by conservative Southern democrats on his proposals for far-reaching domestic reforms, and splits within his cabinet over foreign policy leading to the resignations of Commerce Secretary Henry Wallace and, later, Secretary of State James Byrnes. On the international front he was faced by the increasing hostility of the Soviet Union, and by signs that the British could not much longer supply military and economic aid to Greece and Turkey who were threatened by communist movements. He also faced political fallout from problems in the Far East, where Chinese Nationalists under Chiang Kai-shek and Communists under Mao Tse-tung were warring for control. On top of all else, Truman suffered charges that if Roosevelt were still alive, the nation and the world would have been spared their postwar afflictions—as if everything out of joint was somehow due to Truman.

The historic achievements of the Truman presidency—as well as the most violent attacks on him—still lay ahead. Yet even as I said my goodbyes to him, I wondered if I was really doing the "right thing" by returning to private life. Perhaps I could still render some small service to a president who was under intense pressure and who needed loyal subordinates beyond those he already had in the highest cabinet posts.

My friendship with Harry Truman extended beyond his presidential years up to the hour of his death. Among other things, our poker games were later resumed when I visited Kansas City, and by his choice they were held in one of his favorite settings, the Jewish Country Club. During a particular poker game, I won twenty dollars and he lost twenty dollars. When it came time to distribute the winnings, I said, "Forget it," as I saw him reach for his billfold. He replied, "Now listen, if you don't take this money I'll never play with you again." The high marks he deserved for the conduct of his presidency, denied him when he was in office, were granted him posthumously. He was clearly seen and valued for what I knew him to be all along—an uncommon common man, courageous, open, candid, a solid whole as a president, son, husband, father, friend. He was not addicted to image building or showmanship, to "photo opportunities." His very name became a byword for plain-spoken honesty. His angers were real, his contempts were real, his loyalties were real. As president he held himself "accountable to history," not because he had any inflated vision of being great. I always had the impression that he ceaselessly rubbed his eyes, wondering how he ever got into the White House. He shunned the word "great," saying that he had his hands full in striving merely to be a "good" president. He held himself accountable to history because his oath of office required that of him. To preserve and protect the Constitution to the best of his ability he must be prepared to incur fierce attacks on his policies and person (but not on his family) if that was the price of serving the nation's highest interest.

[II]

In Chicago I moved my family into a rented apartment at 199 East Lake Shore Drive. Ethel organized our domestic life, and I busied myself on two fronts. I met with my Omaha law partners and associates to settle matters bearing on the formation of a branch law office in Chicago. I also met with Nathan Manilow to complete our mutual agreement, to frame the concepts that would guide us when we formed a small management team for the town-building venture.

Manilow was not a bookish man, attuned to the latest work on the best-seller list. He was a first-class promoter and maker of real estate deals at a time when that kind of business was not among the "prestige" occupations open to Jews. In fact, he was never accepted as a member of the Standard Club of Chicago, the citadel of German Jews, and had to be content with membership in the Covenant Club, the refuge of Jews of east European background. He might have "made it" into the Standard Club—despite the vicious divisions of the time between western and eastern European Jews—if he had been a college graduate and a professional man. But he was not a "routine" fellow. He was always alert to new opportunities and was prepared to take risks that would make other men quail. He had my unqualified respect.

My initial arrangement with my brother-in-law Sam Beber had assumed that only part of my time would go to the practice of law, the rest being reserved for the town-building project with Nathan Manilow. When the law office was opened, it was, as noted earlier, conveniently located near the office of American Community

Builders (ACB), the name of the corporation formed to build the new "GI town." Neither Beber nor I could foresee the evolution of his relationship to ACB or mine to the law firm. In his case, he would be drawn deeply into the work of ACB as one of its officers. He would render invaluable service to the corporation as a watchdog over prices, payouts, featherbedding, and contract performance. As one of the brightest graduates of the Creighton Law School, he was aware of his brilliance but had difficulty making and holding friends—because he did not wish to "waste his time" on people who were not of his intellectual level.

As for myself, the town project absorbed so much of my time that my only legal business involved cases where I was consulted about government procedures. At times when I was caught in a fishhook tangle of difficulties common to town-building, I often wished I was merely practicing law and had not agreed to a leadership role in creating Park Forest, Illinois, a community initially of 31,000 people.

Of the perceptions I brought to the town-building venture, events confirmed what I assumed would be a ravenous postwar appetite for homes. The year 1945, for example, saw only 325,000 housing starts nationally. In 1946, despite critical shortages of material and labor, housing starts increased to 1,023,000, followed in 1947 by 1,268,000 new starts and in 1948 by 1,023,000. The boom, largely suburban, pointed to a future where all major cities would be ringed by vistas of new homes, often tightly laid out and looking alike.*

Still, while my associates and I recognized the insatiable need for housing, our aim was to build not just houses but a community whose environment would foster a better life for people of modest means and pressing family needs. Immediate preference would be given to veterans and families with young children. Streets and clusters of homes would be laid out with an eye to the safety of children at play. Religious denominations would receive gifts of land on which to build their institutions. School facilities would be

*Levittown, the emblem of this process, was the largest single subdivision undertaken in postwar America. It was not, however, planned as a total community. It was a leader in providing a great value in a housing facility, but it did not undertake at the outset to provide communal facilities that are essential to a full-fledged town. Yet the exceptional bargains in houses the Levitts made possible set in motion a process that made Levittown an enormous success.

available the moment the first families moved into Park Forest homes. We would provide built-in inducements for tenants to care for rented property as though they actually owned it. Finally, and crucially, ACB at the earliest possible hour would take the lead voluntarily in calling upon the inhabitants of Park Forest to incorporate themselves as a self-governing community.

[III]

The first addition to the ACB management team was the architect Jerrold Loebl and his partner Norman Schlossman, both being Chicagoans by birth and education. Though they had done extensive work for private parties, I first met the pair when they were commissioned on the eve of Pearl Harbor to design Wentworth House, a public housing project on Chicago's south side. I came to know Loebl better when I was commissioner of the Federal Public Housing Authority and he was a member of the architects' advisory committee to the commissioner. I saw in him a gifted architect who combined broad social views with a sound business sense.

With the architects chosen, American Community Builders was incorporated, followed by a formal election of the officers. I became president, Loebl became vice president, and Manilow treasurer. Carroll Sweet, Sr., was too busy on other fronts to be actively involved in the work of ACB, but his son Carroll Jr. eventually joined us.

Early in the planning process, Loebl and Schlossman recruited Richard M. Bennett to augment their own design capabilities. Bennett, a graduate of Harvard's School of Architecture and director of the Yale School of Design, had spent much time in Europe studying the handiwork of master architects. What began as a "trial run" in Chicago in August 1946 evolved into a thirty-year association with a firm later to be called Loebl, Schlossman, and Bennett. Bennett was the "Mr. Design" of the triumvirate, the man in charge of "creativity." ACB engaged the triumvirate for many different projects in the years beyond our Park Forest venture. The three men would become my close personal friends as well.

At an early hour we saw the need for someone who could work with Bennett on overall land planning. The man I secured was Elbert Peets, a graduate of Western Reserve University and of the

Harvard School of Landscape Architecture. I had known him since the first days of the United States Housing Authority when Peets, then chief of the site planning section of the USHA, came to Omaha to examine a project site of the Omaha Housing Authority. Later, when the Resettlement Administration under Rexford Tugwell mounted three "greenbelt town" projects, the one to which Peets was assigned—Greendale, near Milwaukee—remains to this day a model of first-class urban land planning.

As a leader in the new school of land-use planners, Peets accented the integration of new communities with their physical environment. A town plan, in his view, should conform to the lay of the land, meaning that people should live in harmony with the natural contours of their physical setting, not at odds with them. His practical experiences with government-planned communities during the prewar years of the Roosevelt administration, and his wartime studies of housing projects in civilian and military towns, made him a fount of wise counsel. Peets joined us at ACB as a short-term consultant on site planning.

He waged many battles to conserve trees and hills on the Park Forest site, and his arguments on aesthetic grounds were backed by economic facts. To the extent that hills could be saved, so he argued, why go to the costs of bulldozing huge mounds of earth to make a flat plane out of what nature formed with graceful undulating lines? Many developers favored a "billiard table" lay of the land, but the destruction of hills was a personal offense to the pioneer land planners who worked on the New Deal's housing programs.

The ACB management team also needed someone to oversee the selection, design, and contract negotiations of utilities. From among the talented people who had worked with me in the government, the man I picked for the task was Charles Waldman, a Hungarian by birth. Waldman, who held separate degrees in three engineering fields—electrical, mechanical, and civil—had emigrated to the United States just before the depression. At first he worked on rural resettlement projects, but later he headed the section responsible for electrical and mechanical utility systems in the U.S. Housing Authority. Still later he dealt with difficult utility problems at Willow Run, the huge aircraft factory and related defense community which the government built near Detroit during the war. In the usual controversies between government agencies and private parties, he could match his own expert knowledge against the high-priced engineering talent at the disposal of major private firms.

Waldman welcomed a chance to join ACB as the director of utilities and to help in the development of the new town. He soon moved with his wife and son to Chicago and eventually into Park Forest itself, where he proved himself to be an exceptionally able negotiator as well as a cost-conscious engineer.

These persons, along with Manilow and myself—plus the addition of Sam Beber at a later hour—formed the inner core of ACB's management team. In my work as president, I faced the need for personal assistants, one to work in the office and another to work in the field. The first of the two was Hart Perry, a graduate of the University of Chicago who had been my executive assistant in the Division of Defense Housing until he was called up for military service. Carroll Sweet, Jr., my executive assistant for the field, helped shape the profile and set the tone of the community.

Although my associates and I were interested in building a town, and not just tract houses or even a subdivision, ACB like other firms which helped meet critical housing needs made use of the liberal provisions of Title VI of the FHA authority. All builders, ACB included, saw their plans threatened by acute shortages of labor and material, by the virus of postwar inflation which rendered budgets obsolete from one month to the next, and by capricious weather conditions. In ACB's case, we found we were undercapitalized, and this fact led to intense internal debates about how best to uphold a standard of excellence with limited available means. On more than a few occasions, our plight recalled the reply that Daniel Boone gave to the question he was asked when he was in his eighties. Had he ever been lost? "No," said the old frontiersman. "I can't say I was ever lost, but I was bewildered once for three days."

15 □ Mother! The Necessity of Invention!

Before the start of construction in Park Forest, we agreed that the character and size of the market, coupled with the economic profile of residents, would determine our other judgments. They would, for example, determine the amount of land that was needed, the time to be spent in production and marketing, the overhead to be carried, and the capital investment that must be made before the point of profit was reached. All that was clear to us from the start, but it was only half the story. The other half is that the Park Forest venture was at times threatened with collapse due to the impact of forces which neither I nor my fellow executives in the ACB clearly foresaw or were in a position to avert.

[II]

In the relatively short time between July 1946, when I assumed the presidency of ACB, and September 1947, when actual construction at Park Forest got under way, plans made on one front often had to be modified because of what happened on another front.

Our original plan, for example, was to build for sale around three thousand homes on the land Nate Manilow had acquired under options. If we could sell the homes as soon as they were ready for occupancy, the income and profits would reduce ACB's need to make major outlays of its own capital. This was an important consideration because the corporation continued to be undercapitalized, even though we drew two "silent partners" into the venture, with each buying $250,000 of preferred callable ACB stock. One of the two was the Chicago Title and Trust Company; it would receive all the title and trust business generated by the Park Forest project. The other was Henry Crown, whose firm, Material Services Corporation, would be the source of all the concrete ACB would buy for its construction work.

To create a community designed for families with children, we had favored a pattern where houses built for sale would be clustered around courtyards removed from streets. The arrangement would reduce the amount of land we would otherwise have to use if we built a traditional row of individual houses for sale, strung out along a straight line. It would also ensure open vistas, landscaped beauty, and play areas close to home and safe from traffic hazards. FHA officials, however, told us that under existing rules they could not approve FHA mortgages for our design, that the rules barred the grant of FHA mortgages on free-standing homes for sale when the homes did not abut a vehicular traffic way.

The logic here was unassailable. A homeowner should not have to walk across the property of a second party in order to reach his home, but should always have unimpeded access to it. We tried to get the FHA rule modified, based on the way our homes grouped around a courtyard gave everyone equal and ready access to his own property, but the novelty of the design fell outside the conventional experiences of FHA officials. Adjustments to new realities are not quickly made by government agencies any more than they are by individuals in their private lives. ACB could not delay a start on its own work until the process of changing governmental regulations ran its course—though FHA eventually altered its rules due to increases in the cost of land. The story of our search for a solution to the immediate problem we faced was along the lines of the one told about W. C. Fields, an agnostic, who was discovered reading the Bible on his deathbed. "I am looking for a loophole," he explained. Our own "loophole" entailed a shift to the concept of building homes for rent but arranged in a "superblock" form around a courtyard. The plan for rental development suddenly opened up promising new prospects. A rental development, for example, would give us more rapid occupancy and generate the purchasing power we needed to attract merchants. It would also quickly create the human foundations for schools, churches, social organizations, and local government.

With the decision to focus on rental housing, the next step was to arrange the necessary financing, backed by FHA-secured mort-

gages that had yet to be secured. When I took a representative of
the Northwestern Mutual Insurance Company to the site of Park
Forest so that he could see with his own eyes the lay of the land,
he confined his reaction to a disbelieving laugh and the word
"impossible." Approaches to other insurance companies met with
the same negative response. They resisted our arguments that there
was a *town* to be built, not just a collection of houses.

We finally secured promises of financial support from insurance
companies after we engaged the services of Ferd Kramer of Draper
and Kramer, a friend who had business connections with Northwestern Mutual and New York Life. Promises of support were also
forthcoming from the Great Western Insurance Company of Canada through its Chicago representative. This did not, however, give
us a clear road. FHA regulations limited the size of any single
mortgage on a rental project that could be insured, and our initial
needs far exceeded that limit. To qualify for FHA coverage, we
broke part of the Park Forest land assigned for rental housing into
nine contiguous sites. Then we applied for FHA insurance for nine
separate mortgages totaling more than $25 million in 1946 dollars.

At a time when FHA faced the need to get a huge postwar
housing program moving nationally, our approach to a local
project was unprecedented. We made it clear that we wanted nine
mortgages or we wanted none. The case required a detailed review
by FHA officials and frequent meetings. If some of us at ACB
grew impatient because of the protracted review process, the fact is
that the FHA moved with commendable speed. By September
1947 they had approved ACB's submission for nine separate but
related mortgages.

Liberal mortgage arrangements worked to the advantage of all
developers, but the onrush of inflation made every delay in the
scheduled delivery of material an added tax on construction costs.
That was the risk all developers had to face, though ACB may have
fared better than most. Because we were involved in a major job of
town building, we often got better treatment from subcontractors
and the material suppliers who wanted volume which our business
assured. This is a way of saying that we were not geniuses, but
rather that we benefited from the very nature of the Park Forest
project.

Things ordinarily taken for granted in existing urban communities reveal their complexities when a new town is built. ACB, for
example, could not plan a community of 31,000 unless we were

sure beforehand that we could count on an ample supply of good-quality water, on sewer facilities, on "clean" energy, and on police and fire protection. Each of these needs was haunted by problems which were overcome by bold measures—savored in the telling in later years, but touch-and-go at the moment of experience.

[III]

Groundbreaking at Park Forest began on October 28, 1947. After that the work went forward with an eye focused on the funds we could regularly draw down on our FHA-insured mortgages to pay bills as they came due, and the extent to which we kept to our production schedule—all in a race against inflation. Our schedule called for twenty to twenty-four basement foundations to be completed each working day. Nearly all subsequent operations depended on the pace at which basements were completed.

That included the time when the homes for rental would be ready for occupancy. When the plans for Park Forest were originally announced, there was much skepticism about its salient features—preference for veterans, preference for families with children, rentals for three-bedroom homes at rates less than one hundred dollars a month, the promise of support for schools and for religious institutions. But the announcements brought young couples out to Park Forest to see what was going on. Some promptly put their names on the rental lists, and more than a few were ready to move in when the Park Forest site resembled a huge construction camp in a sea of mud—before roads, sidewalks, and landscaping were provided.

ACB's cash-flow calculations depended on the rentals for homes on occupied units. This was the background for a visit I paid one day to Henry Crown, president of the Material Services Corporation. Concrete supplies were desperately short nationally, and many of Crown's long-standing customers were unhappy at delays in the delivery of concrete for their own projects. Because Material Services' own supply sources were being taxed from many sides, they found it increasingly difficult to meet our demands. When we had decided on a goal of twenty to twenty-four finished basements a day, neither Crown's company nor we clearly foresaw the building boom ahead.

Crown offered me a check for a considerable sum to relieve his company from the contract, but I told him the check would do us no good. If we could not get the concrete we needed from his firm, we would not be able to get it anywhere else. That meant we could not keep the schedule for basement completions on which everything else depended, and the life of the Park Forest project as a whole would be imperiled. "Is it as bad as that?" Henry asked. I said it was. "Well," he said, "I'll see what I can do for my other customers." Under conditions where concrete was literally more valuable than the coin of the realm, Material Services continued to supply us with the concrete we needed to maintain our schedule. In this as in other matters, I always found Henry Crown a man of his word, even when there was no written contract to make his promises legally binding.

As rental units were completed and occupied, some members of the ACB management team cited legal and practical reasons why the incorporation of Park Forest should be delayed until its development was substantially complete. But the overwhelming argument in favor of incorporation was our determination from the start to create a people's village, not a developer's fiefdom. We decided to bet on people. When there were only a few hundred rental units leased, and before these were all occupied, ACB convened a "tent barbecue" on a Saturday afternoon in November 1948, and placed two propositions before the tenants in residence and those who were committed by leases. First, they were presented with a list of names for the village and asked to choose the one they preferred. Park Forest was on that list, and it emerged as the favored name. (On the advice of Carroll Sweet, Jr., streets in Park Forest were to bear the names of men who had won the Congressional Medal of Honor.) The second proposition was whether or not Park Forest should be incorporated without further delay. The vote was affirmative; a municipal incorporation committee was formed, an election was held in February 1949, and the village of Park Forest was born, a small but full-fledged municipal corporation.

I am not aware of any prior instance when the landlord encouraged tenants to form an incorporated village and to assume responsibility for planning, zoning, building code, and taxing authority—all of which could potentially be used against the owners. All this in fact created some problems for ACB, but it also kindled the civic senses of the people who moved into Park Forest. It was *their* village. They could use an official voice in talking to the developers, sometimes in a friendly way and sometimes in head-to-head confrontation, but on balance in ways that were of benefit both to the community and the company.

Ethel and I were among the first people to rent homes built in Park Forest, and we were either the first or second family to spend a night in the place. In fact, Ethel and our newborn fourth son, Sam, came straight from the maternity hospital to that new home. In this we shared the experiences of other families with children who moved into Park Forest the moment rental homes were ready for occupancy. Ethel also made a point of calling on each new tenant with a welcoming cake she had baked.

The place somehow seemed to grow children on all sides. It led Ethel and I to prevent our own children from lording it over those in the families of newcomers. I designated Tom, the oldest son, and Jim, the second oldest, as vice presidents of ACB. A Park Forest mother later told us of the time she opend the door of her home in response to a knock and saw a boy of about six. He solemnly introduced himself as James Klutznick, vice president of American Community Builders, and he had a question to ask. Were there any children in the family? If so, he wanted them to know that he would personally do what he could to make their life in Park Forest more enjoyable. Four decades later Jim took the lead in the Chicago area in building "senior life-style" structures for men and women who were getting on in years, did not wish to retire in Florida, but were in need of creature comforts, medical security, recreational amenities—all at a reasonable rental price.

I always savor in memory the excitement generated by the people who came to live in Park Forest and to help make it a community. Most of the men were veterans of World War II, with an educational level well above the average of most developments that were springing up around the country. They were young lawyers, advertising executives, newspaper men, a noted city planner, physicists, upward-bound junior executives in corporate structures. To an astonishing extent, they readily immersed themselves in the tasks of self-government, even though elective offices carried no salary. It seemed to be their way of trying to honor the vision they had during the war years of creating a better world.

There were many natural leaders among the veterans who chose Park Forest as the place to form and rear their families, but many of us thought of one in particular as being "the first among equals." This was Anthony Scariano. As a young lawyer by professional training, he had served in the OSS during the war years, and later worked for five years in the Chicago office of the U.S. Attorney. When he entered the private practice of law, he was encouraged by his friends to seek the Democratic party nomination to a seat in the Illinois House of Representatives. He won the nomination and went on to win the seat during successive elections. Civic and professional organizations that monitored the performance of the Illinois legislature regularly judged Scariano to be the best member of the Illinois House of Representatives. In later years, when he returned full time to the practice of law, he was tapped to serve as chairman of the "blue ribbon" Illinois Racing Board, with a mandate to clean up the regulation of horse racing. He was subsequently elected to serve on the Illinois Appellate Court, and under the merit system was returned to his judicial post almost by acclamation. He was the embodiment of the bright, vigorous public spirit and the practical idealism common among veterans who converged on Park Forest when the place was still very young.

People could choose to be alone in this new community, but it was my impression that very few were ever lonely in it. There was always so much going on to engage their interest. During the daytime, mothers might be part of a movable coffee klatch in Park Forest while children out of doors played within sight of young mothers. At night the place seemed to heave with committee meetings, general meetings, and the sound of debated resolutions or the threats of a "strike" against the ACB. As the resident president of ACB I was the natural object of protest movements. The sometimes disputatious spirit of Park Forest democracy wrote large what I recalled of the spirit of Beth Hamedrosh Hagodol back in Kansas City during my father's day. One night in Park Forest our daughter Bettylu, while playing outside our home, saw a crowd of people headed our way carrying torches. She rushed indoors crying, "Mother! Mother! They're coming to get daddy!" The crowd she feared was simply people leaving a meeting place where they had been debating school problems.

As a community, Park Forest became one of the more closely studied social phenomena in the United States in the immediate postwar years. William H. Whyte caught the spirit of the place in many pages he devoted to Park Forest in his book *The Organization Man*. He observed what while other "developments" in postwar housing were "statistically almost identical to Park Forest," they failed to generate anything like its verve. "The people who went to Park Forest," he wrote, "went there because it was the best housing for the money." Once there, however, under the stimulus of the developers, "they created something over and above the original bargain." Together "they developed a social atmosphere of striking vigor" that was to be "a significant extra" over and above "the material attractions."

By January 1950, 3,010 town houses had been built and occupied at rentals ranging between $75 and $117 a month, at the rate of four hundred new rentals each month. As the months went by—and as still more children were born as the breadwinners in the families were advancing in their careers—it became clear that Park Forest offered a promising market for homes to be sold directly to individual owners.

ACB was not yet in a strong liquid position, but the lure of the new market warranted the start of a new building program wherein ACB offered for sale two-bedroom homes with a brick exterior located on a relatively spacious lot for a bargain purchase price of around $11,000. In response to demand, some five-bedroom homes were also offered for sale at around $19,000 and were snapped up. In one memorable instance, a home purchased at that price was resold for $24,000 before the original buyer even moved in.

[IV]

ACB was not legally obligated to help provide schools for Park Forest residents. But we at once had to face the fact that virtually every family had or would soon have a child ready for elementary school, and with increasing numbers from one month to the next. A school district had not yet been formed, but we recognized that purely from a business standpoint, we must either move promptly to meet educational needs—though doing so would entail heavy capital obligations—or we must decelerate the rate at which we could build Park Forest.

A nationally known educational consultant advised ACB to steer clear of planning school facilities, saying that Park Forest residents should handle the matter on their own. We ignored the learned advice. ACB initially arranged for children to attend schools in neighboring School District 170. When new residents began to pour into Park Forest, however, it became clear that their children could not be accommodated that way. ACB then created a school by converting one of the eight-family units into sixteen classrooms, with ACB meeting the budgetary costs.

To parents, the condition and quality of the schools available for their children was of central importance. With the encouragement of ACB they initiated the formation of a new school district, No. 163, to serve the scheduled influx of families into Park Forest. The school district, however, lacked the bonding power to provide for new schools, so ACB came to the rescue through several legal steps. First, in negotiations with the school district we established a not-for-profit school foundation, directed by selected representatives of the school district and of ACB. ACB then loaned the foundation the funds necessary to meet a specific program. At the same time the foundation contracted with the school district to build a school, subject to competitive bidding, to specifications set by the school district and on land which was a gift from ACB. The school district, in turn, agreed to buy the completed school when its tax base enabled it to issue bonds for that purpose. The purchase price would reflect only the cost of developing the building; ACB would provide operating subsidies until adequate public revenues were available.

As a specialist in municipal law, I would agree with most municipal law authorities that the contract which required the school district to honor its bonds was largely unenforceable. The district had a clear moral obligation to do so, but a hostile taxpayer suit or a decision by a successor school board might have overturned the understanding previously reached with the ACB. The contracts, however, were honored. Referenda for school bond issues were passed by large majorities, and with the sale of the bonds the school board assumed ownership of the schools.

At one time about half the total working capital of ACB was tied up in school loans, new school construction, and subsidies. All but the subsidies and the value of the land was ultimately repaid ACB, and every school building in the original Park Forest plan is on land which ACB contributed. But ACB was well paid. When we turned to the construction of homes for sale, Park Forest's excellent schools attracted buyers despite a slowdown in other developments with homes for sale.

The campaign to build what became known as Rich Township High School started in 1951 on the initiative of a group of dedicated Park Forest parents led by J. M. Patterson of the Standard Oil marketing division and Robert Dinerstein of Standard Oil's research department. A "yes" or "no" referendum on the proposal to build a high school was set for June 23, 1951, and the results startled even those who were its most ardent advocates. The ballot count showed a vote of 1,828 for the high school project, with only twelve votes opposed.

When Rich Township High School opened in the fall of 1953, Jack Star, a Park Forest resident who was a reporter for *Look* magazine, suggested that the village enter the competition to be designated as an All-American City, an award given jointly by *Look* and the Municipal League. The village celebrated its fifth anniversary with special flair. On January 31, 1954, the All-American City certificate and flag were presented to the community; a second All-American certificate was awarded the community at a later date.

The high school went on to win distinctions of its own. The achievement scores of its students were consistently among the top 1 percent in the country. Three-fourths of its students went on to college, and educators from around the country descended on Park Forest to study it as one of the three best schools in the Midwest. All five of my children had part or all of their schooling in the schools of Park Forest, with my oldest son Tom being a member of the first class to graduate from Rich Township High School. As I evaluate the education of my children received in various places, including "elite" private schools, I remain convinced that one of Park Forest's greatest achievements was the excellence of its school system, made possible by the collaboration between an active citizenry and the initial financial support of ACB.

[V]

I followed with equal satisfaction the manner in which the religious needs of Park Foresters were met, starting with ACB's grant of the land on which religious structures might be built.

The needs of the Catholics were arranged for in a straightforward way. In the planning stage of Park Forest, I was visited by Roman Catholic representatives in charge of real estate matters for the diocese. The diocese owned a little rural Catholic church building and a small cemetery of about an acre surrounded by abutting land in Park Forest. The church building was in virtual disuse, and few if any burials were being made in the cemetery. I had hoped we could give the diocese some of our land in return for their little property. The diocese was not prepared to give up its own land, but it readily accepted the gift of our acres of land and promised to build a school building and later a church on it.

We were all so enthusiastic about getting a commitment for a Catholic school and a church that we gave up our effort to get their small landholding in exchange. The diocese had made a lengthy investigation of our program and purposes in Park Forest; their undertaking of a school and church amounted to a seal of approval on our efforts. Saint Irenaeous Roman Catholic Church was built on Park Forest land, and by the early 1950s other related buildings had been erected on the same site, including a chapel, school, rectory, and convent.

Park Forest had no central place where members of the Jewish community could go for help in building a religious edifice. The first started modestly in temporary quarters for religious services and for the religious education of children. Later, with an increase in the numbers of Jewish residents, the congregation that was formed built a Reform synagogue. Still later, a Conservative congregation was formed and built its own synagogue.

Of special interest to me was whether ACB's intervention on behalf of Protestants would withstand the test of time. In anticipation of the way many Protestant denominations would be organizing themselves in the burgeoning village of Park Forest, I asked the Church Federation of Greater Chicago for help in planning for the needs of diverse Protestant groups. ACB would provide church sites, but we wanted advice as to number, size, and denominations to be provided for. The Church Federation responded enthusiastically. Twenty-six denominations agreed to participate in a bold experiment that could merit the descriptive term "ecumenical" in later years. What emerged as a legal entity in 1950 was a United Protestant Church wherein adherents to various Protestant denominations would have their religious needs met in one of several large, strong churches instead of many small struggling congregations. Each person would be identified with the denomination of his or her own choice, but all could participate in the way the service was conducted.

There would eventually be four United Protestant Churches in Park Forest, each oriented to a major Protestant sect. ACB contributed the building sites for all. By the early 1950s I was convinced that the experiment was solidly conceived and would remain a success.

[VI]

Not everything in Park Forest went swimmingly. As the village expanded, there were complications over the water supply. ACB's initial investment in a water system grew much larger with the need for more wells, more softening capacity, and more storage facilities. All along, it had been ACB's hope that the water system would be taken over by the village trustees and thus become a municipal asset. But the village officials hesitated until they were sure they would be taking on a profitable operation. Finally, and with great reservations, the officials agreed to negotiate. But we were far apart on price.

Our studies indicated that if the village bought the water system at a price we were prepared to accept, they would earn enough income to retire the debt on the system. They could also afford to expand the system and still have surplus funds for the general purposes of the village, or for reducing later rates. We observed that municipal owners of the system would be relieved of the federal income taxes we were paying on profits, as well as on the mounting real estate taxes. But the controversy over the purchase price of the water system remained unresolved until late 1957, when the village and ACB finally agreed to a price roughly triple the amount the village had first offered. To consummate the purchase and to allow for expansion, the village was authorized by public referendum to issue water revenue bonds. As I had argued all along, the sale of water not only generated enough revenue to pay the principal and interest on the bonds and to expand the water system, but also to reduce water rates. Even so, the village was annually embarrassed because of a surplus in its water revenue accounts.

For years I have cherished a passage written by a Park Forest newspaperman, Al Englehard, and quoted by William Whyte in *The Organization Man*. Park Foresters had previously enjoyed the bite in Englehard's column in *The Reporter*, called the "Pepper Mill." I was the object of some of his more sweeping attacks, but at one point he paid me a grudging compliment which Whyte chose to reproduce:

> Of itself, harmony between tenant and landlord is a salutary thing, testifying to the tenant's intelligence and the landlord's good will. But the price has been high. Apathy has been the child of Peace, Indiffer-

ence the spawn of Concord.... Since he is a man of many parts, I hope that Phil Klutznick, alert to the disservice he has done us by becoming a sweet and lovable old bug, is even now pondering some issue which will redynamize us. We need a common enemy we can magnify into a monster, whisper about, conspire about, hang in effigy.

16 □ Old Concerns, New Departures

While building Park Forest I was actively involved in other matters, starting with those of direct concern to Chicago's Jewish community. I was no stranger to that community when I settled in Chicago in July 1946. My associations with some of its leaders dated from the 1930s due to my involvements in B'nai B'rith, Zionism, and to the work of the Omaha Federation of Jewish Charities whose innovative operations were studied by Chicagoans. Chicago was the headquarters of District No. 6 of B'nai B'rith, which I visited frequently when I was its president. Other associations dated from wartime contacts.

As of 1946, the economic and political life of Chicago—to touch on the matter briefly—was in transition, from its slam-bang character in years past to its more oblique and complex ways in the years ahead. The dominant figures among the owners of equities in major enterprises—in steel, transportation, construction, food processing, utilities, communications, mail order houses, clothing—were often their managers as well. The man who combined in himself ownership and management functions could not, therefore, readily hide behind assorted masks when things he set in motion flopped. Besides, though Chicago had the size of a great metropolis, its known and visible players comprised a kind of village of their own, where individual entrepreneurs stood out in their distinctive personal strengths or limitations.

"Deals" between Chicago's principal businessmen were deals

between entrepreneurs who did their own negotiations face-to-face, without a battery of lawyers; lawyers were brought into the picture mainly to tidy up legal details after the substantive points of a deal had been settled. It was common for the city's leading businessmen to view Chicago from a proprietary perspective. Chicago was *their* town, and emergencies that threatened it *as* a town, threatened them personally. So, without anyone ordering them to do so, they often came together as an "establishment" to initiate the kind of remedial measures which, by serving the common good, could frankly serve their private good as well.

In 1946, Chicago politics was still dominated by the Democratic "machine" which had displaced the local Republican organization in the early 1930s. Some of its grab-and-get members continued to engage in transactions on the shady side of the law, and such winds of reform as were on the rise were confined to those candidates whom the machine was prepared to endorse for offices at a distance from the loaves and fishes of local politics—that is, governor of Illinois and United States senator.

The Chicago machine's winning ways at the polls owed much to the fact that its leaders, unlike those who presided over disintegrating urban political machines elsewhere, had not aligned themselves with the enemies of the New Deal and the successor Fair Deal. They had identified themselves with the social welfare programs of Roosevelt and Truman and presented themselves as the agents of their local application. They could do this more readily because the heads of the Chicago Catholic hierarchy, starting with figures such as Cardinal Mundelein, were always more spacious in their views of labor and social welfare issues than their counterparts in New York, Boston, or Los Angeles.

The Jewish community of Chicago absorbed to itself the tone of the larger community around it. In 1946, its human base had not yet been reduced by the postwar flight to the suburbs. There were, however, significant shifts of location within the city as Jews who had lived amid the concentrations of Orthodoxy on the west side now gravitated to the south side or to the lakeshore where the center of Reform Judaism could be found.

No man should be the judge of his own case, yet it seems right to suggest that my position within the Chicago Jewish community in 1946 owed much to a combination of three elements. First, while I was known to its existing leadership for some years, I had never been a party to any divisive local dispute. Second, my name at the time kept cropping up with increased frequency in favorable reports published in the metropolitan press about the building of Park Forest. The third element was perhaps the most important. My having held a high-visibility wartime post in Washington implied that I had received the stamp of legitimacy from non-Jews who controlled the levers of supreme power in the nation. Many local Jews, removed by no more than a generation from an immigrant background, and still nagged by doubts about the stability of their place in the structure of American life, may have seen in me a figure secure enough in his relationships with non-Jews to be entrusted with the responsibilities of leadership in specifically Jewish matters.

As of July 1946 the Chicago Jewish community was subject to two major fund-raising drives. One supported relief work overseas, especially on behalf of the Yishuv in Israel. The other dealt primarily with the relief of Jews in Europe. In a speech I was invited to give to Jewish community leaders, I stressed the wastefulness of conducting two separate campaigns. The two should be consolidated into a single campaign, with the funds distributed according to need.

After chairing the committee formed to merge the two campaigns, I was asked also to head the united drive. I agreed subject to two conditions: first, if I were approached to serve as chairman by the two anticipated "top givers," Henry Crown and A. N. Pritzker, and others; second, if the goal set for the united campaign was increased from under $50 million, the total of the earlier separate campaigns, to around $68 million.

My insistence that I should be asked by both Henry Crown and A. N. Pritzker to serve as chairman did not stem from a desire to have them massage my vanity. I had known A. N. Pritzker since my days as a young lawyer in Omaha, when he entrusted some legal business to Sam Beber's law firm where I had begun to work. As for Henry Crown, I have already indicated that he was a source of the extra capital as well as the supply of concrete indispensible to the Park Forest project. To have both men and other backers solicit me to serve as chairman of the drive might help overcome the usual disputes about how the campaign should be conducted. Also, the support of two of the wealthiest participants, through their own gifts, could ensure the success of the campaign.

In this way I became the first chairman of what was known in Chicago as the Jewish United Fund. The goal was substantially raised, and we came close to securing the targeted $68 million in funds. No one after that questioned the merits of a united fund-raising drive, though it seemed to need someone in my position— free from existing emotional entanglements in the Chicago Jewish community—to prove that what obviously made sense would actually work.

[II]

Two other matters engaged my interest while I was engaged in building Park Forest. One involved my relationship with Adlai E. Stevenson. The other involved events of fundamental concern to Jews generally, and my relationships to B'nai B'rith specifically.

I may have casually met Adlai Stevenson when he was the 1948 Democratic candidate for governor of Illinois. But my association with him began after his election as governor by a decisive majority at the same time that Paul H. Douglas won his own contest—also by a decisive majority—as the Democratic candidate for the United States Senate from Illinois. I doubt if there were many other instances in modern American political history when the same election within a state offered the nation two outsized figures who qualified as prospective presidential candidates. At the same time, personal contact between these two men—of radically different backgrounds, emotional charges, and personal styles— was marked by strains that caused more than a few sighs of regret among their mutual friends.

A few days after Stevenson's triumph at the polls, I happened to be in the massage room of the Standard Club in Chicago when an attendant placed a telephone receiver in my hand as I lay prone on the massage table. Stevenson was at the other end of the line. When he learned where I was and in a condition where I had nothing to conceal, he said he would come to the club to see me. I demurred. As governor-elect he was due the courtesy of my coming to him instead. A time was set for a visit in his law office.

When we met he remarked that he had heard good things about my governmental work in public housing during the war and in veterans housing afterward, and of my part in the building of the new town of Park Forest. Then, having baited the hook with praise, he offered me the chairmanship of the Illinois Housing Authority. Because of my background, he said, I could make the authority a model for other states.

I thanked him for his generous words but declined the appointment. In the first place, as chairman I would have to work with six members of the authority who were carried over as appointees of Illinois governors prior to Stevenson. Second, and more important, Temple McFayden, the incumbent chairman of the authority, was the brother of the president of the Automobile Dealers Association of Nebraska, who was my friend and client when I was practicing law in Omaha. I valued that friendship and would not be the hand that pushed Temple McFayden out of his post in Illinois. Hearing this, Stevenson asked if I would be willing to serve as vice chairman of the authority while McFayden retained the chairmanship. I said that if he thought I would be useful in the post, I would agree to serve in it. The appointment as vice chairman followed.

During the next four years I saw Stevenson at random moments but seldom had a face-to-face discussion with him about policy questions related to public housing in Illinois. For that matter, I received no instructions from him regarding positions I was to take on issues that came before the governing board of the authority. The other six members of the board initially assumed that my mission was to carry out "orders" from Stevenson. In time, however, they came to understand that while I would naturally reflect Governor Stevenson's general political attitude, I relied on my own judgment in deciding concrete cases.

Later, when Stevenson was the 1952 Democratic candidate for president, I was not surprised by the celebrated photograph showing a hole which threatened to break through the sole of his worn-out shoe. I knew him by then—as I did later in the United Nations—to be the very model of parsimony in public and private life alike. For my part, I was inclined to believe with Emerson that "true economy does not consist in merely saving coal, but in using the heat wisely while the coal burns." Saying this, I turn to my second and larger concern.

[III]

The end of World War II revealed the extent to which the catastrophic consequences of the Holocaust had been underestimated. Hitler failed to destroy world Jewry, but he destroyed European Jewish communities, especially those in eastern Europe which had been the most vital traditional centers of Jewish culture as well as the mainsprings of the Zionist movement. The same blow, which destroyed the district grand lodges of B'nai B'rith in Germany, Austria, Poland, Czechoslovakia, Bulgaria, and Yugoslavia, hastened the transformation of the Order. B'nai B'rith remained international in form, but it reflected the new prominence of American Jews in matters of concern to world Jewry. By 1947 American male membership in the Order stood at 190,000, and more than 90,000 women had joined B'nai B'rith Women.

The war's end did not, however, usher in peace and harmony among American Jewish organizations. When Germany finally conceded defeat, the differences among American Jews over postwar plans for Jewish survivors reasserted their divisive force. I shared the conviction that American Jewish organizations should work to reconstitute Palestine as a free democratic Jewish commonwealth. The American Jewish Committee and the Jewish Labor Committee, however, were of a different mind. While they urged the immediate entry into Palestine of 100,000 Jewish survivors of the Holocaust, they continued to reject the notion of a Jewish state. Their main efforts instead centered on securing more liberal immigration quotas so that more Jews in the displaced persons camps of Germany could start life anew on American soil. These efforts foundered in Congress.

Among American Jews as a whole, a rapidly growing American-Jewish consensus in favor of the Zionist viewpoint was revealed when the 1945 Roper Poll showed 90 percent of American Jews in favor of a Jewish state and only 10 percent opposed. Even the Central Conference of American Rabbis, a Reform body, for the first time approved a resolution with a pro-Zionist cast—though a handful of dissident Reform rabbis organized the militantly anti-Zionist American Council for Judaism. The council never won much popular support, but it served as a conduit for the discontent over Zionism present in other American Jewish organizations.

Although anti-Zionism was relegated to the fringes of American Jewish communal life, the 1947 convention of B'nai B'rith was still unwilling to support unequivocally the central Zionist demand for the creation of a Jewish state. Instead the Order endorsed the abrogation of the British White Paper to permit Jewish immigration to Palestine, and called upon the United States "to facilitate the establishment of a homeland for Jewish people in Palestine." The convention also approved B'nai B'rith's participation in the pro-Zionist American Jewish Conference, and authorized the formation of a committee of B'nai B'rith members who would represent the Order in an American Jewish Assembly. I was among those picked to serve on that committee if the American Jewish Conference ratified the creation of an American Jewish Assembly as a permanent and formal body.

At the American Jewish Conference in 1947, Henry Monsky suffered a fatal heart attack while he was delivering an impassioned speech in which he urged the conference to transform itself into the American Jewish Assembly. The fact that he tried with his last breath to overcome strong opposition to his master plan afterward accounted for the way he was often referred to as a martyr.

Frank Goldman of Lowell, Massachusetts, a lawyer by profession and the first vice president of B'nai B'rith, became Monsky's successor as president of B'nai B'rith. Then in his sixties, Goldman shared Monsky's outlook on Jewish life and his views about the role of B'nai B'rith in the Jewish community. His personal charm was entwined with a self-deprecating humor. He recalled that when he was first elected president of the Order, he expected a deferential greeting when he returned to Lowell. Instead his wife had left him a note: "Frank, as soon as you get home, go buy the cat some liver."

Goldman's exemplary traits of mind and character made him a leader of the bar, but he stood at a distance from the stream of human forces that might shape the nature of B'nai B'rith's leadership in the postwar world. The Order, for example, included increasing numbers of individuals whose affiliations with B'nai B'rith began when they were AZA members, or later as participants in the Hillel programs on college campuses. By the end of the 1940s, tens of thousands of Jewish men nationally had once belonged to AZA, had served in the armed forces, and had gone on to successful careers in the professions and in business. Moreover, a significant number had assumed leadership posts in local B'nai B'rith lodges, and several had duplicated my own pattern when my election at the start of the 1940s as president of B'nai B'rith District 6 made me the first product of AZA training to attain the presidential post for any district in the Order.

In matters related to the birth of the state of Israel, Frank Goldman reflected the convictions of this new generation of leaders within the B'nai B'rith. Many of them, however, grew restive as time passed and B'nai B'rith as an *institution* was beset by assorted troubles. In the first place, the practice of volunteerism on the home front, stimulated by an eagerness to contribute to the war effort, waned after VJ Day. Second, many American Jews preferred to contribute their dollars directly to the newborn state of Israel rather than to B'nai B'rith programs which helped support American-based Jewish institutions. With a decline in both membership and income, B'nai B'rith strength and prestige seemed to be ebbing.

These trends, combined with some lapses in Goldman's political tact in a matter related to a campus director of Hillel, set the stage for a challenge in 1950 to which I was a party. As the 1950 triennial convention of B'nai B'rith drew near, I was urged by many former AZA boys and by others as well to be a candidate for the presidency of the Order in a contest against the incumbent. Out of cockiness and the conviction that I was equal to any challenge, I succumbed to the pressures of flattery, agreed actively to seek the presidency—and showed a flawed judgment in doing so.

As of 1950, Goldman had served only a single three-year term, and it would have been contrary to precedent to deny him a second term. While it was agreed that B'nai B'rith faced mounting problems, when the votes were cast a majority of the delegates endorsed the view voiced by Sidney S. Kusworm, a member of B'nai B'rith's executive committee and treasurer of the Order. He observed that "Klutznick was still a young man, only forty-two years old, and could have the presidential office for the asking at the triennial convention in 1953. There is time enough for him to wait his turn, but it would be wrong to send Frank Goldman back to his own town in a humiliating defeat." In all this there was an echo of what Sam Beber had told the deadlocked first convention of AZA—that William Horowitz, as "a younger boy," could afford to yield the post of Grand Aleph Godol to his older rival because he was certain to attain the post at the next year's convention.

[IV]

Frank Goldman agreed that in 1953 I most likely would succeed him without opposition as president of the Order. More than that, he showed uncommon generosity in helping prepare me for office. At his invitation, for example, I regularly joined him in settings where decisions were made about issues vital to B'nai B'rith.

A major case in point were the meetings of the "Conference on Jewish Material Claims Against Germany," better known simply as the "Claims Conference." The Claims Conference had been organized in New York by Dr. Nahum Goldmann, then president of the World Jewish Congress as well as chairman of the Jewish Agency. Comprised of representatives of sixteen major Jewish organizations, the conference provided an executive council of advisers to Dr. Goldmann once he began the reparations negotiations with designated representatives of Chancellor Konrad Adenauer. Frank Goldman, in his capacity as president of B'nai B'rith, was one of the vice presidents of the Claims Conference, as I would be after 1953 when I succeeded him as president of the Order.

Claims Conference meetings with Nahum Goldmann gave me a chance to judge the manner of a man with whom I was to have a close relationship in later years. He was a man of exceptional intellect and talent, and his political wisdom found its voice in the distinction he once drew between the politician and the statesman. The politician, he said, cared only about satisfying his supporters or electorate; the statesman's first consideration was for the aspirations of his opponents so as to find an acceptable compromise with them.

In other respects Nahum Goldmann was a man with a high tolerance for paradox. He held eight passports and was a loyal citizen of his successive countries. He spent many years in the diplomatic sphere yet he had little admiration for diplomacy, claiming that it was simply "the act of postponing inevitable decisions for as long as possible." Though he was a consummate politician, he had no great enthusiasm for his own art in the metier. "Politics," he said, "merely confirmed situations which had been created by other causes—economic, social, religious." He was for three-quarters of his life the representative to the world of a people whose very existence as a people was denied, and he was accepted virtually everywhere as the ambassador of a country that remained to be created. He was an architect in the creation of Israel, but he never took up permanent residence there. He was a philosopher and historian, holder of two doctorates from German universities. He was also the publisher of the ambitious *Encyclopedia Judaica*. Despite his vast erudition, his best instrument of persuasion lay in his gift as a raconteur—in his appetite for anecdotes and in his lavish use of them to drive home a serious point on a gale of laughter. The Nahum Goldmann who charmed his interlocutors, including those who were heads of nations, also had the great defects of those gifted with the power to charm—

which is to say, egocentricity, a tendency to authoritarianism, and impatience.

He hated New York, but as New York represented "Jewish power," that is where he spent most of his time when he was in the United States; only once in his lifetime did he ever visit Chicago. He had no illusions about the people with whom he dealt, any more than he had any illusions about himself. As a model pragmatist, he courted any person he believed could serve his political ends even if that person was in other respects a *gruber yung* (roughneck). To justify such courtships, he often repeated the Hasidic story of how ten men had been assembled at the request of a rabbi to form a *minyan* so that prayers could be chanted for the recovery of someone who was ill. A friend of the rabbi protested that he saw among them notorious thieves. "Excellent," replied the rabbi. "When all the heavenly gates are closed, it requires experts to open them." His genius lay in his sure instincts, though in pursuing them he seldom calculated the costs.

Goldmann was not particularly attractive physically, yet many beautiful women were drawn to him, and he to them. He would slyly add that in courting a woman, "truth is of no value." With my own straitlaced, puritanical ways, I was initially put off by Goldmann's spiciness. It took me some time to look past the unappealing aspects of the man and to be drawn to his side because we were agreed on policy matters—and to recognize his authentic genius as a leader fit to hold the highest post in any major nation-state on earth. In addition to my introductory encounters with Goldmann, I learned anew that a measure of unity could be achieved among diverse Jewish organizations in the United States only if one had God's autonomous power to create mountains without valleys. The schoolroom for that lesson was an Atlantic City conference of the National Community Relations Advisory Council (NCRAC) held in 1951. The NCRAC had been formed in 1944 as the successor to the ill-fated General Jewish Council. Its original function was to serve as a consultative forum for Jewish civic defense work carried on by the Anti-Defamation League of B'nai B'rith, the American Jewish Committee, the American Jewish Congress, and the American Jewish Labor Committee. As of 1951, two more national agencies—the Jewish War Veterans and the Union of American Hebrew Congregations—along with twenty-nine community councils were part of the same forum.

In years past, these constituent groups had become embroiled in jurisdictional disputes and often competed for funds. This condition, common to voluntary organizations in the world at large, proved particularly worrisome after the birth of the state of Israel in 1948. Support for Israel drained off the supply of funds which the American Jewish community might have used for its own internal purposes. On the face of things, therefore, it made sense to provide a greater measure of unity among the overlapping civic defense agencies.

But how?

The Large Cities Budgeting Conference, a coalition of the larger Jewish community welfare funds, commissioned Professor Robert MacIver of Columbia University, a non-Jewish sociologist with distinguished academic credentials, to study the question and prepare a report setting forth his answer to it. Professor MacIver's findings, it seemed to me, failed to give full weight to American Jewish history and life. He recognized that there were "irreconcilable social and economic differences" among the groups. Rather than a single, all-embracing agency, he offered a plan whereby responsibilities would be allocated to individual organizations along functional lines. For example, the Anti-Defamation League of B'nai B'rith would be paramount in investigative and counteraction programs and the Amercian Jewish Committee would work in the fields of legislation and litigation. He proposed that the NCRAC form standing committees to control the process of coordination and to settle jurisdictional disputes. What had begun in 1944 as an advisory council would be transformed into a functioning agency.

At the Atlantic City meeting, the Anti-Defamation League and the American Jewish Committee, each of which had a comprehensive community relations program, challenged proposals in the MacIver report that threatened to curtail their work and enlarge the activities of other organizations. After a long debate on the report, the issue was forced to a vote—the most ill-advised move of all. Under the prevailing system of majority rule, where one vote was equal to any other, the sheer weight of numbers favored a combination of national agencies and community councils. In their support for the substance of the MacIver report, they easily outvoted the Anti-Defamation League and the American Jewish Committee who were in opposition. The latter two organizations at once served notice that they would withdraw their affiliation from the NCRAC.

The morning after the night meeting at which the fatal vote was taken, I breakfasted with a community council leader who had led the way in initiating the showdown balloting. He was crestfallen as he surveyed the shambles caused by his paper victory. I might have reminded him that the rule by which Rome built its empire was "conquer but spare," not "conquer and annihilate." Instead I put the moral to be drawn from the disastrous experience into less inflated terms. "In voluntary movements," I said to him, "when you've got the votes, don't use them. That's the time to keep negotiating."

[V]

My bread-and-butter business interest continued to be centered in the further development of Park Forest. My wife and I enjoyed our new Park Forest home, and the older of our five children entered fully into the many activities which this community, teeming with children, offered the young.

For myself, I tried as best I could to be accessible to all residents of Park Forest. In all this I was fortunate in 1951 to secure the services of Tom McDade, who became my assistant-in-chief and jack-of-all-executive-skills. McDade was brought as a boy to Hillboro, Illinois, when his family emigrated to the United States from Scotland. He later attended the University of Chicago until he was called up for military service, during which he was in five major campaigns, including the D-Day invasion. After the war he enrolled in the University of North Carolina, studied urban planning, and returned to Chicago as assistant director of development for the Chicago Housing Authority. When Hart Perry left, I engaged McDade to take his place as my personal assistant.

17 □ Elections and Their Consequences

I was a witness to the truth that Governor Adlai E. Stevenson's 1952 bid for the presidency was mounted on very short notice. Few people knew how deeply he had been shaken by the signs of his wife's mental problems leading to the breakup of his marriage when he was governor. Nor did they know the extent to which he was always haunted by a memory going back to his early youth. At a birthday party for a cousin, he was handed a gun, playfully pulled the trigger, and was horrified by the discharge of a bullet that killed his cousin. He seemed to believe that his life after that should be one of penance. He was painfully uncomfortable when he was the object of public acclaim, and all the more uncomfortable by the need to seek it.

While Stevenson wrestled with the question whether he was fit to be president, the 1952 Democratic Convention, held after the Republicans had nominated General Dwight D. Eisenhower, decided things for him. It reached for Governor Stevenson, drafted him as the party's presidential nominee, and thereby absolved him from his earlier pledge to stand for reelection as governor of Illinois.

Among public men, Stevenson was a democrat who cherished the values of excellence ordinarily associated with aristocrats. His appeals on the major issues of the day were appeals to the reason of reasonable men. He held before a new generation of voters a vision of politics as an ennobling activity. Within my own family, for example, my daughter Bettylu, who was a student at Rockford College in 1952, got her first taste of political work when she immersed herself in Stevenson's cause on the campus. It was a taste that never left her in later years, though her hero went down to defeat.

My own role in the 1952 campaign was confined to financial contributions, and to some suggestions concerning housing matters or other policy issues. I saw more of Stevenson after the election when he joined a law firm in which his former gubernatorial aide, Newton Minow, had also become a member. I used Minow's legal services in connection with some of my personal affairs, and visits to his office sometimes led to chats with Stevenson as well. The immediate aftermath of the election found him a lonely man, but this changed as time went by. He seemed to have discovered that despite his defeat for the presidency he had gained a worldwide constituency which looked to him for leadership.

[II]

In Washington, for the first time in twenty years, the keys to the White House were now in Republican hands. Jewish leaders, with an advocate's case to make, no longer could use their familiar communication channels into the Oval Office, as during the long presidencies of Franklin D. Roosevelt and Harry S Truman. President Eisenhower organized the White House along the hierarchical lines of military command with which he was comfortable, though the arrangement restricted the way political controversies reached him. When it was recalled how President Truman had played his fateful role in the birth of the state of Israel—in direct opposition to many of his chief advisers—the limits which President Eisenhower imposed on direct access made for unease in certain quarters about what to expect from the man if Israel were *in extremis*.

Dwight D. Eisenhower's inauguration as president fell on the fifth year of Israel's rebirth as an independent state. The picture of Israel in early 1953 depended on one's angle of vision. The population of the state had increased since independence day through the influx of Jewish immigrants from nearby Muslim countries such as Iraq, Yemen, Syria, Egypt, and Iran. Local funds for Israel's developmental needs—for schools, houses, land reclamation, health services, training for jobs—were in short supply. But in addition to funds from recently launched Israeli bond drives, the Israeli government had negotiated a $100 million loan from the Export-Import Bank, an astronomical sum at the time. Also, Israel began to receive from the Federal Republic of Germany the first payment in goods of the $700 million in reparations which Nahum Goldmann had gained through brilliant negotiations.

Israel's future, however, was clouded by the rise to power of Colonel Gamal Nasser in Egypt and a new militancy by other Arab states, most notably Syria.

In the new Eisenhower administration, Secretary of State John Foster Dulles initiated what was called an "evenhanded" treatment of the parties to the Middle East conflict. The U.S. continued to withhold arms from Israel, and Israel continued to buy its principal arms from France, an arrangement that would prevail until the Kennedy administration for the first time modified the no-U.S.-arms-for-Israel policy. On the other hand, while U.S. loans and technical assistance to Israel were vulnerable to a cutoff if Israel struck across its border at the bases of Arab marauders, U.S. economic aid and technical assistance went forward to Egypt in increasing amounts.

I believed that any response to these adverse developments called for maximum self-discipline on the part of leaders and rank-and-file members of American Jewish organizations. American Jews, who in common with much of American officialdom, enthusiastically greeted the birth of the state of Israel, needed a "second win" with which to carry on supportive work. They needed clearer perceptions about the real problems besetting the United States in its approach to the differences among Israel, the Arab states, and the Western powers in the context of the Cold War. This situation provided the backdrop for the stage of action onto which I walked in the spring of 1953.

[III]

On the eve of B'nai B'rith's triennial convention in Washington, D.C., I was asked if I would accept the presidency of the National Jewish Welfare Board, the parent body of Jewish Community Centers. I had been closely associated with the work of the board for some time, but I accepted instead the offered presidency of B'nai B'rith—on condition that at the next triennial convention the constitution of the Order be amended to limit the tenure of the president to two three-year terms. I explained that a man who served six years would either be worn out or deserved to be retired. I was unanimously elected president, and the constitution of the Order was later amended as I proposed.

On the morning after the day of my election, I received a telephone call from Nahum Goldmann in New York. Our conversation went like this:

> *Goldmann*: Now that you are the president of B'nai B'rith, we can reorganize the American Jewish Conference. After all, you were for it in 1948.
> *PMK*: Dr. Goldmann, I appreciate your call, but what you suggested is not at the head of the list on my agenda.
> *Goldmann*: Look, I want to come to see you in Washington right away.
> *PMK*: Don't do that. I've got to be here a day or two cleaning up the consequences of my election. I am coming to New York, and I owe it to you to call on you first.

The way things worked out, I met him a few days later in the Jewish Agency office in New York. Goldmann said to me, "Phil, we've just got to reorganize the American Jewish Conference. We can put it together again now that you are president of B'nai B'rith." As I recall, this is what was said next:

> *PMK*: Look, Dr. Goldmann, the president of B'nai B'rith is not like the president of the World Jewish Congress. I am a new president facing many organizational difficulties as it is. In my first act I am not going to take on a subject that divided us in years past and repeat it anew. In retrospect I think it was wrong for us to press for the American Jewish Conference when there was so much resistance to the idea. The American Jewish community is not ready for the kind of centralized discipline you have in mind. But I do have an idea I've been playing with for some time, and I'd like to suggest it to you.
> *Goldmann*: (alert) Tell me. Tell me.
> *PMK*: In the years when I've gone to meetings at the Defense Department or in the State Department as part of a delegation of Jewish leaders, I found myself introducing presidents of other Jewish organizations to each other. For example, I had to introduce Lessing Rosenwald, president of the Council for American Jewry, to Irving Edison, president of the Jewish Welfare Board. I suggest that we should try to get together an informal—very informal—grouping of presidents of major national Jewish organizations.
> *Goldmann*: When do we start?
> *PMK*: Let me think about it, and I'll write you a memo on the subject.
> *Goldmann*: How many organizations would be in it?
> *PMK*: Maybe ten or twelve or fifteen at the most.

Goldmann: (impatiently) When do we start?

PMK: Wait a minute. What I am suggesting is only an idea. Before anything at all is done, we better check with other people.

On returning to Chicago, the memorandum I wrote and sent Goldmann in New York drew on what I had learned in connection with the American Jewish Conference in 1948 and the 1951 NCRAC conference centered on the MacIver report. The lesson was not to try to impose unity on voluntary Jewish agencies.

I argued that the proposed presidents' conference of major Jewish organizations should have a very informal structure. It should have a chairman to call meetings, a secretary to inform the members where and why meetings were being called, and a telephone number and address for the exchange of information. It should have no staff, no platform, no agenda. "American Jews," I wrote,

> are not only in need of Jewish education. We need education about Jews—their ideologies, their institutions. Their organizations, linked through their presidents, would serve the cause of mutual education. At the same time, it could provide a forum where the presidents could debate the terms and frame a common response to any emergency of fundamental concern to the Jewish community as a whole, starting, no doubt, with matters pertaining to Israel.

Goldmann apparently saw in the proposed organization a chance to revive the American Jewish Conference on the basis of consensus around Israel. When he received my memorandum, he lost no time in telephoning me to say, "Let's get to work."

I had already talked to Rabbi Maurice Eisendrath, head of the Union of American Hebrew Congregations. I knew he yearned for a greater measure of *E pluribus unum* among separate, sovereign, and diverse Jewish organizations. When he declared himself in favor of the presidents' conference along the lines I sketched, I telephoned Goldmann to say, "I've got one person committed." He said, "Well, I've talked to the Zionists, and I've got six presidents committed." To which I said, "Not so fast. We don't want another Zionist organization. We want a conference of presidents of major Jewish organizations. We'd better sit down with Maurice Eisendrath to decide which organizational presidents should constitute the group."

He agreed. At a subsequent three-cornered meeting, Goldmann, Eisendrath, and I compiled a list of seventeen organizations whose presidents should first be approached for affiliation with the Conference of Presidents. We subsequently secured tentative commitments from eight or nine leaders, including those at the head of the religious groups Eisendrath had won over. My assigned task was to win over the American Jewish Committee. Irving Engle, its president, was personally inclined to join the Conference of Presidents, but when a proposal to do so was brought before the committee it led to a divisive debate and finally rejection. But sixteen of the seventeen organizations that had been approached did join the new entity, which became a reality in April 1954.* Dr. Nahum Goldmann became chairman of the Conference of Presidents, but as he spent most of his time in Europe or in Israel, the members designated me to act as chairman when he was away from the United States. This was to be of crucial importance during the 1956 crisis over the Suez War.

I did not foresee how the conference would curtail the power of American Zionists in representing American Jewry's pro-Israel sentiments. That, however, is what happened. In later years, pronouncements that issued from the conference or on the personal initiative of an incumbent chairman made me wince either in dismay or embarrassment, so that I questioned the worth of my role as a midwife at the birth. At the same time I became increasingly concerned about the terms of the relationship between Israel, American Jews, and Jews the world over, and I grappled with the question of whether it was possible to provide an adequate institutional forum for the unfolding of that relationship.

---

*The sixteen organizations were the American Jewish Congress, the American Trade Union Council for Labor Israel, the American Israel Committee for Public Affairs, the American Zionist Council, B'nai B'rith, Haddassah, the Jewish Agency for Israel (American section), the Jewish Labor Committee, Jewish War Veterans, the Labor Zionist Organization of America, the Mizrachi Organization of American National Community Relations Advisory Council, the Union of American Hebrew Congregations, the Union of Orthodox Jewish Congregations, the United Synagogues of America, the World Jewish Congress (North American section), and the Zionist Organization of America.

18 □ Getting to Know You

My plan upon being elected president of B'nai B'rith was to devote most of my times to its affairs, and this required a change in the management of ACB. I resigned as president of the corporation and became chairman of its board, while Nate Manilow, who had protracted bouts with illness, assumed the presidency of the firm and held it as long as his health permitted. The day-to-day direction of ACB's operations in Park Forest was in the hands of Tom McDade.

The new arrangement allowed me to travel but also to keep a supervisory eye on ACB operations. Even when my future business interests led me in new directions, the time I spent on "public affairs" absorbed roughly 90 percent of my attention while only the remaining 10 percent went "purely to business." Some of my close associates were heard to mutter that the limited time I devoted "purely to business" was all to the good. It was doubtful they would have withstood my proddings if I were on the scene for extended intervals.

The industrial development that had been part of the original plan for Park Forest never got very far. I remember the enthusiasm with which we offered forty acres of industrial land at a very low price to a large corporation that was planning to build a plant in the Chicago area. The corporation used women employees, and Park Forest was a highly desirable labor market. Many women with children in school were available for employment and actually needed to work in order to supplement the family income. The corporation instead bought expensive land in the northern suburbs of Chicago. Why? We learned that the executives who would manage the plant planned on living on the North Shore and so wanted the plant to be nearby.

The development of the Park Forest shopping mall, a pioneer in the development of the regional shopping center concept, posed other problems—and missed opportunities. The mall developed in phases, as did everything else in Park Forest. First steps included basic services—a food store, a drug store, a dry cleaner, a hardware store, a baker, a shoe repairman, a liquor store. This incremental growth, always within the frame of an overall plan, was the recipe for success. But like all recipes, the outcome depended on the cook. The success of the venture depended on the quality of the merchants and the skill and integrity of the service establishments. There must also be a range of stores. Customers must know they were being exposed to a choice and were not simply the captives of a mall.

At its height, Park Forest's downtown shopping center contained some sixty shops with almost every kind of retail establishment. Goldblatt's was the first major department store to open a branch. Other major stores assumed there was not enough business to justify the risk. In 1955, however, Marshall Field came in when its successful collaboration with ACB elsewhere marked the onset of what was to be a long and fruitful relationship, first with ACB and then with Urban Development Investment Corporation (of which more later). Sears, which came into Park Forest in 1963, was also part of that collaboration.

[II]

International presidents of B'nai B'rith had never made grass-roots tours of all the districts and lodges in the United States, much less in Canada, Latin America, Europe, or South Africa. None had ever visited Israel. I was the first to have direct personal contact with all districts and many individual lodges in the United States and overseas. The onset of the process, which extended over a number of years, dated from my first tour of American districts starting in mid-July 1953. Ethel often went with me on these trips, and at times my children were brought along. When we traveled by car, our chauffeur was William Covington, an admirable human being who served our family with grace and wisdom for more than forty years until he died. The experiences of these trips deeply impressed five-year-old Samuel Klutznick who, on being asked what he thought of B'nai B'rith, answered from the depths of his wisdom, "B'nai B'rith is a meeting."

My approach to the tasks I undertook as president of B'nai

B'rith was grasped by the noted Israeli writer Amos Elon. In the mid-1950s Elon was the Washington correspondent of *Haaretz*, and he sometimes followed my trail. He once wrote that I "symbolized the transition from the first generation of immigrant ideological leaders in the Jewish community in America through the second generation of practical leaders to the third generation that is rooted in its environment and sees itself as American in all things." Leaders of this type, he continued,

> are not Zionists but are enthusiastically pro-Israel. They do not want to emigrate to Israel, but want Israel to succeed, just as they want to see an enriching Jewish life grow on American soil. Their status in the public eye does not depend on their identities as leaders of specifically Jewish organizations. They have achieved individual success in diverse fields in general American society, and they bring to specifically Jewish causes the distinctions they have won elsewhere in other contexts.

In speeches to local B'nai B'rith lodges which I visited after the manner of a fence-mending American politician, I argued that compulsory uniformity was not for us, no more than we could afford pointless interfamily struggles for power and position. Most American Jews, steeped in freedom and the ethos of democracy, could only operate as volunteers in organizations that were themselves congruous with the spirit of the American environment.

From a cultural standpoint I was Jewish to the core of my inner being, but I was not doctrinaire on the fine points of Judaism as a religion. I wished it were true that all Jews were affiliated with a temple or synagogue. Without that affiliation, Jewish life would be bones without flesh and a denial of the root source of Judaism's greatest contributions to civilization. The fact was, however, that no more than 40 or 50 percent of those who identified themselves as Jews belonged to any of the divisions—Orthodox, Conservative, or Reform. The rest remained unaffiliated either as a matter of principle or because of casual indifference. Many of them, however, were deeply concerned with Jewish problems, with Jewish history, and with Jewish literature and culture; many were often in the thick of battles affecting the fate of Jews wherever they might be. One could apply to them a judgment voiced by Jewish sages of old that a formal affiliation with a synagogue was not the only badge of Jewish life, but rather that a "good heart" was the best badge of all. If so, then by their affiliation with B'nai B'rith they could help create and sustain at the local level those secular institutions that were essential to a full Jewish life.

This was particularly necessary in the case of Jewish education. I thought it ironic that at a time when the children and grand-children of Jewish immigrants from eastern Europe were bursting with creative powers in the United States, the quality of Jewish scholarship on Jewish issues was, with some notable exceptions, strangely pallid. In my view a progressive Jewish community and a full Jewish life called for direct and sustained contributions by scholars, the integrity of whose work could stand up under exacting cross-examination by other scholars without regard to their religious affiliation.

My talking and writing on these matters went hand in hand with detailed work on the purely institutional aspects of B'nai B'rith. Working capital must be replenished and budgets balanced. Drives for new memberships were mounted. The B'nai B'rith youth program, under the skilled leadership of Dr. Max Baer, was granted more resources to keep pace with accelerating demands. So was Hillel. More attention was paid to B'nai B'rith women and to rebuilding B'nai B'rith institutions in Europe that had been reduced to ruin during the war years.

The Order's internal structure was reorganized to make B'nai B'rith a more effective "general service" agency and to provide professional guidance for its programs. And we initiated the process that finally provided B'nai B'rith with a permanent head-quarters. Organizations do not live by brick and mortar alone, yet the character and stability of the headquarters of an enterprise is a fairly reliable index to its progress. Before my tenure as president of the Order ended, B'nai B'rith not only had a handsome new home of its own in Washington, D.C., but also had paid off the mortgage on the structure.

[III]

The first two years of my presidency of B'nai B'rith coincided with the climax of Senator Joseph McCarthy's inflamed brand of anti-communism and the onset of the turmoil that followed the Su-preme Court's 1954 decision in *Brown vs. Board of Education*, which repudiated the "separate but equal" principle in public education.

The Anti-Defamation League's resistance to McCarthy reflected the maturation of its commitment to civil rights not for Jews alone but throughout the reaches of American society. Where civil liberties were concerned, it came to the defense of those whose beliefs it otherwise opposed, and it did not hesitate to offer its defense services where the air overhead was ablaze with charges of a "Jewish communist conspiracy."

In the efforts to end government-sanctioned racial discrimination in the United States, the ADL used legal battles as instruments of popular education. The effects distressed some B'nai B'rith leaders in the South, though their reactions stopped short of breaks with the Order as a whole. It was different, however, when the Supreme Court overturned the "separate but equal" precedent dating from *Plessy vs. Ferguson* at the end of the nineteenth century, and ordered the desegregation of the public schools "with all due deliberate speed." The ruling jolted Southern Jews as it did their white Christian neighbors, though perhaps in different ways and degrees.

My reaction as president of B'nai B'rith was immediately to call a meeting of its executive committee, which then issued a statement urging all members to support the Court. Large numbers of B'nai B'rith lodge members and leaders in the South objected to this action. Caught in a society on the threshold of fundamental social change, they opted for the seeming security of white solidarity. The vulnerability of Southern Jews, threatened on the one side by white supremacists and on the other by black activists, was aggravated by their concentration in such visible economic endeavors as retailing.

As president of B'nai B'rith I could scarcely be indifferent to the dilemma of Southern Jews nor to the motives of those who resigned from B'nai B'rith lodges. I was never in doubt about B'nai B'rith's duty to support the principles set forth in the Supreme Court's decision. I did, however, want to see for myself what school desegregation meant to those who had to contend with the practical consequences of what the Supreme Court had ordered. Despite cautionary words from friends who were concerned about my physical safety, I went South, not to the border states but to the Mississippi delta. I traveled from one town to another and met morning, noon, and night with people from all walks of life in the Jewish community, at town crossroads, in private homes, in public halls, in synagogues and temples.

I knew it was easier to make a ringing speech on desegregation from a platform in Madison Square Garden, Chicago Stadium, or the San Francisco Cow Palace than in the Elks Club of a small town in Mississippi. Even an honest speaker will modify what he says depending on where he speaks, or at least modify his emphasis and tone. So I was not surprised to hear bitter words from local people about the role of the national Jewish organizations in the civil rights field. Some of my fellow Jews in Mississippi insisted that they would have no problem at all if we could accept their conclusion that "desegregation was no concern of the Jew." When I pointed out the obvious—that in the quest for equality, the American Jew could expect no more for himself than he was prepared to give others in a similar situation—the average and decent man's reply was to agree and then add in a whisper: "But don't be so loud or so active about it." When confronted by evidence that under the "separate but equal" doctrine very little had been done to improve the quality of life for blacks, their last desperate admonition was, "This is a problem that can only be solved by education, not by law." To which I would answer, "But the law itself is a great teacher."

From the moment I set foot in Greenville, Mississippi, to the moment I left Jackson and went north, I heard Southern Jews repeatedly say:

> You see, we enjoy equal status down here. Our families have lived here for several generations. We are accepted. We are on the boards of directors of banks, presidents of Rotary clubs and chambers of commerce. When B'nai B'rith, which is known as *the* Jewish organization down here, takes a leading part in this controversy, our white non-Jewish neighbors are not so sure of us. You continue what you are doing and we will end up with a strong Ku Klux Klan, economic boycotts, and everything else hostile to Jews in the South.

In reply I would say, "Jewish organizations have taken no greater leadership in this than most of the Protestant and Catholic church groups and social welfare agencies that are not Jewish. What about them?" The customary rejoinder to this was either, "Well, they are not Jews," or, "After all, they're not in the minority."

From among the dimming recollections of names, faces, and places in the course of my Southern tour, one encounter stands out starkly, as though it happened but a moment ago. The leader of the B'nai B'rith lodge in a certain Mississippi town was a principal merchant in the area, popular with the townspeople. He also enjoyed a measure of popularity from the fact that his son-in-law, a colonel in the U.S. army, was an authentic war hero. When I arrived in the town on a Friday morning and placed a call with the lodge leader, he refused to meet me face to face. More than that, he seemed to imply that the best thing I could do for all parties concerned—myself included—was to leave town as soon as possible. He eventually relented, and I arranged to see him under almost cloak-and-dagger circumstances.

I soon faced a man with tears in his eyes and with a tale about how his standing in the town had been gravely imperiled because B'nai B'rith nationally had supported the moves toward desegregation. He revealed that for years he had hoped he might some day be allowed, as a Jew, to join the all-Christian local country club. The invitation to join was at last in clear prospect, but the prospect was clouded over by the local commotion whacked up by the Supreme Court school desegregation ruling and by B'nai B'rith's support for the Court. Now he was isolated.

The start of my trip throughout the South happened to coincide with the opening round of negotiations with the Federal Republic of West Germany on claims rising out of the Nazi confiscation of B'nai B'rith property. So in my talk with the distraught merchant in the Mississippi town I recalled the tragic Jewish experiences in Germany where "nice people" with their self-centered interests chose not to see what was happening to the Jews. When they finally saw and wanted to speak out, it was too late. In the Jewish tradition, I observed, those with power to help avert a wrong who did nothing were implicated in the wrong itself. In this case, what needed to be set right was the wrong that had been done historically to fellow Americans of the black race. The merchant was not won over to the stand B'nai B'rith had taken, but that night, when I spoke in the local synagogue along the lines I've just sketched, I noticed that his daughter and son-in-law were present in the congregation.

Some things shine more brightly when projected against a dark background—as in the case of individual Jews in the South who refused to be cowed into silence during this bleak period. This was particularly true of Label A. Katz of New Orleans, a product of AZA, a debater and orator, a lawyer by profession, a member and then chairman of the B'nai B'rith Youth Commission. Katz's name stamped him as unmistakably Jewish; his speech was rooted in Hebraic and Yiddish cadences, and he could speak to prime ministers of Israel in Hebrew. He was simultaneously the vice president of the Urban League of Greater New Orleans—which worked to improve economic conditions for blacks—and the lay representative of the Anti-Defamation League of B'nai B'rith in a major part of the Deep South. He was intimately involved in coping with the tensions generated by the Supreme Court's decision against school segregation. In contrast to the way the fear of reprisal stilled the voices of many Jews in the South, Katz forthrightly supported the ADL position on desegregation issues. Label Katz succeeded me as president of B'nai B'rith in 1959.

It would be false to suggest that Southern Jews generally, and Southern members of B'nai B'rith specifically, were converted overnight to the cause of desegregation. Yet it seemed to me then, and it seems to me now, that throughout my presidency B'nai B'rith moved with a remarkable self-assurance in its approach to the explosive problems associated with desegregation.

19 □ En Route to Suez

As president of B'nai B'rith I was drawn close to the center of U.S.-Israeli problems and tensions. A limitless cast of actors on the American side of the story helped to shape the course of those relations. What follows is necessarily confined to what I personally saw, heard, and did on the stage where the shifting drama was played out.

[II]

By coincidence, the year of my election as president of B'nai B'rith coincided with unsettling developments for Israel. From across her border with Jordan, Syria, and Egypt came a torrent of violence—military units and marauders, organized under the name of *fedayeen*, who brought mutilation and death to Israel's civilians in frontier areas and sometimes in the heart of the coastal plain. Israel's armed forces often acted to stem the violence, but the result was a heavy toll of Arab and Jewish life and indignant appeals to the U.N. Security Council, usually followed by resolutions that condemned Israel. The State Department at the time seemed to believe that its own troubles in the Arab world had nothing to do with an endemic anti-Americanism in Arab capitals. To judge from Secretary of State Dulles's remarks in a speech on June 1, 1953, the department preferred to believe that the remedy for anti-Americanism lay in large measure in "the need to allay Arab discontent arising from the establishment of the State of Israel."

While the United States and virtually all other Western powers opposed Israel's policy of retaliation against the deadly raids, none suggested an alternative for defending the lives of Israelis. It was asserted instead that "Israel's apparent policy of retaliation increased rather than diminished tensions along the armistice lines." The implied logic seemed to be that tensions would vanish if Israel would stoically allow its citizens to be killed without a response.

A particularly fierce Israeli retaliatory raid at Beit Liqya in Jordan had been preceded by Israel's defiance of a U.N. order to suspend water development in the north. The United States, in support of Arab protests of that water development, had decided to cut off all economic support to Israel already voted by Congress. An announcement to that effect coincided with the tragedy at Beit Liqya and seemed to be prompted by it. The administration's actions, in turn, sparked a firestorm in the American Jewish community, with consequences that placed the Republican candidate for mayor of New York in a painful strait. Secretary of State Dulles, acceding to a request from Senator Irving M. Ives of New York, a Republican, joined in by Congressman Jacob K. Javits from the same state, also a Republican, agreed to meet a representative delegation of American Jews on Monday, October 26. I was asked to join that delegation.

My initial estimate of Dulles would later change, as Abba Eban in his memoirs admits was true for him. I continued to disagree with some of Dulles's judgments, but he earned my respect and sympathy because of the nature of the problems that confronted him. My initial opinion of Dulles, however, was on the low side. He was about sixty-six years old when I first met him in an official capacity, or roughly two decades my senior. Physically he was a rather imposing man, about six feet tall and 190 pounds in weight. His features took their definitive cast from his mouth which was rather thin, stern, and sharply turned down at the edges due to a slight stroke. He could laugh and joke, not viscerally like Nahum Goldmann but cerebrally. Laughter, however, was seldom his dominant mood. When I first judged his mettle, he seemed to fit the mold of a lawyer who has great pride in his own intellect and cunning, confident he can take either side of a brief and outwit adversaries in litigation. Yet for all my initial reservations about the man, I kept in mind the fact that he *was* the United States Secretary of State, and that it was necessary to preserve open lines of communication with him.

At the end of our meeting with Dulles, our delegation issued a statement stressing "the need to maintain Israel as a secure bastion for freedom and peace in the Near East in the interests of the United States and the whole free world." We referred to the economic boycott of Israel openly carried on by the Arab states and their categorical rejection of Israel's constantly reiterated willingness to enter into negotiations for a peace treaty with the Arab states. We expressed "profound regret and sympathy for the victims of the deplorable and tragic incidents on the Israel-Jordan frontier which have cost the lives of so many innocent people on both sides." We urged the government of the United States "to address itself most vigorously to removing the cause of these incidents by striving for Arab-Israel peace." Impeding or delaying Israel's development of its own resources, we maintained, would not advance peace and development in the Middle East.

On October 27, the day after the delegation met with Secretary Dulles—without knowing what his own decision would eventually be—I thought it politic to write him a note in my capacity as president of B'nai B'rith, offering a personal comment on the meeting. It was the first of the "bridges" I intended to build to him. I briefly alluded to my service behind a government desk in wartime Washington, though I noted that my problems were "minute" compared with those he faced daily. I could not agree with the State Department's decision to withhold aid to Israel, I wrote, but I could see that he was "visibly affected by the whole controversy" and revealed "the kind of understanding and interest which are the attributes of a great Secretary of State." Hence I had an "abiding conviction that at the proper time" he would "give evidence of those great qualities" by reversing himself, if need be, to do what I knew he would "find to be full justice."

The arguments of our delegation were far less persuasive than what the Republican party chiefs of New York City had to say directly to President Eisenhower—to wit, that the bright Republican prospects to win the mayoralty would be eclipsed unless economic aid to Israel was resumed. The point told on White House political operatives and from there on the State Department. Dulles sent Assistant Secretary of State Henry Byroade on a peculiar mission to see Abba Eban, then serving as Israel's ambassador at the U.N. He asked Eban to agree to an immediate statement signaling the resumption of financial aid to Israel. "It was," so Eban later sardonically wrote, "the only occasion on which I was pressured by a foreign government to receive and not relinquish something."

After an Israeli pro forma expression of willingness to "comply with the Security Council recommendations on the water question," President Eisenhower announced on October 28 that the United States was resuming economic aid to Israel. I at once sent two telegrams under my signature as president of B'nai B'rith. One addressed to President Eisenhower read, "Warmly applauded" his decision to resume United States economic aid program to the state of Israel. The other, to Secretary of State Dulles, read: "In the realization that the President's statement this morning on the resumption of the economic aid program to the State of Israel must needs be in conformity with the views and advice of our Secretary of State, we take this opportunity to express to you our deep appreciation."

[III]

Israel's troubles in the world arena were matched by those within the country itself. Here the soaring hopes and nerve-wracking risks which marked the politics of purpose in the first four years of independence seemed to have been replaced, temporarily at least, by the politics of fatigue. The emblem of the change was the decision of David Ben-Gurion at the end of 1953 to resign as prime minister and retire to Sde Boker, a kibbutz in the Negev. For more than two decades this buoyant and pugnacious man had sent out sparks of energy on all sides. While his single-minded objective was to realize the Zionist ideal, his personal ambition was not for honors but for the power to dominate. Dominate he did, for though he was a democrat, no one in his party dared contradict him.

By the end of 1953 Ben-Gurion was deeply dissatisfied with aspects of Israeli life—the intensity of parliamentary warfare; an electoral system whose fragmented parts reflected old ideological divisions among pre-state Zionist parties; the consequent need always to conciliate small groups in order to maintain an ad hoc coalition that would enable the government to govern. When he surrendered responsibilities to his successor Moshe Sharet, he was, however, like King Lear who, after dividing the kingdom among his three daughters, wished to retain for himself all the pomp of kingliness. He made it clear that his surrender of power was only temporary—as indeed it was.

Few strong leaders are enthusiastic about their successors even when the successors are handpicked. Trouble between them always seems to wait in ambush. In the case at hand it took the form of an alternative government which Ben-Gurion established at Sde Boker. Israeli leaders dutifully went there not only for inspiration but for their marching orders.

Meanwhile, the appointment of Pinchas Lavon to head the Defense Ministry led to the creation of another center of authority in the state. This was because of Lavon's notion that the Minister of Defense, after the model of a ministry in the British cabinet, had a right to function independently of the prime minister. People who knew Lavon well judged him to be a man of acute intellectual powers, with a broad view of Israel's social destiny. In the defense establishment, however, he seemed driven to prove his militant virility. With Sharet, Ben-Gurion, and Lavon each pulling in a different direction, the fabric of Israel's political structure seemed strained to the breaking point at a time of troubles.

Egypt, while persistently violating Israel's navigation rights through the Suez Canal, had mounted an intensive campaign for the removal of British troops from the Suez area. Coincidentally, Iraq, then under a monarchical rule, together with Jordan and Lebanon, asked for and began to receive American military aid. The Arab League, for its part, maintained a militantly anti-Israel posture.

On April 4, 1954, Assistant Secretary of State Henry Byroade gave a widely publicized speech which could have been construed as a statement of U.S. policy. Its eye-catching passage read:

> To the Israelis I say, look upon yourselves as a Middle Eastern state rather than a headquarters or nucleus so to speak of worldwide groups of peoples of a particular religious faith who must have special rights within and obligations to the Israeli state. Drop your attitude of conqueror and the conviction that force is the only policy that your neighbors will understand. To the Arabs I say, accept Israel. Accept a less dangerous modus vivendi with your neighbor.

In a follow-up address on May 1, this time to the anti-Zionist American Council for Judaism, Byroade solemnly warned that unlimited Jewish immigration to Israel "was a matter of grave concern."

I soon called on Byroade in order to get a firmer sense of the State Department's Middle East policy. He told me that he understood the mind and motives of Colonel Nasser and hence could "do business with him." All else that emerged from that meeting was wrapped in fog. Insofar as I understood Byroade's line of reasoning, I agreed that a genuine "impartial" U.S. policy toward Arabs and Israelis *might* strengthen the hand of the United States in securing Arab support in a peace settlement in the Middle East. But I did not construe "impartial" to mean, "Let Israel give up what it has while the Arabs give up nothing but take all."

While Colonel Nasser was stirring up trouble, the Department of State could scarcely be said to be a calming influence. It brought heavy pressure on Britain to evacuate its Suez base by 1958 on the theory that the Soviet Union's explosion of a hydrogen bomb in 1953 had made the Suez base "untenable." The same theory, if logically extended, would make every other British base in the world "untenable," along with Great Britain itself, the United States, France, and all other members of NATO.

Increasingly it appeared to me and to others who held posts of leadership in American Jewish organizations that there was a conceptual void at the center of U.S. Middle East policy. The Conference of Presidents thus began to hold loosely structured meetings in New York starting in May 1954. Its sixteen constituent organizations were drawn together by an anguished concern for Israel amid the patchwork diplomacy of the Western powers. Talking together led to acting together in public statements, in community meetings, and in consultations with the State Department and other government agencies, and in developing mutually reinforcing personal relationships in the delicate area of international affairs. We also agreed upon a memorandum which I was authorized to present to Secretary of State Dulles when I saw him at the State Department in August 1954. The text urged that

> Israel be brought into American planning for the defense of the Middle East against Communist aggression, that the United States should try to obtain from Egypt unqualified guarantees that Israeli ships be allowed to pass through the Suez Canal freely, and that Arab states

should not be granted arms so long as they refuse to make peace or even sit down at a conference table with Israel.

Dulles's response to the memorandum amounted to a yes-but. Yes, the United States was committed to the survival of Israel. But, whatever it did would be based on estimates of the strategic needs of the United States and its Western allies in their struggle to contain the aggressive expansion of the Soviet Union.

Where did all this leave Israel?

Dulles accepted former President Truman's commitment in the Tripartite Pact of May 25, 1950, whereby the United States, Britain, and France would jointly work to maintain peace in the Middle East. Under the terms of this pact, the three nations agreed to regulate the supply of arms to achieve parity between Israel on the one hand and the combined Arab states on the other. They would not permit armed aggression across the lines specified in the 1949 armistice agreements. The existing status quo would thus be preserved and an arms race prevented. The "lawyer's brief" Dulles spelled out for me along these lines must have seemed a *tour de force* of reasoning to him, but within a year the "brief" was reduced to confetti.

In Israel, 1954 ended on the macabre note of the "Lavon affair," which would shake Israeli politics for many years. In Cairo, a military tribunal tried eleven Egyptian Jews accused of espionage, and two of the accused were soon hung in a Cairo prison. Acting on what appeared to be a set of instructions from Israel, the group had laid explosive charges in public buildings in Cairo in the dim hope that the American and British governments would attribute the bombing to Egyptian instigation. Suspicions about Lavon's part in the affair, coupled with concern over some of his known radical plans for security actions, led the Labor party in Israel to advocate the return of Ben-Gurion to the Defense Ministry. Moshe Sharet, with his fingers crossed, accepted the return. Within a year, following a vote of the Labor party, he would be forced to step down as prime minister in favor of Ben-Gurion's return to the office.

[IV]

Toward the end of 1954 I learned that Henry A. Byroade was to become the U.S. Ambassador to Egypt. With his known sympathy for Nasser's revolution there, it was thought he could win Colonel

Nasser over to the West by engaging him in intimate "colonel-to-colonel" talk; Byroade had been a colonel in the U.S. military government in Germany after World War II. His successor as Assistant Secretary of State for Middle East Affairs was George V. Allen.

It seemed to me that this was the right moment to convene in Washington, D.C., a public meeting of representatives of major Jewish organizations. State Department officers would also be invited to participate in the spirit of Isaiah's morally profound utterance, "Let us reason together." It would not be a case of *we* and *they*. *They* would also be *we*. We were not only Jews but American citizens who had a constitutional right of petition—to ask the officials of *our* government to explain their purposes to us, and to hear our own appraisals of their explanation.

During a mid-December 1954 meeting of the Conference of Presidents, I made the case for the public meeting. I met with Henry Byroade and George V. Allen on January 24, 1955, to discuss the terms of the prospective conference and to invite State Department officials to participate. Byroade, as the outgoing Assistant Secretary for Middle East Affairs, played his cards close to his chest. Allen laid his on the table face up. He said he would welcome a chance to take part in the meeting and would arrange for the participation of other State Department officials as well as those in the various branches of the executive who had an "operational" interest in the Middle East. I reported these assurances back to the Conference of Presidents, and we set a meeting for March 5–6, 1955.

While all this was in motion, I flew to Paris on January 29 for a meeting of the board of directors of the Conference on Jewish Material Claims against Germany. Within days after I returned to the United States, George V. Allen was installed as Assistant Secretary of State for Middle East Affairs, and Henry Byroade reported to his ambassadorial post in Cairo. It was at that very moment that the Soviet ambassador in Cairo made a secret offer of Soviet arms to Nasser, an offer that derailed from the start all the policy hopes pinned on Ambassador Byroade's plan to win Nasser over to the West. Byroade nonetheless regularly sent back reports to the State Department filled with assurances of Colonel Nasser's statesmanlike purposes.

At the March 5–6 session in Washington, the largest representative body of American Jews assembled since World War II, there was plain talk on all sides. But there was no table pounding, no exercises in demagogy, no inflammatory accusations. Spokesmen for Jewish organizations said what was on their minds. Official representatives of the U.S. government said what was on theirs. Yet it would take far more than this unprecedented meeting to change the course of U.S. policy in the Middle East in directions which would serve America's national interest, promote the "legitimate aspirations of Palestinian Arabs," and quiet the nagging fears of American Jews regarding the security of Israel.

[V]

Five days after the end of that conference in Washington, I left with Ethel for a scheduled six-week tour of Europe and Israel. On all extended trips I took as president of B'nai B'rith, I always sent reports of my activities back to the board of governors of the Order. I wanted them to know what I was doing *when* I was doing it. I find that the file copy of my report on this trip between March 11 and April 29, 1955, equals the size of a small book. There is no need here to dwell on the details of that trip. It is enough to touch on my experiences in three places—Geneva, West Germany, and Israel—each for a reason of its own.

In Geneva I spent three days at a conference of nearly a hundred nongovernmental organizations, convened by the United Nations Economic and Social Council and focused on discrimination and prejudice. Two and a half crowded days in West Germany followed, and in Bonn I met with Chancellor Konrad Adenauer. I met the chancellor several times in later years, but my first encounter with him in April 1955 was the most revealing. Here is an extract from my report to the board of governors of B'nai B'rith:

> Chancellor Adenauer welcomed me warmly, and without any ceremony proceeded to discuss the importance of the Jews returning to Germany. In this connection he referred to his deep interest in the restitution work and his profound regard for our mutual friend Nahum Goldmann. We both agreed that Goldmann's attitude in the claims matter had been helpful to Germany as well as to the Jews.
>
> I immediately tried to respond to his suggestions that we should help him to bring back the Jews to Germany. Frankly, I was somewhat shocked by the abruptness and straightforward approach that was taken by this Head of State. I told the Chancellor that I thought the subject of the Jewish return was much easier talked about than achieved. I

expressed the view that there were some very deep emotional upsets that could not be cured merely by an invitation. I even had my doubts as to whether some of them would be cured by time. I hastened to assure him that save for our confidence in him personally and his immediate colleagues I was doubtful that I could even consider discussing the subject in my official capacity.... I emphasized again that I felt that the principal obstacle here was of assurance that the return, if it took place, was desirable.

In response to this view on my part, the Chancellor expressed his complete awareness of the depth of the hurt inflicted by Nazi Germany. He emphasized that he knew what this meant from personal experience, but that he wanted Jews back. He then proceeded to emphasize, as did his ambassador early in March, the degree of the loss to Germany by the departure of its Jewish citizens.

I again told him that it was a very difficult problem to know what was right or what was wrong. This was not a matter that was easily determined by leadership alone. I had seen any number of former Germans of my faith in other countries of the world who had not made adjustments and who would hurry back if they felt that it was the Germany that he said it was and would be in the hands of other leadership than his own. It was at this point that I told him that I had come to West Germany and was going on to Berlin to determine whether or not B'nai B'rith should return with one or two lodges. I then expressed the thought that had occurred to me in our conversations that maybe it would be desirable to send a delegation of former German Jews to see for themselves what the real situation was in West Germany.

He thought this idea was excellent and wished that we would do something about it. We then proceeded to more general topics....

An added note of interest in the report concerns the B'nai B'rith properties in West Berlin. The main property which served as the headquarters and meeting place of B'nai B'rith had the structural features of a baronial home. Located in the area of West Berlin known as Kleistrasse, it was now surrounded by a sea of rubble, a reminder of Allied bombing and Soviet artillery fire. The building had miraculously survived the destruction of war but was rapidly deteriorating. It was not occupied—except for refuse that remained from its use as a Filmhaus by Joseph Goebbels's propaganda organization.

The ultimate value of the building would clearly depend on whether the Kleistrasse area around it would be rebuilt. In my report to the board of governors of B'nai B'rith concerning my meeting with the Burgomeister of Berlin I quote him as saying that the Kleistrasse area would be rebuilt only if the federal government assisted West Berlin in the matter. The city government lacked the money for the project. I added, "As we started to leave, the Deputy Burgomeister said in flawless English, 'Don't worry. Leave here with the certainty that Kleistrasse will be rebuilt, and so will Berlin.'"

After leaving Germany, I contacted Jewish leaders in Europe to discuss the question whether or not B'nai B'rith should return to West Germany. All, with one exception, said we could not escape a return. In my own view, one of the first steps to be taken was to send several former B'nai B'rith members back to Germany to assess the prospects facing Jews in West Germany.

[VI]

I had been invited to Israel by Prime Minister Moshe Sharet—the first president of B'nai B'rith to visit the country. I wanted to see the "rank-and-file" Israeli who, on waking up in the morning, did not jump to attention in an heroic pose to satisfy the expectations of American Jews with deep pockets. I wanted to see the Israeli who washed, dressed, had breakfast, and then trundled off to work. I discovered, as others do, that next to the remarkably varied terrain for so small a country, the most striking thing about Israel was the infinite variety of its people—so varied it was hard to believe all were Jews: Yemenites, Ethiopians, North Africans, Iraqis, Austrians, Bulgarians, Germans, Rumanians, Hungarians, South Africans, some few Americans and Canadians, Russians, and Poles.

On this first trip to Israel I was directly exposed to the tensions between Prime Minister Sharet and then Defense Minister David Ben-Gurion. When my appointments were being scheduled, each seemed to be jockeying to talk to me after I had talked to the other. When I finally sent word that because my time was short I could not wait much longer, it was left that I would see Prime Minister Sharet first.

Jacob Herzog, whom I knew well—and with affectionate admiration from the time he was a minister in the Israeli embassy in Washington—was with Sharet when I called on him. We talked of many things, including Israel's immediate material needs. Sharet, for example, stressed the acute food shortages in the country. In the absence of wheat that could be used as feed grain in addition to human consumption, Israel was woefully short of beef cattle, of milk cattle, and hence of dairy products. I later helped secure Israel its first shipment of fifty thousand tons of U.S. wheat under a U.S. foreign aid program.

At one point in my conversation with Sharet, he asked me to assess the impact on American opinion of a particularly fierce Israeli raid against an Arab village in reprisal for a Jordanian attack on a bus in the Negev marked by the death of a number of Israelis. I said that American opinion, while generally sympathetic to Israel's plight and dilemma, was sharply critical of the scope of the Israeli reprisal. "You are going to see my older colleague tomorrow morning," said Sharet in a reference to Ben-Gurion. "Are you prepared—and willing—to tell him what you've just told me regarding American opinion?" "Yes," I said. "Would you mind," Sharet then asked, "if Jacob Herzog goes with you when you call on Ben-Gurion tomorrow?" I said I was always pleased to have Jacob by my side. It was left that Sharet's staff would clear the arrangement with Ben-Gurion.

The next morning, with Jacob Herzog along, I called on Ben-Gurion in his office. He greeted me cordially, asked about "old friends" in the United States as well as what I had so far en-countered in Israel. He then abruptly raised the same question Sharet had asked. What was the reaction in the United States to the latest Israeli reprisal raid? When I said the reaction was strongly negative, Ben-Gurion pushed back his chair and sprang to his feet. In a voice heavy with the wrath of an Old Testament prophet in the service of the Lord God Jehovah, he cried, "I am not going to let anyone tell me *how* I have to defend my Jewish people." With that, I stood up and turned to leave. "What are *you* standing up for?" Ben-Gurion asked. "Well," I said, "my answer to your question obviously upsets you, and I don't want to continue to do that. So it's best to end this conversation right now." "Sit down!" Ben-Gurion barked. I did. "Now let's talk," he said calmly, as if the eruption a moment before had never occurred.

Of my grass-roots experiences in Israel, one of the most moving was the Passover which Ethel, Jack Morrison, and I spent at Moledeth. We arrived in mid-afternoon at the settlement, which is identified on the map of Israel simply as Moledeth B'nai B'rith, though it is actually the Alfred M. Cohen colony established in the early 1930s by B'nai B'rith as a refuge for the victims of Nazi persecution. Tea was waiting for us in the house where we were to spend the next two nights. At about 5:30 p.m. we watched the ceremony in the fields where grain was cut before the seder began. At eight o'clock three hundred men and women gathered in the old tool and repair house for the seder. It had been scrubbed clean so that all of us could sit down together.

It was the most poignant and joyous seder I have ever experienced anywhere. *We* were the Children of the Exodus. Here, at last, after wide wanderings across the millennia, we were celebrating in Eretz Yisrael a rebirth of freedom. After the reading of the Haggadah came the ritual meal—whose dish of matzo ball soup remains fixed in my memory. It had an exquisite taste, and when I agreed to a second helping, Ethel kicked me under the table—a reminder of Israel's acute food shortage. The ritual meal was followed by songs and skits, usually satirical. A traditional one, performed every year, dealt with the president of the B'nai B'rith who, like the prophet Elijah, was supposed to arrive but never did. This year, however, the skit was changed to show that the president had finally made it. It ended with the words, "Now that he is here, what can we do with him?"

We walked out of the seder—the guard had been doubled that night as it was on all holiday nights—and looked up into a sky that was more beautiful and clearer than any starlit night sky I have ever seen. It was as if the heavens were bestowing a benediction on this spot of earth. Yet the nearby presence of the armed guards served as a reminder of the trials still in store for the Israelis before the benediction could be fully enjoyed.

I made many trips to Israel in later years, for purposes not confined to politics. It was on this initial trip, however, that I drew close to Oved Ben-Ami, an Israeli citizen with a remarkable record in town development besides being the publisher of the *Maariv* newspaper and associated publications. Even before the creation of the state of Israel, Ben-Ami had a notable achievement to his credit. He had created the town of Nathanya, named after Nathan Strauss, the American philanthropist. Under his guidance as mayor, Arabs as well as Jews comprised the population of Nathanya, with no restrictive covenants, "red lines," or other such devices to segregate them.

Ben-Ami had been told by a mutual friend—a Chicago Zionist—of my work in the development of Park Forest. He had come to Chicago to visit the project and to talk with me about it. It was on that occasion that he proposed my joining him in the development of a new community in Israel. The Park Forest project by now was firmly established, and I was strongly taken by the idea of helping to plan and develop a new town in Israel. Here was a good chance for ACB to stretch further such skills and talents in town development as we had so far acquired—and, to put the case bluntly, to profit from mistakes we had made in the planning process.

While I was still in Israel, Ben-Ami took me to the ancient port city of Caesarea, originally built by Herod, "the real estate king," in northern Israel, about halfway between present-day Tel Aviv and Haifa. The site still gave evidence of its richly architectured palaces, temples, amphitheater, hippodrome, aqueducts, and quay. With its natural beauties and the remains of ancient glory as well as strife, it might be made into a "resort town" that could, among other things, be a tourist attraction. It was suggested that the Rothschild interests of France might join forces with us in planning such a town.

The idea of an American Jew out of Kansas City and Omaha joining forces with the House of Rothschild of Paris—and of French history—was not without its charm. Still, when I called on my old friend Golda Meir, then minister of labor in the Israeli cabinet, it was brought home to me that a resort town on the Mediterranean was not what Israel needed at that stage of its economic existence. Hence the developers could not look for any kind of the conventional help which the Israeli government offered entrepreneurs of major and necessary projects. What Israel needed was a new port city which could be a multiplier of jobs for incoming immigrants and could also help promote the development of southern Israel.

I fully agreed with Golda Meir's priorities. So did Ben-Ami. As the Rothschild interests were in a position to proceed unaided in developing the town of Caesarea, Ben-Ami and I shifted our attention to southern Israel where we looked for a site that could be developed as a port city.

Haifa, in the north, had originally been developed as a naval port and for use in matters of defense. It was not intended as a commercial port, and the facilities it offered to exporters and importers were overcrowded. The congestion adversely affected the export of one of the principal Israeli cash crops at the time— citrus fruits and off-season flowers. Haifa oranges, for example, were in lively demand throughout Europe's markets, yet the lack of adequate export facilities meant that crates of these oranges were bruised or spoiled while awaiting shipping. To use the old shallow port of Tel Aviv would increase shipping costs, because oceangoing freighters could not dock flush with the quays at Tel Aviv. They rode at anchor in the harbor while "lighters" carried the cargo between quays and the ships. In the end, the site chosen for the commercial port was Ashdod.

When I consider the extensive engineering studies I wanted as a matter of routine before embarking on any construction venture in the United States, I stand a little in awe of the reasons for my going along with the choice of Ashdod. Briefly, during the Israeli war of independence, Israelis relied on the Bible and the commentaries in order to locate neglected paths, roads, and underground passages. The geographical references turned out to be accurate. So why doubt what the Bible said about the location of a great port? In the Book of Joshua "it was written" that Ashdod, which was assigned to the tribe of Judah, was once a great Philistine seaport. That was good enough for Ben-Ami, and through him, for me.

Like other places in Palestine, Ashdod—located some twenty-two miles south of Tel Aviv and thirteen miles north of Ashkelon—was the scene of major historical events, some of them bloodstained. When I first saw the place it consisted of nothing but sand dunes, a few houses, and a small power station. Yet it would be hard to overstate my excitement when I contemplated the prospect that Ben-Ami, with his associates in Israel, and I, with my own ACB associates in Park Forest, might bring to new life a major commercial port where the Phoenicians had once plied their trade. The emptiness of the place worked in its own way to fire my imagination about what could be.

But there were problems, and their solution was left hanging for some months after my return to the United States. Ben-Ami, for example, wrote me to say that Golda Meir welcomed the job-creating prospects of a port, but Levi Eshkol, then minister of finance, objected, saying that Israel could not afford the $27 million for the estimated start-up costs of the project. Some of his aides insisted that Israel had no need for a new port. The old port of Tel Aviv could be put to use for exports. He wanted Ben-Ami and me to limit ourselves to building houses on the Ashdod site.

When I met Eshkol in the course of a later trip to Israel, I told him, with Ben-Ami's concurrence, that if the port was not built, it was pointless to build houses because no one would come to

Ashdod. Without a port there were no employment outlets in the place except for a small power plant. I urged Eshkol to ignore what his budget-balancing aides told him and to think in larger developmental terms. Further, I said, he would be well advised to get an opinion from an outside expert regarding Israel's need for a new port. I would draw up a list of the most competent masters of ports in the world. He could choose a consultant from the list and ask for a report on the wisdom of providing Israel with a new port. Eshkol agreed, and to my secret delight he chose from the names on the list the master of the port of Rotterdam— the very person whom I would have chosen if I were in Eshkol's position.

The Rotterdam expert was contacted and soon arrived in Israel for what was billed as a study that would take thirty days. At the end of the third day, however, he contacted Ben-Ami to say that the Haifa port facilities were clearly inadequate for Israel's export needs. Most of the Israeli production for export was well south of Haifa, and that made Ashdod a logical place for a new port to be built. After waiting a respectable time, the expert submitted his report, which persuaded Eshkol. As usual, however, there were problems—big ones—before actual work on the new port could start.

20 □ Israel and Dulles

On my return from Israel in the spring of 1955, the Marshall Field people asked ACB to be involved in the construction of the Old Orchard Shopping Center, located on the northern rim of Chicago. Richard M. Bennett, of the firm of Loebl, Schlossman, and Bennett, was entrusted with the overall plan. He keenly appreciated what shopping meant to the American consumer, and especially to the suburban housewife. He believed that "adventure" was an aspect of shopping and that an environment with surprises could help provide it. The shopper should not be able to see everything at a glance; straight lines made for dullness. Vistas should include curves and corners. "It is sometimes difficult," Bennett once wrote,

> for architects to remember that a piece of architecture—the building—should be considered as a frame for the picture of the love affair between a customer and a piece of merchandise. When the frame is too big, the customer is apt to feel that both she and the merchandise are inadequate—too small—to consummate the attachment.

Old Orchard, designed as an outdoor, unenclosed shopping mall with a good mix of high-quality competitive merchants, was meant to attract a year-round patronage comprised of people who would enjoy walking around the mall as part of their experience in shopping. This is where a young landscape architect, Lawrence Halperin of San Francisco, entered the picture; the landscaping assignment was one of the first major projects to come his way. ACB and Field's were willing to spend half a million preinflation dollars on landscaping—a large sum for such a purpose in those days. Halperin himself was afire with ideas for carefully designed walkways, footbridges, garden spots, fountains, ponds, and foliage that would change with the seasons. For the chance to translate his concepts into practice, he grossly underpriced himself, as if the sheer pleasure he found in fulfilling his plan was sufficient compensation. We were so pleased with his work that we would not allow him to suffer financially because of his enthusiasm.

The construction of Old Orchard was headed by Norman Cohn, a graduate in architectural engineering from the University of Illinois and president of Inland Construction, a firm he had founded in 1940. Its operations, after a fast start, were suspended during World War II when Cohn entered the service with the air force engineers. His experience in building runways, hangars, barracks, maintenance buildings, fuel storage dumps, and recreational facilities gave him a postgraduate education in the use of heavy earth-moving equipment—which was as helpful in peacetime as in war. Once out of the service, he reassembled his old staff at Inland and started where he left off.

Within a short time Cohn was building structures for the Pritzker interests in Chicago, besides doing work on Midway Airport and O'Hare Airport before it became city of Chicago property. Soon he was doing work for stores in the burgeoning world of shopping malls.

When Old Orchard was being planned, I had a talk with Cohn,

My parents, Morris
and Minnie, in
midlife, standing on
their home grounds
in Kansas City,
Missouri.

I was twenty-seven years old and
attending a meeting in
Washington, D.C., of special
assistants to the attorney general for
public lands, in 1934.

Vacationing with Ethel and our children at
Buena Park, California. From left, Bob,
Bettylu, Sam, Tom, and Jim.

At work in the library of our
Chicago apartment in 1963,
following the end of my service as
U.S. Ambassador to the United
Nations Social and Economic
Council.

The first of the two-bedroom homes built by American Community Builders in Park Forest in the early 1950s. The purchase price was around $11,000. Five-bedroom homes built later were offered for sale at about $19,000.

By January 1950 more than three thousand town homes like the ones in this photograph had been built in Park Forest by ACB. Monthly rentals started at $75 for a two-bedroom apartment and rose to $117 a month for apartments with three bedrooms.

Water Tower Place in Chicago, built by Urban Investment and Development Company after its marriage with Aetna Life and Casualty Company. As the first high-rise shopping center and multi-use structure in the nation, it changed the character of North Michigan Avenue in Chicago.

The core of the shopping center in Water Tower Place, designed to heighten the visibility of all stores and promote access to them.

A segment of the Chicago "establishment" during the time of Mayor Richard J. Daley. I made a point to, from left, Peter Peterson, then head of Bell & Howell and former Secretary of Commerce; Marshall Field III, then owner of the *Chicago Sun-Times*; and the mayor.

Ethel and I with Father William F. Kelley, S.J., of the Creighton University Foundation.

At the United Nations with World Bank president Eugene Black, following the 1962 U.N. vote that authorized a bond issue and rescued the world organization from a threatened bankruptcy.

After my election as new president of the B'nai B'rith, I and other officers of the Order met with President Eisenhower in the White House in May 1953. From left, Henry E. Shultz, national chairman of the Anti-Defamation League; retiring president Frank Goldman; President Eisenhower; myself; Benjamin Epstein, executive director of the Anti-Defamation League; and Maurice Bisgyer, national secretary of B'nai B'rith.

With Oved Ben-Ami in 1955, walking over the sand dunes in Israel where they later built the port city of Ashdod.

With Moshe Sharet at a formal reception in Chicago in 1957, when Sharet was head of the Jewish Agency.

With Teddy Kollek at the B'nai B'rith triennial convention in Jerusalem, 1959. Kollek at the time was director general in Prime Minister Ben-Gurion's office; he became mayor of Jerusalem in 1965.

When Menachem Begin, left, Israel's prime minister, was an official guest of the city of Chicago, I greeted him with Mayor Michael Bilandic.

From left, Frank Goldman, former president of B'nai B'rith, myself, and Israeli Prime Minister David Ben-Gurion at the B'nai B'rith triennial convention in Jerusalem, 1959.

A relieved Dr. Nahum Goldmann congratulated me upon my election in January 1978 to the presidency of the World Jewish Congress, a post which Goldmann had long held.

From left, Ethel, myself, and Israeli Prime Minister Yitzhak Shamir at a luncheon meeting in 1989.

In the White House for the signing of the Trade Reorganization Bill. From left, Robert Strauss, U.S. trade representative; James McIntyre, White house staff; myself, the Secretary of Commerce; President Jimmy Carter; and Senator Reuben Askew.

As Secretary of Commerce I spoke to a meeting of the U.S.-Rumanian Economic Commission in May 1980.

and we hit it off immediately. After he consulted with Loebl, Schlossman, and Bennett on the preliminary plans for Old Orchard, he gave us a construction cost estimate which we accepted. The Old Orchard project under his supervision started and finished on time, well within budget.

[II]

One might have wished for an equally skilled engineer to cope with the mounting Middle East tensions. They sharply increased the moment Colonel Nasser on September 27, 1955, confirmed that Egypt had entered into an arms deal with the Soviet Union (via Czechoslovakia). The Israeli-Arab conflict at once ceased to be—if ever it was—a regional matter. It became a component in the larger Cold War conflict between the communist bloc and the free world. President Eisenhower at the time was in Denver recovering from a heart attack. It was left to Secretary of State Dulles to formulate the U.S. response.

Dulles had reason to be a shaken man. Only that summer at the Geneva Conference—which gave currency to the phrase "the spirit of Geneva"—President Eisenhower and Nikita Khrushchev, then leader of the Soviet Union, had ceremoniously agreed on a "relaxation of tensions" in the Cold War. Besides, it had been inconceivable to Dulles and to his chief aides in the State Department that Colonel Nasser would place himself and Egypt in the teeth of the Russian bear.

At about this time there was also a change in Israel's leadership following the 1955 general elections. By prearrangement within the Labor party, which still dominated the government, Ben-Gurion returned to his former post as prime minister while continuing as minister of defense. Sharet became foreign minister. In an ideal world, each should have drawn strength from and given strength to the other. Unfortunately, however, character differences made it hard for them to work together. While Ben-Gurion was impulsive, imaginative, daring, and dynamic, Sharet was prudent and analytical, a man with deep roots in Hebrew and Arabic cultural traditions.

On October 11, 1955, with President Eisenhower back in the White House, Israel asked the United States for arms to match Czech shipments to Egypt as well as the flow of British and U.S. arms to assorted Arab states in the Middle East.

While Israel's diplomatic representatives in Washington moved through official State Department channels to press Israel's case for U.S. arms, domestic political support for Israel was fairly widespread nationally. Within the government and the U.S. Senate, impressive Republican and Democratic figures—some of them presidential aspirants—supported Israel's cause. One of these was Vice President Richard Nixon. Others included Senators Lyndon B. Johnson of Texas, William F. Knowland of California, Irving Ives of New York, Hugh Scott of Pennsylvania, Leverett Saltonstall and John F. Kennedy of Massachusetts, Sherman Cooper of Kentucky, Clifford Case of New Jersey, and Hubert Humphrey of Minnesota. In addition, Senators Jacob Javits of New York and Abraham Ribicoff of Connecticut formed a bridge between American official life at its highest level and the American Jewish community, of which they were loyal members.

Sustained by general national support for Israel, they and their counterparts in the House helped enact measures authorizing U.S. credits and other forms of financial aid for Israel. They could not, however, challenge the primacy of the White House and the State Department in the strategic realms of Middle East power and diplomacy.

The realities of the case were brought home to me soon after Israel submitted its formal request for arms; as acting chairman of the Conference of Presidents of Major Jewish Organizations, I secured an appointment with Dulles to lend support to the Israeli case. My argument was neither confrontational nor threatening; it was based, as always, on the nature of America's own interests. Dulles in turn gave me a glimpse of what was going through his mind. Nasser's arms deal with Russia was, he said, "the most serious development since Korea, if not since World War II." In a single stroke it undercut all of Dulles's efforts to lay the grounds for a durable peace in the Middle East. He could not, however, support Israel's request because he did not wish to involve the United States in arms competition. Besides, the balance of military power was in Israel's favor and would not be changed unless and until Russian MIG-15 fighter aircraft actually reached Egypt.

In early December 1955, hard intelligence available to the State Department and the Pentagon confirmed the arrival in Egypt of those MIG-15s. When I saw Dulles at this time, he indicated—as I later learned from the Israeli embassy in Washington—that Israel's military position was being seriously reappraised.

Dulles continued to preach caution for the United States, but he also moved with muffled oars behind the scenes to bolster Israel's military position. He encouraged France to extend its preexisting "special connection" with Israel, even if this meant selling to Israel some of the jet aircraft that France was manufacturing under contract for the U.S. air force. He sent a somewhat similar message to the Canadians. They could, if they wished, sell to Israel two squadrons of U.S.-designed F-86 jets which were being produced in Canada for use by the U.S. air force when called for.

Israel now stood on the threshold of access to Western arms which could help safeguard the military balance between herself and her Arab neighbors. But the door was suddenly slammed shut after an Israeli raid on Kinneret in Syria caused an international uproar. The raid was in retaliation for harassing Syrian artillery fire on Israeli fishing boats in Lake Tiberias. No Israelis had been killed or wounded, but the violence of the Israeli response ordered by Prime Minister Ben-Gurion resulted in an inordinately high number of Syrian deaths. Reports placed the number at more than eighty.

World reaction to the event stopped whatever movement was then afoot for the U.S. to provide Israel with the jet fighters it urgently wanted. In the clash between two Israeli military objectives—the short-term interest in retaliation and the long-term interest in defensive arms—the short-term view triumphed. Still, as often happened in the past—and in the future as well—criticism of Israel's actions was displaced by controversies over Arab-inspired violence. Egypt at this very moment chose to whip up strife within Jordan and to step up the frequency with which it sent *fedayeen* bands deep into Israel. Reports of the resulting carnage tended to mute the furor over Israel's devastating actions in Kinneret.

A new move in Washington was initiated to exhaust every possibility for a peace settlement. Robert Anderson, a close friend of the president and a former Secretary of the Navy, was sent to the Middle East to meet Nasser and Ben-Gurion and explore the idea of a conference between them. He returned to Washington a few weeks later in a despondent mood. Nasser, already inhibited by his closer relations with the Soviet Union, had found ways to evade any meeting with Ben-Gurion. He also darkly questioned U.S. motives in merely trying to bring him to the conference table.

From the failure of the Anderson mission one can date the Eisenhower administration's tilt away from evenhandedness in the

Israeli-Arab conflict and toward an arms balance more favorable to Israel. This tilt had little to do with the imagined political power of the so-called Jewish lobby; rather, it represented a conclusion reached within the administration that the Soviet-Egyptian arms deal potentially threatened America's *own* interests. By means of that deal the Soviet Union had jumped over the barricades of states joined in the Baghdad Pact and landed in the very center of the Mediterranean—an objective that had eluded the tsars for centuries.

The public at large knew little about what was going on behind the diplomatic scenes. Even as Secretary Dulles was revising his position toward Israel, many American Jewish leaders assailed him with fresh and strident criticism. True, Dulles had not sharply reversed the State Department's Middle East policy; yet the foreshadowings of significant policy changes were lost on some in the American Jewish community who responded to slogans and were impatient with complexities. Meanwhile, Israel's diplomats in Washington, such as Minister Reuven Shiloah, signaled to me their gratitude for what Dulles was trying to engineer.

[III]

I had reason to believe that my friend, Adlai E. Stevenson, would again be the Democratic party's nominee for the presidency in 1956, and I also hoped he might win. Still, I could see nothing but harm to American politics in general and the Jewish community specifically if the hostility toward Dulles were allowed to continue. I believed it was necessary to set attitudes right.

The triennial international convention of the B'nai B'rith, set for the early spring of 1956 in Washington, was a good place to start. Its delegates were geographically and ideologically diverse and would closely parallel the varied sentiments of the Jewish community as a whole. I discussed with Robert Murphy, then Undersecretary of State, my interest in inviting Dulles to address the convention on the night of its concluding banquet. We were able to make the arrangement. When it was announced that Dulles would address B'nai B'rith, the Jewish community was surprised, then critical.

At the 1956 convention, B'nai B'rith approved an amendment to its constitution which set a two-term limit for its president and other elected officers. In urging the adoption of the amendment, I remarked that whatever the vote, a second presidential term would be my last, "not because I love the work so little but because I love it so much." The convention also approved my proposal to hold the next triennial convention in Israel.

Dulles, who had been in Paris for a NATO meeting, returned to Washington on the morning of the day he was due to address the convention. On rumors that our banquet hotel would be picketed by anti-Dulles demonstrators, we hired additional security guards. The banquet itself seemed like a grand assize of official Washington. In attendance were a number of cabinet officers, members of the Supreme Court, ambassadors of fifteen foreign nations, more than two hundred senators and representatives, and many senior State Department officers. No pickets had formed outside the hotel, but I continued to be apprehensive when the time came to escort the secretary and Mrs. Dulles from our suite. My concern proved groundless. As his figure came into view, the audience rose to its feet and greeted him with an ovation.

My sense of relief was shared by many political dignitaries who were present. Republican leaders in particular brought to the dinner their own private fears about how a Jewish audience would receive the controversial Secretary of State. Many of them now came to Dulles to shake his hand and comment on "the wonderful greeting" he had received. Senator Everett Dirksen of Illinois, the Republican leader in the Senate with whom I had been on particularly friendly terms, dropped his usual inflated manner of speech and spoke to me without affectation. "Phil," he said simply and directly, "we are all in your debt for what you've done for us this evening."

In his speech Dulles reported on the NATO conference he had just attended. But he was also mindful of the interests of his audience. At a point midway in his text, he included a brief and unequivocal statement on the Middle East. There were grounds for hope of an Arab-Israeli agreement, he said, asserting that Israel "will be maintained in its independence."

Coupled with his presence, Dulles's words had a salutary effect. Through the medium of the B'nai B'rith banquet, the American Jewish community was provisionally reassured that its profound concern about the fate of Israel was also of concern to the Eisenhower administration. It was also a healthy thing for Dulles personally to be accorded a warm and respectful reception from a representative Jewish group. This did not mean, however, that a rainbow was painted permanently across the sky as if to mark the end of all storms between the American Jewish community and the American presidency in connection with Middle East matters. The worst of all the storms lay just over the horizon.

21 □ Touch and Go

Levi Eshkol, a busy man with a fine sense of humor, would often ask the people who called on him to start at the end, saying, "If we have time, we'll go back to the beginning." In May 1956, roughly a year after my first visit to Israel, all who were directly involved in the proposal to build a modern port city on the site of Ashdod, "came back to the beginning." We then had in hand a memorandum by Eshkol stating what the Israeli government was prepared to do in connection with the Ashdod project, and what we as "initiators" were expected to do. Ben-Ami and I accepted the government's general terms; teams of lawyers went to work on the details that would be incorporated in a final agreement; and our technical staffs began to formulate imaginative studies of what the town would be like.

[II]

I was in California in late May 1956 when a telephone call from Jerusalem made me an ad hoc negotiator in a highly charged diplomatic matter. Nahum Goldmann and Shlomo Z. Shragai, head of the immigration department of the Jewish Agency, were at the Jerusalem end of the line. The subject of their urgent call was the fate of Moroccan Jews, specifically a group of Moroccan Jews who were likely immigrants to Israel.

Jews had been in Morocco for some two thousand years. Of the 500,000 who had once lived there, 75,000 to 80,000 had migrated to Israel since its creation in 1948. To facilitate further immigration, the Jewish Agency had established an organization known as Kadimah. In addition, UJA-HIAS, with an office in Casablanca headed by a man who was a member of B'nai B'rith in Marseilles, was concerned with emigration to other parts of the world, such as Brazil, Venezuela, or any place which would accept immigrants.

The French high commissioner in Morocco had routinely issued exit visas to individual Moroccan Jews bent on immigrating to Israel. But on the eve of Morocco's full independence in 1956, the high commissioner in a single stroke issued a blanket exit visa to 8,500 Moroccan Jews. The action might have been prompted by a humanitarian desire to speed the exit to Israel of those Jews who wished to escape the unknowns of life under the new Moroccan regime. Some people, however, believed the action was designed to embarrass the new regime, which Paris doubted could be trusted to deal fairly with its own people.

The new Moroccan regime, angered by the French action and confused over how to process the exit of so many people at once, rounded up the Jews covered by the blanket visa and herded them into retention camps. They were not physically harmed, but the action was psychologically unhinging. At a time when memories of Nazi concentration camps were still fresh, the roundup excited fears among all Moroccan Jews. The Israeli government, too, was concerned about the security of Moroccan Jews in general and the fate of those in the camps.

"Phil," I heard Nahum Goldmann say, "we believe that the intervention of an American can help secure the release of the 8,500 so that they can come to Israel. Will you, as president of the International B'nai B'rith, go to Morocco and see what can be done to help out?" First, I replied, I must determine the attitude of my own government. When I contacted William Rountree, who was then acting as Assistant Secretary of State for the Middle East, he exclaimed, "Where are you? We've been trying to reach you about the same matter. By all means go."

I agreed to go to Morocco on a very tight schedule. I told Rountree that I wanted to take along two leaders of B'nai B'rith in Europe. One, based in London, was Jack Morrison, president of British B'nai B'rith. The other, based in Paris, was Paul Jacob, president of French B'nai B'rith, who could help serve as a translator if I needed one. I then reached Morrison and Jacob, explained the purpose of my mission, and they agreed to join me.

After a flight to Paris on June 6, where Morrison was waiting with Jacob, the three of us continued on to Casablanca where we landed late at night. We reached our hotel around two in the morning, and I was preparing for bed when there was a knock on the door of my room. "You don't know me," the voice on the other side of the door said, "but I have a special message for you." I thoughtlessly opened the door without taking any of the standard precautions as in James Bond films. It turned out there was no reason to be on guard. My caller was one of the Israeli "boys" on the scene, a member of the efficient Israeli intelligence service. He was fully aware of all aspects of my mission and proceeded to brief me on fine points of detail that might prove helpful.

William Porter, chargé d'affaires at the new U.S. embassy in Rabat, came down to Casablanca to meet me with Consul General Lamont. They added their personal assurance of support in addition to official instructions they had received from Rountree. With Morrison and Jacob, I then met the leaders of the Casablanca Jewish community to hear their expressions of concern over "who would be seized next." I could only assure them for the moment that they had not been forgotten by the outside world. The Moroccan government had just ordered the closing of Kadimah, and this was construed to mean that large-scale immigration to Israel was a thing of the past. The fear of entrapment was pervasive among Moroccan Jews, at all economic and social levels. Afterward I wrote to the board of governors of B'nai B'rith:

> I have seen frightened people in my day, but none so afraid as a substantial businessman who called on me just after he heard that the Kadimah had been ordered closed. He shook and trembled as if he suffered from a terrible fever; his answers to my questions were relatively incoherent. He was only certain that he was uncertain. He told me that all the leaders were agreed that as many as could and wanted to should leave before it was too late. I do not want to overdo this aspect, for I realize much of this emotion arises from inner psychological pressures as well as from poverty or economic hopelessness. A great deal arises from the positive urge to go to Israel. But whatever the situation, it was clear to me that there was general agreement on the desire of many to emigrate.

Later in the day at Casablanca, we met representatives of the United Jewish Appeal who were on the scene. They had been trying in their own way to be of help to Moroccan Jews, many of whom had come down from caves in the Atlas Mountains in the hope of getting to Israel. When I asked the UJA people how they could distinguish Moroccan Jews from non-Jews, given their physical similarities, they explained that Jews wore a black instead of a red fez. When in serious doubt, they had another method to determine who was who: they asked the men to take down their pants to show evidence of circumcision. One UJA representative admitted, however, "We can still miss a few."

The next day I received word from Porter in Rabat that he had arranged for me to see M'Barek Ben Mustafa Bekai, chairman of the council of ministers, the equivalent of prime minister. Bekai had been deputized by the sultan to act for him in the matter of the Moroccan Jews, who were being held in the camps though they were covered by French exit visas. I was informed that if I could not settle the matter with him, access to the sultan would be considered.

Like so many other leaders of the Moroccan nationalist movement, Bekai was a product of French schools. He did not subscribe to Nasser's rabid form of pan-Arabism, with its volatile mixture of vicious attacks on the existence of Israel and a confection of Arab rhetorical socialism. He looked to California, not to Nasser, as a model for the development of Morocco's agricultural economy, because of similarity in climate, soil, and rainfall patterns. His manner in greeting me was cordial, touched perhaps with a detached clinical interest. When we met face to face in the sultan's palace, he wanted no one else present, not even a translator. He could speak little English, and I could speak little French, but it was agreed that we would try to understand each other by speaking very slowly. The effect was like teaching a child to talk. It also made for a protracted meeting, lasting two and a half hours and marked by much tea drinking—and mounting pressure on my bladder.

When he asked about my background, I explained that I was currently president of the largest Jewish organization in the United States, or for that matter in the world. I was a lawyer by professional training; I had served in the United States government in high administrative posts under Presidents Roosevelt and Truman, and had been active in private business in the development of new towns and communities.

I went on to say that I did not carry a diplomatic passport. I was a private citizen. But I had consulted with officials in the State Department before venturing on the mission that brought me to Morocco. It was at their urging that I had come to Morocco to try to understand why 8,500 Jews were being held in the detention camps, and, if possible, to secure their release.

I said I fully understood the difficulties Bekai faced in organizing his new government. But his burdens would be complicated if he did not release the 8,500 Jews who wished to migrate to Israel. Many people in the United States, and in the world press, were increasingly aware of the plight of these Moroccan Jews. To imprison them in camps, though they were innocent of wrongdoing, was a blemish on Morocco's own brave struggle to live as a free people. It would be in Morocco's highest interest to release the 8,500 without delay, before a rising tide of international criticism made the release politically difficult.

All this I said very slowly, almost syllable by syllable, in halting French and English. Bekai's attention, except when he sipped his tea, never wavered. He then began his own recital. He reviewed the history of the nationalist movement which he and the sultan had led in their struggle to liberate Morocco from French rule. When France granted Morocco its full independence, it turned over to the sultan a weakened governmental structure. Even when the French issued a blanket exit visa to 8,500 Moroccan Jews, they failed to inform the incoming regime of what they were doing. Bekai, an overworked man, plainly was saddled by the accumulated weight of grievances against France which he wished to get off his chest.

I heard him out and then said two things. First, I had been requested by the State Department not to leave Morocco until every opportunity had been explored to secure the prompt release of the Jews held in the detention camps. Second, I had also been instructed that, as a last resort, I should make every effort to meet with Sultan Mohammed V and appeal directly to him for help.

The moment of silence that followed was one of the longest I have ever known. "Mr. Klutznick," Bekai finally said, "you can go home and convey to your government the assurance that the 8,500 will be at liberty to leave Morocco under the terms of the blanket French exit visa. You have my word on that." I thanked him for his statesmanlike decision and removed myself from his office as quickly as I decently could.

Jack Morrison had been waiting patiently in the courtyard until I emerged. "What happened?" he asked anxiously. "I'll tell you in a minute," I said. "But first tell me if you know where a toilet is. I'm about to burst from drinking tea." I scurried off to a corner of the palace courtyard, which was an odd way to end a diplomatic mission. On returning to the waiting car, I told Morrison all that had transpired. I then placed a telephone call to Casablanca to inform the Jewish leader I spoke to, for transmittal to others, that I had good news but would reserve the details until I was back in their midst.

Morrison and I sped back to Casablanca where we were scheduled to dine with Jewish community leaders. We picked up Paul Jacob and reached the place of the dinner around midnight. When I reported that the 8,500 Jews in the detention camps would soon be released for their departure to Israel, I was treated—for that one night at least—as though I were the Messiah's deputy in Morocco. The Jews at the dinner saw in the promised release of those in the detention camps, a sign that they could continue to live in Morocco if they wished, or could migrate to Israel—as tens of thousands later did. No money I had ever earned through the practice of law or from my business ventures was equal to my joy at this dinner.

Bekai proved a man of his word. The blanket exit visa which the French had issued was honored by the new Moroccan government, and the Jews in the camps were released to journey to Israel and to the new life awaiting them. The timing of the exit was fortuitous. It came before a spiraling increase in Middle East tensions led in the fall of 1956 to the Suez War.

[III]

On my return to Chicago, I had time only to wash up and repack my bags before departing with Ethel and all four of my sons— Tom, Jim, Sam, and Bob—for Latin America. My daughter Bettylu, oldest of the children, remained behind. She was engaged to Dr. Paul Salzman, then in his residency for cardiology, and did not wish to be away from the man she would soon marry.

As the first president of B'nai B'rith to visit Latin America, my purpose was to dispel misconceptions about the Order in relationship to other organizations such as the World Jewish Congress, to assess the strength of the lodges, and to suggest what could be done to overcome their weaknesses. We left by boat from New Orleans for Rio de Janeiro. The four days aboard ship were quite literally the first period of inactivity I had known since the time, as lawyers would say, "when the mind of man runneth not to the contrary." I had reason to be grateful for this rest, considering the taxing round of meetings, inspections, tours, lunches, dinners, speeches, dances, and so on, that began immediately after the boat docked in Rio. The tour continued on to Sao Paulo, then to

Montevideo, and from there to Buenos Aires and to Santiago, Chile. At each stop, B'nai B'rith members from the smaller cities appeared at events scheduled in the principal cities.

One detail stands out in my recollections of this trip. It concerns the damage I personally did to Yiddish as a language. I spoke neither Spanish nor Portuguese, and so on one occasion when I was scheduled to speak in Santiago, Chile, I thought I could get by if I couched my remarks in what I recalled of Kansas City and Omaha Yiddish. I was rather pleased with the impact. Someone who had been in that audience later telephoned me when he was on a visit to the U.S. to extend regards from mutual friends. To my delight, he vividly recalled the speech I had given and thought it was the most extraordinary one he had ever heard. My pleasure, however, proved to be a case of idiot's delight once he explained why he found my speech so exceptional. It was, he said, the worst use of Yiddish—vocabulary, grammar, syntax, metaphors—which he ever remembered.

My experiences in Latin America reinforced my belief that if B'nai B'rith was to become an international organization in fact and not in name only, it must have the institutional means to make policy *as* an international organization. What I had in mind would finally materialize in 1959.

[IV]

Throughout the summer of 1956, Egypt had been negotiating with the World Bank for the financing of the Aswan High Dam. The United States and Great Britain had favored the project, but as Nasser increasingly clashed with Western policy everywhere in the world, disenchantment with him set in. He had brought Soviet influence into the heart of the Middle East and flirted with Communist China as well. He tried by violence to overthrow every Arab regime that refused to accept his authority. He plotted against President Camille Chamoun in Lebanon, against King Hussein in Jordan, against the monarchical regime in Iraq, against the conservative forces controlling the Arabian peninsula, against the newly independent regime of Tunisia under Habib Bourguiba. He continued to order armed raids across Israel's boundaries, imposed a blockade on the Suez Canal, and seized an Israeli ship in violation of its right of passage through the canal. As an added touch to his self-portrait as the "new Saladin," he blocked a

U.S. plan to develop scarce water resources in the Middle East.

If Nasser could receive arms from the Soviet Union as well as vast financial aid from the West without modifying his policies toward the West or Israel, he would become the dictator of the Arab world. Many members of Congress therefore opposed further aid to Nasser without reciprocal gestures on his part.

This was the troubled foreign policy setting in the summer of 1956, at the onset of the second contest between Adlai Stevenson and Dwight Eisenhower for the presidency of the United States.

The Egyptian ambassador to the U.S., Ahmed Hussein, apparently was not aware of these stirrings in the American government. When he returned to Washington from Cairo in midsummer, he seemed to believe that a major American contribution to the financing of the Aswan High Dam project was virtually assured. Instead, when he called on Secretary Dulles he was told that America would not help finance the dam. Without an American contribution, the World Bank could not execute the financing of the dam, and the British contribution would also lapse automatically. Nasser's resentment ran amok, and he hit back at a sensitive Western nerve. On July 25, 1956, the anniversary of his revolution, he announced to a fanaticized crowd in Alexandria that he would seize the Suez Canal and nationalize it as Egyptian property.

Diplomats scurried back and forth during the summer and into the fall, when the U.S. presidential campaign was under way in earnest. Behind the scenes, French leaders close to Israel spoke to Israel's defense ministry about the inevitability of a military showdown with Nasser. Anthony Eden, while not yet drawn close to Israel in the French manner, committed himself to preventing a situation "which could leave the canal in the unfettered control of a single power which could, as recent events have shown, exploit it purely for purposes of national policy."

Abba Eban, before returning to Washington on October 20 from a quick trip to Israel, had a private talk with Ben-Gurion who dwelt on Israel's grave security situation. Ben-Gurion would presently leave for France to meet with Premier Guy Mollet, but he doubted that France would join Israel in operational security measures. If, to his surprise, agreements were reached, Eban "would be feeling certain consequences in Washington." Ben-Gurion did not reveal what he meant by "agreements" with the French. He withheld information from Eban even when the decision to go ahead with an Anglo-French-Israeli operation in

Sinai was made in Sevres, France, on October 23 at a meeting between Ben-Gurion, Mollet, and Selwyn Lloyd of Great Britain. Eban, once back in Washington, continued to stress the danger from Jordan and Iraq when he was asked to account for reports of large Israeli troop concentrations amounting to virtual mobilization.

During these days I had given another 10 percent of my time to purely business matters in order to oversee the completion of the Old Orchard Shopping Center on time and within budget. All the goals were met on October 22, 1956, when the Marshall Field's executives and the ACB team joined in officially dedicating Old Orchard.

Four days later I was back in New York City for a meeting of the Presidents Conference, focused on the Arab League's boycott of Israel. That was on a Friday, October 26. I remained in New York because I had a speaking engagement on Sunday evening. On Sunday, however, I had a noon meeting in my hotel room with Reuven Shiloah, the Israeli minister in Washington, to discuss the Arab League boycott further. At one point in the conversation, when Shiloah telephoned Abba Eban in Washington, I took advantage of the link to exchange small talk with the ambassador and to get his assessment of what he had learned during his hurried visit to Israel. He told me what he actually believed at the time and would soon repeat at the State Department—to his immense embarrassment. Things in Israel, he said, "were like always." Nothing unusual was in the offing.

On Monday morning, October 29, the news reported a massive eruption of Israeli forces across the Egyptian frontier and a subsequent forking movement and parachute drop into Sinai. People in Tel Aviv were as startled by the suddenness of the attack as were those in Cairo, New York, Washington, or Chicago— to which I had returned. President Eisenhower had previously warned the Israelis against taking a "forceful initiative." The fact that his warning had been ignored reached him while he was en route to Florida in his final push for reelection. When he learned how deeply the Israelis had penetrated Sinai, he broke off his campaign tour and returned to Washington. After conferring with the State Department, the Pentagon, and his principal White House aides, he was in a very angry mood.

Eisenhower was convinced that the Israelis had deliberately planned their operation for the final week of the election campaign in order to influence the outcome of the election. Influence it did, but not in ways adverse to Eisenhower's interests. To the contrary, estimates made by the Stevenson camp indicated a shift of three to six million votes in Eisenhower's favor while the nation rallied around the incumbent president—as it traditionally does—in time of danger.

Eisenhower also felt that Israel was "doing a great service to the Soviet Union by diverting world opinion from the struggle of the Poles and Hungarians to break free of the Soviet Union's grip." He cited a U.S. policy statement issued on April 9, 1956, which offered support "for any country that had been attacked." The text had been drafted as a promise of protection for Israel, but the same statement could now be used against her.

Within the American Jewish community, the first reactions mixed bewilderment, hope, and dismay. On the face of things, Ben-Gurion's program of "deeds not words" cast Israel in the role of an unprovoked aggressor. But was it an aggressor, or was it engaged in a preemptive act of defense against an enemy sworn to destroy it? The question was overshadowed by an Anglo-French "ultimatum" to Israel and Egypt giving them twelve hours to agree to a cease-fire.

This particular diplomatic charade was played with such telling effect that Eban, still in the dark about what it concealed, debated the British representative at the U.N. about the justice of the "ultimatum." He realized that something eccentric was afoot only when England and France vetoed a Security Council resolution calling on Israel to withdraw its troops from Sinai.

On October 31 the Israeli government "accepted" the Anglo-French "ultimatum" regarding a cease-fire, but Egypt rejected it. With that, British and French planes began to bomb Egypt as a preliminary to military landings.

The sudden eruption of the conflict found the White House without a star to steer by. Eisenhower now added strong criticism of France and England to his public condemnation of Israel. The position of the United States—arrayed with the Soviet Union against France and England—was more traumatic than the outbreak of familiar violence between Egypt and Israel.

[V]

Meanwhile, the Conference of Presidents was thrust into the forefront as the "voice" of American Jewry. At a hastily called New

206]   *ANGLES OF VISION*

York meeting in the last days of October, members expressed their views in a formal resolution unanimously adopted by the sixteen participants. The text affirmed the conference's full support for the government's efforts to stop the shooting, but it appealed to the White House and the State Department to make a "fresh appraisal" of the causes underlying the conflict.

The emotional involvement of the Jewish community, flushed with anxiety, was evident in overflow public meetings organized by the conference throughout the country. It was widely feared that the fulfillment of a two-thousand-year dream—the rebirth of a Jewish commonwealth—was threatened with destruction, though the fear was tempered with awe over the success of Israeli military operations. Within three days of combat, Israeli forces came within ten miles of the Suez Canal. Most of Sinai and the Gaza Strip was in Israeli hands. Egyptian armies in Sinai had been shattered. Thousands of prisoners had been taken as well as enormous stocks of Egyptian arms and equipment.

The Eisenhower administration's head-on clash with its old allies, England and France, and with its friend, Israel, was driven by an overriding need to stamp out the fires of war before the flames spread, and to rescue the tottering status of the United Nations. In these motives it had almost universal support, even among those who were strongly sympathetic to the British-French-Israeli objectives. The United Nations quickly organized an emergency force to monitor the truce which stopped the war, and, in the process, saved the Nasser regime. In early December the British and French began to evacuate their troops, and the Israelis pulled back toward their own borders. A cooling-off period set in. By December 8, Sherman Adams, then the principal assistant to the president, was able to write to me as president of B'nai B'rith:

> Although the United States Government opposed the resort to force in the Near East by Britain, France and Israel, this did not impair our basic friendship with those nations nor our determination to retain and to strengthen the bonds among us. United States policy is to seek the friendship of Israel and the other states in the Near East....We feel that the way may soon be opened to take possible steps designed to eliminate the sources of prejudice in the Near East.

The humiliation suffered by France at the hands of the United States spurred rise of go-it-alone Gaullism and the crumbling of France's Atlantic orientation. In Britain, the Suez fiasco brought the imperial dream to an end and reminded the British that they no longer had the power to sustain difficult international enterprises without American backing.

22 □ Fallout

I now assumed that all plans for building a new port at Ashdod in Israel could be put into a folder marked "File and Forget." Leaders of a people fighting for their independent existence could hardly be concerned with the details of a contract for the building of a new port city. Here, once again, I was dead wrong.

On December 4, 1956, Ben-Ami cabled me from Israel to say that the government had just executed a definite agreement for the Ashdod project. Precisely because Israel was under heavy pressure from all sides, Levi Eshkol knew it was imperative to offer people assurances that their progress would not be stayed and that their future was secure. So, in a tipsy-turvy play of cause and effect—which often seems the "normal" way things work in Israel—the war stimulated instead of deterred the building of a new town and the development of a new port.

The government specified that the "initiators" should jointly maintain control of the entire enterprise—a proviso which later complicated my lot. Ten thousand acres could be bought or leased by the initiators at an agreed price and in stages as the city developed. Under the terms of the agreement, we would build at least fifteen hundred housing units during the first five years after a master plan for the city was approved by the government, an additional fifteen hundred housing units in the second five years, and in ten years thereafter at least three thousand housing units. It was contemplated that Ashdod's population would ultimately range between 150,000 and 200,000 people.

We were bound by the agreement to invest one million Israeli pounds at the outset (the value of the pound at the time was roughly equal to fifty-five cents) and to mobilize at least ten million Israeli pounds for use at Ashdod in the first five years. The government, on its part, would plan and build the port and port buildings with our cooperation, while we would help the government mobilize at least part of the $27 million in capital borrowed for the building of the port.

Still, definite agreements and final agreements are not always the same thing, in Israel or anywhere else. The Israeli budget was painfully strained due to the costs of the Suez campaign. Who, then, could help finance the construction of the port facilities, and so warrant what Ben-Ami and I were prepared to do in the construction of the town itself? This question was suddenly overshadowed by a nasty political collision between Israel and the United States.

[II]

On the eve of the clash, a delegation of the Presidents Conference met with Dulles in early 1957, when the U.S. breach with Israel appeared to be healing. The British and French had completed their withdrawals from Suez, and the Israelis were moving back in reluctant stages. We were concerned with the mistreatment of Egyptian Jews, but despite official expressions of concern, Cairo was not challenged. The forced exodus of Jews from Egypt—this time without a Moses to lead them—buried any possibility of formal action by the United States. The ancient Jewish community in Egypt became only a shadow of its former self.

Now Israel, having retreated from all Egyptian territory except Gaza and the southeastern coastal strip of Sinai known as Sharm el-Sheik, halted its further retreat. It declared it would make no further withdrawals until it was granted formal assurance on two counts. First, the Gaza Strip, measuring about twenty-five miles long and five to eight miles wide, must not be restored to Egypt as a staging area for further *fedayeen* raids, but rather must be placed under United Nations control pending a permanent peace settlement. Second, Israeli shipping must not again be blocked from navigating the Gulf of Aqaba because of Egyptian coastal guns mounted at Sharm el-Sheik.

Except to keep the sea lanes open, Israel had no use for Sharm el-Sheik—a desolate, unpopulated wasteland, not worth the high price of the drinking water that had to be shipped in. What Israel wanted was an American "guarantee" that an Israeli withdrawal would not mean the restoration of an illicit Egyptian blockade at

Sharm el-Sheik. A U.N. guarantee was deemed worthless and probably unattainable.

Israel's legal right of free passage through the Straits of Tiran was supported by U.S. "elder statesmen" and by key senators, including William F. Knowland, Lyndon Johnson, and Richard Russell. Pressures generated from these sources *outside* the American Jewish community led to an *aide-mémoire* which Dulles gave to Eban on February 11. It stipulated that if Israel withdrew from Sinai and Gaza, the United States would exercise free passage in the Straits of Tiran and would encourage other maritime powers to do the same. To avoid a reversion to belligerency, it would also back the presence of the U.N. force in Sharm el-Sheik and Gaza for as long as necessary. While the United States had been sympathetic to Israeli aims before the war, it viewed the methods used by Israel, Britain, and France to be wrong and dangerous. Israel's legitimate aims, Dulles said, could be achieved by political means.

When this was conveyed to Jerusalem, Ben-Gurion responded that he would not change his stand even if sanctions were threatened. Eban arranged to be called back to Jerusalem for consultations. On the eve of his departure, Dulles told him that if the Israeli government meant to reject even "in principle" the U.S. proposals of February 11, a "catastrophe" was imminent. The theme of this private conversation figured in Dulles's public announcement—in line with President Eisenhower's own angry views—that the United States considered the possibility of sanctions against Israel.

At this very moment, when Eban was en route to Jerusalem in an attempt to get Ben-Gurion to see what was at stake, a group of eight American Jews, of which I was one, was drawn into a peculiar political exercise.

[III]

My personal involvement in the matter began with a telephone call I received from the motion picture pioneer Barney Balaban, an old friend. It seems that Sidney Weinberg of Goldman, Sachs, had brought him a message on behalf of President Eisenhower. Weinberg wanted Balaban to assemble a group of prominent American Jews to meet with Dulles regarding the grave divisions between Israel and the United States. If discussions with Dulles about how to get Ben-Gurion to ease his opposition to the U.S. proposals regarding Aqaba and Gaza were fruitful, President Eisenhower would meet with the group afterward to see if something concrete could be worked out. All this was to occur in strict confidence.

Balaban was furnished a list of eight American Jews who would comprise the group. My name was among them. "Phil," Balaban said to me, "I want you to agree to be a member—you know how serious things are." I reminded him that I was not only the president of B'nai B'rith, but in Nahum Goldmann's absence overseas I was acting head of the Presidents Conference. I was not a free man in the matter. Balaban insisted, "You must be there. Sidney Weinberg says you are the key—precisely because you wear two hats."

I continued to demur, saying that I could not keep strict confidence and yet go. I must be free to call Maurice Bisgyer, the executive vice president of B'nai B'rith, simply to inform him of what I would be doing. And if the meeting at the State Department was followed by one at the White House in the afternoon, Judd Teller, secretary of the Presidents Conference, must be called so that he could convene a meeting of the conference the next morning where I could report what had transpired. I added that there was no way the meeting could be kept secret if eight persons were involved in it. Balaban conveyed my views to Sidney Weinberg, whereupon it was agreed that I could inform both organizations.

The composition of the group seeing Dulles was unusual. Besides Balaban and myself, the other members were Louis Novins, an associate of Balaban; Samuel B. Leidensdorf; Mendel Silberberg, prominent in the Republican party and in Jewish affairs in Los Angeles; and Jacob Blaustein and Irving M. Engle of the American Jewish Committee. Except for Blaustein, Engle, and me, the others had not been intimately involved with Jewish organizations known to be concerned with day-to-day political aspects of U.S.-Israeli relations. They were publicly identified with philanthropic campaigns. Mine was the only name linked to an organization that was part of the cooperative process which made the Presidents Conference the most representative leadership group in the Jewish community. No one on the list was associated with the leadership of the Zionist movement in the United States. This omission may have been due to an innocent oversight, but it was later charged that Zionist leaders had been deliberately ignored by Dulles.

On the eve of our meeting, several members of our group gathered in Barney Balaban's New York apartment to hear President Eisenhower's speech to the American people about the crisis with Israel. He claimed credit for major efforts to allay Israel's concern, but added that if Israel was unreasonable in its refusal to withdraw from the Gaza Strip and from Sharm el-Sheik, the United States would "have to adopt measures which might have far-reaching effects on Israel's relations throughout the world." He did not mention sanctions in his speech (he knew that he could not win congressional support for them), but he did call Israel an aggressor. The term "aggressor" has a technical definition in international diplomacy, and resolutions adopted by the United Nations are careful in its use. Was Israel, provoked by border raids, economic blockades, and other harassments, an "aggressor"? Or was it a nation acting in self-defense? It was a moral as well as a political question.

The president's speech seemed to change the terms of reference for our meeting in Washington, and we debated among ourselves whether to go through with it. We agreed, finally, that we should meet with Dulles for one purpose. We should say that because the president had called Israel an aggressor, it was pointless for us to talk with him about help we might render in the U.S.-Israeli embroglio.

Unknown to us at the time, Ben-Gurion had received a personal letter from General Bedell Smith, whom he regarded as Israel's staunchest friend in Washington. Smith, a slender, scholarly, and bespectacled soldier whose mother reportedly was Jewish, drew fully on the confidence he enjoyed with Israel's leaders. He wrote Ben-Gurion to say he ought to "give some flexibility to Eban" who was "perfectly capable of reaching a negotiation which would ensure stability for many years."

Our meeting in the State Department lasted ninety minutes and was one of the best I have ever attended. Barney Balaban, as chairman of the group, quickly came to the point. What he had to say was along the following lines: "Mr. Secretary, we have had a very serious discussion among ourselves before coming here, and we believe you should understand our position before anything is said. We listened to the president's broadcast last night. In the light of our understanding of the issues involved, we were shocked to hear him declare that Israel was an aggressor. We momentarily thought it would be inadvisable to come here at all, but as you had extended the invitation, we owed it to you to explain in person why we believe it would be counterproductive if we later saw the president. With all due respect, we would like to be relieved of that appointment."

Dulles flushed, was silent for a moment, but finally said, "I can understand that. I wish it were otherwise." Then addressing Maxwell Raab, the secretary of the cabinet who was present, he said, "Max, I guess you can go tell the president the time is released." On turning back to us he said, "I hope we can restore our own relationship on a constructive basis so that we can discuss the problems that concern us. Before we get into a serious discussion, I've just received a note that Ben-Gurion is speaking right now in the Knesset, and Cabot Lodge [head of the U.S. permanent delegation at the U.N.] is monitoring what he is saying. I'll get a call about the matter, and maybe that will change the whole tenor of our own discussion. Meanwhile, I'll tell you what worries us." He no sooner started his exposition about the international situation, when an aide entered with reports of Ben-Gurion's speech broadcast to the Israeli people. "It doesn't change the situation at all," Dulles remarked. To judge from the report, Ben-Gurion had again rejected an Eisenhower plea for withdrawal but had voiced the hope that the door was still open to further negotiations and a satisfactory accommodation.

After Dulles completed a careful exposition of the U.S. position, each of us in turn had a chance to respond. I knew the general sentiments of each man in our group, and I expected unanimity in our views. I did not, however, expect them to be voiced in so outspoken and direct a fashion. Our mood was conveyed by Samuel B. Leidersdorf, who had been Dulles's classmate at Princeton and now headed a large accounting firm. "Foster," he said, "I'm a fellow out of his element. I don't know anything about politics or diplomacy. All I know is this: For our country to try to bludgeon Israel against its own vital interests to do what the United States wants, without assurance that conditions in the Gaza Strip and in the Straits of Tiran will not revert to what they were, is morally wrong." Dulles replied, "I understand you, Sam."

When it was my turn to speak, I said, "Mr. Secretary, you are obviously correct in concluding that we are dealing with a very dangerous condition—dangerous for the United States, not helpful to Israel, and dangerous to the world. On the other hand, Israel itself has a legitimate right to the freedom of passage that has been denied it for years. A formula must be found that will enable her to be secure in that right, and yet withdraw. Whether matters go from bad to worse or the other way around depends entirely on the United States. My report to the heads of the major Jewish organizations which I momentarily represent, and who meet to-morrow morning, will be what I've just said. It is in the interest of the Jewish community to help you find a formula to make it possible for Israel to withdraw from Sharm el-Sheik. Anything else will have nasty consequences from here on out."

We left the State Department after Balaban gave a brief, non-committal statement to newspapermen in the foyer. The story that later appeared in the press suggested that we had been called together by the president and State Department to pressure us to pressure Israel. This was absurd, but when the Presidents Conference convened at nine o'clock the next morning, the atmosphere was as cold and hostile as a polar icecap.

The moment I took my seat as presiding chairman, Emmanuel Newman, president of the Zionist Organization of America, was on his feet. I viewed him as a close personal friend, but he proceeded to assail me with angry questions. What business did I have to go to a meeting of that sort? Who gave me permission to go? How could I be so presumptuous as to act on my own? Had it ever occurred to me that I had placed the Presidents Conference in a false light? Two or three presidents of other major organizations added their charges to Newman's tirade.

In response, I told them of the dilemma I faced when I was asked to attend the meeting at the State Department under a pledge of secrecy. I could not sever my identity as president of B'nai B'rith from my role as acting chairman of the Presidents Conference. What was I to do? I decided it was important to attend. "It was," I continued, "of equal importance that you should immediately know what took place. That is why I arranged this morning's meeting."

I then reconstructed the remarks made by each member of our group. "Instead of complaining about what transpired at the State Department," I concluded, "you should be proud of how the group as a whole bore itself. If you want evidence why we have difficulties with one another—and with the White House and State Department—you have provided it yourself by your rush to judg-ment without evidence of what the others and I did. If you feel I am not qualified to sit here in the absence of Dr. Goldmann, I am ready and willing to leave you right now." That ended the uprising, and apologies followed.

[IV]

Within a week, Eban was back in Washington from his consultations with Ben-Gurion in Jerusalem. At a February 24 meeting at the State Department, he told Dulles that Ben-Gurion had been impressed by the American attitude since February 11 and wanted Eban to bring matters to a conclusion. Eban thereupon proposed that as soon as Israel left Sharm el-Sheik, the American commitment on free passage of the Straits of Tiran should take effect, leaving the problem of Gaza for later solution.

Dulles accepted these suggestions as "constructive." Eban then asked for precise assurances. Would U.S. shipping regularly use the Straits of Tiran for trade, including the conveyance of oil to Elat, when appropriate facilities were constructed? Yes. Did the United States understand "free and innocent passage" to mean passage of all ships of commerce and war, provided their conduct did no injury? Yes. Would the proposed U.N. force to be stationed in the Straits include naval units? Yes, that was reasonable. Would the United States recognize an Israeli declaration announcing its intention to protect Israeli ships and their right of passage if they came under attack? Yes.

But some of Dulles's assurances needed an endorsement by U.N. Secretary General Dag Hammarskjold. And Hammarskjold refused to agree to a U.N. navy patrol in the Straits of Tiran or to recognize that Israel had a legitimate interest in the status of Gaza—leaving Israel with no assurances of security against further *feda-yeen* raids.

Dulles now informed Eban that the prime minister and foreign minister of France, Guy Mollet and Christian Penau, who were in Washington on an official visit, had made a proposal which Eisenhower and Dulles thought might help end the deadlock. If Israel found the French suggestion "interesting," Eisenhower and Dulles would give it their support. The memorandum which Eban then received from the two French leaders suggested that Israel announce complete withdrawal from Gaza in accordance with U.N. resolutions, subject to a clear understanding on the following points: First, the initial takeover of Gaza from Israeli military and civilian control would be exclusively by a U.N. emergency force to be formed. Second, the U.N. would be the agency for civilian administration until a peace settlement was reached. Third, if Egypt created conditions which again led to a deteriorated state of affairs in the strip, "Israel would reserve its freedom to act to defend its rights" by returning to Gaza, and the United States and other similarly minded states would approve of Israel's actions.

The French initiative, when conveyed to Jerusalem, had a decisive effect on the Israeli government's attitude. Eban was now authorized by Ben-Gurion to proceed with negotiations for a settlement based on the U.S. memorandum of February 11 and the new French suggestions.

To seal the settlement, it was agreed that Israel's Foreign Minister Golda Meir would speak to the U.N. General Assembly stating that Israel's withdrawal from Sharm el-Sheik and Gaza was linked to the "assumptions" formulated over the previous weeks.

The speech she actually delivered in the General Assembly had an unusual drafting history. Eban, who helped draft it, was assisted by U.S. State Department officers. The text, before delivery, was endorsed by Washington and Paris. Dulles then secured advance assurance from Great Britain and Canada that they too would support what Abba Eban would later call "the Doctrine of Immaculate Assumptions" at the heart of Golda Meir's speech.

During this tense period, I kept in close touch with Abba Eban and Reuven Shiloah, minister in the Israeli embassy, in order to render such help as might be useful in steadying American Jewish opinion. On the night of the U.N. special session where Mrs. Meir was due to speak, I conveyed to Eban and Shiloah by telephone my admiration for the remarkable political breakthrough they had achieved for Israel. Ethel and I then listened to Mrs. Meir's speech and afterward, at a late hour the same night, flew to Florida. I was so tired and emotionally drained from my work as a "spear carrier" on Israel's behalf that I could scarcely sleep when I reached Florida. The next morning, while relaxing in the bathtub, I received a telephone call from Reuven Shiloah in New York.

"As you know," he began, "John Foster Dulles worked out the deal that will enable Israel to withdraw from Sharm el-Sheik, and he also brokered the French deal which will enable us to withdraw from Gaza. I have since called four or five Jewish leaders here in New York and nationally, and I cannot get a single one to send Dulles a note of thanks and congratulations. They won't touch the idea. Would you at least send him a message of congratulations on behalf of B'nai B'rith?"

My answer to the question was, "Of course. Let's draft the text right now on the phone." This was done; the message was sent off, as were messages of congratulations to President Eisenhower and Prime Minister Ben-Gurion.

I was distressed by the blurred perceptions of some Jewish leaders in their refusal to extend a minimal courtesy to the Secretary of State who had helped Israel win a great political victory. The same blindness could have broken up the Presidents Conference—and there were times in future years when I wished this had occurred.

Few participants or informed bystanders had any illusions about what had occurred during the four months of intense diplomatic maneuvers that began the moment Israeli troops marched into Sinai. The storm that followed was not the kind that clears a foul sky. No one expected the accumulated problems and difficulties of the Middle East to be swept away suddenly. They remained, primed for the eruption of the Six Days War a decade later. What counted for the moment was that a dangerous breakdown in U.S.-Israeli relations had been averted.

23 □ From Ashdod to Oak Brook

With Jews increasingly at risk under Moslem regimes in the Middle East, the prospects for a new influx of immigrants to Israel spurred the building of Ashdod as a port city. There were, however, financial difficulties in bringing to fruition the paper agreements reached in December 1956 between the Israeli government, Ben-Ami and his Israeli associates, and the ACB team in Chicago. Israel lacked the funds to cover its share of the costs in building the port facilities. The Suez War and its aftermath had left its treasury on the threshold of exhaustion.

I had earlier asked Newton Minow, who acted in legal matters for me, to explore the possibilities of funding the Ashdod port in a roundabout way. I had in mind "U.S. 480," the popular name of a law which authorized agricultural assistance to developing nations. I reasoned that Ashdod presumptively qualified for help under the law because it was meant to serve as a port for the export of agricultural products. This view, however, was rejected by U.S. officials to whom it was put by Minow.

As it turned out, Ashdod's financing problems were solved as a byproduct of the Suez War. On Nasser's orders, freighters had been sunk in the Suez Canal to block passage. The wrecked ships now had to be cleared. The canal's facilities in any case were in need of modernization and expansion to serve international commerce, even if the effect redounded to Nasser's benefit.

A World Bank loan to Egypt to help clear and improve the canal provided the grounds on which the State Department could be asked to ensure equal treatment for Israel. In putting that case to a former colleague, Christian Herter, then Undersecretary of State and soon to be Dulles's successor as Secretary, I noted that Israel had received little if any financial aid in the aftermath of the Suez War. Now, however, it urgently needed financial help in building the port facilities of Ashdod. Herter welcomed the "reminder." It would allow the U.S. to do something positive for Israel of a nonmilitary nature to balance what was being done for Egypt. If Israel, he said, asked the World Bank for a loan in an amount equal to the assistance being extended to Egypt, the U.S. would support the Israeli request.

Eugene Black, president of the World Bank, looked closely at the Ashdod project during one of his periodic trips to the Middle East. He was impressed by the commercial case for developing a port at Ashdod, but, as he soon told me, the World Bank could not make a loan to the Israeli government. Israel, he said, was the only nation he knew that could not present a balance sheet that accurately showed its total debt. Why? Black explained that every day of the year, someone somewhere in the world was buying Israeli bonds which were not immediately reported. But he had suggested to Levi Eshkol that the World Bank *could* make a loan to an Ashdod port authority if one were formed. Eshkol had balked. "I could not make him understand," said Black, "how and why the creation of a port authority would enable the World Bank to make a loan to it."

I volunteered to see if I could explain matters to Eshkol. I called my associate Ben-Ami to arrange a meeting with the Israeli finance minister, and a few hours later I was on my way by air to Israel. When I faced Eshkol and repeated Eugene Black's suggestion about the creation of a port authority, Eshkol dismissed the thought, saying that no government of Israel could part with ownership of land. The land was sacred to all the people. "What are you worried about?" I asked. "When you create a port authority, you are not transferring land to a strange institution. You write the law which creates the authority. You appoint or remove the members of the port authority. The authority receives income from port operations, pays its bills, and oversees the construction and maintenance of port facilities. The legal form of an authority merely assures the World Bank that the fiscal affairs of the authority are segregated from Israel's general credit situation."

Among the Israelis I knew who held the post of minister of finance, Levi Eshkol had the firmest grasp of economic details, including those related to economic interdependence among nations. When one of his aides informed him that a serious drought was imminent, Eshkol, upset, asked, "Where?" "In the Negev," the aide replied. Eshkol's face cleared. "For a moment I thought you meant *Kansas*." Yet for all this extensive knowledge, I could tell from Eshkol's astonished look that he had not understood the nature of a port authority. "Why didn't Eugene Black explain all this to me?" he asked. "*Gonif*! How do you know such things?"

"It's my life," I replied. "I have written laws for such authorities in my country, and in court cases even defended their powers and limitations."

An Ashdod Port Authority was soon formed and received a World Bank loan. I returned to Israel for the formal start of the construction of the town and port; while there I called on Ben-Gurion to discuss certain cultural matters pertaining to B'nai B'rith. His abrupt greeting was typical of his "take-charge" style. "Klutznick," he said to me, "I thought you were interested only in public and cultural matters. Now I see you are making a big business deal."

His chiding tone made me uncomfortable. "B.G.," I said, taken aback, "if you mean Ashdod, I will give you a blank check right now. When the Ashdod project is complete, you can fill in the blank check in the amount of any profit I make, and you can use the profit for any activities you wish."

"No! No!" he said. "You must not talk like that. Israel needs

American Jews who come here to invest and to build up our country. To do this, American investors must make profits." I did not expect this old-line socialist and kibbutznick to make a case for profits. The point dropped out of our discussion for the next twenty minutes or so, but then the socialist strain in Ben-Gurion brought him back to our earlier discussion. "Phil," he said, "but *too much profit* you should not make!" A few years later I gave all my shares in Ashdod to major educational institutions in Israel, just as I later gave to Israeli institutions all my shares in the Jerusalem Hilton Hotel, in whose organization and construction I had been a major participant.

The team that organized the Ashdod project consisted of a small number of experts. The main architect was a distinguished Israeli, Y. Perlstein, and his work was backstopped by two widely experienced American architects, Jerrold Loebl, the Park Forest veteran, and Albert Mayer. Other experts were involved in fields such as traffic, water supply, sewage disposal, landscape architecture, road and bridge construction, and market analysis. At my own side was Tom McDade, who put his Park Forest experience to use in drafting memoranda on commercial outlooks, sociological investigations, and summaries of progress.

It would be hard to overstate my excitement in helping to build a new town seven thousand miles from Chicago, rising from sand dunes that afforded a wonderful view of the Mediterranean but little else. We faced more serious construction difficulties than those encountered earlier in Park Forest, as in the instances of sewers and water. In Ashdod the problem of water was painfully simple: it was controlled by a national agency which parceled it out depending on available resources. You got so much and no more, and that fact controlled the building schedule. With sewers, we had to guarantee that the effluent was not wasted but rather was retrieved for agricultural purposes. We were ceaselessly reminded that water was more precious than oil.

[II]

Around the time when the building of Ashdod began in earnest in 1957, and when the Old Orchard Shopping Center, dedicated the previous year, was already a proven success, an item in a Chicago newspaper reported that Marshall Field's had acquired a 160-acre parcel of land directly west of Chicago in DuPage County. The land had once been a corn and hog farm belonging to a family named Ahremo. It was to be the site of another shopping center— called Oak Brook—which Field's would create in the Chicago area. Two days after the story appeared I received a phone call from Hughston McBain, the president of Field's. "Did you," he asked, "read the item about a shopping center near Oak Brook?"

"Yes."

"How would you like to build it for us?"

"If I got involved in the project, what would be its terms?"

"The same as in the case of Old Orchard," he replied. "You reproduce that contract, make it applicable to Oak Brook, and I'll sign it."

I was not entirely a stranger to the Oak Brook area. Some months earlier I had been contacted by an architect who worked for Paul Butler, president of the Butler Paper Company. Butler owned about three thousand acres in the Oak Brook area, which included his private polo field, and proposed to sell some of the land for use as the site of a new town. He wanted to know how to proceed. Through the intercession of the architect, I met Butler in his Chicago office. "I've got this land," he said to me. "What do you think it is worth?"

"I haven't looked at it," I replied. "But what do *you* want for it?" He indicated a selling price. I said I knew only two people in the United States who would even consider buying the property at the inflated price he cited.

"Maybe," said Butler, "I should try to build a town myself on the property. What would be my problems?"

"What is your utility situation?" I asked.

"Well," he said, "we've got Sauk Creek out there."

"You are going to need much more than a creek if you are going to build a town. You need an assured source of water and a functioning sewer system."

"Why don't you and your associates buy some of my land and build a town on it?"

"Frankly," I said, "we can't afford it. We are just finishing a big job at Old Orchard, and a substantial part of our capital is tied up in it. We would not in any case be willing to pay the price you are asking for the land. At most we would pay no more than a quarter of what you want. For your part, you should not sell the property unless you can get cash or its equivalent."

After inspecting the farm property which Field's had purchased at Oak Brook for a shopping center, I signed an agreement to build it on terms similar to those for Old Orchard. Unlike Old Orchard, however, there were long delays before work could begin at the Oak Brook site. Coincident with Paul Butler's decision to build the village of Oak Brook on his own, but before the village had actually been incorporated, some "locals" leaped into a legal vacuum and tried to exploit the situation to their advantage.

These were mostly blue-collar families who lived on small lots just to the west of the proposed Oak Brook Shopping Center. They incorporated a "city" of 350 people and appropriately called it "Utopia"—a name which expressed their hope of acquiring fantastic unearned wealth. To that end they annexed the proposed shopping site—something they were free to do without permission of the landowner because no one yet lived on the site. Their intention was to milk the shopping center by charging high fees for building permits, and by getting a penny from every dollar of shopping center sales. With a population of only 350, and with an expected annual volume of $100 million in sales, the incorporators of Utopia envisioned an opulent style of life for themselves with no need to use the shopping center revenues for any municipal services.

It was a clever gambit. If one had a highly developed aesthetic sense, the craftsmanship involved would merit a grudging admiration even from the intended victim. Instead a court battle followed. It lasted two years before it was finally possible to de-annex the site of the Oak Brook Shopping Center from Utopia, then annex it to the village of Oak Brook, which was by then incorporated and being built.

24 □ Interlude at the United Nations

In midsummer of 1957, I was contacted by Secretary of State Dulles who had a question to ask. Would I accept an appointment by President Eisenhower to serve on the U.S. delegation to the twelfth General Assembly of the United Nations? By tradition, the ten members of the delegation—of which five were alternates—included two members of Congress, one a Democrat and the other a Republican. In years when members of the House stand for election, two senators who do not face election contests are appointed to serve. The remaining members of the delegation are drawn from the ranks of prominent figures in the world of business and labor, the arts and sciences, and the professions.

I was the first head of any leading Jewish organization ever to be offered an appointment to a U.S. delegation to the United Nations, but there were other unusual considerations. For one thing, as president of B'nai B'rith and as acting chairman of the Conference of Presidents of Major Jewish Organizations, I was prominently identified as an advocate of Israel's cause. For another, the offer was made despite the way Arab delegations in the United Nations, along with their communist bloc and Third World allies, continuously attacked Israel, including the very idea of its existence. I construed the offered appointment as a sign of the administration's trust in my purposes—that even when I spoke for the B'nai B'rith or the Presidents Conference in pointed criticism of U.S. foreign policy in the Middle East, I stayed within the norms of democratic adversarial politics, and argued for a course of action I believed was congruous with the interests of the United States.

Something else intrigued me about the offer. While I had plenty of confidence in my abilities as a "negotiator," I wondered how I would fare in a world forum with its clashing interests from every corner of the globe.

I was not, however, entirely free to accept the appointment to the U.S. delegation to the U.N. I would have to arrange for a leave of absence from my post as president of B'nai B'rith—and lay myself open to the familiar charge that I always "skipped around from one thing to another," without ever staying in one place very long.

The board of governors of B'nai B'rith took a kindlier view of the case when I put it to them. They observed that I had devoted almost full time to B'nai B'rith affairs in the previous four years and had restored the organization to a state of health. And it would stand to the credit of the organization to have its president play a part on the world stage as a member of the U.S. delegation. So I accepted the appointment, starting in the fall of 1957, and was delighted to find that my fellow "public members" of the U.S.

delegation included George Meany, president of the AFL-CIO, and Irene Dunne, the actress.

[II]

During the first two decades of its existence, the U.N.'s admission policy appeared to be selective. The original fifty members included twenty Latin American countries, eight European, and six from the British Commonwealth, the Philippines, and Taiwan. Their political outlook, combined with their dependence on American economic and technical aid in the immediate aftermath of World War II, made for an "automatic" American majority in the United Nations. In the next nine years, only nine additional nations were admitted, and the arithmetic meant that the American majority was still protected.

After 1954, however, new members were admitted to the United Nations at an accelerating rate, partly in consequence of the wave of decolonization that swept over the old trading empires of the British, French, Dutch, Portuguese, and Belgians. Once the former colonies attained the legal emblems of nationhood, they applied for and were generally granted U.N. membership. The growth in U.N. membership was also due to the political rehabilitation of the former Axis powers—Germany, Japan, and Italy— plus Spain and eastern European nations that had been compromised by their conduct during World War II. In 1955 alone, sixteen new members became part of the United Nations. Still more had been added by the time the twelfth General Assembly met in late September 1957.

The old basis for an automatic American majority was diluted. A Western majority still prevailed, but it worked through the formation of ad hoc coalitions which might change from one issue to the next. The importance of this development lay in the fact that the General Assembly operates by a two-thirds majority vote on important questions. It is a half-truth to say that the General Assembly can make only nonbinding recommendations concerning disputes or questions not being discussed by the Security Council. The other half of the truth dates from June 1950, when North Korea invaded South Korea. Secretary of State Dean Acheson argued that the U.N. charter gave the General Assembly "authority and responsibility for matters affecting international peace," and could recommend collective action if the Security Council was unable to act because of a veto by one of its members.

Since 1953, the permanent U.S. representative to the United Nations had been Ambassador Henry Cabot Lodge, formerly a member of the U.S. Senate Foreign Relations Committee. Lodge loved his job and worked hard at it. In the 1952 presidential elections, he had managed Eisenhower's successful campaign for the White House and thus had continuous and direct contact with him. He was, in fact, the first permanent U.S. representative to the United Nations to be made a member of the president's cabinet.

I had had earlier differences with Ambassador Lodge, and they had persisted despite the intervention of Max Raab, secretary of the Eisenhower cabinet, who brought us together for a candid discussion of U.S.-Israeli relationships. As a member of the U.S. delegation, however, I found Lodge to be both reasonable and cooperative. He also had the grace to say of himself that he had a "pan-of-popcorn" mind. He wanted his associates at the U.N. to put him on the right track if he tried to jump to quick and puffed-up conclusions. He was properly deferential to Secretary of State Dulles and prided himself on "being a good soldier." But his special relationship with President Eisenhower seemed to have helped him avoid most of the institutional strains I saw at close range starting four years later, when Adlai Stevenson was the U.S. permanent representative at the U.N. and I was the U.S. representative and ambassador to its Economic and Social Council.

The General Assembly transacts much of its business in standing committees. It turned out that my main assignment was to the sixth (legal) committee. I suggested that I hadn't practiced law for years, but Lodge dismissed my cautionary note.

Aside from my regular assignment, I substituted for George Meany on the third, or financial and economic, committee when he was obliged to be in Washington for AFL-CIO matters. I also found myself in the role of a "white knight" for Irene Dunne. She was a grandmother by this time, but her still vital beauty, charm, and celebrity as an actress made her the subject of unwanted amorous attentions from certain delegates. I was pressed into service as her shield.

I also found myself bracing her morale when she once came into my office, which was next to hers in the U.S. delegation's head-quarters. She was carrying a briefing paper that had been prepared by State Department foreign service officers who comprised the staff of the delegation. "Don't they know," she tearfully asked, "that I've only been to a college of music? How am I supposed to know and master what's in the briefing papers prepared for me?" I told her that it might be a waste of time to try to decipher what was in these papers, though if she wished I would try to help her. Otherwise, the members of the committee on which she served would be enchanted to hear her say what came naturally to her tongue.

On the theory that it was possible to make more headway with liquor than speeches, Ethel and I entertained other delegations rather extensively. We also made a special point of accepting invitations extended by the Russians. But I could do nothing about the hostility certain Arabs in the General Assembly directed toward me personally, because of my identity as the president of the B'nai B'rith with a known concern about the interests of my people.

I recalled that Warren Austin, the immediate predecessor of Henry Cabot Lodge as the U.S. representative to the United Nations, had once offered an earnest piece of advice to the warring Jews and Arabs. In the course of a debate on the Middle East, he urged them to sit down and settle their differences "like good Christians." As a member of the U.S. delegation to the U.N. in 1957, it was brought home to me how difficult it was to do what Austin had urged. One Arab delegate to the U.N., who was the head of the Arab League, seemed to have a hard time holding his spittle in check when he could not avoid looking at me. Others did accept personal friendship while remaining true to their policies.

[III]

Among the diverse matters in which I was involved on the sixth committee, one episode stands out in my memory, but not because it "made history." Indeed, I remember it precisely because history was *not* made, but rather because of what it revealed about the volatile moods that can sweep through delegations at the U.N.

The matter at issue came before the General Assembly on the initiative of Judge Morosov, my Soviet opposite number on the legal committee. Morosov, who had served as a Russian judge at the Japanese war crimes trials, called on the General Assembly to define aggression so that it could be punished by a world criminal court which might be created. I laid down a barrage of questions about the jurisdiction, powers, and procedures of the world criminal court that was being contemplated, along with other leading questions. How was the term "aggressor" to be defined, and by whom as the basis of trials before the proposed court?

After much talk in the corridors, many luncheons, late afternoon drinks, head-to-head talks in a corner during receptions, we managed to form a coalition of delegates with sufficient votes to get the proposed definition of aggression referred to the legal committee where a requiem mass and burial awaited it. But before the matter came to a vote, the Russians successfully fired off their first *Sputnik*. The impact of this orbiting satellite on the delegations at the U.N. was beyond belief, except to those who experienced it.

With one thrust of a rocket, *Sputnik* at least momentarily shattered the notion of American omniscience in science and technology. It was the Soviet Union which now seemed to set the pace for major technological advance, and the United States had to struggle to catch up. A luncheon I had arranged happened to coincide with news of the Russian success. Morosov was among those who were invited to attend, and I congratulated him on his country's achievement. He corrected my pronunciation of *Sputnik*, saying it should be pronounced as in *Klootznick*.

There was no logic to the immediate political fallout from *Sputnik*. Yet our voting coalition in opposition to the Soviet proposal for a definition of aggression suddenly began to unravel. Some delegations apparently feared the consequences of offending what now appeared to be the transcendent power of the Soviet Union. My associates and I had to work doubly hard to patch together the frayed coalition. That goal was again within reach when Morosov, while making a speech before the final vote, worked himself up to a high state of excitement and fainted from a heart attack. He was rushed to a hospital where doctors stabilized his condition and set him on a regimen of care that led to his recovery. In the interval, however, some of the delegations who witnessed his collapse spoke and thought of him as a martyr to his beliefs, and seemed prepared to cast a "sympathy vote" on his side of the argument. Again we had to repair the breaches in our coalition. Finally we mobilized sufficient strength to get the Soviet proposal assigned to a commission for further study.

When my brief three-month stint at the United Nations ended, I must have begun to nurse an ambition to return to that forum in a more substantial capacity. From my early youth I was used to making speeches in public forums, and as I matured, the subject of the speeches and their purposes gained in weight and seriousness. But nothing quite equaled the emotional charge I always felt when I stood at the rostrum of the U.N. General Assembly, looked over the sea of faces that reflected all the races and ethnic strains of the world, and then addressed them as *the* world. There were times when I, in common with other delegates to the U.N., grew tired during the apparently interminable debates in the place. Yet a truth that Warren Austin voiced in his own time about the same experience was seldom far removed from my own thoughts. "It is better," he said, "for aged diplomats to be bored by their own speech-making than for young men to die."

25 □ Between Several Worlds

In early February 1958, I left Chicago for an overseas trip that took me to Paris, Rome, and Israel. In Rome I attended a meeting of the Conference on Jewish Material Claims against Germany, and also found time for a Sunday morning audience with Pope Pius XII. In Israel I wanted to visit certain cultural institutions of interest to B'nai B'rith, to button down plans for the Order's triennial convention to be held there in 1959, and to consult with my partner Oved Ben-Ami on aspects of the Ashdod project.

[II]

This was my fourth trip to Israel since the whirlwind Sinai campaign, and each visit led to sharp impressions of a different country. With the help of Bernard Simon, my friend and press aide in the B'nai B'rith who was with me on this trip, I tried to formulate my impressions in a series of articles I wrote for the *Chicago Tribune*. Some of my impressions would change radically with time and events—the Six Days War of 1967; the Yom Kippur

War of 1973; the rise of Menachem Begin and his Likud coalition; the rapprochement with Egypt; and the grim miscarriages of the deep incursion into Lebanon.

As of early 1958, however, it seemed right to choose the phrase "Sinai made the difference" as a common thread for my observations.

It seemed to me that the Sinai victory had opened the door to tensions latent within the country between Israel's native-born *sabras* and old-time pioneers from eastern Europe, and immigrants from the Middle East and from North Africa. The Ashkenazim who came from Europe or the West ran the government. They comprised the civil service, governed the Knesset, commanded the army, ran the shops, led the trade unions, ruled the economy. They and the *sabras* had encouraged the policy of unrestricted immigration, but by the spring of 1958 they were already a statistical minority—outnumbered three to two by what was loosely identified as Sephardic or "oriental" immigration. There were painful strains, even bitterness, between the two groups; a sense of inferiority on the part of oriental Jews, and a sense on the part of European-reared Israelis that the oriental immigrants neither pulled their weight in the economic struggle nor seemed ready to learn how to do so.

To the outsider looking in, the most emotional and combustible of Israel's domestic problems was that of Arab-Jewish relations. For every nine Israeli Jews there was one Israeli Arab, but the Arabs as a whole were not all of the same pattern. Four of five were Muslims, but the Muslims included Bedouins who were lax with the strictures of faith and responsive to the hegemony of the tribe rather than to any political unit. The Christian Arab, on the other hand, could be a Greek Catholic, a Russian Orthodox, or one of a dozen or more Christian sects and denominations. If he was a Druze, his loyalty to the state of Israel made him an object of pride. About Arab-Jewish relations, as of the spring of 1958, I wrote:

> It would be a sentimental error of perception to conclude that Israel has succeeded in wiping out the mutual animosity and distrust between the two populations.... Inevitably, the problem is linked to that of the Arab refugee on the borders, to whom Israel's Arabs are tied by family and by cultural and intellectual kinship. Its solution lies in a negotiated peace.

The city of Ashdod was a microcosm of some of these problems.

When I returned to Ashdod several years after the newly built city received its first wave of settlers, I was appalled by what I saw. Despite the care that had gone into the planning and construction of the city, the living organism that resulted was a far cry from Park Forest. A substantial number of the new settlers were Moroccan Jews who seemed either through carelessness or habit to have imposed the features of a slum on the civic envelope. The gap between the Western Jew and the oriental Jew stood out in all its raw quality. A few years later, however, when I again returned to Ashdod, the features of a slum were no longer visible. New ways of community living had been learned, and Ashdod began to grow and mature into a city whose inhabitants took a proprietary interest in maintaining an upgraded quality of life.

[III]

My return to the United States from that visit to Israel coincided with stirrings among the candidates for the 1960 presidential nominations. Adlai Stevenson was not an active candidate, but he hovered in the political air breathed by Senators John F. Kennedy, Hubert H. Humphrey, Stuart Symington, and Lyndon B. Johnson. Each would have welcomed his open support, yet Stevenson's intentions were perhaps unknown to himself, much less to them.

I hoped that Stevenson might emerge as the Democratic party nominee for a third time, yet in my meetings with him he gave no sign of such an urge. When his attention was called to the way he was praised in the European press for his condemnation of American U-2 reconnaissance flights over Europe, he remarked wryly, "The trouble is, I always run in the wrong continents."

Senator Kennedy was a different matter. In the spring of 1958, he was already campaigning openly or sometimes, depending on his target, quietly. I was an object of the latter approach. Through Sargent Shriver and Hyman B. Raskin, who were lining up possible sources of political support for Kennedy, I was invited to visit the senator in his Washington office. If he meant to "pick me off," it was not because I was a Stevenson man but for another reason: I was head of the largest and oldest Jewish organization in the world and had ready access to people who could bring a measure of strength to a presidential aspirant.

When I walked into Kennedy's office, I was delighted to encounter his aide, Theodore C. Sorensen. I had not seen Ted since he was a baby back in Nebraska, at a time when I was working for his father, Nebraska's attorney general. Ted left Kennedy's office, and I talked alone with the senator for some time. He sat in his rocking chair while I tried to make up my mind whether this was the man I wanted to see as president in 1960.

When our discussion turned to problems of the Middle East, I found Kennedy fuzzy in his views about Arab-Israeli issues. "Look," I said, "you've got to make up your mind where you stand. I'm not here to sell you anything regarding Arabs or Israelis, but frankly, I think you are trying to be all things to all men, and that's not good enough. It just wouldn't work. You've got to decide whether you are for or against some of the things on the move in the Middle East. Being a 'statesman' on such matters isn't going to get you anywhere."

Even when Kennedy disagreed with someone, he paid him the compliment of close attention, as I learned some months later when he delivered a speech on the Middle East before B'nai Zion, a New York–based Zionist organization. He sent me an advance copy of the text with an attached note: "Do you like this better?" Signed "Jack." He had not forgotten our earlier discussion.

After my meeting with Kennedy, I told Hyman Raskin, "I think he's a wonderful fellow, but my guess is he's probably four years early." I took the position out of friendship for Adlai Stevenson and in the hope that political lightning might strike him a third time. I did not join the effort to nominate Senator Kennedy. I told Sargent Shriver, "As long as there's any chance of Adlai Stevenson being nominated, you can't count on me. Once he's out of contention, I'm for Kennedy. In the meantime, I consider Hubert Humphrey as a stand-in for Adlai Stevenson, so I am going to support him."

[IV]

When Adlai Stevenson declined an invitation to serve on the U.S. Commission on Money and Credit, which was being formed in the spring of 1958, he urged my appointment instead. When the invitation came to me, I accepted the opportunity to come to grips with the new problems and demands that had arisen in the world of money, credit, and finance since the end of World War II.

My service on that commission helped me in work I later faced as U.S. Ambassador to the Economic and Social Council of the United Nations. Further, the intimate friendships I formed with other members of the commission, eventually led to my election as a trustee of the Committee for Economic Development and chairman of its research and policy committee, the intellectual heart of the CED. Still further, these associations were instrumental in my appointment as Secretary of Commerce during the Carter presidency.

The Commission on Money and Credit was not an official creation of the United States government. It was privately created and privately financed. It grew out of an awareness that the national economy had outstripped many of the major assumptions and much of the institutional machinery for its existing monetary and credit arrangements. Deciding on the appropriate medium for conducting a reappraisal of the nation's financial mechanism produced many false starts and much infighting between Congress and the executive. Finally, the Committee for Economic Development announced on November 21, 1957, that it would create a privately financed Commission on Money and Credit.

The commission formed in May 1958 was under the chairmanship of Frazier B. Wilde, president of the Connecticut Life Insurance Company, with H. Christian Sonne as vice chairman. I knew some of the other commissioners through past associations; the rest I knew only casually or met for the first time at our initial meeting. The members included Marriner Eccles, the revolutionary and revolutionizing chairman of the Federal Reserve Board during the Roosevelt and Truman presidencies; Adolph A. Berle; Henry Fowler, a lawyer and later Secretary of the Treasury; Isador Lubin, former U.S. Commissioner of Labor Statistics; Robert R. Nathan, former chairman of the planning commission for the War Planning Board; David Rockefeller, chairman of the Chase Manhattan Bank; William F. Schniztler, secretary-treasurer of the AFL-CIO; Jesse W. Tapp, chairman of the Bank of America; Theodore O. Yntema, vice president of the Ford Motor Company and chairman of its finance committee; and Beardsley Ruml, father of the "pay-as-you-go" tax reform and the former treasurer of Macy's.

The costs of the three-year study—$1.2 million—were covered by grants from the Ford and Merrill foundations. Dr. Bertrand Fox, of the Harvard School of Business Administration, and Dr. Eli Shapiro, professor of finance at Massachusetts Institute of Technology, as codirectors of research for the enterprise, mobilized 110 professors who eventually supplied the commission members with eleven thousand pages of research papers.

The commission's job was not to make ex cathedra pronounce-ments on matters of theoretical economics; it was expected to make wise choices among practical policy proposals bearing on the three goals of national economy policy—adequate economic growth, sustained high levels of production and employment, and reasonable price stability.

This would have been difficult even for a small group of disinterested experts. It was all the more difficult for a large and diverse group. Indeed, sharp divisions of opinion emerged in separate task force meetings and then as the full commission argued points of policy and drafted the final report.

The report, completed in late 1960, agreed that a mixed govern-ment and private economic system best met the nation's needs, and that "cooperative action by government and private enterprise was mandatory if the national economic goals of a low level of unem-ployment, adequate rates of economic growth, and reasonable price stability were to be met." We agreed further that the nation and the world were "passing through the most revolutionary phase in human history, in its science and technology, in its political, social, and economic structures." This reality rendered "irrelevant the Jeffersonian proposition about how government is best which governs least." The "critical problems rising from the worldwide revolution called for American responses which could only be forthcoming from a strong central government presided over by a strong president."

Our report argued that national economic policy "was an inte-grated whole." Adequate economic growth, low unemployment, and reasonable price stability could be attained "only if monetary, credit *and* fiscal and debt management decisions were carefully planned, reviewed, and coordinated with other major measures of both the executive branch of government, and of the independent agencies of government."

Many of our specific recommendations were eventually enacted into law or were adopted as guides to policy. Other recommenda-tions got nowhere—and with consequences that were to prove costly.

[V]

As my work with the commission unfolded, construction of the Oak Brook regional shopping center was at last ready to begin after legal and political delays. Sears, for example, was brought into the picture as a major anchor for the center, a matching piece to Field's. This set a pattern for Sears-Field's collaborations in later projects in which my associates and I were intimately involved.

The financing of the Oak Brook Shopping Center also led me to a new relationship with long-range consequences. Since Northwestern Life Insurance Company had helped finance Old Orchard, to everyone's advantage, I was prepared to offer it the same terms for an Oak Brook loan. When I approached Edward Fitzgerald, chairman of the board of Northwestern Mutual, he brought the full membership of his finance committee to the Oak Brook area to look it over. "Our boys," he reported, "are not happy with what they saw at Oak Brook. Unlike Old Orchard, with its lively human traffic, Oak Brook seems lost in rural isolation. Phil, if you really want to go ahead with the Oak Brook project, I'll convince my finance committee to make the loan, but the rate will be higher than at Old Orchard. On the other hand, if you can get better terms with another company, by all means take advantage of what they have to offer." The generous spirit behind the remark was typical of Fitzgerald, and I would count it an honor in later years when he nominated me to be a trustee of the Committee for Economic Development.

I passed Fitzgerald's comment along to Ferd Kramer. Kramer had long worked closely with the Aetna Life Insurance Company and had often urged me to look to it for financing. When he again urged me to do so, I entered into negotiations with Olcott Smith, chairman of the board at Aetna. The agreement we reached for financing Oak Brook marked the onset of close relationships between Aetna and the ventures in which my associates and I had an interest.

During the two years before construction began on Oak Brook Shopping Center in early 1959, I occasionally saw Paul Butler for an exchange of small talk. When he learned that Marshall Field's was moving ahead with the shopping center, he decided to build the village of Oak Brook on some of his own land. He asked if I would join him in forming a utility company to provide water and a sewage system for both the shopping center and the village. I said I would consider it subject to a major proviso based on my Park Forest experience: at some point in the future, the company would be sold to the village of Oak Brook. Butler agreed, and we jointly formed the Oak Brook Utility Company, and, as planned, eventually sold it to the village.

Charles Rhodes, a Field's executive, had specified what the Oak Brook Shopping Center should be like. "We want a quiet, restful, and aesthetically beautiful place to shop away from the noise of the city," he told me. That implied an open mall—an arrangement I always strongly favored unless exceptional factors warranted a closed facility. The case for closed malls—that they invite people to shop in both cold and hot weather—is not confirmed by behavior patterns. The costs of heating and air-conditioning a closed mall are immense, but women, who do most of the shopping, stay home on cold days. They also stay home on hot days while the air-conditioning system inside the closed mall serves only the employees who stand around with nothing to do. The attainment of Rhodes's objective was entrusted to the same team that had built Old Orchard. When the shopping center was completed in 1962, sixty stores opened for business. More stores were added as time went by, but from its opening day the center was a commercial and aesthetic success, and it often influenced the way shopping centers were planned by other developers.

26 □ "Debate" with Ben-Gurion

Soon after the start of construction on the Oak Brook Shopping Center, I was back in Israel for the triennial convention of the B'nai B'rith, the first ever held in Israel. The moment coincided with the tenth anniversary of Israel's admission into the United Nations in May 1949. Israel was so very young that the miracle of its birth could still be felt in its freshness by the B'nai B'rith delegates. They delighted in every symbol of the resurrection of the dead in Israel, the flag, the Hebrew letters on the planes of the Israeli National airline, Israeli stamps and currency with Hebrew symbols, the parade of Israel's armed forces, the debates in the Knesset.

As outgoing president of B'nai B'rith after six years of service, I was able to report to the convention that the Order was in good shape. An immediate postwar drop in membership had been reversed with an in-gathering of thousands of new members. Our budget was balanced, and more funds were going to various institutions that depended on B'nai B'rith for support. Our new international center in Washington was in operation and soon to be free of debt. Funds from West Germany, in compensation for B'nai B'rith property losses under the Hitler regime, and other funds from the sale to the West German government of the B'nai B'rith headquarters building in West Berlin, were put to constructive use in Israel. B'nai B'rith districts in Europe, decimated by the Nazis and by the impact of World War II, were revived and reorganized. B'nai B'rith adult education programs in Jewish studies were professionalized and shored up by budgeted funds. The activities of our youth-related programs were expanded and enriched.

The convention delegates approved my proposal to create an International Council of B'nai B'rith. Its purpose was to transform our overseas representatives from passive witnesses at B'nai B'rith conventions to active partners in matters of concern to us worldwide. After the election of Label Katz as my successor, I was chosen to serve as the first chairman of the International Council.

[II]

The convention became the setting for an unplanned debate on the relationship between the state of Israel and Jews in the Diaspora—and in America specifically. The nature of that relationship had increasingly come to dominate discussion among Jews inside and outside Israel. In earlier years as president of B'nai B'rith, I had dealt as best I could with a proposition that included a slogan about "the centrality of Israel in the scheme of Jewish survival." It was difficult to argue against the slogan without inviting the charge of indifference to the significance of Israel on its *own* terms. I never slighted the important place of Israel in the psyche of Jews; yet it was not frivolous to observe, for example, that to a group of religious Jews, the central issues of Jewish life were Torah and tradition. Besides, a preoccupation with the "centrality of Israel" might lead to the neglect of the needs of American Jewry itself. A weakening of American Jewry would bear hard on Jews everywhere and on Israel in particular.

When he spoke to our convention, Ben-Gurion argued that Jews of the Diaspora were still a minority, even where they lived in the freest and richest countries where they enjoyed full rights. In Israel, Jews were no longer a minority. In Israel they must do everything themselves. They must do all the work on the land, all the work in the mines, all the work in the factories, all the work in the laboratories, all the work in the schools, even all the work in the prisons. In Israel everything was Jewish, just as everything was human. In Israel, one could forget he was a Jew for everything around him was Jewish. The roads were paved by Jews, the trees were planted by Jews, the harbors were built by Jews—even the crimes were committed by Jews.

In Israel, he continued, Jews were "not split as Jews and as human beings but were linked in one human world." This was the fundamental difference between Jewish life in Israel and Jewish life even in countries where Jews enjoyed full and equal rights. "Two hundred years ago, Jews were united by their religion," Ben-Gurion said, "but the thing which now unites Jewry in the whole world, is the Jewish state of Israel."

Here Ben-Gurion posed the question whether the great center of Judaism created in the United States was absolutely safe in its Jewish future. He was raising the question, he said, not because of what happened to Jews in Europe. He was certain that such events would never happen in America. He had something else in mind, and it was the note on which he concluded his remarks:

> There is a legend known in Hebrew as *mitat n'shika*. It tells that when the time came for Moses to pass away, it was not the Angel of Death who was sent, but the Almighty Himself came and kissed Moses, so that his soul departed. *Mitat n'shika*—the kiss of death.
>
> In the past, in several countries, something has happened to Jews who enjoyed riches and good status. They disappeared as Jews by *mitat n'shika*. Unless there are sturdy links between American Jewry, Jews in other countries and the Jewish people in their own country, this fate may even befall that great Jewish community in the United States.

In my own remarks, I noted that all of us took solemn pride in the glory of Israel reborn, and we shared in our limited ways the travails of our brothers there. But just as those outside Israel must understand better the people of Israel, so Israelis must understand the hopes and motivations of Jews who lived outside their border. All of us had been so preoccupied with the emergent aspects of our relationship that we had not examined the events that were transforming Jewish life. I continued:

> Israel's first decade is not a fair measure of either the totality or character of its significance. The newness of the idea—which we have dramatized for ten years—will wear off. In another generation Jews reaching maturity will have lived their whole life, whether in Israel or elsewhere, in the familiarity of its statehood. This reality will tend to diminish the sense of personal glory and gratification that dug deep into our emotions as we of this generation stood witness to the achievement of an age-old dream. Most naturally, constructive criticism will tend to replace the willingness to forgive and forget that has been our relationship in the difficult formative days. The intense nationalism, without which Israel could not have struck her independence, and the swelling joy and sense of sacred commitment that have dominated the Jewish spirit throughout the world during the first decade, will begin to change, perhaps materially.
>
> Inexorable time will erase people and personalities whose roots were planted in an epoch of Jewish experience that will be strange to a nation of *sabras* and to Jewish communities that will not have known a world without Israel. The kind of interrelationships that will arise in the coming generation is not easy to forecast. It is not groundless, however, for us who span the two eras to set up some guideposts that the generation to come, geographically separated, may inherit as a basis for Jewish unity.

I went on to observe that most Jews would continue to live in lands other than Israel—a hard fact for extravagant nationalism to accept. I distinguished among three groups of Jews living outside of Israel. The first were comprised of those in underdeveloped nations with deplorably low standards of living—and often with government behavior to match. Many Jews from these lands would continue to seek their way to Israel, and it was axiomatic that "all of us assist their efforts to migrate." The second were those who lived under forms of government oppressive to their sense of Jewishness and abrasive to their human dignity. Some of them from time to time might escape or be permitted to migrate to other lands, Israel among them, where they could fully restore their Jewish personalities. In any case, in one way or another, "We must keep burning the flame, no matter how small, that is still lit in the souls of men and women of our faith who want to remain so in the face of their adversity."

Then there were those who lived where Jewish life was free

to flourish—the United States, Canada, western Europe, Latin America, Australia, Great Britain, and the like. Their social structures and forms of government did not restrict Jews from being Jews. In this free world, Jewish life could be as responsive as Jews wanted to make it. This was the group, representing about four times the number of Jews then living in Israel, whose relationship with Israel was a key challenge to Jewish life. These Jews must not be taken for granted by the people or spokesmen of Israel, they "must not be characterized in the Israeli mind as available targets for immigration campaigns—and their reluctance to emigrate derided." Of course it was within Israel's sovereign right to encourage immigration, and the "law of return" was one of the great moral justifications for its statehood. But it was both unwise and unproductive "for Israel to anticipate any disintegration of Jewish life in free lands, such as the United States, as a boon to large-scale *aliyah*.

American Jewry, I insisted, with all its faults, was the heart of Jewish possibilities outside Israel. No graver crisis could afflict Israel than the disintegration of Jewish life in America. At the same time, American Jews must understand that their relationship with their Jewish heritage and with Judaism itself was not coincidental with Israel as a state. The striving for personal adherence to Judaism might be easier in Israel than elsewhere, but I feared that too many Israelis and too many American Jews tended to view Judaism and Israel as identical. The tenets of Judaism, no more than those of wisdom, had no geographical bounds.

There were great opportunities for the advancement of Jewish consciousness and religiosity in every Jewish community in the free world. Even in Israel, I observed, nationalism was no substitute for fundamental Jewish bonds of religious faith, any more than philanthropic and secular activity fulfilled the life of the Jew elsewhere. The mission of Jewish existence entailed something more than a political structure or social expression. We needed to be partners in the divine enterprise of a small people holding aloft in tortured days the light of learning and spirit without which men could not be free nor human dignity be attainable. In conclusion, I said:

> Until this moment I have not used the word Diaspora. It is a perfectly good word expressive of the historical dispersion of our people. But in recent years I find the tendency to popularize it as a term of self-exile for Jews outside Israel, with absurd connotations of a second-class Jewishness because they lack the political framework of a Jewish state. . . . The Diaspora must be judged by its people, their work,

and their devotion to the Jewish mission, and not by its geography.

It could complicate the position of Jews in many places if Israel, in her future adjustments, fails to recognize the importance of the religious attitudes of Jews of the Diaspora with whom Israel would have an enduring relationship. It is not helpful in the interactions of a worldwide Jewish community if in these sacred precincts one interpretation of Judaism is denounced in favor of another.... The minimal understanding essential to a wholesome Jewish unity is a mutual respect for differing religious practices to which a Jewry which does believe has committed itself....

Neither Ben-Gurion nor I had the last word in this debate over the relationship between Israel and Jews of the Diaspora. The topic has continued to dominate the agenda of the Jewish people.

27 □ Germany Again

The first meeting of the newly authorized International Council of B'nai B'rith, of which I was chairman, was held in Amsterdam in late fall 1959. The small executive committee was comprised of representatives from the United States, Great Britain and Ireland, France and North Africa, western Europe, and Latin America.

The structural details agreed upon at the organizational meeting in Amsterdam had not yet been set in place when Jews and Jewish organizations everywhere suddenly confronted a plague of anti-Semitic vandalism unique in postwar history. It began when two neo-Nazi youths desecrated a new synagogue in Cologne, Germany, on Christmas Eve, 1959. In subsequent weeks, an epidemic of swastika smearing and anti-Jewish slogans spread over a substantial portion of the world until the frenzy peaked and subsided. In that period, 1,849 anti-Semitic incidents were reported in thirty-seven countries worldwide, including the United States.

Public statements in the United States by church officials and political leaders vigorously condemned the incidents. In the United States the events raised no questions about the inherent strength of American democracy; but Germany was a different story. Democratic forces in the free world, not Jews alone, voiced their fears that anti-Semitism might again become an "export" product of Germany.

The International Council of B'nai B'rith, meeting again in Amsterdam in January 1960, received a report from Benjamin R. Epstein, national director of the Anti-Defamation League of B'nai B'rith, in which he dismissed this fear. The ADL had consistently viewed the postwar German scene with a genuine desire to nurture democracy there. Its earlier studies, starting in 1954 and focused on German education problems and neo-Nazi movements, were recognized as constructive efforts. Based on a recent visit to Germany, Epstein doubted that the world was witnessing an international anti-Semitic Nazi conspiracy.

A few days after this ADL report, I received a personal message from Chancellor Konrad Adenauer asking if I could come to Bonn soon to discuss the anti-Semitic incidents in Germany and what could be done about them. I replied that I would come to Bonn at once. Then came his second message containing an apologetic withdrawal of the invitation. I later learned the reason for the turnabout.

Dr. Henrick van Dam, secretary of the Council of Jews in Germany, representing thirty thousand Jews in a total population of 53 million West Germans, had been incensed by actions of representatives of the World Jewish Congress and the American Jewish Committee. The first had arrived in Bonn armed with "ten point" demands which he put to Dr. Heinrich von Brentano, the foreign minister, and then claimed that von Brentano had endorsed the demands. The second, upon arriving in Bonn, charged publicly that anti-Semitic incidents in Germany were the work of Hungarian Nazis imported for that purpose.

Dr. van Dam had repeatedly suggested that the real cause for some of the strongest criticism abroad was anti-Germanism. In his view, anti-Semitic episodes gave foreigners a pretext to unleash their hostility toward the Federal Republic. He and the Central Council of Jews considered anti-Semitic incidents in Germany as internal matters to be dealt with by the council. The intervention of foreign Jewish organizations was not welcome.

That view, when made known to Dr. von Brentano, was conveyed by him to Chancellor Adenauer, who thereupon withdrew his invitation to me. Within forty-eight hours, however, the invitation was reinstated with apologies, and I had a constructive meeting in Bonn with the chancellor. We considered anew the merits of opening a B'nai B'rith office in Bonn—one that would provide authentic information to trustworthy sources inside the Federal Republic and to people the world over who were sensitive to events in Germany. Clearly, an expanded B'nai B'rith presence in Germany was needed.

Adenauer at the time was eighty-four years old. When he was approaching ninety, and still chancellor, he succumbed to a heavy cold. His personal physician, who could not be of much help, had to bear the brunt of his patient's impatience. "I'm not a magician," the harassed doctor protested. "I can't make you young." "I haven't asked you to," Adenauer replied. "All I want is to go on getting older."

He did not continue to get older. Yet within his long span of life, whose changing fortunes included persecution by the Nazis who ultimately sent him to a concentration camp, what Adenauer achieved stood on a plane of its own among postwar leaders of the first rank. He cannot be credited with the "miracle" that led to West Germany's economic recovery amid a sea of rubble. That "miracle" was presided over by his minister of finance, Ludwig Erhard. What stood of Adenauer's credit involved something of greater importance and greater difficulty. He had the rare moral authority and political strength to make his own consciousness the source of a return to health in the consciousness of his fellow West Germans—to have them take their bearing from the proposition that the state must guarantee optimal room to the individual for independent intellectual and economic development, and their absolute protection under a rule of law supreme over governors and governed alike.

28 □ Dilemmas of Choice

Although Sargent Shriver periodically urged me to join in support of the campaign for John F. Kennedy—or better yet, to persuade Adlai Stevenson to do so—I continued to adhere to my earlier stand. "As long as there is a chance of Adlai getting the Democratic nomination," I repeatedly told Shriver, "you can't count on me." I did attend a luncheon which Shriver gave for Kennedy in the Merchandise Mart in Chicago just after the Wisconsin primary. It was my first face-to-face meeting with the senator since our conversation in his office in the spring of 1958. "I hope," he said to me in his graceful way, "the time soon comes when I can convince you that you ought to be on our team."

When Hubert Humphrey withdrew from the race for the nomination after the West Virginia primary later in May, the contest within the Democratic party shaped up as a head-to-head conflict between Kennedy and Lyndon Johnson. Stevenson's law partners, Newton Minow and Bill Blair, now urged me to meet privately with him. I should try to persuade him to shed his strict neutrality and come out for Kennedy. Although I did not share their purpose, I did meet with Stevenson at his invitation.

"Phil," he began, "I know it looks as if I am playing hard to get until Jack or Lyndon offers me what I want. I have reason to believe I could be Secretary of State if I now endorse either Jack or Lyndon—who then goes on to win the presidency. The fact is that being Secretary of State is the one post I'd rather have above the presidency itself. But Phil, I simply can't declare for either of the two when I gave my pledge to both men, and to Stu Symington as well, that I'd not take sides in the fight for the nomination."

"Look, Adlai," I replied, "there is another reason why you should not endorse either man. No one knows for certain if Jack or Lyndon will have enough votes to prevail in the convention. Suppose the two knock each other out? What will the party do then? To whom will it turn? You owe it to the country, and not merely to the party, to keep yourself available for the nomination in case the duel between Kennedy and Johnson ends in a deadlocked convention."

"Phil," Stevenson now said almost tearfully, "do you really appreciate what it means to run for the presidency—how many babies you have to kiss—how many men and women you have to embrace—how you must ceaselessly be on guard against a single misspoken word? And that's only the start of the price you pay—physical, emotional, intellectual—when you run for the presidency."

"Adlai," I said, without offering him a piece of Kleenex, "it would be a tremendous letdown for the party and for the country if you were not available for the nomination in case of need."

"But if you had to choose," Stevenson said, as if he were suddenly engaged in a calculation of cost-benefits, "which one would *you* choose—Jack or Lyndon?"

"I have no problem with that," I said. "I would choose Jack. He's young, more attractive, and I think he can do a better job than Lyndon in pulling the country together. But I don't think you should endorse either one of them." I gave him bad advice, but in view of the different kinds of advice he was getting from countless other sources, mine was scarcely decisive.

By early July, when delegates to the Democratic convention converged on Los Angeles, Stevenson, evidently against his conscious will, had emerged as the candidate for a mushrooming movement. I was not at the convention, but friends on the scene gave me reports of enthusiasm for Stevenson that was on the rise.

As was learned later, the stirring speech in which Senator Eugene McCarthy placed Stevenson's name in nomination was approved by the Johnson camp in an attempt to break the back of the Kennedy coalition. But there was no stampede for Stevenson. With Kennedy's nomination secured, requirements for a balanced ticket made Lyndon Johnson the vice presidential nominee.

[II]

It was after the Democratic convention that I became involved in John Kennedy's presidential campaign. At the invitation of Robert Kennedy and in the company of Newton Minow, I went to Robert Kennedy's home in McLean, Virginia, to help plan some of the special organizational aspects of the bid for the presidency. Others in attendance included two future members of the Kennedy cabinet—Byron A. White, who was to serve as Kennedy's attorney general before being appointed to the U.S. Supreme Court; and Luther Hodges, a former vice president of Marshall Field's in Chicago, governor of North Carolina, and a future Secretary of Commerce. At the meeting I was asked to work with Luther Hodges on a "businessman's operation" for the campaign.

While Luther Hodges was active throughout the South, the businessman's operation was headquartered in Chicago where it could be close to Shriver. I chaired its executive committee and helped raise money within the business community nationally. A tidy sum was raised, but we often had to play catch-up ball when Shriver committed funds for emergency matters without actually having the money in hand. It was up to the executive committee to find the funds to cover bills as they came due. It was hard pickings at times—compared with the success Lyndon Johnson later had in 1964 with the business community—but when the chips were down, the candidate's father, Joseph Kennedy, was counted on to help out.

Besides being involved on the cash-and-carry side of the Kennedy campaign, I tried to deal with lukewarm or even outright hostility to Kennedy in certain Jewish circles. He had never ruffled Jewish sensibilities by anything he had done or failed to do. But he was saddled with a belief widely held within the Jewish community that his father, Joseph Kennedy, on the eve of World War II, had been an "appeaser" friendly to Nazism. The charge that Joseph Kennedy was an anti-Semite surfaced in different forms and places during the campaign.

In my representations within the Jewish community, I advanced the doctrine of personal accountability for one's own actions. Myer Feldman, who had been on Kennedy's Senate staff for some time, was entrusted with the task of holding the large Jewish community in New York in line. When Mike faced troubles that could not be resolved on the spot, he sometimes contacted me in Chicago. I would then try to arrange some sort of redemptive operation, or would suggest the names of people in New York to whom he could turn for help.

By far the most impressive source of help, however, was Kennedy himself. Governor Abraham Ribicoff and Myer Feldman, aided by Abe Feinberg, brought together about fourteen Jewish leaders of national stature for a private meeting with Senator Kennedy in Feinberg's New York apartment. While there, Kennedy exposed himself to the most searching questions one could put to a presidential candidate. No holds were barred, no punches pulled, no hedging. The questions asked were not about immigration or human rights. Kennedy had written a leading pamphlet on immigration, and his record on human rights was good enough to satisfy the tastes of purists. The questions focused on his father's attitudes toward Jews and toward Nazism.

Kennedy fielded the questions calmly and spoke at length about his feelings toward his father; he was always at his best when he spoke off the cuff about something he understood fully and believed. He explained that a president may have a father who is alive, but the father can't make policy for him. "Nonetheless," he went on to say, "I won't mislead you. I have great confidence in my father's judgments on many things, and I have reason to be grateful for being able to turn to him for counsel. On the other hand, my father respects my own position when it is at variance with his, and with the need to make my own decisions and stick with them." The manly response touched chords of sympathy among Jewish leaders, themselves attuned to the affections and tensions of father-son relationships.

For the Jewish community as a whole, the end of the nagging skepticism about Kennedy and the full turn in his favor date from an event on August 26, in New York City's Hilton Hotel. Leading Zionists of America were to meet there. Through a Chicago Zionist we arranged for Kennedy to be invited to address the delegates. I had previously questioned the choice of that forum because I thought it would be possible to get Kennedy a better setting for a "Jewish speech." Kennedy, fortunately, was not deterred by my doubts. Once he decided to appear at that Zionist meeting, I contributed a few thoughts to what he might say. The speech he gave, however, was his own. It had none of the fuzziness about the Middle East that had troubled me in speeches of his 1958 vintage.

Max Bressler, a Chicagoan and good friend, and the president of the Zionist Organization of America, was responsible for the seating arrangement. He placed me on the dais next to Rabbi Abba Hillel Silver. I saw that when Kennedy was introduced, he glanced at his prepared remarks, laid the text aside, and then proceeded to speak eloquently from memory, without a stammer. He won the audience when he said straight off, "Prophecy is a Jewish tradition, and the World Zionist movement, in which all of you have played so important a role, has continued that tradition. It has turned the dreams of its leaders into acts of statesmanship. It has converted the hopes of the Jewish people into concrete facts of life."

Next, in a reference to Theodore Herzl, the prophet of Zionism, Kennedy noted that when Herzl proclaimed the ideal of Jewish nationhood, it was "a classic case of an ancient dream finding a young leader," for Herzl was only thirty-seven years old at the time. "Perhaps," said Kennedy, "I may be allowed the observation that the Jewish people—ever since David slew Goliath—have never considered youth a barrier to leadership, or measured experience by maturity or mere length of days." He then proceeded to compare the bleak Palestine he saw in 1939 with the "grandeur" he saw in Israel when he returned there in 1951. "Israel," he declared, "was not created in order to disappear. It will endure and flourish. It is the child of hope and the home of the brave. It carries the shield of democracy and it honors the sword of freedom; and no era of the world has ever had an overabundance of democracy and freedom." All this, so far, was overture, music to the ears.

What followed was a thrust to the mind and an appeal to the heart.

> It is worth remembering that Israel is a cause that stands beyond the ordinary changes and chances of American public life. In our pluralistic society, it has not been a Jewish cause—any more than Irish independence was solely the concern of Americans of Irish descent. The ideals of Zionism have, in the last half-century, been repeatedly endorsed by presidents and members of Congress from both parties. Friendship for Israel is not a partisan matter. It is a national commitment.
>
> Yet within this tradition of friendship there is a special obligation on the Democratic party. It was President Woodrow Wilson who forecast with prophetic wisdom the creation of a Jewish homeland. It was President Franklin Roosevelt who kept alive the hopes of Jewish redemption during the Nazi terror. It was President Harry Truman who first recognized the new state of Israel and gave it status in world affairs. And may I add that it would be my hope and my pledge to continue this Democratic tradition—and to be worthy of it.

This was followed by a bill of particulars in which Kennedy indicted the Eisenhower administration for its failures in the Middle East. What could a new president do? The next president, he said, should always be personally available to stimulate every experiment in cooperation, from the joint development of a river, to a reconsideration of the Arab refugee problem, to the crowning mercy of the final reconciliation that could be brought only by a true peace settlement. "In this task," Kennedy said, "I ask for your assistance, your patience, your wisdom, and your support—until we can say to Jew and Arab alike: 'Peace be within thy walls and plenteousness within thy palaces. For my brethren and companion's sake, I will wish thee prosperity.'"

At the end of the speech, as the audience rose for an ovation,

Rabbi Abba Hillel Silver put a question to me: "Is he for real?" Silver, known for his own power as an orator, was a close friend of the Taft family in Ohio and himself a Republican who seldom had anything good to say about Democrats. "Yes," I replied, "he *is* for real." "In that case," Silver said, "he will be getting my vote." The remark symbolized in microcosm the major breakthrough Kennedy had achieved in the attitudes of the Jewish community with that one speech.

[III]

My interest in serving in a Kennedy administration was an iffy thing—maybe yes, but for the time being mostly no. At one point during the presidential contest, a New York operative in the Kennedy camp drew me to one side to say in a conspiratorial voice, "You know, Luther Hodges wants to be Secretary of Commerce if Kennedy wins. You're not a contender for the post, are you?" "If Luther wants it," I replied, "I'm for him. He's entitled to it." Still, the prospect that I might be asked to serve in the new administration if Kennedy defeated Richard Nixon accounts for an understanding I reached in early fall 1960 with the leaders of the United Jewish Appeal (UJA).

When I stepped down from the B'nai B'rith presidency in 1959, I had been pressed from many sides to accept the UJA chairmanship. I managed for a while to hold off these pressures, saying that my business interests needed attention after my six years of concern with B'nai B'rith affairs. In the summer of 1960, however, because of disarray in UJA affairs in key communities, UJA leaders urged me anew to accept the presidency and the chairmanship of the fund-raising campaign. I explained that I wished to remain free of encumbrances in the event Senator Kennedy was elected president and I was offered a place in his administration. This proviso was understood, and I tentatively agreed to accept the UJA positions in mid-December 1960.

Immediately after Kennedy's hairline victory in November, Shriver telephoned me to ask my appraisal of prospects for certain posts in the administration. "And now," he said, "what do *you* want?" "I don't want anything in particular," I replied, "and I am not asking for anything." "Well look," he said, "you've got to be in the new administration. You helped do this, and you did that." "Sarge," I said, "I've been in and out of government enough, and

I'd like to rest for a little while. Besides, I've got some business things I want to do." "No," he insisted, "you've got to come in."

Our conversation resumed when I was back in Chicago. Shriver asked my judgment about the person whom the Kennedy people had in mind to head the Housing and Home Finance Agency—Robert Weaver, an African-American who had once worked with me. I urged his appointment. I learned that Adlai Stevenson was out of the running for Secretary of State, but that he had been offered the post of permanent U.S. representative to the United Nations. "He hasn't accepted it," Shriver continued. "See what you can do about getting him to take it. He's your friend. Right now he's in Bill Benton's apartment in New York. You talk to him." "I don't want to get into the man's business," I replied, "but I happen to think that if Adlai is not going to be Secretary of State, his is the one voice we need in the U.N. I will certainly talk to him."

The membership of the United Nations had increased by more than a third just during the eight years of the Eisenhower presidency, from sixty to ninety-nine members. This made the task of the United States representative much more formidable. When I reached Stevenson by phone in Bill Benton's New York apartment, I ran through all the arguments in favor of his accepting the U.N. post—his consuming interest in foreign affairs and his stature in the world arena. I also dwelt on the importance of his being part of the incoming administration whose leaders were, in a real sense, the direct heirs of his own work as a "public teacher" during the preceding eight years.

In response to my "lawyer's brief," Stevenson said, "I know I am not going to be able to turn down the offered post, but I don't want to accept it before they appoint a Secretary of State. I want to know with whom I am going to be working." His position made sense, and I passed on to Shriver the substance of our conversation.

During this same period, I received a call from a Texas businessman, a friend of Lyndon Johnson and a home builder who had actively supported the Kennedy-Johnson ticket after the nominating convention. "Phil," he said, "we're in a hell of a box. We have it on direct authority that the Kennedy people are arranging to appoint a black man as head of HHFA. We've talked to Lyndon Johnson about it, and he said that if we could get a good alternative candidate, we could defeat him. We want you to be the candidate."

"Let's get one thing straight," I replied. "I've been in the housing agency in the course of my life, and I understand the fellow under consideration to head it is Robert Weaver. Bob has worked with me in years past, and I'm for him. I would not under any circumstances be a candidate to oppose him. Besides, I will do everything I can to defeat you if you try to get someone else to knock him out of consideration for the post—provided, of course, he wants it."

I immediately contacted Shriver so that he would know what was afoot. "If Bob wants to be the head of HHFA," I said, "he should have the job. But if you intend to appoint him, you'd better do it quickly before the opposition to him jells. The home builders are afraid of him. Others are afraid of him." Shriver said he got the message, but then asked a question. "How about yourself?" "Myself?" I replied. "I'm sitting where I am right here in Chicago."

<h2 style="text-align:center">[IV]</h2>

When Stevenson learned that Dean Rusk would be named Secretary of State, he agreed to accept the U.N. appointment. He now had two posts to fill at the U.N.—or, more precisely, to recommend to the president-elect. He asked me "to take one or the other of them. You can be Assistant Secretary of State for International Organizations, or you can be a minister at the U.N. and the U.S. representative to the Economic and Social Council. Now which one do you want?"

"I don't want either one."

"You're going to have to take one," Stevenson insisted. "You helped get me into this whole thing. You could be my man in Washington in the State Department Bureau of International Organizations which deals directly with the U.N. and U.N. agencies."

"And if I don't take that post," I asked, "whom are you considering for it?" He mentioned some of the possibilities. "And whom are you considering for the other post if I don't want it?" He indicated whom he had in mind. "Give me a little time to think the matter over," I said, "and I'll be back to you."

Stevenson's offer in early December 1960 came when I had just been formally elected president of the UJA. Still, given the conditions I had previously set when I agreed to accept the office, I could—so I thought—gracefully bow out of the UJA presidency if I wished to accept either of Stevenson's posts.

I made it a point to read all the material I had on file about the Economic and Social Council of the United Nations. When I next saw Stevenson, I said it was inadvisable for me to go to Washington "to be his man." It was not possible to be an Assistant Secretary of State and yet be responsible to him in New York. An Assistant Secretary of State is directly responsible to the Secretary of State. Besides, Stevenson had a first-rate prospect for the post in Harlan Cleveland. By any test—intelligence, experience, character, vision, administrative ability—he was superbly qualified to be Assistant Secretary of State for International Organizations. Cleveland was chosen for the post, along with a strong deputy, Richard Gardner, a professor of international law at Columbia University.

The Economic and Social Council of the U.N. was another matter. I said I was interested in it but would not accept an appointment on a part-time basis. The council, which included eighteen member states, was one of the five principal organs of the United Nations. Its supervisory jurisdiction covered eight functional commissions and subcommissions, four regional economic commissions, four standing committees, and, by the latest count, fifteen special bodies concerned with world cooperation in the fields of economic and social welfare and cultural development.

It was not possible for the U.S. representative to the council to work at it only part time and yet stay in touch with the thinking of the member states. It was a full-time job. I would have to move to New York and arrange for the schooling there of my three younger sons. I would have to spend between six to eight weeks each year in Geneva. Besides, I wouldn't take the job at the protocol rank of minister. In studying the U.N. records for the previous ten years, I found that nearly all the representatives of the major powers in the Economic and Social Council held the rank of ambassador or higher. It didn't make sense for the U.S. representative to deal with them from a subordinate diplomatic status.

"How can I make you an ambassador?" Stevenson asked.

"You don't make me anything," I replied. "The president does."

Stevenson subsequently talked to Kennedy, who saw no difficulty in arranging my designation as an ambassador.

There was, however, another kind of difficulty in prospect. "Adlai," I said, "I want you to think carefully as to whether you really want me. Remember, a permanent post in the U.N. for an

American Jew at this time is not the easiest thing in the world to carry off. Besides, a book I worked on since 1959—*No Easy Answers*—is set for publication next month by Farrar Straus. It is not autobiographical, but it contains some chapters where I use certain personal experiences as a peg for my reflections about Israel and Israeli leaders. It is in no way an automatic defense of everything Israel has done, but the last two chapters contain an assessment of Nasser and the Arab bloc as well as an assessment of Israel's reactions to them."

"Don't worry about that," Stevenson replied. "You couldn't say anything I wouldn't be able to live with."

"Maybe you should read the manuscript before you express your confidence," I said.

"No, no, no," Stevenson insisted. "I know what you say is all right, perfectly all right.... I want you to take the U.N. post that will be offered to you."

I didn't talk to Kennedy about any aspects of the matter, because I was not going to work directly for the president. I was going to work for Stevenson. I'd been in the bureaucracy long enough to know that you had better make up your mind exactly whom you're working for. I finally said to Adlai, "If you accept my conditions, I accept yours." That seemed to be that.

[V]

The Senate Foreign Relations Committee, under the chairmanship of Senator J. William Fulbright, set January 18, 1961, as the date for the confirmation hearings of Stevenson's nomination as U.S. representative to the United Nations. Hearings on my own nomination as U.S. representative to the Economic and Social Council were set for January 31.

Aside from my impending resignation from the UJA and from the executive committee of the B'nai B'rith International Council, I reviewed my involvement in business enterprises to see which among them should be discontinued. I recognized that it would be inappropriate for me to represent the United States in the U.N. and yet continue to be involved in the building of the city of Ashdod in Israel. I contacted Oved Ben-Ami, my partner in the construction of Ashdod, and explained why I must withdraw from the Ashdod project. Ben-Ami voiced his regret, but volunteered to break the news to Levi Eshkol before I contacted the Israeli finance minister myself.

When I later spoke to Eshkol by international telephone, his voice lacked its usual playfulness. "You can't withdraw from the building of Ashdod!" he cried. "You have a contract with the Israeli government to see it through!"

"I recognize," I said in response to his agitated words, "that from a legal standpoint you are perfectly right. That is exactly why I am asking you to relieve me of the contract. If you don't, I will have to tell President-elect Kennedy that I can't accept the appointment he has offered me—not because I don't want to serve my government, but because *you* won't let me."

"*Gonif!*" he cried from halfway around the world. "You wouldn't do *that!*"

"Oh yes, I would," I said.

The moment of silence at the Israeli end of the phone was deafening while Eshkol digested the import of what he had just heard. "All right," he said finally, "we will work things out to give you relief from your contract." As a realist, he accepted the fact that a "call" from a president of the United States for the services of a willing and consenting individual is a species of "higher law" which takes precedence over other things.

At the hearing for my confirmation, Senator Fulbright, who was known as a critic of the "Israeli lobby" in Washington and of Israeli policy toward its Arab neighbors, quickly zeroed in on my identity with Jewish causes. This did not diminish my admiration for the man; we later became good friends, in close accord on matters that once appeared to divide us. His remarks at the hearing turned on the question of whether I could objectively serve the interests of the United States. An extract from the committee hearing reads:

> *The Chairman*: You have been extremely prominent... and very successful, in the United Jewish Appeal work, and I believe you have been President of the B'nai B'rith, have you not?
>
> *Mr. Klutznick*: I served as International President of B'nai B'rith for some six years, and by virtue of that service, by constitutional mandate, I become for life an honorary President of the B'nai B'rith. In addition, I have served, and do now serve as chairman of its International Council. In that connection I... will, if confirmed, resign from these responsibilities because I do not consider them wholly consistent with

my responsibility in this connection. With respect to the United Jewish Appeal, sir, from youth on I have been interested in activities of this kind. I have been National Chairman, and more lately elected as the General Chairman of the campaign for this year, and President of the United Jewish Appeal. I have already tendered my resignation from those positions in the event I am confirmed. . . .

The Chairman: And you believe that, in representing the United States, you could take an objective and impartial view involving Arab countries? You have no prejudice against assisting Arab countries?

Mr. Klutznick: Sir, I not only have no prejudice against assisting them . . . [We must do what we can] to develop the underdeveloped countries and to assist all people who are in need and who are lacking the capacity to help themselves; and in doing so, to create the atmosphere in which to help themselves, and I do not exclude this from anyone, whether they be Arab, Jews, Buddhist, or anything else. If I did I would not be sitting here.

When Senator Fulbright paused in this line of questioning, Senator Wayne Morse and others turned the tone around. But I was treated by Senator Russell Long to unexpected support.

Senator Long: . . . With your background of having been so active in organizations such as the United Jewish Appeal, you are, of course, necessarily going to have to deal with these Arab countries in many instances. Just from what little I know of you, I know you can work with them. Let me ask you whether these representatives of these Arab countries are going to be able to work with you.

Mr. Klutznick: I hope the fact that I was born a Jew, and not a chauvinistic Jew, but rather a simple believing one, does not disqualify me. In this sense of trying—and I know you believe it—in my serving my country and in serving it in the way that I may best serve it. . . .

I am sufficiently realistic to recognize the merit of your inquiry, and I must say my experience in the United Nations in 1957 indicated that it took at least six weeks before I could meet with the representatives of some of those countries in a way where we trusted each other. I do not think this is necessarily true only of Americans who are Jews. I have seen Americans of other persuasions who have had some difficulties with the countries in the Middle East and elsewhere because of their past history . . . I would hope that my behavior and my participation would demonstrate that it is conclusively possible for an American of Jewish faith to not only do justice but to be helpful to those who historically were cousins of his, now known as members of Arab nations. This I hope for above all.

Senator Long: I appreciate your fine statement, and in a somewhat related problem I undertook the task of persuading Protestants in my state, some of whom found it very difficult to believe that a Catholic could be President without permitting his religion to interfere with his politics. And in some instances I was successful and in some others I was not successful. One point I made repeatedly was that if you never give a Catholic a chance to prove that he can meet the other fellow with complete goodwill, we would never know. And I would hope very much that those with whom you deal, particularly those from the Arab countries, would meet you on the same basis that you propose to meet them, because I think there is a lot to be achieved if they will. Thank you very much.

The committee voted unanimously to confirm. There was, however, a near miss afterward when I was set to be sworn in at the State Department. I was stopped in my tracks by a telephone call from Adlai Stevenson. "The people at the State Department," he said, "have read the galley proofs of your book *No Easy Answers*. They are terribly upset about the chapters on Nasser and the Arabs."

"Well, Adlai," I said, "I warned you this might happen. I'll stay home. It's perfectly all right."

"Oh, no, no," he said. "Don't worry about it. I just wanted you to know."

"Adlai," I said, "I am not going to stultify myself. Now you'd better call me back and tell me it's all right, or I won't come. I told you beforehand what was in that book, and I told you to read it."

There was a follow-up call from Stevenson: "Go down and get yourself sworn in." I did so in the presence of my family, and left with them afterward for the new life that was awaiting us in New York.

A week later, Roger Tubby, acting public affairs officer in the State Department, began pressing me. "Phil," he said, "you don't have to publish the last two chapters of your book on U.S. foreign policy in the Middle East, with Nasser and the Arabs. You can publish those chapters after you leave the U.N. and add a lot more to them."

In the end, it was the State Department people who went to the publisher of *No Easy Answers*. They got Farrar Straus to agree to publish only the half of the book that dealt with domestic matters, and to leave the remaining half about foreign affairs for publication at an indeterminate later date.

29 □ Working Around the Clock

In New York, Ethel and I moved into the old Park Lane Hotel across the street from the Waldorf Astoria, which was the official residence of the head of the U.S. mission to the U.N. The arrangement was suited to the entertainment that is part of the business of politicking at the U.N.

Two of our three older children were now on their own, and a third soon would be. Bettylu, our oldest child and only daughter, and her husband Dr. Paul Saltzman were established in Chicago where Paul specialized in internal medicine. They now were parents of a child, with a second on the way.

Tom, the oldest of our four sons, had married Ellen Diengott when he was a junior at Oberlin and she was a student at Smith College. With Tom's graduation from Oberlin in June 1960, the young couple returned to Chicago where Tom planned to enter the University of Chicago Graduate School of Business. But the world of action was more to his taste, and he arranged a job in the Oak Brook office of the Draper and Kramer firm that would be managing the rental properties of the new development.

Jim, our second-oldest son, was completing his senior year at Lake Forest Academy on Chicago's North Shore, and soon decided to attend Princeton. With the move to New York, our two youngest sons, Bob and Sam, were enrolled in the Riverdale School, a private institution. They lived in the school dormitory during the week, but they joined Ethel and me on weekends. Time would show that the pair were affected in radically different ways by their formative years in New York City. Bob eventually placed as much distance as he could between himself and the big city, and established himself in Boulder, Colorado. Sam, on the other hand, fell in love with the excitement of New York. As a youth at Riverdale, he often spent his free hours watching sessions of the

U.N. In later life, he made his permanent home in New York City, where he divided his attention between the world of the theater and the world of finance.

[II]

Aside from foreign service veterans such as Charles Yost, the political appointees who comprised the full-time membership of the U.S. delegation under Stevenson were Francis Plimpton, Stevenson's former roommate at the Harvard Law School and his deputy at the U.N., and Jonathan Bingham, U.S. representative on the U.N. Trusteeship Council. The part-time members included Marietta Tree, U.S. representative on the Human Rights Commission, and Jane Edison Dick, one of Stevenson's intimates from Lake Forest.

Except for the head of the U.S. mission at the U.N., the government in those years provided no housing and little "representation" allowances for the other members of the mission. The rest of us had to draw on our private resources to cover the costs of such matters. My rent alone at the Park Lane Hotel annually came to $25,000 (at 1960 prices)—a sum equal to my salary, before taxes.

In the world of the U.N., which had no real equivalent in the world of Washington, entertainment was not fun and games. The rounds of breakfasts, luncheons, cocktail parties, and suppers were as much a part of U.N. diplomacy as *aide-mémoire*, debates, resolutions, and reports of commissions. I tried to attend every social function to which I was invited, regardless of the political source of the invitation. I also hosted parties attended by representatives from communist countries, from Latin America, from the newly independent nations, and from the traditional Western allies of the United States. The real menu at these parties was a confection of wheeling and dealing bearing on pieces of official business.

An aspect of Stevenson of which I was aware in previous years, became all the more vivid for me when I was associated with him at the U.N. This was his obsessive concern with saving money, whether it was his own or the government's. In traveling together on official business, I noticed that his battered bag cried out for a replacement before it disintegrated, but Stevenson was majestically indifferent to it. On one occasion—over a weekend in Switzerland—I glanced down at his odd-looking pair of shoes and teasingly asked why he chose to wear them. "Well," he explained earnestly, "you remember the 1952 presidential campaign picture which showed a hole in the sole of one of the shoes I had on. After that, I must have received in the mail several hundred pairs of shoes sent me from around the country. I'm wearing a pair from that stock right now, and I have far to go before I wear out the rest which I have on hand."

When we lunched together in New York City, Stevenson would ordinarily return to the U.S. mission in his official car. Once, however, at the end of a lunch, he said to me, "Do you mind if I drop you off at the mission? I've got to go over to Brooks Brothers to buy a tuxedo." "Are you," I said, "still buying tuxedos there like a college student?" "Yes," he answered, and then went on to defend himself. "I was at a formal dinner party in Washington," he explained, "and as I was being seated next to the hostess, I looked down and there were my tux trousers with a big rip. I had worn those trousers for only ten years. I don't know why they couldn't have lasted longer."

[III]

At the U.N., Stevenson and I were not always of one mind on policy issues. There were differences, for example, in our perceptions about events in the Middle East. I was not personally involved in articulating U.S. policy; that was Stevenson's responsibility, backstopped by his able deputy, Charles Yost. It was understood, however, that if a Middle East problem arose which had a U.S. *domestic* political angle, Myer Feldman might call me to ask for a discussion at the White House about the matter.

An early visit of this kind concerned a presidential decision on the allocation of funds to certain Middle East countries by the U.S. Agency for International Development (AID). Feldman informed me about the pending discussion of the issue at the White House, and added that others due to be present were Arthur Goldberg, Secretary of Labor, and Abraham Ribicoff, Secretary of Health, Education and Welfare. I asked Stevenson if he objected to my taking part in such a meeting. "Of course not," he said. "Go down to Washington and help out in any way that you can."

That particular White House meeting remains fresh in my memory for a special reason. Once our conversation was over, President Kennedy said to me, "Mr. Ambassador, when you get back to New York, tell Governor Stevenson to do this and so regarding what we've decided." "Mr. President," I replied, "I can't do that. I work for the governor and am his subordinate. I don't think you would want me to appear to be giving him an order." President Kennedy looked at me as though I were a strange apparition, but he broke the strained moment by saying, "You are quite right." He then turned to Feldman and said, "Mike, will you see to it that *I* tell Governor Stevenson what he needs to know and do."

Although my personal affection for Stevenson was deep and abiding, I came to sympathize with Secretary of State Dean Rusk because he was dogged by the problem of Stevenson's very existence. The nature of the case was vividly brought home to me when Stevenson, the Rusks and their daughter, and Ethel and I had dinner together in New York and then went on to see the show *How to Succeed in Business Without Really Trying*. My seat was next to Rusk's. At intermission, none in our party headed outward. All remained seated. I noticed that few people in the audience had moved toward the lobby. Most were on their feet staring in ways which brought our own row into view. "Mr. Secretary," I said to Dean Rusk, "they've certainly got their eyes fixed on you." "No, Phil," he said as he pointed to Stevenson, "not with *him* sitting there."

30 □ Storm in the Congo

The outgoing Eisenhower administration had bequeathed to the Kennedy administration a crisis in the Congo and Laos, and the making of a third one involving Cuba. At the U.N. I was straight off immersed in matters related to the Congo crisis.

The violent events which shook the Congo at the start of the 1960s are today but dim memories to most Americans. Three great issues were entwined in the turmoil: Would the United

Nations survive as an institution or die of financial and political bankruptcy? Could the U.N. play a leading role not merely as a forum for debate but as an agency that could help build a nation out of tribes? Would the communist bloc countries, led by the Soviet Union, secure a foothold in the heart of the African continent—and at the same time place a halter around the neck of the U.N. secretary general?

Between July and October 1960, sixteen new African nations were admitted into the United Nations in almost pell-mell fashion. The giant Belgian Congo, renamed the Republic of the Congo after being granted independence, entered the United Nations on July 11, following the formation of a central government with Joseph Kasavubu as president and Patrice Lumumba as prime minister. The bunting had scarcely been removed from the independence celebration when violence flared between major Congolese tribes, followed by a mutiny in the Belgian-officered Congo army. With police joining the mutineers, the attacks on the officers were accompanied by widespread looting, onslaughts against Belgians generally, and the rape of Belgian women. In the wake of the disorders, fifteen thousand Europeans left the Congo while Belgian forces in the country, reinforced by units sent from Belgium, intervened to protect the Belgian residents who remained.

The Congolese government broke off official relations with Belgium, and Lumumba asked the United Nations to intervene. His request had a strong advocate in Dag Hammarskjold, the U.N. secretary general. Hammarskjold had sought to make the U.N. the chosen instrument of mankind in its quest for salvation—he referred to himself as a "secular pope." He kept out of the area of direct Soviet-American confrontations, such as Berlin, but concentrated on peacekeeping in the Third World, with himself as commander-in-chief of the peacekeeping forces.

Hammarskjold drew on the authority vested in his office and sent a U.N. force to suppress the civil strife among the rival Congolese, particularly the critical clash between the "central government" and the rich breakaway Kantanga province. The Soviet Union denounced this action and mounted what became a protracted campaign to replace the secretary general with a *troika* or triumvirate representing three groups of nations—communist, Western, and uncommitted. Hammarskjold, standing his ground, rejected the plan as prejudicial to the interests of smaller and new nations.

He survived the first Soviet onslaught, but the Soviets had another string to their bow, and it was aimed at cutting down the whole of the U.N. operation in the Congo. The most vulnerable point in the fall of 1960 was the U.N.'s financial crisis, chiefly because of the situation in the Congo. The U.N. finances its activities through direct assessment of members, voluntary contributions, and a combination of the two. Among other failings, the Soviet Union, other communist members, the Arab states, and some others had refused to pay their assessments or contribute in any way toward the costs of maintaining the U.N. emergency force in Palestine.

By November the U.N. had no more than 32 percent of the funds needed to support its Congo operations, and it was reprieved from bankruptcy only through two acts of grace. Certain governments did not present bills for services rendered the United Nations, and the outgoing Eisenhower administration made substantial advance cash payments to the U.N. on behalf of the United States.

By December 1960, political divisions in the Congolese republic became all the more menacing. Provinces withdrew from the central government and resisted by force any attempt to bring them back to the fold. Unable to discover any central government capable of exercising control, U.N. representatives in the Congo faced an even greater crisis when Lumumba, who had been held captive in Leopoldville by his rival, General Mobutu, was flown to Elisabethville, the capital of Katanga. He was reported to have been ill treated during the journey that placed him in the hands of a mortal enemy, Moise Tshombe. Fears of reprisals by Lumumba's supporters were accentuated by reports of violent turmoil in areas loyal to him.

That was the prevailing picture in the Congo when Kennedy took office in January 1961. His first State Department appointment was former Michigan Governor G. Mennen Williams as Assistant Secretary for African Affairs—also the first person to hold that newly created post. The financial aspects of the U.N. operation in the Congo were precarious in the extreme when I joined the U.S. delegation at the end of January.

[II]

Any hope of a *rapprochement* among the contending factions in the

Congo was shattered by the announcement on February 10, 1961, that Lumumba had escaped his captors in Elisabethville. Three days later came news of his death. It was widely held, both inside and outside the country, that this was a case of political murder—a conclusion later officially supported by a U.N. investigating group. The Soviet Union seized on the report of Lumumba's death to resume its campaign against Hammarskjold.

In the Congo itself, news of Lumumba's violent death led to reprisals in pro-Lumumba areas, and in one of these, the province of Kivu, the civil administration collapsed. In an attempt to forestall further turmoil, the U.N. Security Council agreed on February 21 to take "all appropriate measures" to prevent civil war, "including...the use of force, if necessary, in the last resort." It also ordered the immediate withdrawal of all Belgian and other foreign military and paramilitary personnel.

As U.S. representative on the budget committee of the General Assembly, my task was to win approval for a special assessment that would keep a U.N. force in the Congo, sustain the U.N.'s nation-building work there, and avoid a general U.N. bankruptcy. At Hammarskjold's request, I also served as a member of a miniature "troika" which worked with him privately on matters pertaining to the financing of all aspects of U.N. work. A Russian ambassador represented the communist bloc, and the scholarly Burmese U Thant represented the "neutral" or unaligned members.

On my part, I used every form of polite arm-twisting in an effort to secure support for a new special assessment. But any headway I made was suddenly put at risk by the United States' disastrous invasion of the Bay of Pigs. All of us in the U.S. delegation at the U.N. were unstrung by news of that event, though we tried to wear our best smiles and speak in cheery holiday voices.

[III]

The impact of the Bay of Pigs bore especially hard on Adlai Stevenson. At a tense moment in the Security Council debate on a long-standing Cuban complaint that it was the victim of U.S. aggression, he made embarrassing assertions which he could have avoided had he been given advance information about the invasion. He was all the more hurt because of the personal affection he held for President Kennedy.

In the hectic days that followed the Bay of Pigs disaster, I heard Stevenson talk aloud about quitting his post at the U.N. because he had been denied full access to the CIA plans. I did not, however, take him seriously. I knew that while he could talk about all sides of an issue, he was not really talking to you. He was ventilating *himself*, trying to get *you* to say something.

(The most striking example of this trait occurred in July 1965 when he was still in the U.N. and increasingly unhappy about American policy toward the conflict in Vietnam. I had lunch with him before he left New York for Geneva and later for London— where he collapsed and died on a sidewalk. At that lunch, I listened to Stevenson dwell at length about resigning his U.N. post but did not interject a word of my own. He suddenly became aware of my silence. "Phil," he said, "you're not saying anything."

"Adlai," I replied, "there's nothing to say."

"What do you mean?"

"You're not going to quit."

"Why do you say that?"

"Adlai," I explained, "you're not Phil Klutznick. You are Adlai Stevenson. You can't quit and just walk away from the U.N. The question isn't whether you believe President Johnson is wrong. If you quit, you've got to lead an opposition, and you're not prepared to accept that battle nationally. Until you are, you can't quit." He looked at me without further comment.)

After the Bay of Pigs fiasco, I worked to rebuild my shaken coalition of votes in the budget committee. Stevenson struggled in the Security Council to cope with the political fallout there. After protracted politicking in the delegates' lounge and corridors of the U.N., after ceaseless plate-side chats, and after much shuttling between New York and Washington, we managed to work out an assessment formula that was acceptable to the poorer nations represented on the budget committee. The key to the formula was a larger U.S. contribution to support the U.N. operation in the Congo, thereby permitting a reduction in the special assessment for the poorer member nations.

The General Assembly approved the assessment after a plenary session that came to an end at five o'clock in the morning. As each delegation announced its vote, I kept a tally for Stevenson. "I don't understand you," he said when the results were in. "With the stakes as high as you know they are, you've sat here coolly making your little marks on the tally sheets." "Don't let appearances fool you," I said. "You should feel my back. My shirt is soaked." I added that something must be done to assure that the financing of the U.N. would not depend on last-minute relief measures.

31 □ In the Thick of Battle

The work of the Economic and Social Council, which goes forward year-round, comes to its sharpest focus at annual summertime sessions in Geneva. Gathered there are delegations from the eighteen member nations, representatives of six functional commissions and five regional commissions, assorted special committees, and the autonomous intergovernmental agencies that report annually to the council—the World Bank, International Monetary Fund (IMF), International Labor Organization (ILO), World Health Organization (WHO), Food and Agricultural Organization (FAO), and the United Nations Educational, Scientific and Cultural Organization (UNESCO).

At these summertime sessions one could see, even during the Cold War years, the brighter side of the U.N. picture in contrast to the dark underside visible in the New York–based Security Council and General Assembly, with their naked clashes of power. Although political differences also hovered above the Geneva meetings, opportunities for economic and social cooperation in many areas were earnestly pursued.*

*The council, through UNICEF, was concerned with matters such as adoption laws, institutional care, economic measures to assist families, legislative and administrative measures for the protection of children, and the creation of a reference center devoted mainly to technical information services related to child welfare. Again, the council assisted governments in developing services for the prevention of disability and the rehabilitation of handicapped persons; and in providing training of personnel in underdeveloped countries for work in population control, community development, prevention of crime, treatment of offenders, housing, and health care.

Also, the council's programs related to migration of refugees and population were dovetailed with the ILO's interest in migratory movements and manpower programs; with FAO and land settlement; with WHO and the control of diseases; with UNESCO

Before the 1961 session of the council was due to convene in Geneva in July, I had to persuade Adlai Stevenson to make the U.S. "economic and social speech" before the council. He had argued that I should make it, but I insisted that the issues at stake needed to be addressed by a U.S. spokesman with his prestige. I would handle all the nuts and bolts of the session, but only he could make the keynote utterance. He reluctantly agreed to come to Geneva. At the last minute, however, the State Department pressed him to visit Latin America to reiterate U.S. concern with the well-being of the region—all the more important because of continuing fallout from the Bay of Pigs misadventure. It was agreed in the end that an able foreign service officer on my staff would prepare a draft speech for Stevenson and would have it ready for him when he arrived in Geneva from his tour through Latin America.

When an exhausted Stevenson arrived in Geneva, I was at the airport, draft speech in hand. He asked what I thought of the text. I said it covered all the essential points, but that it needed his distinctive touch. Twenty-four hours later I was treated to a textbook specimen of Stevenson's work as an editor and writer. The substantive notes remained substantially the same. It was the spaces between the notes which he filled—to make the difference between a speech that spoke and one that sang.

When he delivered a speech, Stevenson sometimes added "asides" which were not part of his prepared text, but which popped out like a slice of bread when browned in a toaster. So it was now. At one point he suddenly observed that if the people of the Federal Republic of Germany drank as much coffee as did the Soviets, it would surely help certain underdeveloped regions of the world that exported coffee. It was his way of illustrating the interdependence of world economies.

It happened, however, that the Federal Republic of Germany had only recently been admitted to the United Nations; in many eyes, it still had a distance to go before its "legitimacy" was reestablished. It was attending its first ECOSOC meeting. I

and schools and literacy; and with the U.N. High Commission for Refugees. In addition, the council through the Commission on Narcotics and Drugs, was involved with all aspects of the international control of narcotic drugs. The whole of this economic and social work was subject to review in Geneva at the summertime sessions of the council, followed by the preparation of formal reports to be transmitted to the General Assembly.

thought it inept of Stevenson to make it appear—even by means of a single illustration—that the implied "failure" of the Federal Republic of Germany to consume more coffee was somehow perverse and a cause for economic affliction in coffee-producing countries. He could have made the same point by exhorting the Russians or French instead to do one thing or another.

My unease was later displaced by relief. At the reception I gave for Stevenson, protocol put me next to him in the receiving line. I braced myself for a counterattack by the West Germans as they drew near. Instead, their spokesman was lyrical in his praise for Stevenson's "statesmanlike" approach to the problems besetting the world's economic order. It occurred to me again that world affairs do not always respond to logic.

[II]

While I was in Geneva, events in the Congo remained uppermost in my thoughts. Continued attempts by the U.N. to stabilize the political situation there regularly unraveled under the impact of continued treachery, assaults on the U.N. peacekeeping force in the field, and promises by Congolese rivals which were not kept. U.N. forces suffered severe setbacks in the heavy fighting, while the outbreak of new hostilities brought a new storm of criticism directed at the U.N. Great Britain and France both claimed that the U.N. army in the field had exceeded the charter in what now seemed to be an offensive operation.

In the interval, Edmund Gullion was designated by President Kennedy as the new U.S. ambassador to the Congo, a fortuitous appointment. Gullion, a foreign service officer who had once served as a special assistant to Dean Acheson, was a veteran of missions in both Southeast Asia and North Africa. He was aware that the question of Katanga had become a crucial test not merely of the U.N. but of America's intentions throughout Africa. Every new state meticulously scrutinized our actions to detect evidence of support for Tshombe, whom the rest of Africa regarded as the "white colonist's black man." Gullion's concern was shared by G. Mennen Williams and Wayne Fredericks in the Bureau of African Affairs in the State Department, and in the U.N. by Stevenson, Harlan Cleveland, Richard Gardner, and me. The State Department's Bureau of European Affairs, on the other hand, opposed our view and instead shared the British and French criticism of the U.N. operation in the Congo.

During the council's summertime session, Ethel and our three younger sons—Jim, Bob, and Sam—were with me in Geneva. At the end of the session, Ethel moved on to Paris with Sam and me. Jim was to be my companion on a fact-finding mission to the Congo, undertaken with the concurrence of the State Department. I wanted to get at the reasons why certain friendly states did not contribute to the U.N.'s fund set up in 1960 on the initiative of the Eisenhower administration as a means to fight inflation in the Congo.

In Leopoldville, when I walked into the stores, I saw how stocks of goods were depleted while many other shops were shuttered. The streets were quiet, with none of the noise and bustle commonly associated with life in a capital city. Here, then, was the key to the riddle. Unlike the state of affairs in a more sophisticated Western-style economy, the Congolese who had moved to the city, when faced by hard times either moved back to the bush or were supplied with foodstuffs by their tribes. There was no significant inflation.

Meanwhile, off in Katanga, Tshombe, who was contemptuous of Americans and confident of his own strength, was also confident that British and French criticism of U.N. operations against Katanga would bring that activity to an end. Nonetheless, he agreed to meet with a worried U.N. Secretary General Hammarskjold at Ndila, North Rhodesia, for discussions looking to a cease-fire. A few days before the General Assembly convened in September, Hammarskjold and his aides, en route to his meeting with Tshombe, were killed on September 18 in a plane crash.

[III]

Most General Assemblies of the United Nations have their distinctive tensions. This was particularly true of the sixteenth when it convened on the third Tuesday of September 1961. First, it was rumored that the plane crash in which Dag Hammarskjold and several of his aides were killed was a result of sabotage by unnamed parties. Then there was the special excitement generated by the arrival of President John F. Kennedy at the United Nations for his maiden speech before the General Assembly.

The powerful appeal of this youthful figure seemed to transcend existing ideological divisions among the U.N. delegations. Kennedy used his first appearance before the U.N. to call for a Decade of Development. The president believed he ought to discuss something beyond disarmament and political issues, and he knew that most of the representatives were from developing countries.

The idea of a United Nations Development Decade, as formulated in Washington, had a compelling rhetorical appeal. But when I saw the text as prepared for delivery in New York, I observed that "it was a blank check that might present the United States with untold problems in the future." The practical implications and costs of the idea had plainly never been worked out.

By the time the president spoke, delegations were already maneuvering to choose a new U.N. secretary general. One leading candidate for the post was Ambassador Cella of Tunisia, who was serving as president of the sixteenth General Assembly. As it happened, on the day President Kennedy appeared before the General Assembly, Adlai Stevenson arranged a late afternoon reception in his honor to which the heads of all the delegations and missions were invited. Ambassador Cella, as president of the General Assembly, joined President Kennedy and Stevenson as part of the receiving line. My own task as a member of the U.S. delegation was to coax the guests to move toward the president and through the handshaking routine "with all due deliberate speed."

In this way I found myself standing directly opposite Cella at the moment when Golda Meir, the Israeli foreign minister and head of the Israeli delegation, drew close to President Kennedy. The pair knew each other from his pre-presidential years, and the president's greeting seemed to add a warm and intimate personal element to the "correct" protocol for official courtesy. Onlookers noted, however, that as Mrs. Meir moved toward Ambassador Cella, the latter turned the line of his shoulder away as if to avoid a handshake or even a greeting. Perhaps he inadvertently turned away. But if his gesture was meant to be a calculated snub in order to win support for his candidacy as secretary general among Middle Eastern and other delegations hostile to Israel, the result was a self-inflicted wound. When his subtle act was reported by the press the next morning, Cella's candidacy was doomed. He could never surmount the opposition of key Western delegations, including that of the United States.

This was the situation when Adlai Stevenson asked the principal associates on the U.S. mission to the U.N. to meet among ourselves and then return to him with a list of candidates whom the U.S. could back for secretary general. It was understood that the candidate would have to come from a "neutral" nation, and that if "he had a little color it would help." At the meeting which followed, I proposed the name of Ambassador U Thant of Burma. As noted, I had worked in harness with U Thant and a Soviet representative in economic matters, and I had found U Thant to be a fair-minded, thoughtful man, deeply committed to the success of the U.N. as an institution.

After further investigation, Stevenson endorsed this recommendation and passed it on to Washington, where the decision was also favorable. U Thant had the support of the principal delegations in the U.N., including that of the Soviet Union, and he was presently elected by a unanimous vote.

[IV]

The bread-and-butter issues which were always of prime concern to the developing nations fell within my province as the U.S. representative to the second committee of the U.N. and as ambassador to the Economic and Social Council. On this account I came to manage the U.S. side of the negotiations for the U.N. Decade of Development, with their overload of tensions between haves and have-nots.

Several of Stevenson's social friends, for whom he had secured appointments to posts on the political side of the U.S. delegation at the U.N., maintained country homes around New York City, to which they retreated for long weekends. After the noise of the days in between, the quiet of the countryside no doubt helped them hear themselves think. The most highly placed among these friends, however, always seemed in need of rest from the strains of looking down his nose at anyone on the U.N. scene who was not of his class—white, Anglo-Saxon, Episcopalian, Ivy League, and "old money." True, his sniffishness was not confined to delegates from impoverished Third World countries. It also extended to members and staff of the U.S. delegation who did not fit his criteria for virtue and wisdom. I was among those who did not.

My own schedule, which bore the imprint of habits formed early in life, called for a seven-day workweek. When I looked in the mirror I did not see a Great Sufferer but rather someone who found his best holiday in work. In a seven-day week I was able to maintain close contact with delegates from the developing countries, many of whom were new to the U.N. and to New York City. Through informal discussions in settings conducive to greater candor, I could assess how far they were held captive at the U.N. by the domestic politics of their home countries, or were in a position to "write their own instructions."

Although the Cold War dominated the politics of the U.N., I did not believe it necessary for the U.S. to emerge the victor in every dispute, regardless of what was at issue, simply to collect the trophies of invincible power. I believed that some second-level disputes, especially those judged important by small or underdeveloped countries, could be handled after the manner of "loss leaders" in merchandising—meaning that the United States could by design concede victory to adversary countries in order to brace their interests in U.N. procedures for the adjudication of conflicts.

Still, instances arose when even small moves had to be resisted because the culture of the U.N. invested them with large implications. A case in point arose after weeks of negotiations over a program for the Decade of Development. On the eve of the final vote, my Soviet counterpart approached me with an offer: If the U.S. would agree to a change of nomenclature—from a U.N. Decade of Development to a U.N. Decade for the Elimination of Colonialism—the Soviet Union would support the renamed program. It did not require X-ray eyes to see through the ploy. The proposed change, if agree to, would enable the Soviet Union to claim that it marched at the head of all human forces determined to liberate themselves from bondage to the colonial empires of Western European nations. When I passed the Soviet offer on to Harlan Cleveland and Richard Gardner in the State Department, I knew in advance what my official instructions would be. I was to say that the proposal was "unacceptable."

In the end, the General Assembly, by unanimous vote, approved the start of a U.N. Development Decade. The results however, never lived up to its initial promise. U.S. financial contributions to the Decade were trimmed to a relatively small amount.

All the while, the U.N.'s general financial condition went from bad to worse. By December 1961, the arrears in contributions totaled $129.4 million. As against this, the U.N.'s net resources were only $15.5 million, leaving a net deficit of $113.9 million. As acting secretary general U Thant, like Dag Hammarskjold before him, tried to collect contributions in arrears from member states. The sixteenth General Assembly went a step further when it asked the International Court of Justice for an advisory opinion as to the legal effects of past assessments against member states.

The advisory opinion delivered much later held that special assessments were legally binding on member nations, and that those in arrears in their contributions for two full years could, under Article 19 of the charter, lose their vote in the General Assembly. The same article went on to state that the "General Assembly must permit a member to vote if it is satisfied that the failure to pay is due to conditions beyond the control of the member." The question whether the Soviet Union could lose its vote in the General Assembly, because of its continued failure to pay its share of the special assessment for the upkeep of U.N. peacekeeping forces in the Middle East and the Congo, later became the subject of an acrimonious debate, but the provisions of Article 19 were never applied to a super power.

The size of the U.N. deficit at the end of 1961, when placed alongside the budget deficit of the U.S. government, was so small as to border on the invisible. But within the U.N. context, the deficit meant that the U.N. must either scrap its peacekeeping functions or face imminent bankruptcy in the most precise sense of the term. As the U.S. representative on the financial committee of the General Assembly, I dealt with this prospect in a speech I made before the committee on December 15, 1961, after the General Assembly passed a resolution authorizing more special assessments—$80 million—in support of the Congo operation. I said in part:

> My government throughout this whole exercise has demonstrated its willingness to meet the problem more than halfway. So have others. We who have paid our bills have no more voting strength than those who have elected to ignore the mandates of this organization. It is for the many who may suffer from the padlocking of these doors to assert themselves now. My government would deeply regret the indecent demise through default of the moving ideal embodied in this organization, but there are limits to our patience. . . .

A chance to play a part in rescuing the U.N. from collapse because it couldn't pay its bills was among the experiences I have often relived in retrospect. The rescue operation began when some of us in the U.S. government—at the U.N. headquarters in New

York, in Harlan Cleveland's office in the State Department, in the Bureau of the Budget—along with World Bank president Eugene Black, were considering how the financing of U.N. operations could be placed on a sound, long-range basis. We finally agreed that what we were aiming at could be achieved if the U.N. were to authorize a $200 million bond issue, of which the United States would agree to purchase up to half the total.

There was a precedent for the bond proposal. The U.N. at the start of its existence in New York had secured a $65 million interest-free loan from the United States with an amortization period of thirty years. The loan was authorized by Congress, and amortization payments were included annually in the regular budget of the United Nations and were paid promptly.

Despite the precedent, however, it was clear to me that if the United States appeared to be the initiating source of a proposed $200 million U.N. bond issue, the measure could very well founder on the rocks of Cold War polemics. As it happened, I had become increasingly close to U Thant after his election as acting secretary general. He had a sick wife and was often lonely. We spent many free evenings talking informally and confidentially about U.N. problems. Once Washington agreed to support the U.N. bond issue, I put the matter directly to U Thant. The bond proposal, I said, had to come from him personally if it was to be acceptable to the financial committee and then to the General Assembly.

The bonds would bear interest at 5 percent per annum, and the principal would be repaid in twenty-five annual installments. The bonds would be offered to member states of the United Nations, members of the specialized agencies, members of the International Atomic Energy Agency, and approved nonprofit institutions and associations. The political safety-catch in the proposal was that the interest and amortization payments on the bonds would be included in the regular budget of the United Nations. Unlike the case of the special accounts established for the U.N. emergency force and the U.N. force in the Congo, no member state had ever refused to pay its assessed percentage of regular budget expenses.

U Thant, who still was serving only as acting secretary general, risked the displeasure of a sizable bloc in the U.N. when he personally unveiled the bond proposal. I worked closely with him to line up a mix of nations who would formally sponsor a pro-bond resolution in the General Assembly. More politicking followed to muster support for the proposal. Some delegations balked because the sale and eventual retirement of the bonds would not affect the liability of states for paying past contributions still unpaid. In the end, however, when votes were cast, the proposal passed fifty-eight to thirteen, with thirty-three abstentions.

[V]

Although the vote was favorable, I had a simmering concern over lack of support from the political sector of the U.S. mission. Perhaps my nerves were as frayed as my bones were weary. I could throw off irritations over the way Stevenson could ignore the real personal needs of people working for him. I found it hard, however, to put up with more fundamental slippages. I reminded Stevenson that before I agreed to join him at the U.N., it was "expressly understood that an effort would be made to bring about a closer coordination and integration of the economic and social with the political." Yet by the end of 1961, nothing had been done toward this end. Stevenson tried to mollify me when I told him that I was reassessing my usefulness at the U.N., but the problems that disturbed me were left unresolved. I could not leave the U.S. mission at that time because U.S. participation in the purchase of U.N. bonds depended on a favorable vote in Congress.

My attitude toward the way the case was handled in Washington is reflected in a long exit report I wrote after I eventually left the U.S. mission. I enumerated the repetitive miscarriages in the relationship between the U.S. mission at the U.N. and the Department of State, along with suggestions about ways to better that relationship. My sharpest criticism dealt with Washington's handling of the U.N. bond issue. I wrote in part:

> The strategy of how the Congressional bill was to be drafted and whether or not there was to be a matching provision was determined without anybody in the U.S. mission being consulted for advice or guidance. I, for example, was opposed to any purchase of bonds by the United States under any circumstances except on a matching basis. This would not only have been good for the United States; in my judgment it would do no harm to the United Nations. Yet I who handled the matter all the way through in the United Nations, was never afforded a chance to express that view. When I finally was called to testify, I had

actually to hem and haw through both the inaccuracy in the Secretary of State's statement and my attitude on what I considered to be a key provision, namely the matching provision. Never in the time that I have known the Congress and through several years when I appeared before the Congress to support money matters during the Second World War did I find myself in such a confused and uncomfortable position. It was altogether unnecessary and could have been avoided quite easily.

Because of a rising tide of criticism of the U.N. in the United States, it was necessary to find someone on the Republican side of Congress with sufficient authority to "stare down" the critics of the proposed bond issue. The U.S. mission at the U.N. settled on Senator Everett Dirksen, the Republican minority leader in the Senate. Adlai Stevenson, as the head of the U.S. mission, was the logical man to approach Dirksen, but he declined the part, saying to me: "You know Dirksen. Talk to him and see what he will do."

In talking to Dirksen on the basis of our friendship going back to World War II, I explained what was at stake in the U.N. bond issue, buttressed by documents I underlined for him. He soon let me know that he would speak in the Senate in support of the bond issue and would work his side of the aisle drumming up Republican support for it. True to his word, he pulled out all his oratorical stops and won sufficient Republican support for the measure to ensure its passage.

When I returned from a trip to Tokyo, I wrote to Adlai Stevenson on April 9, 1962, asking to be relieved of my responsibilities at the U.N. The letter said:

> I certainly have no desire to leave while you or the U.N. are under any kind of attack, unless, of course, it would be helpful if I did. Short of any desire on either your part or that of the President that I leave earlier, there are one of two logical cut-off dates which would not materially interfere with any of my future plans. Naturally, I would like to be permitted whenever you think it proper to present my formal resignation in person to the President. No one knows about this letter except Ethel, you and I.... For obvious reasons, if I am to stay for sometime I would prefer it be kept secret as long as possible. Any other course would merely further handicap my ability to perform.

The cutoff dates I suggested would be either at the end of the summer meeting of ECOSOC or at the end of the next General Assembly if it was "felt that the completion of either the Development Decade negotiations or the fiscal problem could be aided" by my presence. Both these matters were "very much my concern," and especially because the "State Department did not present the whole program that we envisioned." It was left that I would discuss all this with Stevenson at a later hour, but, as usual, other pressing matters overrode the planned discussion.

[VI]

Affairs at the U.N. in 1962 unfolded at a pace as hectic as in the previous year, with all the usual Cold War tensions. Yet, my present recollection is focused on only one matter in particular. From the earliest days of the U.N., communist and other nations inveighed against the sins of "colonial exploiters" (and there were many), which they associated with the free-market system. The U.S. did not respond to this line of attack. In my time at the U.N., however, I believed it was necessary to make clear the benefits and achievements of the market system as against the distortions, corruptions, and wastefulness of the command economies glorified by the communists. Much to the surprise of many, the U.S. mission got the 17th General Assembly to adopt a ringing endorsement of free-enterprise principles. This success—almost three decades before the communist economies of Russia and eastern Europe professed their own failures—was virtually unnoticed. Yet it was an unprecedented "first" among international organizations comprised of sovereign states.

Despite my criticism of Washington's treatment of the U.S. mission at the U.N., I cherished the chance to serve there. The work could be fatiguing, exasperating, baffling—but always fascinating. Among other things, I valued the fact that I could work closely with Eleanor Roosevelt, who in 1961 had been appointed for a third time to serve as one of the rotating members of the U.S. delegation to the U.N. Her previous appointments had been in 1945 and again in 1949–1952 when she chaired the U.N. Commission on Human Rights and played a major role in the drafting and adoption of the United Nations Declaration on Human Rights. I have already indicated that my first association with her dated from the late 1930s when I was among the people she brought together at the White House in support of programs for young people. Now, in 1961, we worked together on the full agenda of human needs addressed by the Economic and Social Council.

Mrs. Roosevelt was seventy-seven years old at the time. Her age and her lifetime achievements would have justified her retreat from the thick of battles at the U.N. Instead she was a vigorous presence on the U.S. delegation, did her homework, and was an unfailing source of wise counsel about what to do and how to do it. She was always busy but always found time for courtesy, and she was particularly careful to respect the sensibilities of the wide variety of human beings who comprised the delegations to the U.N.

Beyond comparison with anyone I knew in public life, she embodied the old truth that virtue is best when it is unaware of itself, for she never made a great noise to call attention to her good deeds. When she conferred a benefit on anyone, she never remembered it; when she received a benefit from someone, she never forgot it. By the route of her sympathetic imagination, she entered into the experiences of other people and made them her own. I felt diminished within myself when she died in 1962 at a time when I was still serving in the U.N.

One detail of her funeral service at Hyde Park is worth recalling because of what it says about the obscene fears that were part of the Cold War psychology of the time. I was among the circle of friends whom her family had invited to the funeral service, aside from the official delegations of mourners. We were all in a cottage on the Hyde Park estate waiting to be called to the service in a nearby chapel. The start was delayed by almost an hour, and it was not until later that we learned why. The Russian diplomats who came to the service brought a large floral wreath for the bier, but U.S. security men delayed their entrance. As a precaution against hidden bombs, they dismantled the wreath, flower by flower, and then reassembled the display when none were found. Only then were the Russian diplomats permitted to enter the chapel and the service begin.

In a later hour, when the Eleanor Roosevelt Foundation was formed, Adlai Stevenson served as chairman of the enterprise, but at his request I chaired the finance (or fund-raising) committee. The work struck me as an enlarged version of my father's thankless job as treasurer of Beth Hamedrosh Hagodol in Kansas City.

I formed durable personal friendships with U.N. representatives from countries not numbered among the great powers. One of these was Ashraf Ghorbal, an economic aide to the Egyptian delegation and a few years later the Egyptian ambassador to the

United States. I also formed a close friendship with Charles Malik, the principal figure in Lebanon's permanent mission to the U.N. My relationship with this pair alone would answer Senator Fulbright's fair and pointed question at my confirmation hearing—whether I, being Jewish, could work with representatives of the Arab world.

At the end of my two years at the U.N., the satisfaction I had found in my work—despite real grounds for irritation—succumbed to family imperatives. Ethel was worn out from entertaining and world travels. The physical price of her support for my work showed up in a medical problem which required her hospitalization. She was restored to health without further complications. But when she was first hospitalized, I thought it best to undergo a physical checkup to get at the cause of some troublesome symptoms I had previously chosen to ignore. To my astonishment, and jolting sense of mortality, it turned out that *I* was the member of the family who was in need of surgery for a growth—which fortunately proved to be benign. I was fifty-five years old, and aside from reasons of health, it was time for me to leave the U.N. and pick up the threads of my life that had been suspended back in Chicago.

32 □ Return to Chicago

During the time I was inactive in the affairs of American Community Builders (ACB), Nathan Manilow and Sam Beber, my two principal partners, set new policies for its management and were pleased with the results. I was not so sure. Nor was Jerry Loebl, who had an equity share in ACB for his work in creating Park Forest. To gain the support of my principal partners on certain questions required more emotional and physical energy than I wished to expend on purely business matters. It seemed best to sell my interest in the Park Forest venture to Manilow and Beber, and to seek other business opportunities. Jerry Loebl also sold his interest in ACB to Manilow and Beber, and we thought the two of us might join forces again at some future hour.

When I entered the business world following the sale of my holdings in Park Forest, I first formed what was called Klutznick Enterprises. In the half-year between January and June 1963, its offices were in the family's Chicago apartment, and Ethel couldn't wait to get the whole thing out of her hair. My oldest son Tom, who had been working for Ferd Kramer on various matters, now became associated with me. When my younger sons Jim and Sam came of age, they too became my business associates. Bob, a Colorado resident, preferred to do things his own way, though he had a share in the total family assets. Every family seems to have its pathfinder in father-son relationships, and the son who breaks new ground makes it easier for the others to come into their own as well. Tom was the pathfinder in our case. His brothers benefited from his experience, for at an early age he proved to be a young man of uncommon business acumen and energy, and he had the courage to face up to father when he disagreed with my views. On the other hand, when my five children cast formal votes regarding business matters in which all had an equal interest, there were times when the vote was four to one against Tom. He may have been right on substantive grounds, but I took care *not* to play the part of a supreme court, reversing the judgment of four of my children in favor of one.

Klutznick Enterprises eventually was kicked out of the family apartment and into an office at 1 East Wacker Drive. At the outset we were essentially just managing a package of investments that belonged to the family—interests in Old Orchard and Oak Brook, and a residual interest in Park Forest. Sometime in the spring of 1964, a chance to be involved in large-scale development activity called for resources beyond our immediate means. So it made sense to bring in some familiar investors in past ventures, plus Lester Crown, the son of Henry Crown. The investors who came together formed a limited partnership which we named KLC Ventures Ltd., from the initial letters of the partners' last names: the K for both Philip Klutznick and Ferd Kramer, the L for Jerrold Loebl, and the C for Norman Cohn and Lester Crown. The name could be logically explained, but when asked about it I often said it meant "Kant Lose Cash." One of KLC's first ventures was to organize a new firm called United Development Company to build and market residential properties. An early project, Regent Park in Arlington Heights, near the Randhurst Shopping Center, was one of the first in the region to be offered as condominiums.

Having had a taste of action on a world political stage, I frankly found it hard to concentrate again on money-making ventures, though, as Samuel Johnson observed, "A man's never so innocently employed as when he is trying to make money." In any case, I soon welcomed a chance briefly to return to the world of government when I was asked by President Lyndon Johnson to conduct a survey of housing problems in Brazil. There had just been a change of regimes in Brazil, and the United States wished to encourage the new government to pursue development programs of immediate benefit to masses of people in the country. The five-man team of housing specialists I formed included Ferd Kramer, Irving Gillick, and Harry Johnson, with their interests in savings and loan associations, and Tom McDade, a veteran of Park Forest.

The detailed report we issued at the end of thirty intense days in Brazil contained practical suggestions as to how Brazil could pursue the planning, construction, transportation, and slum clearance related to a major housing program. We also suggested timetables, cautioned against trying to do too much all at once, and urged that government and private enterprise work in tandem. In this connection, I faced the bemusing need to explain to Brazilian officials that an "insured mortgage" meant that the *lender* was insured, and not, as they thought, the *borrower*. I recalled that there were Americans, including myself, who were similarly confused when the FHA "insured" mortgage was first introduced in the United States.

[II]

In the spring of 1963, I accepted an invitation to deliver the commencement address at Regis College in Denver, whose president was the brother of the president of Creighton University. While in Denver I found time for a second look at what was then a bare, windswept stretch of grazing land to the northeast of the city. The land was owned by the descendants of Joe Miller, who had emigrated to the United States from Russia in 1880 and had settled in Colorado where he married and fathered seven sons.

The Millers at one time were the largest cattle producers in

Colorado, but the guide who took me to see this stretch of land—now known as Montebello—was Joe's grandson, Mickey Miller, a lawyer by profession. His wife was the daughter of one of my close B'nai B'rith friends, Judge Charles Rosenbaum. When I first saw the land in 1952, I suggested to Mickey that it would take about a decade before the growth of Denver would make it worthwhile to consider developing it. After my second look, I sent a member of the KLC organization out to Denver to check on all the benefits claimed for the Montebello property—rail access, availability of utilities, a chance to make a city out of the property, perhaps to annex it to Denver or to Aurora.

The report confirmed the representations that had been made to me. About a year later, a series of contracts were signed between KLC Ventures and the Miller family, plus a firm of Denver builders known as Perl-Mack. This combination laid the basis for the development of Montebello as a successful "town within a town" and its eventual absorption by Denver in September 1965.

[III]

Meanwhile, the KLC team planned and built the River Oaks Shopping Center at the south end of Chicago near Calumet City. In contrast to Oak Brook and Old Orchard, where Field's had made the initial land purchase, Sears took the lead in the River Oaks project. Field's came in as a second partner after a suggestion I made to the president of the firm. He had doubted that Field's had enough regular customers in and around Calumet City—a factory town—to justify a branch store in River Oaks. I suggested that he check the list of charge account customers with addresses that fell within the reach of the proposed shopping center. The result showed an astonishing number of accounts in the area. So Field's came in, and in time, sixty other enterprises also opened in the center.

The planning and development of the residential and other elements adjacent to the shopping mall were as significant as the mall itself. What we learned about the matter at River Oaks was further refined by the United Development Corporation in its work in Village Green, the Park of River Oaks, and projects of later years—New Century Town; Stonebridge on Cherry Creek in Hazel Crest, Illinois; Chateaux of Chambord adjacent to Oak

Brook; Village-on-the-Lake in Hazel Crest; High Hill farms in Algonquin, Illinois; Fox Valley East; and Orland Park.*

While many new business prospects were put to KLC, in the words of my son Tom the firm was still run "as a family store," with all of its advantages and disadvantages. People with an ownership share in KLC included financiers, real estate men, architects, construction engineers, and merchants whose successful collaboration in earlier ventures fostered a "handshake basis of mutual trust." On the other hand, some shareholders in KLC might have a natural interest in receiving a dividend, and satisfying that interest without regard to other factors could reduce the firm's ability to finance a growing backlog of new business. Also, some of KLC's principals were aging, and the distribution of their assets could upset the equilibrium of ownership interests in KLC.

After protracted discussions about these matters, KLC passed from the scene on April 1, 1968. The structure of a newly named enterprise that took its place—Urban Investment and Development Company—provided for flexibility in both operations and financial participation. It was now possible for those who wanted to sell or to expand their ownership interests in KLC to do just that.

The new arrangement had important institutional implications which were succinctly stated by my son Tom. He observed that "for the first time since the days of Park Forest and American Community Builders we had a unified corporate structure, organized so that we would be in a position to make any fundamental move we might contemplate in the decade of the seventies. That is, we could either merge the firm with a larger one, or 'go public' in order to meet the capital requirements that the future would undoubtedly demand. Implicit in what we did was the notion that we would not restrict our future activities just to the Chicago metropolitan area and to Denver. We were to create a new enterprise that would be national in scope."

[IV]

The creation of UIDC in the formal mold of a corporation meant

---

*Fox Valley East, located west of Chicago, was annexed to Aurora, Illinois. Orland Park, southwest of Chicago, was annexed to the existing suburb of Orland Park.

that people in the enterprise had to relate to one another on a new basis. In the previous KLC setup, I was the only person who had a title—namely, chairman. Now, for the first time, my other associates acquired formal titles. I remained the chairman, but Norman Cohn, on becoming president of UIDC, merged his company, Inland Construction, into UIDC as a subsidiary. My son Tom became executive vice president of the new firm, while Tom McDade and George Goldman—two veterans whose services dated from Park Forest days—became senior vice presidents.

No more than six years had passed since Tom's graduation from Oberlin with a major in economics. He had deliberately placed himself under the tutelage of a series of hard taskmasters from whom he absorbed a rare fund of knowledge about the management of shopping centers, the sale of residential properties, and the construction of homes. Perhaps he might never have entered the real estate development business if he were not my son. At an early age he showed a strong independent streak, as in his passion for flying—which led him to earn a pilot's license not long after he entered Oberlin as a freshman. But, as was true in my own case after I accidentally entered the realm of housing through my professional interest in law, the more Tom encountered the world of property development, the more it claimed his interest. As executive vice president of UIDC, he soon showed himself to be an exceptionally able negotiator with a keen sense of market trends, and a man well endowed with all the qualities of an institution builder—a talent for planning, finance, accounting, and the recruitment of able staff.

We also persuaded Mickey Miller to leave his law practice and join UIDC, subject to our opening an office in Denver. Miller soon was involved in the construction in Denver of what became the Lincoln Center, a thirty-story high-rise office building with 250,000 square feet of leasable space and parking for five hundred cars. The Lincoln Center building was only marginally successful at first, but we were convinced that the project might eventually work out very well. With patience this proved to be the case.

[V]

A series of land acquisitions served as the basis for Urban's New Town program, which was often called the "minitown" program or, in Tom McDade's phrase, the "microtown in a macro region."

As my colleagues and I observed the results of the successful shopping centers we had created at Old Orchard, Oak Brook, and River Oaks, we saw how potentially successful shopping centers could lead to the development of entire communities—something in which we had not been directly involved since the building of Park Forest.

When Urban considered the prospect of creating a minitown, some simple principles guided our approach. The location should be appropriate for a regional shopping center, and the center should be developed first because in that way we could get back most of our capital through the business the center generated. We could then proceed to develop the remaining land slowly but surely. Second, the optimum size for such a new town, based on our trial runs, seemed to be a 640-acre section of land. This was large enough to promise a reasonable profit without too greatly taxing our capital. If the price was right, and the land adjoined high-density settlements, more land could be bought as an investment—because a minitown formed in a growing neighborhood could not only generate profits but enhance property values in the surrounding area. Guided by these concepts and organized for action, Urban proceeded to buy land around the outer margins of the Chicago metropolitan area.

When the microtown concept was first formulated, Urban organized a planning group to consider all the complex social and economic factors inherent in such a project. To head the group we were fortunate to secure the services of Robert E. Merriam. Merriam, a graduate of the University of Chicago, had worked with me in Washington on housing matters; he combined a spacious social vision with extensive experience in practical government. He had served as an alderman of Chicago's famous Fifth Ward, had run against Richard Daley for mayor of Chicago, and had served as deputy director of the U.S. Bureau of the Budget under President Eisenhower.

The minitown concept involved Field's and Sears from the beginning. The three original regional shopping centers of Old Orchard, Oak Brook, and River Oaks were located in the "second ring" around Chicago. All were within a range of fifteen to eighteen miles from downtown Chicago, north, west and south. The minitowns were to be located further out in what we called the "third ring."

The New Century Town, a prototype of the minitowns Urban

built, had an interesting legal history. We thought that the nearby village of Libertyville, a prosperous community set amid "gentleman farms," was a logical choice for a negotiated annexation once the land for the New Century Town was purchased. We were encouraged to believe that the annexation agreement would go through, especially when Libertyville's mayor and his associates reached a provisional but carefully worked out understanding with Urban.

It was all in vain. When the heat was turned on by the Libertyville Countryside Association in opposition to the proposed annexation, some proponents reversed themselves. They thought that unless New Century Town was to be part of Libertyville, it would not be built at all. To cover their retreat, however, they proposed to Urban that a plebiscite be held on the issue of annexation. When I met with the opposition leaders, I explained that Urban, Marshall Field's, or Sears did not make plans contingent upon the outcome of a popularity contest. When the opposition leaders nonetheless continued to insist on a plebiscite, we formally withdrew the application we had filed for annexation and instead entered into negotiations with Vernon Hills.

Vernon Hills, a relatively small, unsophisticated new community eager for development, lay close to the site of the 640 acres on which New Century Town was to be built. With no change in the terms previously negotiated with Libertyville, Mount Vernon annexed the site of the New Century Town. The result? New Century Town's shopping center is in precisely the same physical place it would have occupied if it were part of Libertyville, and with precisely the same traffic flow—subject to one difference. Instead of Libertyville getting the sales tax and other real estate revenue from New Century Town, the revenue went to Mount Vernon, making it a very prosperous little community, half of whose total annual municipal budget is covered by sales tax revenues it gets from the shopping mall. Ironically, the man who sponsored the petition that blocked the annexation of the New Century Town to Libertyville moved out of Libertyville six months later.

33 □ Uncertain Trumpets

In the years after my return to Chicago from United Nations work, my business interests were not confined to projects undertaken by KLC or by Urban. I also served as chairman of the board of the American Bank and Trust Company of New York and on the board of Swiss Israel Foreign Trade Bank in Geneva. I was president of the Oak Brook Utility Company, a board member of Mortgage Guaranty Insurance Corporation and CIC Leasing, both in the United States and its counterpart in Israel, and a partner in Jerusalem Hilton Associates which was building the Jerusalem Hilton Hotel. In addition, I had what was called a "participatory partnership" in Solomon Brothers. I heard other people say that if I spent all my time developing proposals for lucrative business ventures that crossed my desk, I might have been included in the list of *Forbes'* wealthiest. But a life devoted solely to the process where money makes money was not to my taste, any more than it was to the taste of my father.

[II]

My involvements in matters of concern to the general society and those of special concern to the Jewish community often were concurrent. Yet it might be clearer for me to recall some matters separately as they evolved in the years immediately after 1963. So I start with my work as chairman of the research and policy committee of the Committee on Economic Development (CED).

The committee was and is comprised of a carefully selected group of businessmen and scholars who study public policy questions and the implications of proposed solutions. Old-line business organizations such as the U.S. Chamber of Commerce and the Material Manufacturing Association often seemed to be captives of their regular staffs, with their own stable of "kept economists." The CED, from the outset, was different. The research and policy committee was served by a staff of independent-minded economists and leading executives, chosen from the elite in the professions and business. The CED's bylaws effectively preserved the independence and integrity of its staff and of the research and policy committee. In fact, the long dissenting footnote to a CED report became an honored feature of the organization's intellectual life.

In my time as an active trustee of the CED and as chairman of its research and policy committee (I am now a life trustee), the public issues we addressed amounted to an inventory of the major problems facing the United States in the 1960s and 1970s. For example, we tried to assess the costs and benefits of President Johnson's War on Poverty while America's involvement in the Vietnam conflict was escalating. In the realm of civil rights, we dealt with the shortfall between the gains made through equality-of-opportunity legislation and what still had to be done to close the gap between the laws on the books and the actual state of affairs in the workplace. We had something to say about access to and equality in education at all levels of instruction, as well as the urgent need to deal with the impact of social change and housing problems in American cities.

Our studies covered many other matters as well. They included the costs and availability of adequate medical care, the mounting deficits in the U.S. balance of trade, the growing instability in the international monetary system, the need to help developing countries get their products into international trade channels, the impact of science and technology on the changing world of work. We paid special attention to the realities of inflation coincident with unemployment—a phenomenon which Gunnar Myrdal named "stagflation." Our reports on all such matters, backed by testimony before congressional committees, carried weight with the architects of presidential and congressional policies. My work with the CED helped prepare me for some of my later tasks as U.S. Secretary of Commerce under President Jimmy Carter.

[III]

My attitude toward U.S. involvement in the Vietnam War passed through three distinct phases. Emblematic of the first were my remarks to the Council on Religious and International Affairs when it met for a two-day conference in October 1965. By then, manpower requirements for the U.S. involvement in Vietnam had outstripped the resources of U.S. forces such as the Marines. Men drafted into the army under Selective Service were being committed to combat roles in Vietnam. Three of my four sons—Tom, Jim, and Bob—were of draft age. Yet in my remarks to the council I said that I favored the U.S. effort to safeguard South Vietnam from being absorbed by communist North Vietnam. More than that, I praised the Johnson administration's self-restraint in the way it managed the U.S. military role in Vietnam.

By March 1967 it was painfully clear that U.S. power could not win one vital objective which held the key to the whole Vietnamese matter. It could not provide the anticommunist majority of South Vietnam with the will and capacity for sustained self-government. In the absence of that will and that capacity, America could not "win the war" *with* the South Vietnamese; winning it *for* them led to operations where *we* appeared to be the aggressors in the eyes of the very people we ostensibly had come to help.

I used the forum of a B'nai B'rith meeting in New York to urge that the U.S. "earnestly reexamine its political motivations in Vietnam" and "expedite its efforts toward negotiations or diminish its military commitment." We were learning the "limits as well as the strength of America's huge military arsenal." To those who said, "We can't quit Vietnam now," the answer must be, "If it is in the national interest, why not?"

I added that the point of our Vietnam policy was all the more dubious when placed alongside the fact that we were "amending our Cold War posture by bits and pieces"—as in the partial test-ban treaty, agreements on the use of outer space, increasing trade relations with Eastern Europe, a softening attitude toward acceptance of Red China into the United Nations. In my view, we had permitted our Vietnam commitment to control our foreign policy to the neglect of vital American domestic needs. "Preserving freedom of choice in Vietnam may be vital, but it is even more vital to make the United States a showcase for the effectiveness of democracy and freedom in eliminating slums and poverty," I observed.

I had always been on friendly personal terms with President Johnson since his Senate days. I admired the way he held the country together in the period immediately following the assassination of President Kennedy. He had been strikingly successful in securing the enactment of key social and economic measures that had not been attended to since the heyday of the New Deal. I had no reservations when I joined in organizing bipartisan business community support for him in the 1964 presidential contest. But when my criticism of his Vietnam policy came to his attention, I learned that he thought I had joined in a band of people bent on destroying him personally. Nothing of the sort was remotely true. Even though I came very late to oppose his policy on Vietnam, I was sympathetic toward President Johnson in his painful ordeal. But he was in no mood to believe that a critic could also be a friend.

[IV]

The situation of Jews in the Soviet Union became an urgent concern in the 1960s and 1970s. Earlier, the rapid process of Jewish assimilation in the Soviet Union—through mixed marriages and the suppression of any kind of Jewish activity during the 1930s—seemed to indicate the approaching end of the great Jewish community in Russia. But the Holocaust and the emergence of the official Soviet anti-Semitism (disguised as a campaign against "cosmopolites") brought a sharp turn in the identity of the remaining Jews.

A new wave of Jewish feeling arose even among highly assimilated Jews, while the struggle of Palestinian Jews for political independence and for the creation of a Jewish state after World War II gave focus to these feelings. This incipient or new birth of Jewish nationalism, however, was severely suppressed in the Soviet Union by the Stalinist terror. Leading members of Jewish intelligentsia were executed, and plans were formulated for the general expulsion of all Jews from the European parts of the USSR. The "thaw" of the early Khrushchev years caused many Soviet Jews to hope for another period of possible coexistence with other nationalities in the great empire and possibly for renewed integration in Soviet life. But it was a case of hope deferred due to increasing social and nationalistic tensions and more anti-Semites, some of whom achieved positions in the Soviet leadership.

Soviet Jews reacted to anti-Jewish measures in diverse ways. The very few who preserved their religious beliefs—as was true of the members of Habad—intensified their devotion and even succeeded in increasing their numbers. Some tried to immerse themselves in the great Russian mass, particularly in the non-Russian border territories where they were in any case the standard-bearers of

Russian culture and champions of Russification. Others started to regain their Jewish identity and to show interest in Jewish cultural achievements, in Israel, in the Jewish past and future. Because many Soviet Jews belonged to the white-collar professions and to the creative intelligentsia, this process of soul-searching passed into a very intense form. There was a sharp increase in dissident activity and in Jewish nationalist and Zionist activity, marked by a rise in applications by Soviet Jews for the right to emigrate to Israel—and by the countervailing Soviet policy of harassing those who did apply.

By the mid-1960s, charges against the Soviet Union for mistreatment of its Jewish nationals became a subject of grave international concern. The force of the case against the Soviet Union on this and other counts—including a mean-spirited delay in granting a simple request by some Soviet Jews for authority to make a minimal supply of matzos for Passover—spoke for itself.

Against this background, I was invited to address a "Public Rally to Protest Soviet Anti-Semitism" held in Philadelphia's Independence Square on March 28, 1965. It was easy to cite the counts of the indictment against the Soviet regime on the charge of anti-Semitism. But I believed it was best to avoid roughing up the air with anti-Soviet polemics. Doing so would feed the paranoia of the Soviet leaders and stiffen their resistance to humane policies for Russian minorities. Thus my remarks at the public rally were largely couched as an appeal to the self-pride of the Soviet authorities:

> We are not here to shake our fists at the Soviet Union. We are here to plead that the Soviet Union do justice to herself by giving meaning to her international commitments—as in her support for the United Nations Declaration of Human Rights—by letting those people go who cannot adjust to her new society.
>
> The essence of what we ask of the Soviet Union is that she accord to all of her nationals—to Jews as well as to all others—what she claims to seek for peoples who were previously subject to colonial domination elsewhere in the world. It is only the weak who lack the courage to face up to problems such as those that account for our rally here. Certainly the Soviet Union has the internal strength to end this controversy if she but wills to do so. The solutions are easier and far more certain to bring peace than a continuing harrowing and acrimonious debate.

Avoiding a strident anti-Soviet tone was a mark of my approach in these years to the plight of Jews in the Soviet Union. No one could gauge with mathematical exactness what Soviet Jews wished for themselves as Jews. But on the eve of Israel's Six Days War and immediately afterward, it was generally said in Jewish circles that Soviet Jewry was subdivided into four distinct groups. The first and smallest, numbering about twenty in all, received the most attention from the Western press and from Jews outside the Soviet Union. They were the "Prisoners of Zion," men and women who had been arrested, "tried," and sentenced to Soviet prisons as "enemies of the state" because they had been prominently engaged in Zionist activities.

The second group, also the object of much attention outside the Soviet Union, were the "refusniks"—about two thousand in all—who insisted on a "rule of law" in place of the arbitrary manner in which Soviet authorities denied Jews the right to engage in specifically Jewish cultural and religious activities. The third group, about 400,000, was comprised of Jews who either had applied for exit visas or were in the process of doing so. The fourth and by far the largest group of Soviet Jews—about two million in all—were the "Jews of Silence."

Most Jewish leaders in the United States and in Israel believed that Russian Jews who wished to remain Jewish could do so only by emigrating to Israel; those who preferred to remain in the Soviet Union would be lost to the Jewish people. These leaders thus devoted most of their energy and resources to the cause of the "Prisoners of Zion," the "refusniks," and the "emigrés." They believed it was not possible to foster any kind of effective Jewish cultural life among the "Jews of Silence."

The conclusion reached by Dr. Nahum Goldmann, president of the World Jewish Congress, and I—independently of each other—initially placed us in a decided minority among Jewish leaders. We both believed that it was wrong to write off the "Jews of Silence" in the Soviet Union. This group, representing the majority of Soviet Jews, was the best-educated segment of the Soviet population. True, it was secular minded and almost totally ignorant of Jewish history, but it was marked by an awakening interest in Jewish cultural matters.

Dr. Goldmann and I agreed that until the great mass of Soviet Jewry had access to literature published within Russia that would help quicken their Jewish cultural awareness, such literature must be prepared outside Russia and brought into the country for dissemination. It must be comprised of texts that could hold a reader's interest *as* literature, and it must be apolitical, meaning free of anti-Soviet overtones, so as not to endanger disseminators and readers alike.

By the end of the 1970s, the minority position which we had taken years earlier came to mark the outlook of most major Jewish organizations—not only toward Jews in the Soviet Union but in Eastern Europe as well. The aggregate Jewish population in Eastern Europe exclusive of the Soviet Union, though dwindling, was still significant. Whether the surviving Jewish communities in Rumania and Hungary—the largest in Eastern Europe—became a museum, respected and preserved, or a cemetery, abandoned and forgotten, depended in large measure on external interest and influence. Rumania and Hungary had genuine programmatic needs. The others—as in Poland, Yugoslavia, Bulgaria, and Czechoslovakia—had more limited but no less real needs for old-age facilities, cultural activities, contacts with the Jewish world, and the like. Beyond that, there was also an obligation to rescue, study, preserve, understand, and interpret what was left of the outstanding Jewish civilization of modern times.

This perspective lay behind a proposal made by Dr. Nahum Goldmann at a meeting of the Material Claims Conference in 1964, when direct payments by West Germany for redistribution to Israel and to Jewish entities elsewhere (exclusive of pensions) appeared to be winding down. He would earmark some portion of the remaining capital to create what he called a Memorial Foundation of Jewish Culture. It would be a foundation dedicated not merely to the remembrance of a tragic and vanished past but to a more affirmative goal—to help replace the scholarship of those Jewish intellectuals who had been destroyed by World War II.

Some Jewish leaders strongly objected. They argued that the claims payments by West Germany must be confined to meeting the physical needs of Jewish survivors of the Holocaust, and must not be diverted for any other purpose. As an officer of the conference, I spoke in support of Goldmann's proposal. Even the Jewish survivors of the Holocaust, I argued, could vanish physically as Jews unless they were nurtured by a renewed culture on soil where Jewish culture faced extinction. Goldmann's proposal was adopted, and the Memorial Foundation for Jewish Culture, formed in 1965, came to be funded out of payments by the Federal Republic of Germany on Jewish claims.

The foundation's eventual funding capacity, based on the interest earned from the conservative investment of its capital, was small relative to the funds annually expended by local, national, and international Jewish institutions and agencies. If the foundation was to "reach the unreached, to educate the uneducated, and to commit the uncommitted," it needed a clear order of priorities governing the use of its limited resources. To help all was to help none. In the decade between 1965 and 1975, however, the foundation's program proceeded haphazardly. Proposals seemed to be approved or rejected on the basis of personal preferences, without a system of accountability. It was left to me in my time as president of the World Jewish Congress and as president of the foundation to develop, with the help of Dr. Jerry Hochbaum and others, procedures designed to fulfill the original promise in Nahum Goldmann's spacious vision.

34 □ Watersheds

The Six Days War in June 1967 was a watershed in Israel's history. The swift victory which left the Arab world paralyzed also shocked the Israelis amid their euphoria. Those who still lived emotionally and intellectually in the past had to face the fact that they could either lay to rest the nineteen-year-old security nightmare they had known or invite new dangers within new borders—in a setting where they were still surrounded by sixty million Arabs and their collaborators. In other words, Israel for the first time since statehood seemed to hold the political initiative, rather than have its fate dictated by the big powers.

But when this small nation between June 10 and 16, 1967, exploded to twice its geographical size, warning flags began to flap in the winds. The "national consensus" within Israel about what it was or wanted to be—and the semblance of internal unity forced on disparate elements by common external danger—would now come under heavy internal siege. There would be ideological differences over the very meaning of Jewish history and of Judaism as a religion, along with profound differences in approach to the political, economic, and demographic problems inherited with the doubling of Israel's territorial size.

One could sense from the highly charged emotional mood of the hour the makings of future strain between the Israeli state and society and at least a segment of the Diaspora. Challenging questions that used to be asked only in academic journals or settings soon moved from the wings of public consciousness to center stage wherever ordinary Jews talked to one another about Israel. Was Israel, for example, in which Jews everywhere now found a new source of immense pride, to consider itself empowered to act for *all* Jews in the Diaspora? Were Jews in the Diaspora duty bound to support uncritically every act and policy of Israel? Were Diaspora Jews entitled publicly to dissent from the acts and policies that emerged from the play of Israel's internal politics?

[II]

I was in Israel in the days immediately after the triumphant end of the Six Days War, and was swept into the emotional tide of a moment in Jewish history still too immediate and overwhelming to be grasped in all its significance. I literally trembled inwardly as I walked through the streets of a Jerusalem no longer divided—now, in its entirety, the fully redeemed Jewish capital. At the ancient West Wall which was all that remained of the second Temple—and which was now free from the rule of Jordanian guns—the scene was noisy and dusty. There I shared the ecstacy of a random mingling of the devoutly pious worshiping in prayer shawls, the nonobservant, the historically minded, and the curious. Yet I was not so carried away as to be blind to a paramount reality which faced Israel and its leadership. In the course of a series of six articles I wrote in Jerusalem which were later published by the *Chicago Tribune*, I observed:

> The hope for a tranquil and not just tranquilized middle east remains blurred by Arab divisiveness, clouded by Soviet intentions, and hardened in its complexities by the sudden and sweeping—and in some respect, permanent—changes in geography. Having decisively won a war its government did not want and desperately, almost sacrificially sought to avert, Israel is now confronted with the more perplexing task of groping for what it wants most: the security of a genuine and durable peace.

This means simply, recognition by the Arabs of Israel's existence and right to live. Given that—an acceptance of Israeli sovereignty and all it implies in international relations—the points of contention between Israel and the Arab states (excepting the status of united Jerusalem under Israeli rule) are probably open to negotiations at the present time. The longer the interval that elapses before negotiations begin, the more Israel may consolidate her own positions. Then much less may remain open for negotiation.

Just after the Six Days War, I took part in a conference called in Jerusalem by Prime Minister Levi Eshkol, who asked Dr. Nahum Goldmann and others—myself included—to create a new universal organization as a basis for Israeli-Diaspora relations. At that conference, committees were appointed to develop a worldwide organization which could serve as a recognized bridge between Israel and the Diaspora. The whole of the effort, however, foundered the next year when the Council of Jewish Organizations (COJO) met in Geneva, and for two main reasons. First, the atmosphere in Jerusalem in July 1967 had been more charged with a keen awareness of the paramount interest of the Jewish people *in their totality* than was the case in Geneva a year later. Second, organizational and personal jealousies in the voluntary section of Jewish (or any other) society are as remorseless as political jealousies.

The failure to create an institutional mechanism did not mark an end to further concern about Israeli-Diaspora relations. I once heard my mentor, Dr. Mordecai Kaplan, voice his anguish over a growing gulf between Israel and the Diaspora, and then direct his disciple Dr. Moshe Davis to start work at once in framing the terms for a "new covenant" which would bind the world Jewish community together. He assigned me to convene a meeting of world Jewry at the foot of Mt. Sinai to ratify the terms of the "new covenant."

I also heard Menachem Begin offer a solution of his own to the institutional needs of the Israeli-Diaspora relations. He proposed the creation of a Jewish equivalent of the English House of Lords, whose seats would be occupied by Jewish "notables" from around the world. Begin did not explain how they would be chosen or what their actual powers would be vis-à-vis the Israeli Knesset.

In the end, nothing came of Kaplan's "new covenant" or Begin's

"Jewish House of Lords." But the problem remained of how Israel and the Diaspora should be related to each other—about the right of Diaspora Jews to criticize Israel, about whom the state of Israel actually belonged to, about the religious, philosophical, and sociological case of the state as well as its political and military stance.

It was easier in one respect to be an Israeli than a Diaspora Jew. Either in person or through his political party, the Israeli could disagree with his government, but his loyalty to a reborn Israel was not questioned. The whole world could hear the noise of internal conflicts among Israelis, but few Israelis charged that their disputatious fellow citizens were destroying the unity of the Jewish people. But if a leader in the Diaspora openly disagreed with a particular policy or act of the Israeli government, he would be scolded by claques at the service of the Israeli establishment. Or, if he held a high post in a national or international organization based outside Israel, he would be reproached by Israeli officialdom centered in Jerusalem.

In the years ahead, I often returned to the riddle of the relationship between Israel and the Diaspora. Amid changing circumstances, I always believed there could be no fruitful relationship if, first, the Diaspora were to be merely the giver and lender, and Israel the taker and borrower in economic affairs; and second, if Israel were to be the decision-maker, and the Diaspora the follower in political and international affairs. The relationship could be fruitful only if there was mutual candor between the leaders and people of Israel as a sovereign state, and Jews elsewhere who felt a special relationship to that state and shared some portion of its success and failure. In wrestling with the issue, I once formulated some propositions in a memorandum I addressed to myself, and later sounded them in speeches and articles.

1. We who believe in Jewish peoplehood must recognize that a partnership between the sovereign state of Israel and Jews scattered all over the world cannot be a full and equal partnership on either side. Israel through its democratically chosen government has a responsibility for the maintenance of its political viability in the world. As a state, it may assume positions and take actions which even its own citizens resent. Their remedy is to change their government. But, the Diaspora cannot expect, nor should it argue for a role in governmental decision-making within the sphere of the state's legitimate concern for its duties as a sovereign. Jews who are not citizens of Israel can protest, declaim, and orate, but the final decision rests with the state.

2. There are other areas in which the state acts but in which the Diaspora has a grave concern and where its counter actions could affect what the state does. This is the most dangerous ground for the state and the Diaspora. That is the case where the interests of peoplehood get mixed up with Judaism as a religion, and where its religion gets mixed up with sovereignty and politics. I firmly believe in the desirability of a religious tone for Israel as a state and as a people. But its distortion in modern terms makes it more difficult for a large part of the Diaspora to accept certain acts of the state even in the rightful exercise of its sovereignty. . . . Many Jews could live with the requirement of rabbinic marriage and divorce provided it included all properly ordained rabbis, whether Orthodox, Conservative, or Reform. But to excommunicate many recognized rabbinic functionaries of the Diaspora in Israel must sooner or later poison the wells of cooperation between large parts of the Diaspora and the state of Israel.

3. A very touchy problem concerns the out-migration of Jews in lands where they may find themselves dispossessed, harmed, or unwanted. Israel has and will continue to have a need for immigrant manpower for a variety of reasons. Yet conditions can arise where it might be possible to secure the immigration of a community of Jews who are prepared to go anywhere but Israel, or, under some circumstances, it might be best for them and for the rest of us to seek to better their conditions in the land of their origins until such time as they might choose to immigrate. Decisions of this character involve the whole of the Jewish world, not alone the government of Israel or the quasi-public bureaucracy of the Jewish Agency as an arm of the World Zionist Organization.

My stands in particular cases and controversies arising within the context of Israeli-Diaspora relations sometimes coincided with and sometimes ran against the grain of a significant body of Israeli public opinion, or of the "official" position of the Israeli government. But more often than not they coincided with the views of Dr. Nahum Goldmann. Although our agreement was unplanned and a result of independent reflection, it accounted for the talk in some circles that I was no more than Goldmann's shadow.

35 □ Between War and Peace

In the six years following Israel's stunning victory in the Six Days War, I held no official post in any major Jewish organization in the United States (aside from being an honorary president of B'nai B'rith and a member of its board of governors) that would allow me face-to-face meetings with American policy-makers concerned with Middle East affairs. But through my personal friendships with congressional leaders on both sides of the aisle, and with key figures in both the State and Defense Departments, I joined in helping to make the case for the supply of arms to Israel—to offset the Soviet Union's massive shipments of arms to Egypt and Syria. Also, through close contacts with Israel's diplomatic representatives in the United States, and with government and opposition leaders whom I regularly met during my frequent visits to Israel, I looked for signs of any movement in the direction of a peace settlement with Israel's hostile Arab neighbors.

[II]

Great orations on the subject of peace did not bring it any closer. "Only the Lord," as Ben-Gurion used to say, "could create by uttering a word. He said, 'Let there be light,' and there was light. But not mortals." Peace could be attained only through deeds, and while Israeli opinion was divided on how to bring peace closer, the Arabs appeared to move steadfastly toward war.

On August 29, 1967, an Arab summit conference in Khartoum involved the leaders of eleven states: Egypt, Iraq, Jordan, Lebanon, Saudi Arabia, Kuwait, Libya, Sudan, Tunisia, Morocco, and Algeria. Syria was not represented, but Yassir Arafat's Palestine Liberation Organization (PLO) was. Inspired by Egypt's president, the conference adopted "the basic principles to which the

Arab states commit themselves." These were the celebrated four no's: no peace with Israel, no recognition of Israel, no negotiations with Israel, no concessions on the question of Palestinian national rights. The oil-producing states also assured Nasser that they would continue to provide financial aid by replacing the revenue that Egypt would lose by keeping the Suez Canal closed.

Meanwhile, the Soviet Union poured equipment and advisers into Egypt and Syria in a massive effort to rearm and expand their armies. Worries over Israel's security were intensified after French President Charles de Gaulle, whose country had been the chief supplier of arms to Israel, imposed an embargo on further arms shipments to Israel, including fifty Mirage V jets on which Israel had already paid two-thirds of their cost. Israel, at the end of 1967, then turned to the United States with a request to buy fifty Phantom jets. To meet that request the U.S. would have to cross policy lines set during the Kennedy administration when the U.S. agreed to sell only defensive weapons to Israel.

The first U.S. reaction was reserved. In January 1968, Prime Minister Levi Eshkol followed through with a visit to President Johnson's ranch. The talks were friendly, but Johnson refrained from a definite commitment to supply the planes. He wanted first to examine the Soviet Union's position on arms limitations which he had discussed at the Glassboro Summit meeting with Soviet leader Aleksei Kosygin. The Soviet invasion of Czechoslovakia in August 1968, coincident with the Democratic presidential nominating convention, undercut U.S. attempts to reach an arms limitation agreement with the Soviet Union applicable to the Middle East. So, in October 1968, Johnson publicly approved the sale of the Phantoms to Israel.

Word of this approval came during the B'nai B'rith's triennial convention in Washington. I had been asked to address the convention, and in doing so underlined two points. First, the sale of the Phantoms was a major turning point in the history of U.S. military aid to Israel. By that act the U.S. recognized Israel as its partner in the defense of the Middle East against Soviet expansionist designs. Second, if Israel was to be a partner, it was wrong for the United States to ask retail prices for the military aircraft it sold to Israel.

Simcha Dinitz, Israel's ambassador to the United States, was present in the hall when I addressed the convention. Afterward he drew me aside to say that I should not have spoken as I did. Israel desperately needed the Phantoms; to question the price being charged for them would anger the administration and imperil Israel's standing in the White House. I said I understood his concern, but I had not spoken at the B'nai B'rith convention as a representative of Israel. I had spoken as a United States citizen, questioning a detail in the conduct of *my* government. Let the Israeli government call me what it would. I would happily be its "Shabbes Goy," taking the blame for speaking out on matters where its official representatives to the United States must be silent.

The fact that 1968 was a presidential and congressional election year undoubtedly worked in Israel's favor. Richard M. Nixon, as the Republican nominee, stated his position on the issue of arms to Israel on several occasions during the election campaign. In a speech to B'nai B'rith, for example, he declared his support for "a policy that would give Israel a technological military margin to more than offset her hostile neighbors' numerical superiority. If maintaining that margin should require that the United States supply Israel with supersonic Phantom F-4 jets—we should supply those Phantom jets."

Nixon's statement on the need to provide Israel with a "technological military margin" represented an advance on the previous phrase "balance of forces" used by the Kennedy and Johnson administrations. But aside from the actual sale of the Phantoms during the early months of the Nixon administration, there was no real follow-through on Nixon's stated policy. It became apparent that his administration meant to advance U.S. interests among the Arab states as well as in Israel. Restraint in its military supplies to Israel was one means toward that end.

This restraint occurred against the background of a continuing "war of attrition" between Israeli and Egyptian forces on opposite sides of the Suez Canal. In that war, which lasted almost three years from the time of its onset in October 1967, Israel's forces clearly had the upper hand. One of the results was, however, that the Soviets sent in more missiles manned by Soviet personnel, and more aircraft with Soviet crews to bolster the shaken morale of Egyptian forces. Within Israel itself, meanwhile, there was a change in the political leadership of the nation when Prime Minister Levi Eshkol died on February 26, 1969. The Labor party selected Golda Meir as its nominee for the premiership, and her selection was approved by the Knesset.

On August 8, 1970, Egypt, in response to a peace initiative by

William Rogers, President Nixon's Secretary of State, and battered by the war of attrition, agreed to a cease-fire with Israel. The Israelis agreed to return to negotiations under U.N. auspices in the search for a peace agreement with Egypt.

While these negotiations were going forward, there were violent eruptions within the Arab camp. Lebanon was swept by a remorseless civil war. In Jordan, PLO terrorists attempted to assassinate King Hussein while their contemptuous action toward other Jordanian authorities brought them into direct and open conflict with the Jordanian army. Fighting broke out in the Amman area. Truce announcements were made on both sides, but the battles continued.

The Syrians then rushed an armored force to aid the PLO, crossing the Jordanian border on September 18 and, accompanied by Iraqi units, advancing toward the capital, Amman.

The Jordanian army attacked the Syrian invasion force, inflicted heavy casualties, and drove it back to Syria. Egypt's chief of staff flew to Jordan, bringing to Hussein and Arafat an appeal from Egypt, Libya, and Sudan to cease fire. When it was clear to Hussein that he had the upper hand, he accepted an invitation by Nasser, flew to Cairo, met Yassir Arafat, and reached an agreement with him—at least on paper.

The next day, September 29 1970, Nasser died of a heart attack. But the clashes between the PLO and the Jordanian army continued until early April 1971, when the Jordanian army, after a three-day battle, wiped out the remaining PLO armed formations in Jordan. Those who had not been killed or taken captive fled, mainly to Lebanon. Hussein, however, was for the time being isolated in the Arab world.

Nasser was succeeded in the presidency of Egypt by his vice president, Anwar Sadat, who was little known to the world and seemed a cipher compared with Nasser. There was no movement on either the Egyptian or Israeli side to bridge the differences that kept them apart. Egypt said it was prepared to end the state of war with Israel but not to sign a peace treaty. It demanded that Israel "settle the refugee problem" and withdraw not only from Egyptian territory but also from the Gaza Strip and the rest of the Arab lands, retiring to the prewar borders. Israel, for her part, indicated that she was ready to enter into peace negotiations with Egypt without prior conditions, but she would not return to the June 4, 1967, borders.

[III]

On a happier front, the renaissance of Hebrew language and culture in Israel, stimulated by the very existence of Israel as a state, caught the imagination of the world of learning. What the nineteenth-century German-Jewish advocates of *Wissenschaft des Judentums* had in mind but did not achieve—namely, academic study of Jewish history and culture as a recognized component of world civilization—was being advanced under the powerful spur of Israeli scholarship. Students of various faiths and backgrounds, seeking the source of Judaism, came to Israel for graduate and postgraduate study. The works of eminent Israeli scholars were taught at universities in many lands, including Christian denominational schools.

Within American colleges and universities, the example of Black Studies programs—and the existence of the state of Israel—stimulated an outcropping of courses related to Jewish studies available to the entire student body and not just to those who were Jewish. A large missing piece in the picture was the focus of many discussions I had in Israel with Dr. Moshe Davis, head of the Institute of Contemporary Jewry at Hebrew University, and with Professor Ephriam Katzir, then president of the state of Israel, whose office was the official sponsor of the institute that Davis headed. What, in fact, was the *actual* state of the teaching of Jewish civilization in colleges and universities beyond the world of Israel itself? What *should* such teaching be like?

If Jewish subjects were taught as part of a general curriculum, the university campus could become a place for self-discovery by Jewish youth. All this was easy to state, but it was also haunted by an issue which went to the heart of the academic enterprise—namely, the potential tension between university goals of knowledge and scholarship and Jewish group goals of identification and commitment. We hoped, however, that a balance could be found between Jewish studies as a component of world civilization and Jewish learning as intrinsic to Jewish self-fulfillment.

Nahum Goldmann, as president of the World Jewish Congress, was of the same mind. Along with Arye Dulzin, acting president of the World Zionist Organization, we managed after much importuning to secure from these two groups support for a major research project entrusted to Moshe Davis. He was to survey the teaching of Jewish civilization in colleges and universities in different parts of the world, including Christian denominational colleges and those with few or no Jewish students. The survey would also focus not only on accredited course offerings but on the entire support structure of the academic enterprise—syllabi and textbooks, library resources, research, publications, and faculty.

Moshe Davis, aided by his devoted wife and others, spent more than a year on his pioneering venture. In his preliminary report to the Commission on Formal Jewish Studies Programs of the Memorial Foundation for Jewish Culture, he stated that the sudden and swift expansion of Jewish studies programs was a curse as well as a blessing, particularly when the teachers whom students encountered could not compete with those in the established disciplines. The problem "for Jewish studies in a university environment is how to ensure that those involved in the teaching of Judaica are ranking scholars of broad intellect who, though specialized, can make a contribution to the entire academic community."

Davis went on to observe that the legitimization of the scientific study and teaching of the entire experience of the Jewish people—its religion, history, thought, and culture—created the need for a new vocation in Jewish life which transcended the seeming contradictions between Jewish commitment and high scholarship. In addition to the modern *professions* of rabbi, educator, and social worker, there was "now the need to shape the profession of University Jewish Scholar in the image of the university." A creative service vocation, however, could not be forced into Jewish corporate life. "It must be defined, planned, and nurtured for the University setting rather than rely on transplantations from other vocations." The case was complicated by the fact that existing Jewish institutions, such as rabbinical schools and teachers' institutes, were not geared either conceptually or structurally to deal with the opportunity for university-based Jewish learning.

> How then [Moshe Davis asked in his report] can we meet the problem of creating a new vocation? On one point there must be full agreement: scholarship as a profession will not be achieved by crash programs. The training of scholars is a highly expensive and demanding enterprise, and the funds for this effort must be garnered at the very start of any combined program. Secondly, every conceivable existing source and institution should be exploited. Beyond this, it is suggested to establish regional centers of specialization in North America and Europe working in coordination with Israeli universities.

The genetic seeds contained in this 1973 report bloomed eight years later when Yitzhak Navon, then president of Israel, announced the formation of the Jewish International Center for the University Teaching of Jewish Civilization; I was the chairman of its board of regents. The aim of the center, under the auspices of the president of Israel but directed by Moshe Davis, was to initiate, stimulate, and coordinate institutional programs without itself becoming a competing academic institution.

[IV]

All such projects contemplated in 1973, and much else besides, were put on hold by the eruption of the Yom Kippur War. The shocks that marked its outbreak on Saturday, October 6, 1973, were not likely to be forgotten by any Israeli who lived through the event nor by overseas Jews who viewed the war from afar. Faith in the all-seeing eye of Israeli intelligence was shaken by the initial success of the Egyptian and Syrian surprise attack.

Washington's formidable oil lobby demanded that Israel not be backed against the Arabs, given the embargo on shipments of Middle East oil to the United States and the sudden doubling of the price of oil. Among America's NATO allies and Japan, the fear of losing access to Middle East oil engendered a mood of hysteria, leading to Israel's political isolation. Not a single Western European country in the NATO alliance allowed even transit landing of American planes bringing arms to Israel. When Israel regained the military initiative on both the northern and southern fronts, Western European nations and Japan, seeking to end the Arab embargo on shipments of oil, joined the Soviet Union and the United States in pressuring Israel to accept a cease-fire—to which Sadat in Egypt agreed. The cease-fire was followed by protracted negotiations on the "disengagement of forces," featuring Henry Kissinger's celebrated shuttle diplomacy as he moved between Cairo, Jerusalem, and Damascus to narrow the differences between the parties.

The agreement with Sadat was reached first. From Israel's standpoint, it was designed, under Dayan's influence, to give Sadat grounds for claiming that he had attained something that had been beyond Nasser's reach, and to reduce any further Egyptian motive to wage war against Israel. Israel, for example, pulled back not only from the West Bank of the Suez but some distance from the East Bank as well. A U.N. emergency force was inserted between the Egyptian army and the new Israeli line drawn in the Sinai. Under an agreed reduction of forces, Egypt could retain only minimal military strength east of the Suez Canal. None of this, however, solved the basic problems in Israeli-Egyptian relationships, or those standing in the way of peace in the "occupied territories." The hope was that the disengagement of forces would facilitate a discussion of such problems. The search for a disengagement agreement between Israel and Syria on the other hand, seemed to elude everyone for months.

Two events cut across these negotiations.

First, David Ben-Gurion, who had moved out of the arena of active politics in Israel, died of a cerebral hemorrhage on December 1, 1973. As the architect of the state of Israel and the leader of the nation in its formative years, Ben-Gurion had made decisions of genius and vision, though he had also had his share of personal vendettas against other Israeli public figures. If his word was law in the early years of a reborn Israeli state, in his later years some of his former colleagues became his sharpest critics. Yet Moshe Dayan, who sat at Ben-Gurion's bedside when he was semiconscious and a few days from death, recalled that there was no trace of bitterness on the man's features. "He looked," so Dayan wrote in a memoir, "immersed in deep thought. His features were touched by an unusual softness and seemed utterly calm. He was leaving a long and stormy life in a state of tranquility," though Israel itself was far from tranquil.

The second major event grew from the fact that PLO forces had turned Lebanon into a central base of operations after being driven out of Jordan. They now numbered about five thousand, and the Lebanese government proved ineffective in halting the attacks they mounted from Lebanese soil against Israel's frontier settlements. On another front, it was not until June 5, 1974, that daily clashes along the Israeli-Syrian border finally stopped, to mark the formal end of the Yom Kippur War.

Israel paid a high price for its extraordinary victory in battle. It lost 2,500 men while defeating an attacking army of one million troops equipped with the most modern weapons. The shock and sense of helpless frustration that swept over Israel had critical consequences for the politics of the country. I was in a position to witness the onset of that public mood.

[V]

I had come to Israel immediately after the main battles on the southern and northern fronts had ebbed and it was possible for civilian aircraft to land at the Tel Aviv airport. The airport remained under tight military security. The military was still fully mobilized—a condition that accounted for the exceptional "courtesy" shown me when I checked into the Tel Aviv Hilton. In the absence of the usual staff, the manager of the hotel served as my bellhop.

The immediate cause for my visit was a meeting in Tel Aviv to make a decision about plans for what is now known as Beth Hatefusoth, the Nahum Goldmann Museum of the Jewish Diaspora, located on the campus of Tel Aviv University.

In 1959, Nahum Goldmann had unveiled a proposal to the World Jewish Congress for a special kind of museum in Israel. The one he had in mind would "present both to the non-Jewish world and the Jewish people, and most especially to the younger generation of Israelis...the nature of the phenomenon which the Diaspora represents in Jewish history, as well as the reasons for the miraculous survival of the people throughout two millennia of dispersion and persecution."

I agreed to join a committee of "experts" from the United States, Israel, and Great Britain to plan and bring the proposed museum to fruition. Goldmann insisted that *he* knew nothing about construction work while *I*, by contrast, was an "expert" in the field.

The commonly accepted design for historical exhibits is the chronological sequence, starting with antiquity, progressing through the Middle Ages, and ending with modern times. But the geographical dispersion of the Jewish people precluded this approach. In Jewish history, where both time and space are variables, a completely novel principle of organization for the museum had to be formulated in order to express the consecutive and concurrent complexities of Jewish existence.

It also became clear to the planners of Beth Hatefusoth that it was virtually impossible to reconstruct the history of the Diaspora in a satisfactory manner through the use of original objects. The problem was not time or money; it was simply that there were no material relics which, even when assembled, could adequately reflect 2,500 years of Jewish life in the Diaspora.

When we saw that it was impossible to fill the rooms with authentic objects, the planning team subordinated the concept of "historic preservation" to an educational goal—namely, to convey emotional and informational messages to visiting public. This meant finding a way to integrate the simultaneous histories of Jewish communities in different countries into workable conceptual frames—which would do justice to the numerous migrations, the dissolution of old established communities, and the birth of new ones. It meant disentangling the fundamental elements of Jewish history from the infinitely complex and subtle choreography of geographical movements. These difficulties dogged the work of the planning committee and delayed its progress until the members began to think in terms of a *thematic* structure suggested by Abba Kovner, a former leader and survivor of the Warsaw ghetto uprising.

Six major themes were chosen which, in the opinion of the planners, encompassed the cardinal aspects of the life of Diaspora Jewry throughout the ages: family, community, faith, culture, relations with the non-Jewish environment, and the return to the land of Israel. Each theme would constitute the core of the permanent main section of the museum. There was to be no division into countries and eras, though an audiovisual display, to be presented in a dome-shaped auditorium, would depict the migrations of the Jews in the chronological order and in relation to events in world history. Further, where a thematic picture of the past could not be satisfactorily conveyed through authentic objects, a series of "nonauthentic" exhibits could be constructed which in combination would evoke the desired result.

A final agreement on the plans for Beth Hatefusoth did not settle all the problems that arose after the 1973 meeting in Tel Aviv.

Some thought the museum should be located in Jerusalem, but Nahum Goldmann insisted on Tel Aviv, which he claimed was an authentic Jewish city built entirely by Jews. Nahum Goldmann did not initially want his name associated with the museum but consented when the museum neared completion. Finally, the costs of building the museum, beyond what the Israeli government contributed, were met by individual Jews in the Diaspora, by the World Jewish Congress and the B'nai B'rith, and by the Memorial Foundation of Jewish Culture which drew on its capital for the first and only time. Since its opening in May 1975, the museum has become one of Israel's best-known cultural learning centers.

[VI]

In the wake of the Yom Kippur War, elements within Israel's Labor party—who favored concessions to the Arabs and limitations on Jewish settlements in the administered territories—asserted themselves, and pushed through a new party platform. Their earlier program had called for Israeli settlements in the administered territories—Judea and Samaria, the approaches to Rafah and the Golan Heights. In the new platform, the desire to stress Israel's striving for peace accounted for the fact that the word "peace" appeared no less than seventeen times throughout fourteen articles.

Meanwhile, popular protest movements across a wide political spectrum sprang up in the country. Ultranationalist groups, for example, demonstrated against any withdrawal from the Golan Heights, but the extreme left urged the exact opposite. There was, however, a common element in the clashing protest movements: all demanded a change in the leadership of the country, and all pointed accusing fingers at those whom they considered responsible for the military and political shortcomings revealed by the Yom Kippur War. The participation of many young widows and bereaved parents of men who had fallen in battle gave a special emotional appeal to the protest movements.

The mood of discontent was compounded by the continued terrorist harassment of Israel's border towns on the northern frontier, and by unhappy contacts with people in occupied territories. At first Israel could point to a seemingly peaceful and humane occupation. Statistical facts showed that the people of the West Bank, and to a lesser extent the Gaza Strip, were enjoying unprecedented benefits in employment, housing, schools, student enrollment, agricultural production, and health care. It was difficult for many Israelis to understand why, if things appeared to be so good in the occupied territories, the hostility of the Palestinians toward Israel intensified with the Israeli occupation. It was hard for many Israelis to face up to the consequences of structural inequality inherent in any occupation. As I wrote at the time:

Even an occupation that regards itself as liberal and enlightened corrupts the relations between the occupying and the occupied, irrespective of the good intentions of the former and the efforts to reach mutual understanding made by either party. Any government of military occupation is an imposed government whose decisions—even the most nobly intended—always arouse suspicion and provoke opposition and revolt.

36 □ The Marriage of Urban and Aetna

In March 1970, a little less than two years after Urban Development had been founded, it was acquired by Aetna Life and Casualty Company, then the largest multiple life insurance company in the United States with assets of eight billion dollars. The acquisition came at a time when the real estate industry had become attractive to the organized economic market because of the boom under way in home building and development. Privately held home-builder firms began to look like juicy plums in the eyes of major corporations bent on acquisitions that fit in with their diversification programs.

Some of the acquisitions predictably proved disastrous. In their eagerness to buy home-building firms, some corporations rewarded the home builders too generously and thus undercut any motive for them to stay on and operate the home-building firms as subsidiaries of the parent corporation. The result was that cave-ins followed many mergers and acquisitions of home-building firms made during the late sixties and early seventies.

Fortunately, Urban at the time was not vulnerable to these negative factors. It was not primarily a home-building company. Rather, it was an investor and a long-term operator of the properties it had built and owned. In the meantime, Aetna had grown into a firm of remarkable vitality and initiative. With expanding investments, mostly in stocks, bonds, and mortgages, it had a large and successful mortgage lending department. But it had not seriously considered getting into the real estate business until it saw that Prudential, another large insurer, was doing so. The example stimulated Aetna management to consider it for themselves. John Filer, head of Aetna's diversification program and later its chief executive, approached me with an acquisition offer based on his personal knowledge of how Urban conducted its business.

From Urban's perspective, a proposed acquisition by Aetna would provide us with the means to finance major developmental projects beyond the Chicago region and Urban's outpost in Denver. The proposed deal, however, nearly fell through at the last minute. In the presence of Filer and his team of experts, I protested that the offered price was too low. I noted that in their assessment the "experts" had failed to include the millions in cash that Urban had on deposit in banks. Filer was taken by surprise but said to the experts, "That's all, gentlemen." They filed out of the room and we brought our negotiations to a mutually satisfactory conclusion.

When Urban became a subsidiary of Aetna in 1970, the lineup of the firm's officers remained unchanged for several years. I continued to serve as chairman of the board and chief executive officer. Norman Cohn, whose background was in construction, continued as president, and my son Tom continued as executive vice president. By this time my second-oldest son, Jim, had graduated from Princeton and had completed a tour of duty in the air force. He was keenly interested in development work, and a place was found for him on the rental side of the Urban setup. Within a few years he took on the major task of rentals for Water Tower Place on North Michigan Avenue in Chicago.

Urban was now inundated with offers of new ventures, and each had to be examined with dozens of criteria in mind. In late 1971, for example, we heard rumors that the First Bank of Denver, the largest bank in the region, meant to construct a new building. Mickey Miller, who continued to head Urban's Denver office, strolled by the bank one day and decided to make an Urban pitch to its management. The bank by then had gone through twenty-six different construction plans with another outfit, but the officials agreed to negotiate with Urban. A proposal was worked up, only to meet with the objections of the Aetna representatives on Urban's board. How, they asked, could Urban consider a plan for a half-million-square-foot building when the First Bank said they would take only 150,000 square feet? How could Urban contemplate so large a structure when the Lincoln Center in Denver was leasing at a snail's pace? In reply, I said to the Aetna people, "Look, if we want to have a presence in the city of Denver, and have a chance to build a major building for the biggest bank in the region—even though the economy is now in a down cycle—you don't pass it up. We have to decide if we want to be in business in Denver or not." That's all I said. The project was unanimously approved. The program eventually included the Energy Center, a twenty-nine-story high-rise, and a mixed structure consisting of the Arco Tower and the Marriott Hotel.

When I turned sixty-five, I decided to give up my active day-to-day role as chairman and chief executive officer of Urban. In addition to my sons Tom and Jim, my third son Sam was now working for the firm, albeit out of the Denver office. My youngest son Bob had a stock interest in the firm but continued to keep his distance from it by half a continent. Norman Cohn, who had been president of Urban, moved up to be chairman of the board and was succeeded as president by my son Tom. When Cohn eventually decided to retire, Tom became chairman and chief executive officer.

Although I was no longer involved in the day-to-day management of Urban, it was at this time that I negotiated the acquisition of the land that made possible the construction of Water Tower Place on North Michigan Avenue in Chicago.

[II]

As far back as the early 1950s, my then partner Nathan Manilow had been interested in the idea of a high-rise shopping facility. Manilow had his eye on some land in Miami Beach and wanted to develop it for use by retail shops. The land, however, was too expensive and too small for a normal shopping mall. Manilow spoke of a high-rise structure as an alternative, and he thought of using the Stevens loft building on State Street in Chicago as a model for what he wanted to do in Miami Beach. I persuaded him that the rents would have to be low and could not produce sufficient income to carry the cost of the land and construction. At the same time I believed that a high-rise shopping center might succeed as a commercial venture provided it had a different market and a more clearly defined structural concept.

I never stopped thinking about that possibility. The more so when Gerald Sivage, president of Marshall Field's, asked me to help Field's develop a new store to be located on Chicago's near north side. The notion of a high-rise shopping facility now appeared to me to be much more feasible than anything I had thought possible.

Several sites considered for the Marshall Field store proved to be too costly or were unavailable. But one location near the north end of Michigan Avenue seemed to have real possibilities. It was owned by the liquor firm of Joseph Seagram and Company, whose principal stockholder was the Sam Bronfman family. Sam was an old friend whom I used to see in New York when I was working at the United Nations. I would sometimes bring U Thant with me for lunch in a restaurant which Bronfman frequented. We would talk about many things on those occasions, including Bronfman's low regard for the real estate business. I remember him saying that he was getting a low return in rentals from the millions he had invested in the construction of the Seagram Building; if he had used the same funds to buy whiskey, its appreciation in value would have put him far ahead. Later, when he sold the Seagram Building for a handsome profit, he may have changed his tune. He often alluded to the vacant land that Seagram's owned on Chicago's near north side, and he suggested that when my days in the United Nations were over, we should be partners in a business venture involving the development of that land.

Bronfman originally meant to use the land as the site of a regional office building for Seagram's. But because of his dim view of the real estate business, he decided not to go ahead with his plan. Seagram's instead used the sixty-thousand-square-foot lot for a distinctive billboard advertising its liquors and other products— probably the costliest billboard in the world. Bronfman was in no hurry to sell the land. He had acquired it for less than a million dollars and had received offers for as much as $7.5 million. Still, whenever the vacant property on North Michigan Avenue in Chicago entered our discussions, Bronfman always promised he would never sell the land without talking to me first.

Meanwhile, I continued without success to look for other sites suited to Marshall Field's needs. Sometime in 1973, however, I received a call from Bronfman's daughter Phyllis, who had a message from her father. He was ready to sell the land on North Michigan Avenue. Was I interested? When I asked Phyllis how much her father wanted for the land, she replied: "He said you know exactly how much." I recalled from past conversations with Bronfman that he would some day sell the land, but not for less than ten million dollars.

I persuaded Field's to participate in the deal up to ten million dollars, and established the fact that land adjoining the Seagram lot could be secured from its owners, the John Hancock Life Insurance Company. I then telephoned Sam Bronfman to make a date to meet him in New York.

My conversation with Sam began with a long review of the fate and fortunes of our mutual friends. But at last I said, "So what about this land? I know what you want for it, and I'm prepared to discuss its acquisition. But who makes this kind of deal only by an exchange of letters, without talking face to face?" Sam agreed. "You are right about that," he said, "but you know I will not sell it for a cent less than ten million dollars, and there is no sense in wasting my time or your time haggling over that price."

"You mean," I asked, "you will sell it to me for ten million?" He said, "Yes." So I said, "Give me some paper." With that I wrote on it: "To Joseph Seagram Company. The Urban Investment and Development Company, a subsidiary of Aetna Life and Casualty Company, offers $10 million for this site [as described], to be effective immediately upon acceptance." I then dated the letter and signed it, "Philip M. Klutznick—on behalf of Marshall Field and Urban Investment and Development Company."

Sam looked at what I wrote and to my surprise put the paper into his pocket. "Look," I said, "I didn't come here to talk. I came here to do business." "Well," he said, "I can't accept your offer." "Why?" "I am not the president of Joseph Seagram Company," he explained. "The president is my son Edgar." "Well," I said, "you'd better get Edgar and your lawyer in here right away, or I want my letter back." Sam seemed to sense that he had overplayed his game of cat and mouse. "Don't get angry," he said. He buzzed for his secretary and asked that she contact Edgar and the lawyer. The pair were waiting nearby until the moment was ripe for them to join the negotiating process. After the lawyer looked at what I had written, Sam asked him: "Is that an offer?" The lawyer replied, "Yes, it is." So now Sam turned to his son and said, "Edgar, sign it and accept it on behalf of the company." This he did.

I then called Newton Minow, my lawyer in Chicago, to say that I was sending him a copy of the handwritten offer I had signed. I read the simple text to him, and he said, "It looks like you have a deal." Minow was to work out the fine points with Bronfman's lawyer. He later telephoned me to say, "When I got together with the lawyer for the Bronfmans, the two of us just laughed. We couldn't find anything wrong with what you wrote and what was signed, but we have never seen a ten-million-dollar deal like that." I didn't know whether Aetna would agree to go along with the purchase, but if they disapproved I was prepared personally to cover the costs of the land acquisition. After a period of hesitation, Aetna agreed to back the deal.

Hancock was willing to sell some of the land it owned adjacent to the Seagram's site. The only condition it set was that any structure built on the land would not obstruct the view of people who lived in the apartments of its Hancock building. This we readily agreed to, and the land in question passed into the hands of Urban. Still more contiguous land became available when one of the owners of the nearby Pearson Hotel died, making the property available for purchase by Urban. It was still a good small hotel, but by leveling the structure to get at the space on which it stood, the blossoming of Water Tower Place was made possible in full.

We now began to plan a "multiuse structure" which would include major retail stores, a range of restaurants for every palate, floors for offices and professional suites, many more floors for luxury condominium residences, a Ritz-Carlton Hotel, a live theater-in-the-round, a four-unit motion picture theater, waterfalls, green plants, and a glassed-in elevator.

The design of the building was essentially the work of Edward Dart, who had become a partner of what was renamed in 1965 as Loebl, Schlossman and Dart. The visual interest of the building was to be its interior. In fact, the building can be said to have been designed from the inside out. It was also agreed that the two major anchor stores, each with its own escalators and elevators, would stand on opposite sides of the entrance way to the mall with its dramatic escalator to the mezzanine. The mall itself was served by both escalators and elevators, so that traffic could move faster than conventional wisdom thought possible.

The interior of the mall, as designed by Warren Platner Associates, aimed to provide a lively, spacious feeling. C. F. Murphy Associates, in collaboration with Loebl, Schlossman and Dart, managed the engineering of the structure and brought to the task an innovative way to "pour the building into place." There was a heated argument over the exterior of the building. Ed Dart, the architect, and I wanted to clothe the building in reddish granite, but Marshall Field's wanted marble—and gray marble was the choice.

The day-to-day supervision of the construction of Water Tower Place fell to Paul Keim, a veteran of the construction of John Hancock Building. The technical problems to be overcome were compounded by uncertainty in the planning stage over matters such as the number of floors to be occupied by the anchor stores, the number of apartments to be built in the tower, and the effect on costs of strikes and dollar inflation.

Meanwhile, negotiations for what turned out to be 130 retail stores moved through a complex maze. Field's, of course, was one major anchor, but it was Urban's view—and Field's agreed—that another major store was needed to ensure the success of the venture. Neiman-Marcus had expressed interest, but it was willing to take only three floors instead of the eight which we felt were indispensable to the plan. Lord & Taylor wanted more entries in the Chicago market under Urban's auspices, so its management agreed to come into Water Tower Place on being assured they would get access to an Oak Brook site as soon as store property there became available. Once the two major retail anchors were in place, the task of filling a seven-level atrium mall with a dazzling array of fine specialty shops was more easily handled.

The hotel part of the project had its own problems. An admittedly crazy idea which I advanced didn't work out. I suggested to the Brashears family, the owners of the Drake Hotel, that they sell their hotel to Urban and then take on the operation of the Water Tower Hotel, thus making the Drake location available for something new which Urban could build. The Brashears did wish to get out of the hotel business, but they were not ready to give up the Drake. The firm of Cabot, Cabot and Forbes agreed to take on the hotel project but overreached themselves elsewhere and were in trouble before the construction of Water Tower Place was finished. In the end, after what seemed to be a ceaseless game of tag, a deal was made with the Ritz-Carlton interests to operate a hotel with 450 rooms, a ballroom, meeting rooms, and restaurants. The high standards implied in the Ritz-Carlton name served as a magnet that drew other quality enterprises to Water Tower Place.

The question of how many floors of the structure should be set aside for condominium apartments found opinions divided. Even after forty floors were agreed to, differences persisted over the total

314]   ANGLES OF VISION

number of condominium units. To end the argument, I decreed 160 apartments in all. That was that. The figure worried Urban's mortgage department, the more so when the apartments at first sold very slowly. In retrospect, however, the greatest mistake we made, in our desire to sell apartments, was not to hold out longer for higher prices. Within six years after the apartments were ready for occupancy, some resold at four times their original purchase price.

If I can lay claim to the role of a founding father of the Water Tower Place project—supported by the confidence of Gerald Sivage of Field's—the successful completion of the project owed much to the leadership of Norman Cohn, Paul Keim, and my son Tom, who were directly responsible in getting the project finished.

Water Tower Place opened in the fall of 1975. From its very first day there was no question of its popular appeal. Its larger economic significance was caught by the *Chicago Sun-Times* in an article on November 15, 1975:

> Not even North Michigan's greatest boosters anticipated the impact of Water Tower Place on the retail volume and real estate values along the street. The stunning increase in business, estimated at 35% by the Greater North Michigan Avenue Association, has begun to have repercussions all along the Magnificent Mile and several blocks in each direction from it.

Water Tower Place changed the entire character of developments by other interests along North Michigan Avenue. It served as a model for developers in other cities, including Donald Trump in New York. Aside from all else, Chicago officials judged that the structure annually drew more visitors than any other in the city. In the years ahead, I was involved in a number of *pro bono publico* advisory roles in connection with public projects. But for all practical purposes, my part in the building of Water Tower Place was the last major venture from which I stood to benefit financially. The future of Urban and its relationship with Aetna was in the hands of my son Tom. In its happiest phase, it led to such massive and successful undertakings as the development of Copely Plaza in Boston.

37 □ The Brookings Report

My concern for Israel's future—the prospects of more powerful weapons of destruction in a future war, the divisive issue of the occupied territories within Israel—induced me to accept an invitation to join a Brookings Institution "Middle East Study Group."

In February 1975, David Owen, director of foreign policy studies at Brookings, concluded that Henry Kissinger's shuttle diplomacy had reached a point of diminishing returns as a means for permanent peace in the Middle East. While the "interim steps" of that diplomacy had reduced tensions along Israel's borders with Egypt and Syria, a prolonged stalemate was now a prospect unless new momentum for negotiations could be generated. Toward that end, peacekeeping efforts should focus on laying the ground for a comprehensive settlement between Israel and its Arab adversaries.

It was Owen's belief that a small but representative group of Americans, studying the Arab-Israeli question from diverse viewpoints, could emerge with a formula for a possible comprehensive settlement in the Middle East. Later, a grant from the Rockefeller Foundation to Brookings enabled Owen to organize the Middle East Study Group, chaired by Roger W. Heynes, president of the American Council on Education.

At the first organizational meeting, Charles W. Yost was proposed as director of research for the report which the group would eventually issue. Although Yost was my friend and former colleague on the U.S. mission to the United Nations, in his presence I dissented from the proposal. I said that beyond comparison with anyone I knew in the diplomatic area, he was "probably the most competent technician on the Middle East." Yet any study group report that bore his name as the sole director "would never be accepted as fair and impartial by the American Jewish community." This was because he had previously published views regarding the need for Israeli concessions as the price for peace in the Middle East.

Yost, a realist, agreed to serve as codirector instead of director of the study group. He also agreed to the suggested choice of a Jewish codirector, this being Professor Monroe Berger, a Middle East specialist at Princeton University. Most other members of the study group either had direct experience in governmental affairs or were prominent academic scholars. The lineup, besides Heynes, Yost, Berger, and myself, included Robert R. Bowie and Nadav Safran (Jewish) of Harvard University; Zbigniew Brzezinski of Columbia University; John C. Campbell of the Council of Foreign Relations; Najeeb Halaby, former head of Pan American Air Lines (and identified with the Arab cause as the father-in-law of Jordan's King Hussein); Rita Hauser (Jewish), a prominent lawyer; Alan Horton, of the American University's field staff; Malcom Kerr (fated to be the victim of terrorists in Lebanon) and Stephen Spiegel (Jewish), both on the faculty of the University of California at Los Angeles; Fuad Khouri (Arab) of Villanova University; William Quandt of the University of Pennsylvania (who later was to play a major role in the Camp David accords); and A. L. Udovitch of Princeton University.

Meetings of the group, modeled after those of the Committee on Economic Development, were regularly held every month, lasting one or two days. The discussion ventilated all the formulae advanced post-1975 for a general settlement (including a federation from the West Bank and Jordan) as well as all the problems encountered (including the question of who should speak for the Palestinians).

Some members were especially sensitive to the concerns of the Israelis; others were specially sensitive to those of the Arabs. All, however, genuinely tried to understand the concerns of Israelis and Arabs alike. In the words used by Jean Monnet in a different connection, all were on one side of the table while the problem was on the other.

The report of the study group, when published at the end of December 1975 after six months of work, began by stressing the United States' strong moral, political, and economic interests in a stable peace in the Middle East. Satisfaction of the Israeli requirement would involve "binding commitments by the Arab states to a stable peace—that is, commitments to recognize and respect the sovereignty of Israel, to refrain from the threats or use of force against it, to desist from other hostile action against it, and progressively to develop with it normal international and regional political and economic relations." Satisfaction of the Arab requirements would involve Israeli withdrawal to the June 5, 1967, lines, "only with such modifications, as well as such particular arrangements for Jerusalem, as might be agreed upon." It would involve the right of the Palestinians to self-determination in one form or another, consonant with Israeli requirements.

The heart of the report dealt with integrated terms for the proposed settlement. Here the text read:

> So that both sides may be persuaded to make the concessions which this integrated accommodation between peace and withdrawal would require, it will be necessary that, until comprehensive peace agreements stipulating the whole range of commitments be concluded, their implementation be staged over a period of years. The stages would be clearly defined in the agreements. Each stage would be undertaken only when the agreed provisions of the previous stage had been carried out. Under this procedure Israeli withdrawal and Arab movement toward normal relations would proceed in tandem. A mechanism would be provided for phased implementation.

It is enough to single out what the report had to say about two matters, of which the first was the "principle of Palestinian self-determination" and "an acceptable means for putting that principle into practice." The report stated that a settlement "cannot be achieved unless Israel accepts the principle of Palestinian self-determination and some generally acceptable means is found of putting the principle into practice." In this connection it mentioned two possibilities: an independent Palestine state, or a Palestine entity voluntarily federated with Jordan.

As for who should speak for the Palestinians, the report observed: "It is not clear to what extent the Palestine Liberation Organization (PLO) can negotiate on behalf of the Palestinians on the West Bank, in Gaza, or in Jordan, to whom it does not have ready access." Further, the PLO had not publicly recognized Israel's right to exist. Nor had Israel recognized the PLO or agreed to accept the establishment of a Palestinian state. "Nevertheless," the report added, "it can certainly be said that a solution to the Palestinian dimension of the conflict will require the participation of credible Palestinian representatives who are prepared to accept the existence of Israel."

The second of the two matters to be noted concerned the status of Jerusalem, a city which embraces sites that are among the most holy for Muslims, Jews, and Christians, besides being the capital of Israel. The report suggested that "it might be wise to leave the resolution of the issue of Jerusalem to a late stage of the proposed negotiations." Yet any resolution should meet the following criteria: unimpeded access to all the holy places, and each under the custodianship of its own faith; no barriers dividing the city to prevent free circulation throughout it; substantial political autonomy for each national group within the city, within the area where it predominates:

> All such criteria could be met either within a city under Israeli sovereign jurisdiction with free access to the holy places, under divided sovereign jurisdiction between Israel and Arab states with assured free circulation, or under either of these arrangements with an international authority in an agreed area, such as the old walled city, with free access to it from both Israel and the Arab states.

Before the report was published, its terms were known to the Israeli government, and I found myself subject to earnest advice from Israeli sources not to sign my name to it. At the same time I received a telephone call from Rita Hauser, a member of the study group who wanted to know if I intended to sign. When I asked what lay behind her question, she revealed that she was being subect to sustained pressure from Israeli sources not to sign. I told her that I intended to sign the report. Despite its imperfections—which flowed naturally from the compromises that had been reached over six months of work—something good might ultimately come of it. Rita signed, as did all the other Jewish members of the group.

Within Israel, press reaction was mixed. The *Jerusalem Post*, for example, confined itself to a summary of the report, coupled with an account of how the Israeli embassy in Washington had urged Jewish members of the study group to refuse to sign the document. *Davar*, the organ of the Labor party in Israel, published two long articles about the report. The first was simply a translation of the text. The author of the second article noted that the recommendations of the report on the Palestinian issue were at variance with the official Israeli government view. On the question whether the Palestinians should be given the opportunity to choose independent statehood or federation with Jordan, the Israelis clearly preferred the latter. Yet it was the author's view that "if a settlement is reached, it will probably be along the lines of the Brookings study."

Soon after the Brookings Report was issued, I was treated to a personal experience whose nature would be repeated with greater intensity in later years. On the one hand, I received many letters of support from individual American Jews whom I knew had been devoted advocates of Israel's cause in earlier years but whose later silence led me to believe they were dead. It turned out that they had been in good health all along. They had lapsed into silence after being accused too many times by other American Jews of having "betrayed Israel"—because they had openly questioned the wisdom of official Israeli policy toward the occupied territories. On the other hand, some of my friends among American Jews were sharply critical of the report and of me for signing it.

Meanwhile, any hope for new life in the Middle East negotiating process was overcast by two events. One was the intensified civil war in Lebanon which absorbed the attention of Arab states in the region. The other was the 1976 presidential election in the United States. After Jimmy Carter's election, the Brookings study group met anew and prepared a statement in December 1976:

> It would be imprudent and unsafe to attempt to leave the situation in the Middle East frozen for any prolonged period. Even though further results may not be obtained quickly, the process and momentum of negotiation must be maintained. In their absence, moderate policies and leaders could be superseded by more intransigent ones, and the security of all parties be gravely imperiled by the failure of all to act while the time was ripe.

The study group recommended the dispatch of an American emissary or emissaries to the Middle East at the earliest opportunity to consult with the governments primarily concerned about the next steps toward peace. What kind of substantive contribution could the U.S. make in 1977 to overcoming inevitable deadlocks between the parties?

> It should make its contributions not by presenting any preferred solution at the outset, but by making clear from time to time, as the negotiations proceed, views concerning the broad lines of a settlement that are in harmony with the conclusions set forth in the Brookings 1975 Report.

In the months that followed, everyone—including the participants in the Brookings study group—was treated to a mixed bag of surprises.

38 □ Enter Jimmy Carter

My leadership posts in various sectors of American life—in business, in public service, in national Jewish organizations—made my Chicago address a port of political call for aspirants to major elective office. In most cases, the results were confined to what Lyndon Johnson, in his pungent diction, would describe as "pressing the flesh." Aspirants stated where they were coming from and what they hoped to do if they got to where they wanted to go. They also voiced the hope that I would personally support their "cause" and would persuade my associates to do so as well. On my part, I asked questions, listened carefully, made mental notes and wished them well. That was that, but in some cases, generally involving candidates whom I knew for a number of years, I served on their advisory and fund-raising committees.

My early relationship with Jimmy Carter, however, fell outside this pattern. I never met him when he was governor of Georgia, never exchanged letters with him, nor did he visit me in Chicago during his bid for the 1976 Democratic presidential nomination. My contacts with his campaign were limited to friends who worked for his nomination, some of whom were later his appointees when he won the presidency.

One among these was Richard Gardner (later U.S. ambassador to Italy), who held a distinguished service chair as professor of international law at the Columbia University Law School. I had worked closely with Gardner when he was Deputy Assistant Secretary of State for International Organizations and I was U.S. ambassador to the U.N. Economic and Social Council. Another was Zbigniew Brzezinski (later National Security Council Adviser), a professor of international relations at Columbia; I came to know him through his work for the Brookings Middle East Study Group of which I was a member. Then there was Cyrus Vance (later Secretary of State), a lawyer by profession, whose personal history included service in vital governmental roles.

As Deputy Secretary of Defense under President Johnson, Vance had worked amid the tumult over the Vietnam War, had witnessed the evolution of U.S. policy during the 1967 Arab-Israeli War, had been a mediator in the Greek-Turkish conflict over Cyprus, and had participated in the 1968 Paris talks on Vietnam. Yet his views about U.S. power and diplomacy were little known even in circles comprising the "foreign policy establishment," and perhaps for the following reason. Unlike Henry Kissinger at Harvard and Brzezinski at Columbia—before each got a handle on the levers of power in Washington—Vance was under no academic imperative to publish articles and books concerning policy choices in international relations.

In earlier years, I had dealt with Vance at times during my assignments from President Johnson, or in my interests in the policy aspects of U.S.-Israeli relations. He prompted a question I sometimes asked myself when I judged other men. The question was not whether they were "brilliant." Brilliant men—with an imperious temperament and a flawed moral character—can be the stuff out of which private and public tragedies are made. The question was whether I would be willing to be governed by them. In Vance's case, the answer was an unqualified yes.

He was a candid, fair-minded man with a finely tuned sense of equity. He never promised what he could not perform, but what he believed he could perform he promised, and then tried by every honorable means to make good. Being deliberate and reflective in manner, it was not in his nature to affect the theatrical pose of a hard-nosed practitioner of *realpolitik* who scoffed at moral sentiments in the face of policy decisions. He tried as best he could to get at objective evidence of what was true, whether on the side of sunshine or of a storm.

I knew that the trauma of his experiences during the Vietnam War made him skeptical about what could be gained by sending U.S. troops into Third World conflict, and also taught him the need to be patient amid the ups and downs inherent in any diplomatic negotiations. I also knew that he shared my own attachment to the United Nations and never took cheap shots at the organization. He believed, as I did, that though its faults reflected those of humanity in the mass, the United Nations had also shown that it could render indispensable help in reducing international tensions.

Zbig Brzezinski was from a different world than Vance. Being myself the son of immigrants from eastern Europe who scratched for a living before they took root on American soil, I had more than ordinary respect for what Brzezinski had to overcome as a Polish immigrant in order to "make it" in the intellectual world. He had received his doctorate from Harvard University and, as a professor of international relations at Columbia, had emerged as a prolific author whose writings were focused on the Soviet Union and eastern Europe. He had had little experience in government except for a brief period on the policy planning staff of the State Department, but he had served for a while as the academic head of the Trilateral Commission, in which Carter had also been an active participant. It was in that context that Brzezinski emerged as the equivalent of a foreign policy mentor to the future president.

When Brzezinski worked with the Brookings Middle East Study Group, I could see, as others did, that he was adept in providing a broad frame of reference for policy debates. Theoretical formulations of governing concepts came easily to him. I sometimes wished, however, that he would cross-examine his tendency to assume that because of his specialized knowledge of the technical aspects of foreign affairs, he was also qualified to speak authoritatively about their domestic political dimensions. In fairness to Brzezinski, I should add that other intellectually proud people have been known to share the same tendency—or its reverse, which is to assume that their mastery of the nuances of domestic politics means an equal mastery of external matters.*

Shortly before the 1976 Democratic presidential primary in Ohio, I received a telephone call from Vance, asking me to make a financial contribution to Jimmy Carter's bid for the Democratic

---

*When I was U.S. Secretary of Commerce (1979–1980) in the Carter administration, I gained an insight into Brzezinski which differed from the public persona he had cultivated as a hard-nosed expert. Shortly before I left for an official trip to Poland, as U.S. chairman of the U.S.-Polish Joint Economic Commission, Brzezinski, with unaccustomed shyness, put a question to me. Could I determine from the communist authorities in Poland if he would be permitted to return there for a visit? He seemed to have a kind of romantic homesickness for the country, though as he explained the matter to me, the purpose of the visit was to take along his two sons so that he could introduce them to the land of their family origin.

nomination. Not much more was said in our conversation, but I agreed to send Vance a check once he returned from a trip to Italy.

At the time I was deeply involved in a major *pro bono publico* project for the city of Chicago. The project began on a day when a group of Chicago businessmen, of which I was a member, held its regular meeting on the fifty-sixth floor of the First National Bank Building. Assorted civic issues were on our agenda, but a new one quite literally came into view when some of us pressed against the great windows of the meeting place and took in the ground-level scene. We could see the old Dearborn Street railroad station, rusting and weed-clogged railroad tracks, empty land strewn with rubbish, along with ramshackle structures that dotted the extent of the neighborhood.

The station, an architectural showplace in its day, was in an advanced state of decay, and the neighborhood around it, once a hive of economic activity, seemed lifeless. As we talked about the scene below, we agreed that the station was salvageable, and that the abandoned rail yards and blighted city blocks cried out for redevelopment. The more so because few parcels of land so close to the heart of the city were still available for new commercial and residential construction. If the area were redeveloped, it would generate new tax revenues for the city. People could live in affordable homes of their own, in condominiums or in rental apartments—all close to their places of work or to the cultural resources concentrated nearby. They could walk to work or to most other needs or diversions, sparing themselves the exhaustion of travel by overloaded public transportation or by bumper-to-bumper commuting from the suburbs.

Those of us who saw the future in this light did not look to the federal government to redeem the Dearborn area. Instead, we formed a limited-dividend corporation, and issued sufficient stock to get the redevelopment project under way until it gained a momentum of its own. A number of Chicago-based corporations purchased the stock with the understanding that they might not get back the full amount they paid in; at best, they could expect only to break even. But what they lost on their investments they might offset in claims for tax losses. They could also share the satisfaction of having contributed to the success of a civic project that was as worthy as it was practical.

I was made chairman of the executive committee of the corporation formed to plan the redevelopment of the Dearborn area. Two others on the committee were my friends Tom Ayers, chairman and chief executive officer of Commonwealth Edison, and Ferd Kramer. The fate of the venture, however, was in the hands of Chicago's Mayor Richard Daley. This was because a key precondition for its success was the city providing the necessary municipal utilities—including schools—just as it usually did in other areas earmarked for development.

The mayor's syntax and pronunciation were sometimes the despair of English grammarians and the butt of jokes by local humorists. But when it came to the governance of a great, vibrant, brawling city—where people had sharp elbows as well as broad shoulders—it would be hard to find his equal. He was not without fault or flaw, and the mores and problems of his time defined the limits of his power. While Chicago's magnates might laugh behind his back when they repeated his latest howler, in his presence they deferred to his talent. They knew that if he bound himself to a project in the interests of the city as a whole, things happened. He was always *there*, a good listener and questioner, a man ready to be persuaded by a rational argument. His sense of timing and his calculus of net gain were critical factors in what he bound himself to do, but once he brought into play his will to decide, he also assumed personal responsibility for the consequences of the decision.

Mayor Daley was not as academically learned as the key figures in his own planning department. He was endowed, however, with a kind of bifocal outlook: he appreciated attractive possibilities as well as immediate realities. He recognized the initial costs to the city of the Dearborn project. But his grasp of how the economic and social revival of a neighborhood would mean an enlarged tax base accounted for the decisive support he gave to the project. In fact, before the development the city collected only about forty thousand dollars annually from the entire Dearborn area. Afterwards it began to collect several million annually—with far more in prospect as new commercial enterprises took root and as town houses which once sold for $34,000 continued to increase in value so that some of the same houses in later years were resold for up to ten times the original sales price.

From time to time, as our executive committee faced new problems, we turned to Mayor Daley for help. That was the case shortly before the 1976 Ohio presidential primary when Tom Ayers, Ferd Kramer, and I arranged to see the mayor in his City

Hall office. Our conversation was often interrupted by the buzz of a secretary who indicated the nature of an incoming call, but one particular buzz differed from the rest. Daley turned to us and said, "Would you mind if I bring in a man who believes he is going to be the next president of the United States? I will talk to him for only a short while and you need not leave." We said we wouldn't mind in the least. There was a signal to the secretary, and presently in walked Jimmy Carter, well groomed and smiling. That was the first time I met him.

Human beings don't look like presidents except in the eyes of the beholder. Our presidents, taken in the mass, have been long, short, lean, and fat in body; erect, stooped, and squat in posture; red, black, blond, and bald in hair; straight-toothed, buck-toothed and false-toothed. Among twentieth-century presidents, Theodore Roosevelt was of medium height and nearsighted, with a high voice and a keyboard display of dentistry. In the case of Calvin Coolidge, an observer who was a professional portrait painter remarked that his face was "grammatically flawed"; it should have "grown an apostrophe above his narrow lips to indicate a deletion of life." And Herbert Hoover, said the sculptor Gutzon Borglum, looked as though a "rose would wilt if you put it in his hand." Not until most men are on their way to the White House do their physical traits seem appropriate in a president.

When I first met Jimmy Carter, I wondered to myself, as I once did in the case of John F. Kennedy, whether I was actually looking at a future president of the United States—or whether I wished him to be one. But my encounter with Carter was too brief to permit even a conjectural answer to the question. I gained the impression that I faced a "good man," but beyond that I could determine nothing more.

A few days later I received a telephone call from Carter which suggested that despite the sea of humanity in which he swam, he could separate out individuals according to how they fit his needs; and that he was inclined to do many things for himself which another person in his position would have entrusted to an aide. The purpose of his call was to ask—based on our brief encounter— for a financial contribution to his campaign. I indicated that I had previously arranged to send Cy Vance a check for that purpose.

When I conveyed to Mayor Daley the substance of my conversation with Carter, he advised me to wait until after the Ohio primary before I actually mailed the check. The outcome of that primary, as Daley correctly calculated, ensured the Democratic nomination for Jimmy Carter.

I was at the time serving as chairman of the governing board of the World Jewish Congress and was being urged by Dr. Nahum Goldmann to accept the presidency of the congress when he retired in late 1977. With Jimmy Carter's election as president, I neither sought a post in his administration nor was I contacted regarding my possible interest in one. I was, however, in a position to stay abreast of policy developments within the Carter administration as they bore on Arab-Israeli relations. One of my personal lines of communication ran toward Vice President Walter F. Mondale, a friend of many years. Another ran toward Secretary of State Cy Vance who, because of my link with the Brookings group, would call me from time to time to get my reactions to proposals being floated within the State Department regarding the Middle East.

In addition, I had access to lines of communication outside the administration. One, which stemmed from my earlier roles in Jewish organizations, led to the Israeli embassy in Washington, to the Israeli delegation at the United Nations, and, on occasion, to members of the Israeli cabinet. The other, also of long standing, led to Ashraf Ghorbal, the Egyptian ambassador to the U.S., whose friendship I had made when we both served in the United Nations during the 1957 General Assembly and in the early 1960s. At Ghorbal's request, I had helped arrange meetings where he and representatives of other Arab countries could confer with Jewish leaders in the United States. So I had ample notice that from the very start of his presidency, President Carter meant to press for a solution to the Arab-Israeli conflict.

[II]

Aside from the Brookings study report, the Carter administration inherited from the administration of Gerald Ford a number of transition papers on the Middle East. In urging the incoming administration to use its full influence for a settlement, the transition papers contemplated a revival of the 1973 Geneva formula—a multilateral conference of all the parties under the cochairmanship of the United States and the Soviet Union. Geneva, however, might only be symbolic—"a cover for serious negotiations which would take place elsewhere." The Soviets did "not seem essential to the negotiating process itself," but the United States would still have to decide whether to aim for partial or comprehensive agreements, how to handle the Palestinian representation question, how to take into account the impending Israeli elections, and how to develop contacts with the negotiating parties.

In consequence of President Carter's decision to reconvene the Geneva conference by the end of the year, his new Secretary of State, Cyrus Vance, left for the Middle East in mid-February 1977 to start the process. In Israel he found Prime Minister Rabin prepared to try for a negotiated settlement, comprehensive or partial. In other capitals—Cairo, Damascus, Amman, and Riyadh—he found a generally positive if guarded attitude and a sense of urgency. President Sadat was particularly anxious for a resumption of negotiations with active American involvement.

It was Vance's view that until Prime Minister Rabin visited Washington in early March, the United States—for domestic reasons—should proceed cautiously in its moves toward a Middle East settlement. He knew that the president's eagerness for an early resolution of the long-standing Israeli-Arab conflict could further alarm congressional circles and the American Jewish community, which already feared that any settlement would be at the expense of Israel.

Prime Minister Rabin arrived in Washington, and made his desires clear to President Carter. First, Israel did not wish to leave the Golan Heights. Second, because the question of a territorial compromise in the West Bank would figure in the forthcoming Israeli election, he could not speak about it except to say that Israel would not agree to a total withdrawal. Third, he agreed that the "bulk of Sinai" could be returned to Egypt in exchange for peace. Fourth, he opposed the creation of a new Palestinian state but leaned toward the creation of a Jordanian-Palestinian state. Finally, he urged the United States not to press the idea of a unified Arab delegation at Geneva.

Carter and Rabin both "went public" in Washington after their formal negotiations were over, each trying to woo American opinion. Carter let it be known that U.S. support for Israel would suffer if Israel refused to participate in the Geneva talks because of the "technical fact" that the PLO would be part of the negotiations. Rabin, for his part, with impending elections hanging heavy over his head, refused to accept a PLO in any guise as a party to the negotiations.

William Quandt, who became an aide to Secretary Vance after the election, later wrote that the Israeli Labor party was fatally weakened in the election by continued U.S. public pressure on Rabin to yield on points that would enable President Carter early in his administration to "solve the Middle East problem." As it happened, however, Rabin also came under fire in Israel on a technical charge of currency violations, dating from his time as Israel's ambassador in Washington—a charge that capped allegations of corruption involving prominent figures in the Labor party. In the upshot, soon after Rabin's return to Israel from Washington, he resigned as prime minister and was replaced on an interim basis by Shimon Peres, a man with whom he would be uneasily yoked in the years ahead.

Roughly a month after the meeting between Carter and Rabin, Egypt's President Anwar Sadat arrived in Washington in mid-April for discussions with Carter. He was already a media star in the United States because of earlier negotiations with former Secretary of State Henry Kissinger, who had praised him as a statesman and man of vision. State Department officials recalled that Sadat in 1974 and again in 1975 had indicated that he might be willing under U.S. auspices to negotiate partial agreements with Israel. This encouraged the notion that he was ready to resume the peace process, but it was not clear how far he was prepared to go in getting out of step with other Arab parties.

The record of Sadat's introductory encounter with Carter—the first the president had ever had with an Arab leader—now reads like an outline for the protracted game of hide-and-seek between Egyptian and Israeli leaders that would unfold in the months ahead.* Sadat was adamant on two points: first, no Israeli soldiers should remain on Egyptian territory; second, because open borders and diplomatic relations between Egypt and Israel involved questions of "sovereignty," they should not be part of the bargaining for an overall Middle East settlement.

Other points in the record indicated that Sadat, from the start, was within hailing distance of Rabin's position. He was, for

---

*Vance, in a reference to Sadat, later wrote: "Strong on principle, weak in implementation, he appeared to expect concrete solutions to flow automatically from political level agreements on the essentials." Brzezinski, from the start, had his own doubts. He later wrote that he was "worried about Sadat's ability to distinguish fact from fiction."

example, flexible on the idea of a Palestinian homeland, adding that any proposed Palestinian state should have some link to Jordan. He preferred that there not be a single unified Arab delegation to the proposed Geneva conference, because that would reduce his own flexibility in the negotiations. He would, however, accept some such arrangement if President Carter thought it was indispensable to the peace process. He also preferred that the United States produce some proposals acceptable to the parties even before Geneva—an arrangement that would enable Egypt to go to Geneva as a "showcase exercise," simply to sign the agreements.

In late April, with the Rabin and Sadat meetings in Washington behind him, President Carter left the United States for a quick trip to the Middle East. A key question he put to the Arab leaders he met was whether the PLO would agree before a Geneva conference to accept U.N. Resolution 242 with its formula of "territory for peace." Under that formula, Israel would return most, if not all, the territory occupied in the 1967 war, in exchange for which it would be recognized by its Arab neighbors. All parties—Egypt, Israel, Jordan, and Syria—would be expected to negotiate security arrangements applicable to their respective borders. The Palestinian "voice" would somehow find expression in the negotiations, and some sort of "solution" to the refugee question would be found.

By early May, the new administration's diplomatic initiative was almost four months old. U.S. officials believed that all Arab leaders favored the idea of a Geneva conference, but they wanted significant progress beforehand in resolving Arab-Israeli issues. In other words, they wanted not open-ended negotiations at Geneva but an American plan which the U.S. would impose on Israel.

And what of the Israelis?

President Carter's approach to the Arab-Israeli conflict depended for its success on the presence of an Israeli partner willing to accept the concept of "territory for peace" with each of its Arab neighbors. With a government in Israel led by Labor, he had a fair chance to make U.N. Resolution 242 the centerpiece of a successful Geneva conference. That was not to be. Although the president was becoming more sensitive to the opinions of American Jews regarding Israel, he had not yet grasped the effect of his statements and policies on Israel's domestic politics. He was soon treated to an unwelcome surprise.

39 □ The Odd Couple: Begin and Sadat

From the birth of the state of Israel, American officials had dealt with successive Israeli governments led by the Labor party. Israeli prime ministers such as David Ben-Gurion and Golda Meir, along with Laborite ambassadors to the U.S. such as Abba Eban, had developed deep ties to Washington power centers as well as to the American Jewish community. This was far less true of Menachem Begin. He had been a major player in the internal politics of Israel for more than three decades, but he was little known in Washington. Leaders of major American Jewish organizations knew in general terms where Begin came from and what he stood for, but it is my impression that not many had sustained contacts with him before the 1977 Israeli elections.

In my own case, when I first visited Israel in 1955 as president of B'nai B'rith, I wanted to meet Begin; I was given to understand that he was aware of my background and wanted to meet me. Yet Oved Ben-Ami, my later partner in the project to build Ashdod, struck a cautionary note. My coming together with Begin must be done quietly, he said. If it was learned that I had spent time with Begin, some of the ministerial heads of the incumbent Labor government might be wary of me. The actual meeting with Begin, held in his Tel Aviv apartment, took place under what struck me as the conspiratorial cover of darkness, at around ten o'clock at night. Perhaps other American Jewish leaders who visited Israel avoided contact with Begin because of the seeming political quarantine under which he had been placed by other political leaders.

[II]

Begin had derived his beliefs from the revisionist wing of the Zionist movement, Betar, led by Vladimir Ze'eve Jabotinsky. But his terrible personal trauma as a Jew in central Europe at the time of Hitler's rise to power, followed by the loss of nearly all his immediate family in the Holocaust, provided the emotional charge behind his words and gestures. As the fiery leader of the preindependence Irgun movement, he was inevitably associated with the terrible massacre of Palestinian villagers at Deir Yassin and with the bombing of the King David Hotel. After independence, his Herut party, which he made the centerpiece of a coalition of parties known as Likud, staked out an ideological claim to all of Eretz Yisrael, defined as both Palestine and Transjordan.

History and religion, and not security considerations alone, were the sources of Herut's insistence on retaining control of Judea and Samaria, the names Begin invariably used in referring to what other people called the West Bank. The two areas had been the center of ancient Jewish kingdoms. If Israel had no valid claim to *them*, so Begin argued, what right did Israel have to Tel Aviv and to the coastal strip with which it had only tenuous historical ties?

Begin had served as a member of the national unity government between 1967 and 1970 but had resigned in mid-1970 when the cabinet, led by Golda Meir, agreed to accept U.N. Resolution 242 with the understanding that its withdrawal provisions applied to all fronts. In my eposodic meetings with him over the years, I always found him to be as courtly in manner as he was formal in dress. When my views about the problems of peace in the Middle East matured after the Six Days War—and were publicized—Begin was aware of the extent to which they differed from his own. Yet with one exception to be noted later, he always embraced me warmly when we came together.

I was personally unhappy with signs that Menachem Begin and his close political associates appeared uncaring about the yearnings of Palestinians in the occupied West Bank for a self-governing homeland of their own. In discussing these matters with Begin, I argued that there was no profit in a policy which called for the perpetual use of power to secure military victories that had no diplomatic conclusions. Self-adulation among the victors could lead to self-destructive recklessness, while the true greatness of a people was revealed when it made friends of its enemies. Begin shrugged off all such arguments. The experiences of the Holocaust ruled his historical outlook, and he seemed unwilling to conceive of Jewish life in Israel in other than apocalyptic terms.

On the eve of the 1977 Israeli elections, few American officials thought Begin would succeed in his bid to become prime minister. Nor can I recall any head of a major American Jewish organization who expected him to be the victor. My guess is that Begin himself was surprised by an election result so favorable to the Likud bloc which he led. Leaders of Labor were stunned. They knew how their election prospects were weakened by U.S. pressure to make concessions toward a Middle East peace, but they apparently failed to acknowledge the negative effects of internal matters.

In addition to "scandals" within the Labor party, there were the grievances of a growing number of Sephardic voters who turned to the Likud bloc for relief. Ben-Gurion as early as 1956 clearly saw the emergent problem posed by Sephardic immigration from Middle East countries to Israel. He said that the Israeli government must assume active responsibility for integrating *all* Sephardim into an Israeli society which was radically different from the one they knew. In the end, Labor was the victim of a conviction common among many Sephardim that they had been personally consigned to the role of "hewers of wood and haulers of water."

President Carter used the word "shocked" when he described his reaction to Begin's election. The whole of his approach to a Middle East peace had been premised on what he believed Israel's pragmatic-minded Labor party leadership might be induced to accept. Begin was an unknown entity for Carter. The president and his staff were unprepared to deal with a proud man of deep ideological convictions who combined a Talmudist's talent for fine-spun legalistic arguments with a master politician's grasp of the arts of brinkmanship.

[III]

Among President Carter's chief lieutenants, Brzezinski "the activist" pressed for a confrontation with Begin. Secretary Vance, however, was of a different mind. His argument *against* publicly pushing Begin too hard was rooted in a factor of which I was keenly aware. It was that even within that portion of the American Jewish community which opposed the West Bank policies of the Likud bloc, the administration's public decrying of Begin decisions was sometimes construed as an attack on Israel itself. Thus, even those American Jews for whom Begin was an "embarrassment" rallied to his side as a way of affirming their support for Israel. At the same time President Carter lost some of his political capital within the American Jewish community which by right should have remained intact.

Soon after Begin became prime minister of Israel, Secretary Vance began to develop concrete ideas for moving the peace process forward, starting with a decision to invite Begin to Washington. He also sought to reconvene the Geneva conference with as much prior agreement as possible. For the West Bank and Gaza, Vance spoke of the possibility of a trusteeship as well as a referendum by the residents regarding their political preferences. The idea of trusteeship was designed to inject the concept of a transitional phase into the negotiations over the West Bank, while the possibility of a referendum would get around the question of PLO participation.

Begin's first official visit to Washington unfolded as a series of cordial meetings with the president and his immediate White House aides, with Secretary Vance directly, and with Carter in private. Begin agreed with Carter's desire for a comprehensive peace settlement, though in Begin's language the goal was expressly defined as "peace treaties" between Israel and its neighbors. While he seemed ready for negotiations with the Arabs at Geneva, he did not favor a unified Arab delegation, no more than did Sadat before him. Such an arrangement, he said, was "illogical." Nonetheless he was prepared, as was Sadat, to *accept* a unified delegation for the face-saving purpose of convening the conference. After that, however, negotiations should go forward on a nation-to-nation basis.

While Begin adamantly opposed any dealings with the PLO as a recognized body, he agreed that Palestinians could be represented in the negotiations and that Israel would not inspect their credentials. As for the Egyptian territory that Israel still held, he promised substantial withdrawals. On the other hand, Begin's views on the West Bank and Gaza were more rigid than his predecessors. He had agreed to accept U.N. Resolution 242 as a basis for negotiation, subject to the personal way he construed its meaning. The resolution had been previously understood to imply some degree of Israeli withdrawal on *each* front of the conflict, in return for Arab commitments to peace, recognition, and the security of Israel. But the ambiguous way in which the administration construed Begin's acceptance of the resolution led him to issue a "clarification" *after* his visit. He explained that while he agreed that

U.N. Resolution 242 applied *to* all fronts, it did not mean that Israel had to withdraw *from* all fronts. In other words, he had no intention of withdrawing Israeli forces from the West Bank. At the same time, he made it clear that he did not expressly promise to heed Carter's plea for restraint regarding settlements in the occupied territories.

Begin's stubborn stand was thought by Washington to be campaign rhetoric and a negotiating ploy. The White House did not have to wait long before it was treated to a poke-in-the-eye reminder that he meant exactly what he said. The day after Begin returned to Jerusalem from Washington, the Israeli cabinet conferred legal status on three settlements established under the previous Labor government—settlements which Carter believed to be illegal.

[IV]

In the late summer and early fall, movements toward a Geneva conference became tangled. In the Arab camp there were sharp disagreements as to who should "broker" the PLO involvement in the conference. The PLO camp itself was split by the question of whether or not to accept U.N. Resolution 242 as a basis for negotiating with Israel. Israel, meanwhile, became the target of sustained criticism by United States officials because the Begin government had not marked time until the Geneva conference but instead had approved new settlements in the occupied territories despite President Carter's request for restraint. And when Israeli-backed Christian militiamen in Lebanon attacked Palestinian positions, and Israel intervened militarily in support of the Christians, it appeared that Begin had violated his promise to Carter that Israel would make no moves in Lebanon without first informing Washington.

I shared the unease of many American Jews who were devoted to the cause of Israel but could not understand why Begin seemed to assume that he could serve Israel's highest interests by acts which wore the face of arrogance and duplicity. Later, I came to understand that Carter's grand design was put at risk less by Begin and far more by two other factors—the unwieldy shape of the conference itself, and the way Sadat assessed Geneva in the light of his own domestic needs. Sadat believed he could cut a bilateral deal with Israel for further withdrawals from Sinai, but he feared that this prospect would be imperiled if the deal became entangled at Geneva with Syria's demands. Syria's Assad could justify taking part in peace talks with Israel only if they resulted in a Palestinian state.

Begin and Sadat had not yet irrevocably decided to bypass Geneva, but both were eager to see how far they could move toward a mutual agreement without American involvement. Secret channels were used for Israeli-Egyptian contacts, but no alarm bells sounded in Washington when Moshe Dayan in mid-September 1977 disclosed them to Secretary Vance. The Carter administration, frustrated in its efforts to bring all the parties to the conference table, finally decided to go over the heads of the regional parties. The United States and the Soviet Union, as cochairs of the proposed conference, decided to work out an invitation which the two countries would jointly issue to all prospective participants. After discussions with the Soviets, President Carter authorized the release of a communiqué on October 1, 1977. Its key paragraph read:

> The United States and the Soviet Union believe that, within the framework of a comprehensive settlement of the Middle East problem, all specific questions of the settlement should be resolved, including such key issues as withdrawal of Israeli Armed Forces from the territories occupied in the 1967 conflict; the resolution of the Palestinian question, including insuring the legitimate rights of the Palestinian people; termination of the state of war and establishment of normal peaceful relations on the basis of mutual recognition of the principles of sovereignty, territorial integrity, and political independence.

President Carter, however, had not taken care to cover his political flank before the statement was released, while Secretary Vance, in a rare lapse, had neglected the domestic aspects of the administration's initiative. Thus Congress had not been fully consulted, nor the press briefed, nor American Jewish leadership contacted. Israel's neoconservative American friends, offended by the fact that the Soviets had been prominently brought into the Middle East picture, took the lead in attacking the communiqué. Liberal Democrats were also against the statement, primarily because it seemed to press Israel too hard on the Palestinian issue.

If the Israelis could relax while the Carter administration regrouped, Sadat could not. His relations with Syria were under increasing strain. At the end of October he informed President Carter that he would personally be taking a "bold step" in pursuit of peace. The nature of that step was disclosed on November 9, when Sadat, in an address to the Egyptian National Assembly—with Arafat present as an onlooker—stunned his listeners by saying he was prepared to go anywhere for peace, even to talk with the Israelis in their Knesset in Jerusalem. At first, no one was sure whether the statement was just another of Sadat's rhetorical cadenzas. But it soon became clear that he really did intend to go to Jerusalem and was anxious to be invited by Begin. Carter and his advisers admired Sadat's bold decision and shared his belief that the visit would help break down psychological barriers on both sides.

40 □ The Road to Camp David

Sadat arrived at the Ben-Gurion Airport after sundown on Saturday, November 19, 1977. It so happened that I witnessed his appearance before the Knesset. Earlier that fall, Dr. Nahum Goldmann stepped down from the presidency of the World Jewish Congress, and I was elected to succeed him. Soon afterward, I received a telephone call from Begin. "Now that you are president of the World Jewish Congress," he said, "we can work together on many things. Please come to Jerusalem so that we can talk." I agreed and set the time of my arrival in Israel for the morning of November 19. Later, when I learned that Sadat was due in Israel the same day, I contacted Begin to suggest a change of time. "No, no, no," said Begin. "Come as scheduled. Sadat won't be here very long. When he leaves, you and I can talk. What's more, I have a place reserved for you in the visitors' gallery of the Knesset when he speaks."

[II]

The picture of Sadat's arrival in Israel, beamed to television viewers around the world, made my own heart skip a beat. Here was the face of the former enemy, a man who had been Nasser's lieutenant-in-chief, and who on his own had been the architect of the Yom Kippur War which took a terrible toll in Israeli lives. Here was a man who had once embodied the hectic fevers that gripped Arab nations in their sustained enmity toward Israel. Now this leader of the strongest Arab state was on Israeli soil not through force of arms but peacefully, not as a victor or vanquished but to explore a new agreement with Israel in his own interests.

I thought of the snarling three decades of Arab-Israeli relations that had preceded it, how many lives had been uprooted or shattered in the name of absolutes, how many plans that could have improved the common life of people in the Middle East had been shelved in favor of allocating scarce resources for arms. Now, suddenly, there was a rekindling of hope that something better might be in store for all the inhabitants of the region. It was a prospect that warranted the eloquent, single-sentence Hebrew prayer: "We thank thee, O Lord, for having brought us safely to this moment."

Sadat's campaign to get what he wanted from the Israelis started the moment he descended from his aircraft onto the tarmac, where a bipartisan cluster of Israeli leaders comprised the receiving line. While he had something to say to each, the high point of the drama occurred when he reached former Prime Minister Golda Meir. Sadat, smiling broadly, embraced the woman who had been his embattled adversary in the years immediately before and after the Yom Kippur War.

In his speech to the Knesset on Sunday morning, Sadat hewed to his known line on the Arab-Israeli conflict, except that on American advice he omitted any reference to the PLO and instead urged the Israelis to respect Palestinian sentiments. What counted, however, was not what he actually said or failed to say. What counted was his physical presence in the Knesset to sound a call for peace and an end to war. As to Begin's reply, I agreed with the local mavins who thought it was "stilted"—perhaps almost deliberately so—compared with the force of his soaring oratory in other highly charged circumstances. It was left to Shimon Peres, the Labor leader, to address Sadat in a generous and graceful way.

Sadat himself apparently expected the Israeli government to respond to his presence in Jerusalem with enormous concessions, though he had previously been warned by a U.S. diplomat in Cairo that concessions overflowing from a grateful heart were not Begin's style. Still, in the heady atmosphere of the hour, it was easy for many people to believe that a formal treaty of peace between Egypt and Israel was within immediate reach.

Sadat and Begin met privately after the public exchange of views in the Knesset, and Sadat then flew back to Cairo. That evening I called at Begin's home according to our previous arrangement. We were not alone: Begin's wife sat in on the meeting as she often did when meetings were held in their home—to watch over her husband with unflagging attention, and no doubt also to serve as his auxiliary memory chamber. I naturally questioned Begin about his reactions to Sadat's visit, but his reply was little more than a dry "We shall see what we shall see."

Our conversation turned to other matters. Nahum Goldmann, my predecessor as president of the World Jewish Congress, had often clashed sharply with Labor party leaders over policy issues, and his relationship with Begin was one of mutual dislike. Now Begin meant to impress on me the conviction that our personal relationship would be different, that we could work together in amity. This may have seemed important to him on two counts. First, it was common knowledge that many Diaspora Jews, and especially those in the American Jewish community, had found his public manners to be lacking in civility. Second, as he thought of how he meant to conduct his future negotiations with Sadat and with American officials, perhaps he anticipated that his public manners would continue to prove offensive to many Diaspora Jews. If so, perhaps I could help to explain his true purposes to his critics.

Now that I was president of the World Jewish Congress, Begin said, I should become part of his inner circle. When I said, "Hey, wait a minute!" he countered with another proposal. I should agree to serve on the executive committee of the Jewish Agency, which ostensibly acts as a bridge between Israel and the Diaspora.

My reply amounted to a restatement of what I had told all prime ministers of Israel, starting with Ben-Gurion. Before the birth of the state of Israel, the Jewish Agency had fulfilled quasi-governmental functions stretching from the Yishuv in Palestine to Diaspora Jews. With the creation of the state, however, most of the agency's useful functions were now carried on by the government. The agency now seemed to serve only as a source of positions for Israelis, most of whom preferred to be in the government itself. It should therefore be abolished. If the agency was to be reformed to serve as a bridge between Israel and the Diaspora, then Diaspora Jews, elected to serve on its executive, should agree to move to Israel and stay there in a watchful role for the length of their tenure. I was in no position to do anything of the sort as president of the World Jewish Congress.

One of the hidden sources of Begin's strength as a leader was his capacity to "wear down" those whom he could not otherwise win over to his views. They sometimes could become so physically and mentally exhausted that they would give in to him—a reality that would be experienced by President Carter, Secretary of State Vance, and President Sadat. Perhaps he counted on this talent with me. For the time being, we merely agreed to meet periodically in order to discuss what the World Jewish Congress could do to help the state of Israel. In particular, I mentioned the need for a new plan for the country's economic development.

[III]

Within a month after Sadat's visit to Jerusalem, high hopes for peace began to evaporate. Sadat, faced by growing hostility in the Arab world to his "opening" toward Israel, thought he could turn the flank on his critics if he convinced Begin to pledge that Israel would withdraw not only from the Sinai but from the West Bank, Gaza, and the Golan. Begin, for his part, wanted to reach a peace agreement with Egypt divorced from the "Palestinian question." Both the Egyptian and Israeli visions of peace, and especially their view on how to proceed with negotiations, remained sharply at odds.

Major differences also prevailed within the Begin cabinet. Moshe Dayan, without a party label or a party following, was serving as foreign minister, and Ezer Weitzman, who had distinguished himself as an Israeli air force commander during the Six Days War, was serving as defense minister. Both men, despite their military backgrounds, strongly favored constructive peace negotiations with the Egyptians and an end to the kinds of actions—such as the building of new settlements on occupied territory—which

threatened to derail any peace moves. Although both were over-
ruled by the Begin cabinet, neither resigned. They could not see
how Israel's best interests would be served if the negotiating field
were abandoned to the hard-line "hawks."

On December 16, Begin was in Washington for a meeting with
President Carter who urged him to be more responsive to Sadat's
initiative. Begin, however, refused to state publicly that Israel
would withdraw from all the occupied territories in line with U.N.
Resolution 242. Instead he countered with a concession which was
fated to undergo a kind of "genetic evolution" in the months
ahead—namely, that there would be a transitional period of self-
rule within the territories. I saw Begin privately on the occasion of
this visit, armed with arguments why he should do all within his
power to keep the peace process moving forward.

On Christmas day 1977, Begin arrived in Egypt for the first
time. Accompanied by Dayan, Weizman, and Attorney General
Aharon Barak, he met with Sadat and his advisers in Ismalya, on
the banks of the Suez Canal. In keeping with the pattern established by Sadat's trip to Jerusalem, no American representatives
were present. For the moment, both sides preferred direct negotiations. Begin and Sadat, however, were unable to agree on anything
of substance—though Begin had the impression that his proposals
regarding Sinai and "self-rule" for the Palestinians met with a
positive response. The Egyptians by contrast, seemed to feel that
Ismalya proved that direct talks with Begin were hopeless and that
the Americans should be brought back into the picture. They were
all the more convinced of the need to do so when the Knesset,
dominated by Likud, voted on December 28 in favor of Begin's
peace plan—which included features Sadat had already categor-
ically rejected.

In early January of 1978, President Carter, who had invested so
much of his physical energy and political capital in an attempt to
resolve the Arab-Israeli conflict, left for a tour of Middle East
capitals in a bid to keep his peace initiative alive. He met with
Jordan's King Hussein in Amman, followed by a meeting with
Saudi leadership in Riyadh, and then a stopover in Aswan to see
Sadat. In the course of that stopover, Carter spelled out his
well-known views on the need for a real peace and an Israeli
withdrawal in the context of security and normal relations. He
then added, "There must be a resolution of the Palestinian problem in all its aspects. The solution must recognize the legitimate

rights of the Palestinian people and enable the Palestinians to participate in the determination of their own future." The Israelis were not quite sure what all this meant, but they took comfort from Carter's earlier statement in which he said that the PLO, because of its intransigence, had removed itself "from any immediate prospects of participation in the peace discussion." The Arabs were also not sure what to make of the Aswan Declaration, but the text acquired the status of acceptable compromise language in later Egyptian-Israeli talks and was eventually incorporated into the Camp David accords.

While President Carter was in the Middle East, I had gone to Rome as chairman of a delegation representing major Jewish organizations around the world. We were to have an audience with Pope John Paul, and I had worked with members of the delegation on formal remarks I would make to the pope once he received us. A member of the Vatican curia who was in charge of arrangements asked for and was given an advance copy of the text, which was presently printed in the official Vatican newspaper. In turn we asked for an advance copy of the pope's remarks, but we were informed that the Vatican could issue no text of papal utterance before an actual audience. With that, some members of our delegation took a stand on "principle": if the Vatican was not prepared to deal with us as equals—to exchange text for text—we should cancel our audience with the pope.

I could think of nothing less likely to be helpful to Jewish interests anywhere, including those in Israel, than for our non-government delegation to pick a public fight with the Vatican over this issue. Yet the argument festered until I contacted Israel's ambassador to Rome, who soon convinced the delegation to stop the squabbling and proceed with the scheduled audience.

On the day of the audience, I was chatting with other members of the delegation in the receiving room when I felt a tap on my shoulder. It was Pope John Paul. "Do we," he asked, "have to make speeches?" "Your Holiness," I replied, "my speech has already been printed in the Vatican newspaper. So I must give it." "All right," the pope said with a sigh as he moved away. I gave my previously published speech, and he replied in courteous but friendly language. Then he hopped down from the throne and I introduced him to the members of the delegation. He addressed each in his native tongue. When he came to Dr. Zalman Abramov, the leading Israeli representative within our delegation, we had previously arranged for Abramov to take the pope by surprise by inviting him on the spot to visit Jerusalem. It didn't work out that way. When the pope learned that Abramov lived in Jerusalem he exclaimed, "Jerusalem, I want to go there!" He did not say when. As of this writing, he still has not gone there.

[IV]

In early February 1978, Sadat was scheduled to come to the United States for an official visit with President Carter. Beforehand, Ashraf Ghorbal, my longtime friend who was Egypt's ambassador to the United States, asked if I would arrange for a small group of American Jewish leaders to meet with Sadat in the Egyptian embassy in Washington.

I failed to see anything "dangerous" in what Ghorbal asked, though I sounded out the White House about the matter—to be certain that such a meeting would not be viewed as meddling in diplomatic negotiations. The White House was all in favor of the idea.

On a Sunday before Sadat was due to arrive in the United States, a Miami newspaper published an interview with him in which he spoke candidly about the problems of dealing with Israel, and about the interests of the Arab world in championing the Palestinian cause. The interview was immediately construed in some American Jewish circles as evidence that Sadat was anti-Israeli and even anti-Semitic (though the Arabs themselves are a Semitic people). That is not how I construed the interview with Sadat, but the American Jewish community was still acutely sensitive to any criticism of the state of Israel and its leadership.

At this point, my friend Rabbi Alexander Schindler, chairman of the Conference of Presidents of Major Jewish Organizations, convened a meeting of the conference to consider contacts between American Jews and Sadat. I tried to reach Schindler by phone to tell him about the meeting I had already scheduled with Sadat, but he did not get my call until after the conference adopted a ban on such meetings. I did not cancel the event set for the Egyptian embassy; to do so would be an affront to the president of Egypt and to the White House as well.

The scheduled meeting in the Egyptian embassy, held during a pause in the official U.S.-Egyptian negotiations, was marked by spirited exchanges not only about the possibilities for a settlement in the Middle East but on the relationship between the American Jewish community and Israel and its perceptions of dangers to that state. President Sadat throughout the encounter was ebullient and charming, but I could not tell whether his attitudes were affected by what he heard from our group. Later, however, I learned why the White House was anxious for the meeting to happen. They wanted Sadat to know that American Jews would support moves toward peace if the proposed terms were fair to all parties in the Israeli-Arab conflict.

When Sadat's talks with Carter ended, an apparent agreement was reached on an American-Egyptian plan of action. The Egyptians would advance certain proposals which Begin would certainly reject. Given an Egyptian-Israeli deadlock, the United States would put forward a set of compromise proposals built around Begin's autonomy plan but clearly limiting autonomy of the occupied territories to a transitional stage, followed by an agreement based on the principles of 242, including withdrawal. The Americans were already known to be exasperated with Begin, but they also soon found Sadat to be a baffling partner in a strategy of collusion. William Quandt, in his authoritative account of the Camp David peace process, described the problem:

> Sadat spoke of the need to pressure Begin to agree to withdraw from the West Bank and Gaza, but at the same time he seemed to have left Carter with the impression that he really wanted only a fig leaf behind which to conclude a bilateral Egyptian-Israeli peace. He talked of the need to bring Hussein into the negotiations, but in private and in public he was abusive toward Hussein and other Arabs, spurning American advice that he should quiet his rhetorical attacks on those whose cooperation was being sought.
>
> Instead of working with Carter toward the minutely detailed plan he professed to want, Sadat constantly surprised the Americans with his views. Sometimes he said he was ready for the Americans to put forward a proposal; then he would say there was no rush. He suggested that the foreign ministers should meet, but even before they had done so he had told [Ezer] Weizman [who was acting for the Israelis] that their talks would fail and that an alternative approach should be considered....

[V]

A trip I made to Israel at this time led to a discussion with Begin not about issues of war or peace but about what was literally a domestic housekeeping issue. The entire matter reminded me anew of how difficult it was to get Begin to modify his hard-set views. "Phil," Begin said to me at the outset of our discussion, "you know a good deal about housing. Why can't you get American Jews to contribute funds expressly for the purpose of building houses in Israel?" I recognized the real need for more and adequate housing in Israel; it had been a prominent issue in the 1977 political contest in the country, with both parties promising to overcome acute shortages. In reply to Begin, however, I observed that if a campaign were launched in the United States for that purpose, the funds raised might be at the expense of a cutback in contributions to the general purposes of the United Jewish Appeal. "Well, Phil," Begin then said, "why can't individual Jewish communities in American cities adopt a 'sister Israeli town' and raise the funds needed to build houses in it?"

I agreed that such an arrangement might be possible in individual instances. But there was a more practical and immediate way for Israel to get the funds it needed. I referred to U.S. legislation which authorized and in fact encouraged U.S. Savings and Loan Associations to make loans to friendly foreign nations for use in financing housing construction. A large pool of S&L funds in the United States was (at the time) available for investment abroad under existing legislation. I was certain that Israel could qualify as a borrower—the more so because prospective lenders would be virtually certain that the American Jewish community would never permit the government of Israel to default on the loans it was due to repay.

Begin, hearing this, asked, "How much interest would we have to pay?" I said that this could not be determined before the loan was negotiated. The price might be 1 percent under or over the average market price. "Phil," Begin at once replied, "in the name of Israel I will not pay interest." I observed that Israel paid interest on the bonds it sold in the capital market. What difference would it make if it paid interest on borrowed funds used to build houses in Israel? In fact, by borrowing funds and repaying them, Israel would establish its creditworthiness. It could then go back to the same credit source for more loans to be used for development.

Begin's insistence that he would "not pay interest" struck me as a tipsy-turvy reversal of the attitudes I had encountered in the "kibbutznick" socialist ministers of earlier Labor governments. Ben-Gurion had favored arrangements whereby American investors in Israel could make "a profit" (albeit "not too much"). Levi Eshkol and Pinchas Sapir understood in a businesslike way that loans, carrying interest, made the wheels go round in the world of economic growth. Begin, by contrast, seemed to think that the Diaspora, and the American Jewish community in particular, should provide Israel with development funds as a gift. Nothing I said could change his mind about "not paying interest."

[VI]

On March 7, or roughly two months after a joint Egyptian-American plan of action had been formulated at Camp David, the Egyptians submitted to the White House "Basic Guidelines for the Solution of the Palestinian Question." The contents of the document were disappointing. It was supposed to detail the Egyptian concept for a transitional regime in the occupied territories. Instead it was an exercise in sweeping generalizations—all pointing to so wide a gap between the Egyptian and Israeli positions that no American compromise could possibly bridge the difference. Sadat was asked to submit another proposal more in line with Washington's earlier understanding. At the same time, the United States maintained its pressure on Begin to be more "flexible" in his relations with Sadat.

President Carter's domestic political capital was already stretched thin by his fight to secure Senate ratification of the treaty contemplating a U.S. withdrawal from the Panama Canal, and, concurrently, to win Senate approval for the sale of U.S. military aircraft not only to Israel but to Egypt and Saudi Arabia. Then, four days after the Americans received the unacceptable Egyptian plan for a solution to the "Palestinian question," PLO guerrillas in a calculated attempt to disrupt the negotiating process, attacked an Israeli bus along the coastal road and left more than thirty Israelis dead. Within days the Begin government launched Operation Litani, an Israeli invasion of southern Lebanon designed to drive the PLO from the area and to form an occupied "security belt" to prevent further terrorist raids across the border.

President Carter was appalled by the PLO attack, but he refused to accept the Israeli response. He believed it was excessive and risked compromising the negotiations with Egypt. Caught between a hammer and an anvil, Carter lent U.S. support to the U.N. resolution which called for Israel's withdrawal from south Lebanon and the creation of a U.N. force to patrol the area. Lebanon remained an irritant in U.S.-Israeli relations well beyond the Carter presidency.

In early July 1978, on the eve of my departure for Israel in connection with affairs of the World Jewish Congress, I was invited by President Carter to join him and Vice President Walter Mondale at a "working dinner" in the White House. Seven or eight men prominently identified with aspects of Jewish life in the United States were also invited.

The discussion at dinner began with Carter's candid account of where he stood in his search for a peaceful solution to the Arab-Israeli conflict. His concept for a comprehensive peace conference at Geneva, with all parties at interest on hand, was not yet dead. But he had concluded that an Israeli-Egyptian accord, calling for an Israeli withdrawal from the Sinai in return for a peace treaty between the two countries, was attainable. He believed that "Sadat was pretty much in line with the direction in which the Americans wanted to move." But he worried that Begin's unyielding attitude— and particularly the terms for the future of the West Bank and Gaza—would jeopardize even an Israeli-Egyptian agreement on Sinai.

He described for us how far the United States had moved in an attempt to satisfy Begin's objections. It had come out strongly against an independent Palestinian state, had consigned the PLO to obscurity, and no longer even spoke of a Palestinian homeland. Second, the U.S. had publicly agreed that U.N. Resolution 242 allowed for border changes, and had dropped all references to "minor modifications." Third, the U.S. had spoken of an Israeli military presence in the West Bank and Gaza for an interim period and beyond, which Israel viewed as an endorsement of a permanent military presence. Fourth, the U.S. had conveyed the impression that Israel would remain in control of a unified city of Jerusalem, would have a veto over the return of refugees, and could retain existing settlements in the West Bank. Fifth, the U.S. had suggested to Israel a mutual security treaty and forsworn the manipulation of military and economic aid as pressure on Israel. Finally, the U.S. had made it clear that an Israeli withdrawal from the West Bank and Gaza would depend on the attainment of full peace, security, and recognition.

But, Carter asked, what had the United States received in return from Begin? Only a vigorous defense of his "self-rule" proposal; a repetition of his claim that everything was negotiable and that there were no preconditions; and a vague promise to give the United States some idea of what would happen after a five-year interim period on the West Bank. While Dayan, Weizman, and Barak recognized the sterility of this approach, they could not alter it without U.S. help. So, asked President Carter in conclusion, what could we suggest the United States might do to overcome five months of stalemated negotiations, and to get Begin to accept the principle of "withdrawal for peace" when it came to the West Bank?

The answers were a variation on the theme of "Mr. President, if you could do this for Israel, if you could do that." Nothing I heard was to my taste. When the table had been circled and it came my turn to speak, I said,

> Mr. President, as president of the World Jewish Congress, I am not here as a representative of Israel or anyone else. I am here to talk about peace. If there are some things the United States can still properly do for Israel, let them be done. But that is not the real issue. The real issue is the kind of peace all of us want. It is a peace in the interests of the United States as well as of Egypt and Israel. I suggest that you might want to bring the Israelis and Egyptians together with the Americans in the same proximity, and thrash out what is good for all parties.

Our dinner meeting was meant to be "off the record," but a participant leaked to the Israeli embassy in Washington a garbled version of what was said; the version was soon published in the Israeli press where it caused a stir. I was quoted as having said, "I am not here as a representative of Israel," leaving out the rest of my remarks and thus conveying the impression that as president of the World Jewish Congress I had no interest in Israel's plight. I sent a message to Begin indicating how I had been misquoted. When questioned, Begin said he had received a message from me saying I had been misquoted, and that was all he knew.

When I saw Begin in Israel, he did not rise to embrace me in greeting as was his habit. He sat behind his desk, cold and distant in manner. "Mr. Prime Minister," I said, "before we start to speak, you should know what I think about the response you gave when you were asked about what I had said in the White House." "What was wrong with my statement?" Begin asked. "It was," I said, "not enough. When you were questioned about my explanatory message you should have said, I believe Phil Klutznick." With that,

Begin's eyes welled up with tears. He rose from his chair and embraced me in a gesture signifying that he did believe what I told him. We were friends again—though we were far from being of the same mind on the quest for peace.

41 □ A Treaty Is Achieved

Against the near breakdown in direct negotiations between Begin and Sadat, President Carter on July 30 decided to hold a summit meeting with Begin and Sadat at Camp David; Secretary Vance would go to the Middle East to issue the invitations. In Carter's view, the gap between Begin and Sadat did not seem great, but their mutual distrust prevented them from reaching any kind of agreement. He now explained to his advisers—who might have made suggestions along the lines of my own at the White House working dinner—that Camp David would provide an ideal setting where Begin and Sadat might discover their common commitment to peace in the Middle East. He was fairly certain that both men wanted an agreement at least on Sinai, with or without a link to the broader settlement of the "Palestinian issues" centered in the West Bank and Gaza.

The president's decision to call a summit meant high political costs to him if the venture ultimately failed. If it produced any measure of agreement between the principals, the president and his administration would reap substantial domestic and international political gains. Begin and Sadat readily accepted the invitation to the Camp David summit, and President Carter's advisers at once began to prepare for the meeting scheduled from September 5 to 17.

The thirteen days of talks—and I here draw on William Quandt's summary—duplicated in microcosm the pattern of the preceding year and a half. Each party came to Camp David with prepared positions and strategies, with ambitions and illusions. Issues central to the controversies of the past were debated over and over again, sometimes with fierce belligerence, sometimes in good humor, sometimes in a mood of despair. Hopes rose and fell, followed by sober realism and another round of revision and reassessment. Normal domestic political constraints were eased somewhat because the participants remained secluded from the public and conducted the talks in almost total secrecy. As to how matters finally turned out, Quandt had this to say:

> By the end, the process came to resemble an endurance contest in which the party that could least afford failure was brought under the greatest pressure to make concessions. This turned out to be Sadat....
> Begin's steamroller tactics, coupled with his willingness to leave Camp David without any agreement if necessary, proved to be more successful than Sadat's flamboyant concept of confrontation. For unlike Begin, Sadat was not prepared to leave Camp David empty-handed. At a minimum, he needed a clear agreement with Carter. But Carter now wanted an agreement between Begin and Sadat, not the appearance of American-Egyptian collusion against Israel.

On September 17, with President Carter as a witness, Sadat and Begin signed two agreements. The first stated general principles for dealing with the West Bank and Gaza. The second, loosely tied to the first, detailed the formula for reaching an Egyptian-Israeli peace treaty. Both agreements were precise on some issues and vague on others. Both were subject to different interpretations and also consigned many divisive problems to the future. Each party, however, believed it had gained something through the agreements, and both also knew that hard bargaining still lay ahead. At the signing ceremony, Carter, Sadat, and Begin exchanged gracious comments, pledged themselves to keep working for peace, smiled, and clasped hands in a picture seen around the world.

Camp David set the framework for peace negotiations that extended over the next five months. Difficulties over filling in blanks, over attempts to revise the basic formula, and over seemingly "technical points" threatened a rupture between the principals. At last, however, a formal treaty of peace was agreed to by Egypt and Israel. Its text consisted of a thick file of documents, and three indexes dealing with the minutiae of security arrangements, maps, and the resumption of diplomatic relations. Very real blood, sweat, and tears shed over the years lay behind these formal words and graphs. Yet I have often wondered how many people in the wide world except for the negotiators—and perhaps some scattered Ph.D. candidates—read every line in the treaty and its annexes.

On the eve of the ceremony in which the Egyptian-Israeli peace treaty was signed, I was invited to meet with Sadat in the Egyptian embassy in Washington. After the signing I was with him again, alone except for Ambassador Ghorbal. During our conversation over a glass of wine, I suggested that as part of Sadat's economic development plans for his country, he might want to consider an Egyptian version of the TVA model to be financed by government and private capital derived from three sources: Egyptian, American, and Israeli. Sadat questioned me closely about the TVA but then threw a halter around his signs of interest. He could not afford, he said, to move too fast with any development schemes involving Israeli participation because of a widespread fear among Egyptians that Israel would try to dominate the Egyptian economy. At the same time, he invited me to Egypt for further discussions, ostensibly about economic matters.

I made the trip later in the year with the understanding that I would pay my own expenses and those of my wife. My son Tom, who joined our party, also paid his own expenses. Inside Egypt, however, the government provided us with elegant accommodations and with security guards. When we traveled by car, I noticed to my embarrassment that an advanced patrol brought all other traffic to a halt. I asked to be spared what I thought was excessive personal courtesy, but I was told that the traffic was stopped as a precaution against any unpleasant incident that might befall the president of the World Jewish Congress. In fact, the security coverage extended even to my habit of rising early in the morning to swim in the pool of the Hilton Hotel in Cairo where we were staying. Two guards outside my room usually dozed the night through, but when I tried to slip past them in the morning, both awakened and accompanied me to the pool. Later on I learned that neither guard could swim.

During sessions when I was alone with Sadat, he reviewed the strained state of his relations with the Americans and Israelis despite the peace treaty. I made it clear that my position as president of the World Jewish Congress in no way meant that my personal views would carry great weight with either Begin or the White House. I could, however, promise to convey to both an accurate summary of what I heard Sadat say about the peace process to date.

At the same time, with Vice President Hosni Mubarak as my guide—this was the first of the meetings I had with him in the years ahead—I was shown development towns, manufacturing plants, farms, cattle breeding, housing projects. Toward the end of my visit, when I again met with Sadat, one of the persons present was a high official who was identified as a housing expert, and another who was the minister in charge of agricultural development. The latter was Sayed Marei, a former speaker of the Egyptian House, who also had close family ties to the Egyptian president; his son had married one of Sadat's daughters.

I was asked to comment on what I had been shown, and so made some technical suggestions about Egyptian town planning as well as its program for home construction from prefabricated materials. My comments about other economic matters went against the grain of certain Egyptian practices, but Sadat said he welcomed my frankness. When he asked what I thought was his greatest economic problem, I replied that the obvious answer was Egypt's need for an adequate food supply to meet the explosive growth of its population. To feed that population, Egypt was forced to import food and pay for it in scarce hard currency.

At the risk of irritating Marei, I went on to say that his farming experts could profitably study the methods used by Israel to overcome its food deficit. I recalled that at the time of my first visit to Israel in 1955, I asked Prime Minister Moshe Sharet what Israel needed most. He answered, "Fifty thousand tons of grain," because without an adequate supply of grain, Israel could not raise cattle for meat and cows for milk. I played a modest role in securing the grain for Israel under an existing U.S. foreign aid program, and Israel initiated fundamental measures of its own to overcome its food shortage. In fact, Israeli agriculture developed to a point where its surpluses led to the saying that Israel's greatest enemy had become the cow. Marei visibly bristled when I suggested that his experts could learn much from Israeli agriculture, including how to conserve water. Sadat, on the other hand, slapped his leg in a sign of agreement and said to Marei, "What did I tell you?"

During most of my meetings with Sadat, I was struck by the fact that he was attended by only a few associates. Aides always hovered around the principal ministers of Egypt as well as the prime minister with whom I visited. But when I sat down with

Sadat to hear from him what I knew he wanted me to transmit to sources in the United States and Israel, he was usually alone. He was always charming in conversation, urbane, seemingly open-minded. He appeared to have complete confidence in himself and in what he was doing, though I sensed he was not always thoroughly briefed about issues in dispute.

Many faults, of course, are found in world figures after they pass from the scene. They can be undervalued after their death just as they can be overvalued in their lifetime. They soon become the subjects of books which thrive on disclosures of hidden personal details and motives. This is common to the revisionism that follows in the wake of a leader's death, but I have been struck by the tone of the complaints about Sadat in memoirs of Egyptian notables who were once his close friends. Muhammad Heikel, for example, an Egyptian journalist of the first rank, at one point describes Sadat as a man on a flying trapeze, someone who adored being adored and called a great figure. At another point, he refers to him as an actor with a history of enjoying and participating in amateur dramatics. The trouble was, so Heikel concluded, he was an actor without a scenario to govern his movements from one thing to another so that they would be consecutive in nature.

There may be a solid core of truth in this judgment, but it is not, in my view, the whole truth. I recall Oscar Wilde's remark that the "fact that a man is a poisoner is nothing against his prose." If Sadat was a man on a flying trapeze, or an actor who adored being adored, that does not discredit his achievement in helping to secure a peace that was as much in the interests of Egypt as of Israel.

42 □ Back to Government

In the summer of 1979, Juanita Krebs, who had served with distinction as Secretary of Commerce in President Carter's cabinet, submitted her resignation, citing family reasons, and the White

House began what proved to be a drawn-out search for a successor.

I did not know what was in prospect until early November when Robert Strauss, then chairman of the Democratic National Committee, flew into Chicago for some speech-making. On the way back to Washington he disclosed to a mutual friend seated next to him in the plane that I was being mentioned for the Commerce post. If I were offered the appointment, did my friend think I would accept it? I learned that my friend sensibly answered that the only way to find out was to ask me.

On the morning of November 14, while in Omaha, I received a telephone call from Stuart Eisenstat, White House economic adviser to President Carter. The president, he said, wished to see me as soon as possible either that day or the next. I explained that I was due to attend a formal dinner that night in Omaha given by Creighton University, my alma mater, where I was to be awarded its Manressa Medal, the third recipient in more than 130 years. I said I would come to Washington the next day.

In Washington I met successively with Eisenstat, Juanita Krebs, and Vice President Mondale. Each talked only about the post of Secretary of Commerce, and each also voiced the hope that I would accept it if it were offered me by President Carter.

Toward the end of the working day I saw the president in his office. He spoke first of his achievements and hopes. He also spoke of his problems. These included the recent seizure of the U.S. embassy in Teheran, the Soviet military push in both Africa and Afghanistan, and the constraints facing his administration as it grappled with inflation, budget deficits, deregulation, a buildup of defense forces, and sagging U.S. world trade. When he turned to the matter immediately at hand, he said I was "nearly everyone's candidate for the post of Secretary of Commerce" and that the appointment had not been offered to anyone else.

After questioning me about my experience at all levels of government, including service under Presidents Roosevelt, Truman, Eisenhower, Kennedy, Johnson, and Ford, he asked if I "liked administration." I replied that few people I knew really liked the grind of administration, but it had been my experience that there was no escape from topside drudgery if "a job was to get done." Carter, with disarming candor, admitted that at the outset of his presidency he had allowed himself to be bogged down in the details of hands-on management. He had since been impressed with the need to unload as many tasks as he could properly delegate either to his White House aides or to the heads of executive departments and agencies.

All this was prologue to the question, Was I free to take the post of Secretary of Commerce if it were offered to me? I said that I had always been ready to serve in any capacity, great or small, whenever a president, Republican or Democratic, thought I could perform useful services. As to my financial position, I retained an economic interest in some enterprises but was only marginally involved in their day-to-day management. Barring an economic disaster, my wife, to whom I had been married for forty-seven years, was well provided for, but I would have to discuss with her the prospect of a physical move back to Washington. One complication was that I had been president of the World Jewish Congress for only a short time, and to serve as Secretary of Commerce I would have to arrange a leave of absence from the WJC. President Carter saw no problem in that kind of arrangement. Perhaps he understood, without my saying so, that if I accepted the post of Secretary of Commerce I would hold it for only a year before the 1980 presidential elections, and no one could foretell the outcome of that contest. As I rose to leave, President Carter told me that Vice President Mondale would call me regarding the outcome of our discussions.

Around eight o'clock the next morning, the vice president telephoned me in my Chicago office to say, in the formal voice of a manifesto, "I am authorized on behalf of the president of the United States to tender you the office of Secretary of Commerce, subject to confirmation by the Senate of the United States." Then he dropped the inflated tone and said simply, "Phil, please take it." I replied that I would welcome an opportunity to serve under President Carter, subject to my being able to take a leave of absence as president of the World Jewish Congress. Vice President Mondale said he had been informed of that proviso.

I had already checked with my family in the event a cabinet post was offered. My wife, as usual, was willing to support anything I wanted to do. I then alerted certain officers of the World Jewish Congress, and approached Edgar Bronfman to take on the acting presidency of the congress. I have indicated elsewhere that his father, Sam Bronfman, was my friend of many years. His relationship with the World Jewish Congress, like my own, was based on his intimate friendship with Dr. Nahum Goldmann. When Goldmann retired from the presidency of the WJC, Sam also retired from the place he had held in its Canadian-American section. As Goldmann's successor in the presidency, I urged Edgar Bronfman to fill the void at the head of the Canadian-American section created by his father's retirement. The son, to the father's delight, agreed to do so.

Edgar Bronfman, when approached to serve as the acting president of the World Jewish Congress, was reluctant to assume the work that might be entailed. He nonetheless asked how long he would have to serve. I said it would be until the next scheduled regular election of a WJC president. After some hesitation, he finally consented to my proposal, and the officers of the WJC supported my arrangement with him.

Meanwhile, Newton Minow, my attorney, worked with my youngest son Sam to prepare the required financial reports for the White House and the FBI as required by the confirmation process. All this was in order within a few days, and soon President Carter announced my appointment. Among the cabled congratulatory messages I received, one was from President Sadat and another was from Prime Minister Begin. American press reaction was favorable.

Because different sources ascribed different political motives to the president's decision, I particularly welcomed a note struck by Carter personally. Much had been made about my age at the time of my appointment—I was seventy-two. At the swearing-in ceremony, the president remarked that I was "still young in every measurement of human life, still innovative, still dynamic, still aggressive, still filled with the wonder of life, still determined to stretch mind and heart to encompass new friends, ideas, and knowledge about God's world."

Some of my thoughts at the time of the swearing-in ceremony touched on family memories. Both of my parents had been dead for a number of years. My father, who had lived to see me appointed by President Roosevelt to the wartime post of commissioner of Public Housing and Administration, had been felled by a fatal heart attack while sitting in his beloved Beth Hamedrosh Hagodol in Kansas City. My mother, who survived him, had lived long enough to witness at least the early phase of my financial success with community development, starting with the building of Park Forest. But how would they have assessed what neither one lived to see? What would they have said about a society where the son of an immigrant father from eastern Europe, who first made a living in Kansas City by selling and repairing shoes—but whose real interest lay in volunteer work for the sick and the needy—could attain a post in a president's cabinet? What would they have said about a society where the son of an immigrant mother from eastern Europe, who firmly managed the small resources of her Kansas City family so that none of its children were in want, could come to head a government department whose 45,000 employees served to promote the well-being of American business? I am certain they would have compressed their appraisal into two familiar words: Golden America.

Memories of my parents fused into reflection about AZA, the junior auxiliary of B'nai B'rith which had been brought to birth by a handful of Jewish boys from small and medium-sized Midwest towns. I could recite by heart the names of the "AZA boys" of my generation who had gained distinction in American life. When I looked at members of a younger generation, I was struck by the extent to which AZA continued to be a training ground for Jewish youth destined for leadership in American life. Inside the Carter cabinet, when I faced Secretary of Transportation Neil E. Goldschmidt, I faced another "AZA boy," this one from Oregon.

I thought about how my lifelong concern with the needs of the Jewish community paralleled my concern as an American with the needs of general American society. I had never sensed a divided loyalty, because my strongest commitments—intellectual, moral, emotional, financial—spanned these dual realms of my existence as a human being. I was, however, judged differently by some Jewish bystanders who saw me give up a post I held for a relatively short time as president of the World Jewish Congress in order to accept a cabinet appointment.

I was not indifferent to this criticism, yet it seemed to me that I had on my side the teachings of Judaism's sages who stressed the importance of serving the welfare of the community as a whole. "Separate not yourself from the community," Hillel had said, and other Jewish sages added: "If the community is in trouble, a man must not say, 'I will go to my house, and eat and drink'... but a man must share in the troubles of the community, even as Moses did." Under the roof of American pluralism, there are communities within communities, where people with common backgrounds, needs, and interests pursue aspirations special to themselves and know special troubles—just as they share in the aspirations and troubles of the larger community of which they are a part. In my own case, on intellectual, moral, and temperamental grounds, I could no more separate myself from *either* the Jewish community or the larger American community than I could separate myself from the air I breathed and yet live.

43 □ In Commerce

Ethel arranged for our creature comforts when we returned to Washington. We resided in an apartment in the Watergate which suited our needs. Even before my confirmation I was provided with an office in the Department of Commerce and plunged headlong into the unfinished tasks of my predecessor as well as countless new business.

I called on the senators from Illinois—Charles Percy and Adlai Stevenson, both being personal friends—and both offered to escort me on the day the Senate Committee on Commerce, Science and Technology passed on my fitness. I also called on members of that committee and was assured that I would be quickly confirmed.

Meanwhile, I had to absorb the key laws governing the work of the Department of Commerce as well as the regulations that the department itself had issued, covering a wide range of domestic and foreign operations. To digest all such legalisms was like sitting down to a meal where the appetizer was a battleship, the entree an aircraft carrier, and the dessert a nuclear submarine. I also had to get on top of the department's changing institutional structure, with its respective jurisdictional lines and entanglements, and also get to know the heads of the various operations.

Today the executive branch of the federal government strives for a more rational organization than was the case during the presidency of Woodrow Wilson, when black bears were placed under the Department of Commerce, brown bears under the Department of Agriculture, and polar bears under Interior. But no matter how rational the organization, every cabinet officer must do more than preside from the top over a vertical structure—with time off for dealing with the White House, the Office of Management and Budget, and Congress. He must also maintain a complex network of horizontal relations with rival veto groups within his own department, with others who think their interests might be affected by his actions, and with their surrogates in both the executive and legislative branches.

In addition to all else, he must be aware of the "institutional memories" associated with his predecessors. Some of my predecessors as Secretary of Commerce were recognizable historical figures—Herbert Hoover, Harry L. Hopkins, Jesse Jones, Henry A. Wallace, and W. Averell Harriman—whether or not their most significant work was as head of Commerce. Others among my predecessors could be identified only by looking at the name plate beneath their official portraits. In all cases, however, how things were done in their day became invisible but potent reference points for how things should be done. Aging civil servants sometimes had to be persuaded to do things differently.

After my confirmation, I adverted to a practice I had followed when I was the head of the government's public housing program. At regular intervals I met with all chiefs of departmental sections and subsections for a candid discussion of the department's operations—to bring them abreast of the administration's policy as it affected their work, and to hear their reports and criticism in return. I also moved quickly to establish effective lines of communication with congressional committees, with other cabinet officers, with White House staff members, and with executive agencies lodged within the Office of the President, such as the Council of Economic Advisers, the Office of Management and Budget, the Office of Science and Technical Policy, and the Council on Environmental Quality.

Because I was already on friendly terms with most members of President Carter's cabinet, I was able to work on important legislative and administrative matters even while I was awaiting my confirmation. For one example, Congress had enacted but the president had not yet signed a new trade bill, transferring to Commerce from the State Department operations involving foreign trade such as the sale of American goods and commercial ideas abroad—though the sale of agricultural products remained in the hands of the Department of Agriculture. The measure, which

created the International Trade Administration, was no mere shuf-
fling of boxes on the organizational chart. Commerce agencies
such as the Census Bureau, the Patent and Trademark Office, and
the National Bureau of Standards had long provided information
bearing on trade, and the department had for some time maintained forty-seven export promotion offices throughout the United
States. The reorganization added to these long-existing capabilities
several new ones. The information resources available to business
were increased through the creation of a new Bureau of Industrial
Economics. U.S. marketing capabilities were buttressed by the
transfer of the commercial attachés resident in sixty-five countries
from the State Department to the Department of Commerce, in a
new Foreign Commercial Service. Commerce also took over the
antidumping and countervailing duty regulations formerly handled
by the Treasury Department. The object was to make Commerce
the key coordinator for U.S. foreign trade policies as a whole, with
their linkage to domestic commerce as well.

In private business, even though executives have certain co-
ercive powers—whether in the form of a carrot or a stick—it is
never easy to move personnel around. But it is much harder to
shift personnel between government agencies. Most government
workers make their careers under the roof of a single agency. They
depend for promotions on the recommendations of superiors who
have known them for many years. They are protected against an
uprooting by the grievance procedures of the civil service, or the
foreign service, or the military service, not to overlook their
personal links to members of Congress. All this and more like it
compounded the pain and complicated the tasks entailed in moving personnel and operations from State to Commerce. Fortunately, my long-standing friendship with Secretary of State Cyrus
Vance enabled the two of us swiftly to solve problems when our
respective staffs could not agree on who and what was to be
transferred to Commerce.

[II]

My appointment came at a time when moves toward a détente
with the Soviet Union were overtaken by events which implied a
resumption of the Cold War. In Iran the shah's regime had
collapsed, and after months of turmoil, Iranian militants had
stormed the U.S. embassy in Teheran and taken sixty-two Ameri-

can hostages. Full power in Iran was in the hands of the Islamic authority of Ayatollah Khomeini.

In Afghanistan pro-Soviet leftists had seized power in 1978 and concluded an economic and military treaty with the Soviet Union. Then, in December 1979, coincident with a massive Soviet military airlift into Kabul, a Soviet-backed coup installed a stronger pro-Soviet leader in place of the leftist. There followed a full-scale Soviet invasion of Afghanistan, in which Soviet forces fanned out over the country fighting rebels.

What should the American response be?

At the end of night-long discussions in which cabinet members were involved, President Carter's decision was to rely chiefly but not exclusively on economic initiatives, both to send a warning and to contain Soviet expansionism. On the political front the president chose to invoke the United Nations process: at no time in its history had the U.N. voted so overwhelming a condemnation of a major power as it did regarding the Soviet invasion of Afghanistan. The president's economic response had two parts. First, all grain shipments to the Soviet Union were embargoed except for what remained of eight million metric tons committed under a five-year government-to-government contract. The embargo covered seventeen million tons of grain formerly approved but not yet in the pipeline. Second, a halt was ordered to all other exports to the Soviet Union pending a review to develop new criteria for shipments—a task that involved at least seven different departments and agencies, each with its own export and policy-related interests.

To prepare the necessary regulations and to provide the inevitable daily interpretations of administrative provisions, the president created an interdepartmental committee—State, Defense, Treasury, Agriculture, Commerce, Labor, and National Security Council. At the end of the night-long session where this was done, the president turned to me and said, "And you, Phil, will act as chairman of the committee." I asked if I could see him after the meeting adjourned, and he nodded his assent.

Later, when we were alone in the Oval Office, I put a question to him. Why did he choose me to be the chairman? His reply, as usual, was lean and crisp. "You are," he said, "a new boy on the team. No one as yet has had a chance to get into many arguments with you. Besides, the new Trade Act soon to be signed expands Commerce's authority and operations in the export field." Days later, I was at a ceremony in the White House where the act was in fact signed by the president.

The moment the embargo went into effect, I was a party to highly charged political discussions with senators and representatives from farm states who were enraged by the ban on grain shipments to the Soviet Union. They lowered their voices by a few decibels only when they learned that the administration had designed a number of measures to cushion the impact of the embargo on farmers. The implications of the ban also had to be explained to foreign governments. Among the Warsaw Pact countries, the embargo applied only to the Soviet Union. The others were put on notice that if they did not transfer to the Soviet Union the products on the embargo list which they imported from the U.S., we would not change our dealing with them.

Meanwhile, it was recognized from the start that for the embargo to be effective, the cooperation of our allies was indispensable. This was not always easily secured. In some instances it was never secured at all. The French, for example, turned to their own competitive advantage the constraints which the embargo placed on U.S. firms doing business in the Soviet Union—though they masked their moves with layers of legalisms about how they were upholding the sanctity of their own contracts. Japan was a pleasing case on the bright side of the picture. Soon after the embargo was announced, an official Japanese delegation arrived in Washington to discuss Japan's business deals with the Soviet Union. In a friendly gesture—repeated in other contexts when I was Secretary of Commerce—the delegation turned over a list of joint Japanese-Soviet ventures and asked for advice as to which should be dropped. There was no need to single out more than a few projects. We would not ask them to stop their explorations for oil in the Soviet Union when a 60 percent boost in oil prices by OPEC had increased existing inflationary pressures.

When the interdepartmental committee reviewed a $25 million phosphates contract between the Soviets and the Armand Hammer Company, Hammer's counsel vigorously challenged our authority to do so. After long discussions, the committee voted to withhold export licenses for the necessary material. Under committee rules, Hammer now had to be informed of our decision by five o'clock on the day it was made. I tried to reach him, but as usual he was en route somewhere in his plane. A member of my staff got through to one of his key aides and stressed the urgency of my message. An hour later Hammer telephoned me, flying south over Washington, D.C. I expected him to explode when I told him about the committee's decision to suspend his phosphates contract, but the opposite happened. "That," he said, "is a stroke of genius." "How so?" I asked. "Well," he said, "now I can tell Brezhnev that you didn't cancel the contract. You merely suspended it and maybe he ought to be helpful in return." Typical of Hammer's genius, he again turned a defeat into a victory.

As chairman of the committee that administered the embargo, I knew in intimate detail how some American firms with a history of normal business relations with the Soviets were hard hit by our negative votes. Armco, for one, was forced to give up a profitable contract to build a steel plant in the Soviet Union. IBM, for another, was forced to restrict the sale of its computers to the Soviets. These difficulties might have been eased if all of America's allies had faithfully supported the embargo to check further Soviet aggression.

A conversation about the embargo I had with Helmut Schmidt, then chancellor of West Germany, remains fresh in my memory, mainly because of the distinction I drew for his benefit on the spur of a polemical moment. The circumstances were these. Nahum Goldmann telephoned me from overseas to say that the World Jewish Congress planned a dinner in Amsterdam in honor of his eightieth birthday. He was anxious that I attend and speak at the dinner, adding that Chancellor Schmidt would also be present. I replied that I wanted very much to be with him, but I must first clear matters with President Carter, because if I went to Amsterdam, a Secret Service detail would have to be assigned to go with me. When I discussed with President Carter what was in prospect, he readily approved the trip. More than that, he suggested that at the dinner in Amsterdam I talk frankly to Chancellor Schmidt about his public criticism of the U.S. embargo on trade with Russia.

At the Goldmann dinner I sat next to the chancellor. During our chat, Schmidt stated emphatically that he was opposed on principle to economic boycotts. They were, he said, both meaningless and ineffective. When I parried this by saying that the U.S. response to the Soviet invasion of Afghanistan was not an economic boycott, he reacted as though he faced someone suffering from brain damage. "What," he asked, "do you mean by *that*?"

I said that when Soviet troops invaded Afghanistan, the possible responses by the United States ranged from bad to terrible. We could ignore what was going on while the Soviet Union pressed ahead with its expansionism. Or President Carter could place a hotline call to the Kremlin and threaten a military clash if the Soviets did not stop their thrust. Or the United States could actually wage war against the Soviet Union in order to isolate it from the rest of the world. As none of these three actions was acceptable, what was there left for the United States to do? It was to initiate not an economic but a *political* boycott, whose aim was to warn the Soviet Union that it invited a self-inflicted wound if it persisted in its armed rule of Afghanistan. I doubt if Chancellor Schmidt was impressed by my distinction between an economic and political boycott, but I felt better for having drawn it.

[III]

Among other matters that converged on my desk, I have a clear recollection of my experiences with the 1980 census. The census count by law could not start until January 1, 1980. That meant that approximately 300,000 census takers nationwide had to be hired overnight and trained for their work. This massive job was not made any easier by the predictable fact that the Department of Commerce would be sued by some cities and states on the grounds that they were the direct victims of a census undercount—or the indirect victims of an overcount which unfairly favored other cities and states.

The chain of command for the physical conduct of the census moved on a line that extended from the director of the Census Bureau, to senior civil servants and their immediate subordinates in the bureau, and so on down to the lower ranks of the civil service that comprised the regular staff of the bureau. My own involvement in the 1980 census occurred in connection with a mismatch between the costs of conducting the census and the availability of appropriated funds—a recurrent problem with the census known to both my predecessors and my successors as Secretary of Commerce.

The 1980 census was already under way when the director of the Census Bureau reached me at our office with a message of distress. The bureau, he said, was running out of funds to pay for its army of census takers. Unless more funds were made available at once, many census takers would have to be let go, and the census itself would suffer. I at once contacted Speaker of the House "Tip" O'Neill and arranged to be in his office at 10:30 the next morning. He, in turn, arranged to have present the chairmen of the committees of the House who had a say in such matters.

At the meeting, he told the chairmen, "This young man"—I was O'Neill's senior by some years—"is trying to do a good job in conducting the census. He needs money or he will have to fire people. Now you go back to your shops, go through your motions, and issue a favorable report. Then I'll get the House quickly to approve of the appropriation and will also arrange for quick action in the Senate." O'Neill then turned to me. "And Phil," he said, "be careful about the census in my own home town. I don't like the reports I've been getting. I want the count to be accurate."

My experiences with the 1980 census made me a critic of the census methods. Aside from the fact that many people are not at home when the census taker calls, untold numbers of people hide from the census takers. I would scrap the head count and would instead use proven statistical methods whose results, like expert testimony, would stand up in court.

While the U.S. census was under way, the government of the People's Republic of China was making preparations for a first census of its own,* and a delegation from Beijing came to the United States to study up-to-date American methods. When the members called at my Washington office, I urged them not to imitate the American-style head counts but to use advanced statistical techniques. The delegation was underwhelmed by my advice. When I later learned that China relied on head counts, I had fanciful visions of Chinese census takers, abacus in hand, trying to find one billion of their fellow citizens in their homes spread over 3,768,726 square miles.

As Secretary of Commerce I was often reminded that U.S. census data were used by limitless public and private sources for

---

*The first census of China's total population to be accepted by Western scholars as reliable was the one taken by the People's government between July 1953 and March 1954. Earlier estimates, by Chinese and Westerners, of the country's population ranged from 250 million to as many as 600 million. The 1953–1954 census, which excluded Formosa, placed the size at 582,602,417. In the next quarter of a century, China's population almost doubled. World Bank projections currently estimate that by the year 2050, China's population will be approximately 1.7 billion.

limitless purposes. So, in one of the "exit memoranda" I wrote with my successors in mind, I brought together all my arguments against head counts and in favor of a change in the law to permit the use of statistical methods. My advocacy altered nothing, but the problem I sketched was discovered anew by Robert E. Mosbacher, Secretary of Commerce in the Bush administration. During a luncheon he gave for some of his predecessors, he reviewed the challenges he faced as secretary and dwelt on the surprising difficulties he had encountered in preparing for the 1990 census. I sympathized with his plight, I said, and mentioned my memorandum of a decade earlier. Mosbacher indicated that he had heard about that particular memorandum, but apparently no one had thought to take it out of its resting place in departmental files.

[IV]

When I took office as Secretary of Commerce, one-sixth of the fiscal year was over, and it appeared that employment levels and inflation were bound together in an ill-fated destiny. In successive presidencies after Truman's, and especially from the 1960s, it seemed technically impossible to reduce inflation without causing a decline in economic growth and a rise in unemployment—or, conversely, to stimulate economic growth and employment without also accelerating inflation. It also seemed politically impossible for administrations to sustain anti-inflationary policies when even the slightest sign of economic downturn triggered political pressure for expansionist fiscal and monetary programs. Fear of unemployment, rather than fear of inflation, dominated economic policy-making in Republican and Democratic administrations alike.

In an economy where everything from human behavior to the worth of money was distorted by inflation, units of value which once served as a standard for decisions were set on their heads. As costs pushed up prices, companies faced increased costs in all aspects of their operations, including employee compensation. Those who operated with borrowed money had to borrow more at higher interest rates to do the same volume of business at higher prices. Those who borrowed from banks increased the money supply and thereby added to the inflationary push. When banks were "loaned up" from their own deposit sources, borrowing continued from other financial intermediaries and with a further inflationary cost-push. As the wage and price spiral continued upward, fewer goods were sold, production dropped, unemployment rose, and the worst of two conditions—inflation *and* unemployment—laid siege to individuals, families, and firms that could not escape the constraints of the marketplace.

Signs of a recession were plainly visible in January 1980, but the inflation rate continued to rise until it reached 18 percent annually, with the prime rate reaching 20 percent. Against this bleak background, President Carter on March 10 announced a new anti-inflation policy. Among other things, the president believed that a balanced budget would have a significant psychological impact on the American public and, more immediately, in financial markets—a view shared by many members on both sides of the aisle in Congress, and by many influential sources of opinion in the financial community, the academies, and the press. I naturally hoped that events would adhere to the president's line of reasoning. My doubts, however, were nursed by reflections about the inexhaustibly queer things that can go on in the world of economics.* The administration's move to bring the federal budget into balance entailed an initial $14 billion cut in the $450 billion budget for fiscal 1981, in an economy of $2 trillion. To reach the targeted cut, each department of the executive was directed to reduce its expenditures by 10 percent across the board.

I was among the first department heads in the executive to make the cuts. I was still relatively new in my job and had not helped to formulate the departmental budget under which I was operating. And any love affairs I might have with some programs, or distaste for others, had not yet had time to jell.

The credit restraints of the new anti-inflation program were based on the Credit Control Act originally passed in 1969 at the request of the Nixon administration. Under the act, the president

---

*For one example, the disastrous economic collapse of 1929–1930 began when federal income—despite two election-time tax cuts—exceeded expenditures sufficiently to reduce government debt by approximately seven billion dollars; when the consumer price level had been steadily declining; when there was virtually no unemployment though five million new workers had entered the labor force; when increased labor productivity was substantially greater than what was previously thought to be normal; and when corporate profits increased by over 75 percent while corporate taxes were low, the maximum being 13.5 percent. For another example, the sharp recession of 1937–1938, which set back the New Deal recovery program, got under way when the budget was technically in balance and when the gross national product had regained 80 percent of its value at the time of the 1929–1930 collapse.

could authorize the Federal Reserve Board to "regulate and control extensions of credit" in eleven specific areas.* Once the 1969 act was invoked by President Carter, the Federal Reserve Board moved quickly, though perhaps not enthusiastically, to outline the terms for credit control. Its choice of words, however, were so ambiguous that many honest people wondered what they could, in fact, lawfully do within the harness of credit control. Credit card usage, for example, dropped off dramatically, as did the demand for loans to buy autos, furniture, appliances, and other credit-sensitive durable goods. Some bewildered consumers stopped using any kind of credit almost as a patriotic gesture; consumer debt plunged, and installment credit sharply contracted. By the end of June 1980, the monthly volume of new credit was 28 percent below the peak in September of the preceding year; total consumer debt in the second quarter declined by almost nine billion dollars—the largest percentage and dollar drop since World War II. The credit control program which had been partially rescinded on May 22 was terminated on July 2. The recession by then was in full swing.

The credit control effort, topped by the recession, may have helped to dampen inflation psychology and reduce the annual inflation rate to around 10 or 11 percent by midsummer of 1980. But when output and demand were slowed to the point of recession, the condition triggered large countercyclical spending, large increases in transfer payments, and a large shortfall in revenue. In this way, the initial aim of a fourteen-billion-dollar reduction in the budget disappeared in a recessionary deficit of fifty billion dollars.**

*Taken in the aggregate, the powers which the act granted to the president for application by the Federal Reserve Board exceeded anything Congress had delegated to the executive even during World War II or at the peak of the postwar inflationary boom.

**I have often wondered what a government financial statement would look like if the value of all the things the government owns—including one-third of the entire land mass in the Western states—could, in fact, be assessed, give or take a few trillion dollars. A figure on the books still assigns the White House a value of $12,500—the cost of its original construction almost two centuries ago. But the actual market value of the nation's assets in land, mineral resources, ores, forests, hydroelectric power, ships, aircraft, research and development laboratories, etc., etc.—not to overlook the skills of its people—would probably blow the fuses of any computer into which the raw data were fed.

The President Carter I knew was a stranger to the political art of escape and evasion. White House policies, framed after discussions with many members of the executive and Congress, sometimes failed to work. But Carter never hid behind his advisers, as if to suggest that *they* made the wrong decisions while he was busy with other matters. He was always the captain on the bridge, always morally prepared to assume personal responsibility for the consequences of decisions made on his "watch."

His conviction that power and responsibility are joined in a president was not shaken by his—and the nation's—ordeal over the sixty-three hostages held in the U.S. embassy in Teheran by Khomeini's zealots. President Carter in person or through Secretary of State Vance explored every possible diplomatic avenue to secure the peaceful release of the hostages. Nonetheless, the president was increasingly assailed on the grounds that he was "indifferent" to their fate, "forgot" them, "did nothing" likely to secure their release, allowed America to be "jerked around" and "humiliated" by Iranian goons. Night after night on the six o'clock news, Walter Cronkite, once identified by President Lyndon Johnson as the "voice of Middle America," concluded his broadcast with a toll of a mournful bell as he counted another day of Americans held hostage.

All this was something new in the experiences of living Americans. In dinner-table conversations, in boardrooms, in lecture halls, in bars, in letters to the editor, no plan to secure the release of the hostages was too futile or absurd to be given consideration. The American air grew thick with the polemics of political cynics who, with the 1980 elections in mind, claimed that the plight of the hostages was due to President Carter's "weakness."

The stage was thus set for a pathetic event.

At around 5 a.m. on the morning of April 25, 1980, a call from a White House operator awakened me in Chicago where I was to make a speech later in the day. I was told to stand by for President Carter's linkup with cabinet officers—a conference by telephone with the president. He revealed to us that a U.S. attempt by military means to rescue the hostages held in the U.S. embassy in Teheran had failed from star-crossed mechanical causes. Eight Americans had been killed and five injured. "I want you to know," the president said simply, "that I am taking full responsibility for the failure." He then read the public statement he would issue.

I did not know at the time who among the president's intimate advisers had spoken for or against the desperate gamble—though when Secretary of State Vance later resigned, it became clear that he had been among those who opposed it. But that was for the future to show. More immediately, I was as stunned as were the other cabinet members who had no hand in planning what ended in a crash in the Iranian desert. The shock gave way to grief over the loss of young American lives, to some sense of how the president's anguish was held in check by his strict self-discipline as a commander, and to a surge of renewed admiration for the way he calmly absorbed all blame to himself and thus shielded his advisers against attack.

[V]

I have often contrasted President Carter's assumption of personal responsibility to the reaction of American business executives who refuse to assume any share of blame for the ills of American industry—for the trade deficit, for the decline in productivity, for the inability of certain American industries to compete successfully in the world's markets or even to maintain price and quality competition in America's domestic market against imported products. Some of those ills are, in fact, due to causes beyond the control of American industry. But as Secretary of Commerce I was disturbed by the gap between the huge sums granted to U.S. institutions engaged in research—$350 million in a typical year— and the extent to which industry failed to apply the results of that research. I was disturbed by a related fact—that much of the advanced technology that enabled Japanese factories to do simple things well was first developed in the United States, only to be ignored by American business executives.

The steel industry was a prime example of this. Sometime before I became Secretary of Commerce, ingenious Americans had developed a system for steel production known as "continuous casting," which accelerated the manufacturing process at lower unit cost. The system was offered to American steel companies, but none saw fit to take it—perhaps because few manufacturers are inclined to accept the costs and risks of change until forced to do so. The Japanese, on the other hand, bought into the system at once. With the competitive advantage they gained, they proceeded to clobber major American steel companies in the competition for markets. The Koreans and Brazilians in turn followed the Japanese lead, until American steel companies were drowning in a flood of foreign steel in U.S. markets.

Most American businessmen are committed—at least in theory—to the idea of a free market, with no "interference" by government. Of course, a true free market means a profit *and* loss system, and not just profits alone. When American businessmen experience losses, however, funny things are known to happen to them on the way to a free market. They often veer off on paths that lead to government doors and to the sources of help behind them.

When things continued to go from bad to worse for the American steel industry, its executives looked to practical measures and not to economic shibboleths to ease their plight. What kind of measures? I formed a consultative group chaired by David Roderick, president of U.S. Steel, with members drawn from the conference of steel producers and from the Department of Commerce. Against the background of work accomplished by this group, President Carter convened a White House conference to focus national attention on the plight of the steel industry and on proposals to improve it. The main proposal called for joint presidential-congressional action to limit for a defined period the amount of foreign steel imported into the United States. During that specified period, American steel companies would modernize their productive capacities to meet foreign competition.

The White House conference successfully drew national attention to the afflicted state of the American steel industry, but the proposal to limit foreign imports was attacked on the ground that it would create more inflation. The opposition generated by the anti-inflation camp within the administration itself scuttled the program momentarily, but the president soon asked me to reinstate the consultative group under David Roderick. This time I persuaded representatives of the steel industry to accept representatives of government and labor in the group as well, so that we might formulate a comprehensive plan to bring the American steel industry back to competitive health.

As a result of the committee's meetings, labor and management in the steel industry modified their usual demands on each other. The president endorsed and Congress approved radical committee recommendations for relief from inequitable tax burdens, encouragement of long-term investments, rebuilding of infrastructure for the steel industry, and quotas on imports of foreign steel. Braced by these means, the American steel industry made extensive capital investments which brought its facilities fully abreast of the state of the art in steel production. The industry as a whole—and not just individual companies with a special product for a special market—became competitive with foreign-produced steel.

David Roderick, in a speech before a group of Chicago businessmen in 1989, pointed me out in the audience and remarked that when I was Secretary of Commerce I had helped "save the American steel industry." I appreciated his generous choice of words. It would be closer to the truth to say, however, that I merely helped bring all parties at interest together—and kept them together—until they agreed on the means by which they could save one another.

The gap between research funding and the failure of industry to apply the results of research—as exemplified in the steel industry—were addressed in a package of remedial measures which I sought to carry forward as Secretary of Commerce (they had been prepared under the direction of my predecessor, Juanita Krebs). The steps included changes designed to improve the patent system and streamline federal patent and regulatory policy; clarifications by the Justice Department of its antitrust policy as it affected industry-sponsored joint research and development; and a new cooperative program between government and the private sector to develop and advance fundamental technologies of industrial production.

At the end of February 1981, with the president's encouragement and approval, I established within the Department of Commerce a new Office for Productivity, Technology and Innovation, headed by an assistant secretary. The office included a Center for the Utilization of Federal Technology—meaning the technology developed in a great range of agencies, many of which were part of the Department of Commerce: Bureau of Standards, Maritime Administration, National Telecommunications and Information Agency, National Oceanic and Atmospheric Administration, Minority Business Development Administration. The object of the center was actively to market federally owned technology to the private sector, to work with federal laboratories to assure the transfer across industries of technology suited to industry needs and opportunities, and to develop strategic technologies for a wide range of individual firms and industries. The watchword of the new Office of Productivity, Technology and Innovation was cooperation instead of confrontation between government and industry.

My earlier work with the Committee for Economic Development had brought me into contact with many of the key players in the American economy. I hoped that they could help serve as the connective tissue for various cooperative ventures between government and private industry. Many producers, for example, did not know how to reduce waste in their production process, or how to make use of their waste products. The Bureau of Standards worked on the problem and chose Detroit as the place for a conference to disseminate what it had learned. Other conferences were held at the Bureau of Standards' home outside Washington, D.C. One of these, which I initiated because of my background in the construction business, was addressed to the question of why it costs so much to build anything in the United States. What was wrong? What could be learned from, say, Sweden that could shorten the many different steps in construction common in the United States?

Some of my actions in these areas drew criticism. Of course, in my time as Secretary of Commerce I assumed that someone would always find fault with what I did or didn't do. Still, the exact reasons for opposition could be surprising.

A case in point stemmed from the fact that American manufacturers of women's shoes were being outbid by competition from Italian and other imports. While I was in Italy on official business, I stayed in Rome with U.S. Ambassador Richard Gardner, an old friend, who arranged for me to meet with his staff and with Italian officials. I learned in this way that in the changeable world of women's fashion, Italian manufacturers managed within a few months to adjust their production lines to new styles while American manufacturers lagged months behind. On my return to the United States, I discussed these findings with my associates in the Department of Commerce. We then arranged a round of meetings between representatives of the American shoe industry and key figures in the Commerce Department's newly created Office of Productivity, Technology and Innovation. In the upshot, industry representatives agreed to join us in creating a Cooperative Generic Technology Center—to help the American shoe industry stay competitive. Philadelphia became the site for the center.

A surprise followed. I was sharply criticized by orthodox adherents of free-market doctrine. In their view, the work of the center disrupted the economic efficiency inherent in an absolutely free market where the most fit among firms survived while the inefficient fell by the wayside. I was at a loss to understand why anyone would decry a joint government-industry attempt to train personnel to meet the challenges and develop a technology of benefit for the *whole* of an imperiled American industry.

I encountered criticism in another quarter when I publicly stressed the need to amend our antitrust laws so that firms engaged in similar lines of production could join in research and development projects from which all alike could benefit. That need was vividly underlined at the time when the American automobile industry was being beaten over the head by foreign competitors. How could the Carter administration help American firms win back their share of domestic and world markets? The question was in the air when President Carter convened a White House meeting in which the presidents of seven major American automobile producers were joined by three cabinet officers, of which I was one. The other two were Secretary of the Treasury William Miller and Secretary of Transportation Neil Goldschmidt.

The automobile executives urged the administration to reduce the high interest rates prevalent in the economy. This, they argued, would reduce the costs of financing the purchase of new cars and thereby increase consumer demand. My own view was that the manufacturers would also be well advised to consider how they could improve the quality of their cars. In the absence of such steps, a reduction in the costs of financing would enable consumers to buy more new foreign cars because of *their* quality.

At a follow-up meeting in Detroit involving the same parties, Secretary of Transportation Goldschmidt opened the discussion with a comment about the administration's desire to help the embattled automobile industry. He referred in passing to a newly enacted environmental protection law which would require changes in the emission-control mechanisms on automobiles. The moment he touched on the subject, the president of Ford Motor Company jumped to his feet. "I am," he said, "under a court order which bars my participating in any discussion or cooperation with my competitors regarding ways and means to meet the new automobile emission standards." His statement brought the meeting to an abrupt end. The seven presidents at once went their separate ways, and the three cabinet officers headed for the waiting government plane which flew us back to Washington.

I later learned that each of the seven major American automobile companies spent in the neighborhood of fifty million dollars in developing new emission-control mechanisms for their respective cars. Avoidable costs were piled on top of avoidable costs to increase the aggregate price of American cars in both domestic and world markets. I publicly urged the need to "modernize" the antitrust laws in line with the new competitive realities confronting many American industries, and permit collaboration when it was in the public interest. Congressman Peter Rodino, chairman of the House Judiciary Committee, honestly believed that my proposal, if adopted, would increase the power of giant corporations to foreclose the role of small and medium-sized firms in the American economy.

From my perspective as Secretary of Commerce, I saw that many American firms which produced goods for export virtually ignored vast markets in the developing world. For example, developing countries in 1980 as a group bought 39.4 percent of all U.S. exports, an amount greater than that purchased singly by Western Europe, Canada, or Japan. In that year it was estimated that two million U.S. jobs, or 6 percent of all U.S. manufacturing jobs, and one of every four U.S. cultivated acres depended on consumption, investment, and import demands among developing countries. If this market ceased to exist for agriculture, the result would be a 20 to 25 percent loss in U.S. gross farm income.

With all this in mind, I had my able associates in the Commerce Department work on plans to expand the marketing of American products in the world arena. This not only included more participation in trade shows but arrangements whereby "traveling salesmen" representing the U.S. would seek new markets in both the developing and developed world. A chance to put those plans into practice depended on the reelection of Jimmy Carter as president. This was not to be. What happened during the Reagan presidency to plans for expanding overseas markets could be seen in the fate of the Commerce Department's "traveling salesmen." Their number almost vanished. It was another case of political dogma triumphing over common sense.

44 □ My Other Self

"Think of it always, talk about it never." Winston Churchill's remark about an issue in Big Power diplomacy applied as well to an aspect of my work as Secretary of Commerce. I always drew a mental line between my official acts and my private concerns about matters related to Judaism and to Israel. But I never thought it necessary publicly to dwell on the existence of that line, any more than I dwelt on the care I took to avoid even the appearance of conflict between my private economic interests and the public policies I advocated or administered.

But I never hesitated openly to identify myself with the nuances of American cultural pluralism. I still smile to myself when I recall the following instance: The president of a Jewish seminary in New York telephoned me to say that the trustees of the seminary wished to award an honorary degree to President Carter. Could I encourage the president to say yes when asked? I did so. The president could not attend the ceremony but suggested that his wife Rosalynn might go to New York to accept the award in his place, and I would accompany her and say a few words.

Matters worked out that way except for an improvised detail. After the citation was read, I responded partly in broken Yiddish on behalf of the president. Bemused laughter rippled through the audience, followed by a joyous roar after I concluded my remarks. The president of the seminary laconically observed, "What a remarkable country all of us live in. First we use English when we bestow an honorary degree on the president of the United States, and the president's representative, with reciprocal courtesy, responds in Yiddish."

I savor another episode of the period related to cultural pluralism. I had been informed that Dr. Mordecai Kaplan, at the age of 103, had been placed in a nursing home in Riverview, New York. From the time I read his *Judaism as a Civilization*, I looked to him as my mentor and counted myself among his disciples. I was anxious to call on him, and so I kept an eye on my calendar to see when I was due to be in New York and could detour my schedule long enough to get to the Riverview nursing home.

The 1980 presidential campaign was by then in full swing, and my role in the contest, in common with other cabinet officers, was to speak on behalf of President Carter before targeted audiences. When I was scheduled for a speech at the Harvard Club in New York City, I routed myself, accompanied by two other disciples of Dr. Kaplan, to Riverview before the hour when I was due at the club.

He was in a wheelchair, freshly scrubbed and dressed, awaiting my visit. But because of his declining health, he lacked the strength for sustained conversation. He would have something to say, followed by a retreat into what seemed to be a catnap, and would then be alert for another brief conversation. He was alert when the time came for me to leave, and one of his disciples asked if he had a parting word to convey. He did, and the word rose from the depths of his innermost being, past the mists and infirmities of his physical condition. "I have always loved the Jewish people," he said softly but firmly, "because throughout their long history they have been tempted to be honest."

En route to the Harvard Club, it occurred to me that I had not yet ordered in my own mind what I might say to the members. All of a sudden, however, Dr. Kaplan's parting words gave me my text. Only a few Jews were in the audience at the club, but I recalled my visit with Dr. Kaplan and cited his ground for "loving the Jewish people." I then applied a paraphrase of his statement. "I have been a member of the Democratic party most of my adult life," I said, "and particularly since the days of Franklin Delano Roosevelt, because as a party it has always been tempted to be honest." I added that if Dr. Kaplan had the physical energy to do so, he might have gone on to say that no human being or institution is free of sins of omission or commission. But it was important for individuals and institutions alike to follow "the temptation to be honest" with themselves and with common humanity of which they are a part. I then made the pitch for integrity in political life.

About this time I met with Edgar Bronfman, who was serving as acting president of the World Jewish Congress in my absence. Bronfman asked if I planned to return as president of the congress in the event President Carter failed to be reelected. I countered with a question of my own. Was Bronfman prepared to serve as the duly elected president of the organization? Yes, he said, he had developed a liking for the job.

In that case, I said, all he had to do was declare his availability for the position and it most likely would be his. Despite the many demands on his time as head of Seagrams, Edgar had shown himself to be eminently qualified to lead the WJC, and he had an able backup staff headed by Israel Singer. I had already spent many years as the head of national and international voluntary Jewish organizations, and no good purpose would be served by my clinging to such positions when able younger men, such as Edgar, were ready to fill them.

The time of the plenary meeting in Amsterdam, where a new president of the WJC was to be elected, coincided with the windup of the Carter campaign for the presidency, and I could not leave my desk in Washington. In a taped message which was meant to be read at the meeting, I congratulated the organization on its achievements under Edgar Bronfman's effective leadership. I hoped the message would work to quiet the gossip within the WJC that I was eager to reclaim its leadership.

Besides the election of Edgar Bronfman—at which time I was accorded the honorific status of president emeritus—a major subject for the Amsterdam meeting concerned a project I had initiated two years earlier. In 1978 I had persuaded Baron Guy de Rothschild to chair a commission to make a comprehensive study of Israel's economy for submission to the WJC—the first such study since one done by Robert Nathan and his associates soon after Israel was reborn as a state. The commission, though financed by the WJC, was independent of it. To that end, I helped recruit commission members from the ranks of preeminent Jews in the Diaspora as well as Israel, from industry and commerce as well as from the "starred" names in university scholarship. After the Camp David accords between Israel and Egypt, I encouraged the commission members to enlarge the study so that it became a report on the "economic implications for both Israel and for world Jewry, of an Israeli-Arab peace."

The completed report was submitted to the WJC meeting in Amsterdam. On reading the text of an advance copy sent to me, I was reminded anew of Dr. Mordecai Kaplan's reason for loving the Jewish people. The text provided ample evidence that the members of the commission had, in fact, "succumbed to the temptation to be honest."

[II]

In the months following the Israeli-Egyptian peace treaty, movements toward a larger Israeli-Arab settlement within the framework of the Camp David accords were frozen in place. I met Begin
and Sadat several times in connection with my official work as
Secretary of Commerce. Conversations about specifically commercial matters almost always veered off into discussions of Israeli-
Arab problems; it was correctly assumed that I would report back
to President Carter and to the State Department the substance of
anything new that might crop up. Very little was in fact new. On
Begin's side, I repeatedly heard why he was convinced that Israel
would be in mortal danger if the status of the occupied territories
was altered in any way. On Sadat's side, I repeatedly heard why the
Israeli-Egyptian peace treaty could not lead to the usual diplomatic
and commercial exchanges among nations formally at peace with
each other. At the same time, the PLO's most vocal factions
insisted as usual that they would never accept any United Nations
resolutions as the basis for negotiations with Israel. Also as usual,
Arab polemicists in the "rejectionist states" continued their shrill
attacks on Sadat as a "traitor."

Copies of the Rothschild Commission report were mailed to all
Israeli leaders and to the Israeli press. The text was not an official
report *of* the World Jewish Congress, but it is not hard to
understand why its findings and recommendations discomfited
Prime Minister Begin and his Likud party. The reason appeared in
the first paragraph of the text, wherein the commission made it
clear that it did not accept some of the key assumptions on which
Begin and Likud justified their conduct to Israelis and Diaspora
Jews.

The first paragraph stated that the lack of progress toward peace
beyond the Israeli-Egyptian accords was not solely the fault of
Egypt or the Arab rejectionist states alone. Israel too had its share
of blame. An essential step on the road to peace depended on
Israel's willingness to agree on the autonomy of the occupied
territories "or an alternative formula which will be both consistent
with Israel's security needs and acceptable to the Arabs most
directly concerned." Other passages were equally forthright about
a range of domestic, economic, social, religious, and political
problems. One, for example, was Israel's system of proportional

representation which allowed Begin to make his minority Herut party the cornerstone of the Likud coalition of minority parties. The prophetic passage here read:

> It is clear that Israel's basic problems can effectively be dealt with only by governments capable of making politically difficult decisions. The present proportional representation system which results in coalition rather than majority governments has not been able to now produce governments with this capability. We therefore subscribe to the view expressed by many Israeli leaders in the past that this system, which has malfunctioned so persistently and with such grave consequences, should be reformed.

The report challenged the conventional view that Diaspora Jews should not publicly object to decisions of the Israeli government—a view rooted in the notion that Israel is in a "front-line" position. Arguing to the contrary, the report stressed the entwining of Diaspora Jewry with Israel's fate. Diaspora Jewry had a duty as well as a right to be open and candid in its dealing with the Israelis, many of whom were "ignorant of actual conditions among Diaspora Jews."

The report also dwelt on the implication for the Diaspora of an Israel living under stable conditions for peace. It noted that while Jewish communities within the Diaspora had their own special needs, all had heavily taxed themselves in order to send funds to Israel to help cover the costs of its security and other programs. Several million more Jews lived in the United States, for example, than lived in Israel. Yet Jewish education in the United States suffered from a lack of financial and institutional resources because a high portion of Jewish community funds went to Israel. An Israel at peace with its neighbors would enable American Jewish communities to apply a greater share of their resources to their own educational, religious, and social development.

As Secretary of Commerce, whatever I might have said publicly about the report was confined to its analysis of the economic opportunities for foreign investment in Israel. Obviously I could not comment on the political aspects of the report, much as I agreed with its conclusions. After my return to private life, I was again free publicly to amplify my uneasy conviction that Begin and his associates in Likud were gravely imperiling Israel's highest interests.

[III]

As a member of President Carter's cabinet, did I achieve all the programmatic ends I had in view? No, I did not. Time was very short. Except when I was free to use the discretionary powers a Secretary of Commerce enjoys, my successes as secretary were confined to those which Congress and the president could be persuaded to support. Some measures which I believed could materially advance American economic development were put on hold by the president. He agreed with their merits but believed they must yield pride of place to other claims. Had he been reelected, he would have brought those measures forward and thrown his authority behind them.

Had he been reelected and asked me to continue as Secretary of Commerce, would I have agreed to do so? The answer most likely is yes—though, in truth, if I ever had a compelling political aspiration it was to be returned to the United Nations as a leading U.S. representative. Even so, I would have accepted the offer of a reappointment as Secretary of Commerce because of my experiences in the post. I did not always have "nice days" as Secretary of Commerce, but I had exciting days, challenging days, wondrous days, surprising days. These I valued. I also had days which drained all of my physical and mental energy, yet left me with a sense of never having been more alive.

As for President Carter, a fateful hand was dealt him by history. He had to contend with problems of national and international life which outstripped the reach of conventional theories. He had to think anew, act anew, and get the nation to do that as well. He vivified the old truth that leadership implies followership, or, as Machiavelli put it, "Before there can be a Moses, there must first be a children of Israel who want to get out of Egypt." Yet despite the inertia that marked the response of many Americans to his call for changes in their perceptions, he in fact succeeded in setting many important things in motion—the human rights program, the program for deregulation, the start of a defense buildup, the onset of an assault on inflation, and many more innovative measures for which he has never been given his just due.

When I took my leave of him, I could only hope that in common with some of his predecessors in the White House, he would be vindicated by history. To put matters more directly, I hoped that sooner or later the sense of what former President James Madison wrote to former President Thomas Jefferson would be true of Jimmy Carter, "...that a sufficient evidence [would] find its way to another generation, to ensure, after we are gone, whatever of justice may be withheld whilst we are here." I believe the process of finally according Jimmy Carter the justice due him is gathering force at the time of this writing.

45 □ On Active Duty with the Future

I was packed and ready to return to Chicago by the time the new Reagan administration took office. Back home I had no intention of trussing myself up in a pose of dignified retirement. I was still sound of body and, I hope, of mind. Still, at the age of seventy-four, what was I to do with myself? I could review my investments and wipe away the dust that had settled over them while I was in the cabinet. What else? I received recurrent invitations to take part in promising new business ventures, but I declined them with thanks. I did not need more income, and in any case I would only give away my share of the profits from any new business venture. After weighing various alternatives, I thought I could make the best use of my time if I did three things. First, I should go through my papers and arrange them with an eye to possibly writing a memoir. Second, I should at once return to the boards of the cultural enterprises in which I was active for years past. They included the Memorial Foundation for Jewish Culture, a renewal of my work as chairman of the board of regents for the University Teaching of Jewish Civilization, and chairman of the International Friends of Beth Hatefusoth (the Nahum Goldmann Museum of the Diaspora). They also included work with civic bodies formed to support development projects in Chicago. I have already alluded to the executive committee I chaired in connection with the Dearborn Park project south of Chicago's Loop. Later, in the time of Mayor Harold Washington, I served as cochairman of two of his task forces. The first formulated proposals to maintain a healthy steel industry in the Chicago area. The second proposed means for dealing with the staggering problems of the Chicago Housing Authority and the demoralizing physical conditions of life for 150,000 Chicagoans who lived in housing projects controlled by the authority.

My third prospect loomed largest in my mind. It was to resume working for peace in the Middle East. Limitless actors and conflicts of interest are at play in the immense theater where issues of war and peace run their fateful course; the scope of what one person can do in this theater may be very small. I had no illusions on that score; still, I hoped that I might stir more people to join in a common effort to advance the cause of peace.

This accounted for my decision to accept an invitation from the Seven Springs Center, a private foundation, to join a four-member fact-finding "peace mission" to the Middle East. The other members were Gerry Greene, president of the Seven Springs Center and a retired foreign service officer; Harold Saunders, a resident fellow of the American Enterprise Institute and formerly Assistant Secretary of State for Near Eastern and South Asian Affairs; and Merle Thorpe, president of the Foundation for Middle East Peace and a public-spirited Washington lawyer.

The center's mission to the Middle East was prompted by several developments: the change of administration in the United States, a full year's lapse in Arab-Israeli peace negotiations, the possibility of a new United States peace initiative in the Middle East, the widening of the war between Iraq and Iran, and an Israeli jet attack on an Iraq reactor near Baghdad which was believed to have a capacity to produce nuclear weapons. They also included an election in Israel which saw Prime Minister Begin survive only by means of a narrow coalition he had assembled.

The purpose of our group was not to draft a detailed prescription for an Arab-Israeli settlement. That was something to be negotiated between official representatives. We aimed to conduct an independent assessment of the Middle East situation, in the hope that we might augment the existing fund of knowledge and help clarify the way ahead for official policy-makers.

In addition to Israel and Egypt, the mission was to visit Jordan and, at my express request, Syria and Saudi Arabia. I had previously visited Jordan and the West Bank but had never met face to face with leaders in Syria and in Saudi Arabia. I knew of them through newspaper reports, magazine articles, and books, but there is no substitute for firsthand contact. Because the mission planned to call on Syria's President Assad, I applied for a visa to that country only to have my application rejected. When word of this reached the Syrian ambassador to the U.S. with whom I had earlier worked in Washington, he called to convey his apologies, saying that he would personally appeal the decision. The visa was soon granted, and I later learned what lay behind the initial rejection.

It seems that an American Jewish political figure had visited Syria on an official congressional junket; was shown all he wanted to see, but at a press conference after leaving Syria he raked the Syrians fore and aft. The functionaries in President Assad's office in Damascus assumed that I might act the same if I were let into Syria, and so they decided to bar my entry. The Syrian ambassador to the U.S. made it clear to the functionaries that my public manners were different, and that to deny me a visa would be a personal insult.

[II]

The formal report of our mission, when published in 1981, became the centerpiece of a hearing in December before the U.S. House of Representatives Committee on Foreign Affairs. Here I draw on the notes and letters I wrote in the course of the mission to convey a sense of what I saw and heard.

At about the time of our arrival in the Middle East, Prince Faud of Saudi Arabia issued an "eight-point" plan for peace in the Middle East with an implied recognition of the existence of Israel as well as new terms for granting "autonomy" to Palestinians on the West Bank. In Egypt one could sense a seething discontent among people who claimed that Egypt had received nothing from the peace treaty with Israel—a conclusion which was reciprocated in Israel. Egyptian Islamic fundamentalists, bent on exploiting that discontent, whacked up bloody street riots in pursuit of their own goals. The Sadat government, in turn, had cracked down on and arrested a number of Islamic fundamentalists, but the smell of more trouble to come hung heavy in the air.

In other Arab countries the overwhelming sentiment rejected the Camp David accords. Few people could be persuaded that the accords were only part and not the whole of the peace process. No head of state, except Sadat in Egypt, was willing to provide active leadership along the lines of the accords in order to extend the peace process. Some said that the PLO alone spoke for the Palestinians and should be included in all negotiations. Others disliked the venue for the negotiations even if it were shifted from Camp David to Geneva. Those who supported the talks favored an international forum which would work to diminish the influence of what they called the "biased mediator" (the United States), the "traitor" (Sadat), and the "land-hungry zealot" (Begin). The prevalent view among the Arabs was that there was no alternative to an "independent Palestinian state, including Arab Jerusalem." They did not insist that such a state be formed at once, but its creation must be accepted as a goal, or at least not rejected *now* as a possibility.

To some Arabs, everything that had happened before, at, or after Camp David was the fault of the United States—because nothing at all could happen unless the United States willed it. Adherents to this view coupled it with a diatribe against the "Jewish lobby" which, so they insisted, "controlled the United States." At the same time, I was struck by the extent to which West Bank Arabs were cut off from any clear view of American Jewish attitudes—or from the search by some American Jews for knowledge about conditions in the Arab world. When some West Bank Arab leaders, for example, learned that I was going to visit Syria and talk with President Assad, they saluted me as a "hero." I tried to make clear that I was no such thing: I had not previously visited Syria because I most likely would not have been admitted into the country when I was president of B'nai B'rith International, or later, as president of the World Jewish Congress. This explanation did not diminish their applause for my "courage."

The "Begin legend" infected many judgments. He was viewed as both the source and the personification of all Arab-Israeli troubles. His stream of pronouncements about the historical and religious claims of Jews to Eretz Yisrael were always cited as insurmountable barriers to a peaceful solution of the Arab-Israeli conflict. The terms on which he had won reelection enabled him to govern only on the basis of a narrow coalition, but his return to office was recast by Arabs as a landslide, and as proof that few Israelis really wanted peace. No analysis of election statistics could shake adherents of this view. Even the measure of resilience which Begin had shown at Camp David was dismissed as out of character or as part of a "conspiracy" which would free him to annex the West Bank and East Jerusalem.

I shared the view of other members of our mission that facing the PLO problem really meant facing up to the two-state solution. Little was said by Arabs about "driving Israel into the sea"; but we thought it odd that the PLO still refused to play its strongest bargaining card—namely, a pledge that it would "recognize Israel." We also wondered if the Begin government or any other government in Israel would have the will to put a two-state solution to a vote of the people. In the absence of such a will, it was doubtful that a meeting between Israeli and PLO leaders, as proposed by many Arab figures we met, could serve a constructive purpose. Unless the PLO disappeared, there was little chance that a lasting and undisturbed peace in the Middle East could emerge naturally.

A positive note concluded the memorandum I wrote to myself at the end of the mission to the Middle East. I found, among other things, an increasing acceptance of the notion that Israel was not about to disappear. Arabs were not overjoyed by the achievements of the Israelis in developing remarkable strength and efficiency, but they were quite realistic about the way things were. I believed this factor could add to the possibility of attaining a livable and fair peace settlement. Even states long known to wish the demise of Israel openly affirmed that this was neither possible, nor likely, nor even desirable if the "legitimate rights of the Palestinians" were recognized as contemplated by U.N. Resolution 242. The last lines of my memorandum read:

> I came away fortified in my long-held conviction that the only settlement, if one is to come, that will be lasting, is a settlement negotiated by the states directly involved. A mediator like the U.S. or an international group can and should be helpful. But a peace imposed and enforced from outside will not last. The feelings on the issues at stake arouse too much passion and emotion on both sides to leave the resolution of the dispute to middle men or proxies. My preference would be to build on or by the side of Camp David, though this may not be possible at least as of now. Yet peace has been too long deferred to permit pride of accomplishments like Camp David to stand in the way.

The report, published by the Seven Springs Center, was widely circulated—and I was, as usual, widely attacked by some Jewish organizations because I had been a party to it. They charged that I was "playing the PLO's game" of "dividing American Jewish opinion" so that the "PLO would be free to stab Israel in the back." Still, the positive impact the report might have had was undercut by the force of events. They included the assassination of Anwar Sadat on October 6, the intensification of the conflict between Iraq and Iran, and the final stage of Israel's withdrawal from the Sinai and the eventual return to Egypt of full control of all Sinai areas in April 1982—about the same time Israeli jets bombed PLO strongholds in Lebanon. A PLO terrorist attack which wounded the Israeli ambassador to Great Britain then set in motion a chain of bloody reactions. On June 6, Israeli forces, in a coordinated land, sea, and air attack, invaded Lebanon ostensibly to destroy all PLO strongholds in a twenty-mile area along Israel's northern border. Syrian forces rushing to the aid of the PLO were engaged by the Israelis in the Bekka Valley on June 9, where the Syrians suffered such heavy losses in the air and on the ground that they quickly agreed to a truce.

The world at large, and a significant segment of Israel's own population, construed the invasion to be the first time Israel had gone to war without its security being directly threatened. Nor did the Israelis stop after they cleared PLO combat formations out of the twenty-mile zone. Defense Minister Ariel Sharon, with the approval of Prime Minister Begin, pressed the advance in Lebanon until Israeli forces encircled Beirut on June 14 and began a sustained bombing of West Beirut where most of the remaining PLO forces were holed up. The televised picture of a city under siege caused the same revulsions among viewers as did the televised pictures of conflict in Vietnam in the 1960s and early 1970s. That the destructive fire which overwhelmed parts of the city came from Israeli instead of U.S. guns did not make the picture any prettier.

This was the beginning of the end of the perception of Israel as Little David, armed only with a stout heart and a slingshot, overcoming the Goliaths in the Moslem world with their massive concentrations of weapons. Israel, which appeared to have the physical strength to act at will in Lebanon, lost its innocence in doing so.

[III]

During this period I had several meetings in Paris with Pierre

Mendès-France, the former prime minister of France, and with Dr. Nahum Goldmann. Mendès-France had seldom if ever spoken out publicly on Arab-Israeli issues, though I knew he was privately committed to the cause of Israel's security. At one of our meetings, he spoke passionately about the way Israel allowed itself to become mired in the "quagmire of Lebanon," and added, "The wisest thing I did in my political career was to get France out of Vietnam, and perhaps the worst thing I ever did was to encourage President Eisenhower to have the U.S. move into Vietnam." He implied that conquerors, good or bad, must always pay a price for their strength, and not the least of the price is that they lose their ability to measure it.

Dr. Nahum Goldmann and I lacked Mendès-France's intimate political knowledge of "the quagmire of Lebanon," but we shared his distress over the course of events in that country, and their linkage to the larger Arab-Israeli conflict. Part of the bitter irony of that conflict was that it produced successive figures who were awarded the cherished Nobel Peace Prize—Ralph Bunche, Henry Kissinger, Menachem Begin, and Anwar Sadat—and still there was no peace. There were only moments of truce, moments of an armistice, all overtaken in turn by more armed clashes with ever more powerful weapons of destruction.

Mendès-France, Goldmann, and I did not flatter ourselves into believing that we three, unaided, could reverse events. Yet we could not be silent, or indifferent, or look with unseeing eyes on the endless rounds of killing. We could at least cry out for a new heart and a new spirit, cleansed of the sins of fraud and falsehood, of arrogance, of insolence, of hypocrisy, of running to do evil. After much anguished discussion among ourselves, Mendès-France, Goldmann, and I joined in drafting a statement which became known as the Paris Declaration, and which we released to the world press on June 30, 1982. The text spoke for our fundamental convictions:

> Peace need not be made between friends but between enemies who have struggled and suffered. Our sense of Jewish history and the moral imperatives of this moment require us to insist that the time is urgent for mutual recognition between Israel and the Palestinian people. There must be a stop to the sterile debate whereby the Arab world challenges the existence of Israel and Jews challenge the political legitimacy of the Palestinian right for independence.
>
> The real issue is not whether the Palestinians are entitled to their

right, but how to bring this about while ensuring Israel's security and regional stability. Ambiguous concepts such as "autonomy" are no longer sufficient, for they too often are used to confuse rather than to clarify. Needed now is the determination to reach a political accommodation between Israeli and Palestinian nationalism.

The war in Lebanon must stop. Israel must lift the siege of Beirut in order to facilitate negotiations with the PLO, leading to a political settlement. Mutual recognition must be vigorously pursued. And there should be negotiations with the aim of achieving coexistence between the Israeli and Palestinian peoples based on self-determination.

Many reactions to the Paris Declaration were favorable, but some Jewish voluntary organizations were critical of its content or timing, or again assailed me personally in language which suggested that I was a blockhead and a knave.

I had been invited to speak before a Jewish audience in Omaha on an anniversary occasion, but after the release of the Paris Declaration the editor of the principal local Jewish newspaper insisted in his columns that the invitation be withdrawn or, failing that, that my talk be boycotted. The invitation was not withdrawn, and the place where I was to speak was packed with Omaha Jews. They were as devoted to Israel's well-being as any community of Jews anywhere in the world, but they had suffered in embarrassed silence by the course of events in Lebanon. They were ready to hear someone give voice to their own "temptation to be honest." It turned out that I spoke for *them* and not for the editor—who misread his own community. I said what I believed. Searching questions were asked. Real dangers were noted by members of the audience. But the honesty of the exchanges accounted for a standing vote of approval at the end of the meeting.

Within the Arab world, two responses to the Paris Declaration were particularly pointed. One was from Sadat's successor, Egypt's President Hosni Mubarak, who applauded the text and privately invited Mendès-France, Goldmann, and me to visit him in Cairo. The other was from Yassir Arafat, who in the course of a reported speech also welcomed the declaration and publicly invited us to meet him in Beirut. Mendès-France balked at going to Beirut for that purpose. Later, Mubarak sent another invitation addressed to me personally, because, sad to say, Mendès-France and Nahum Goldmann were no longer alive. Both died within a few weeks of each other, while the stir over the Paris Declaration was still in the air. Until his last breath, Goldmann labored in support of the proposition that the supreme goal of his life—a secure Jewish state—could be reached only if Israel and the Jewish Diaspora worked to attain a lasting friendship and cooperation with Israel's Arab neighbors. Because of the indivisible connection between what Goldmann privately believed and what he said and did publicly about Arab-Israeli relations, he became an object of bitter criticism by some Israelis who had once been his comrades-in-arms in the struggle to establish the state of Israel.

As it happened, on September 1, when I was en route to Israel for Nahum Goldmann's funeral, President Reagan unveiled his plan for Middle East peace. I recalled the birth pangs that preceded the Camp David accords and so knew that the Reagan program would not be quickly accepted. I welcomed it as a step toward the resumption of the stalled Arab-Israeli negotiating process. Former President Jimmy Carter pointedly endorsed the object of President Reagan's plan and said it "conformed to the letter and spirit of the Camp David agreement." But within a few days, the Begin cabinet rejected the Reagan proposals.

In Lebanon itself, meanwhile, after massive Israeli bombing of West Beirut, the PLO agreed to evacuate the city. Pledges were given regarding the security of the Palestinians in the refugee camps of West Beirut, and the bulk of the PLO's combat formations boarded ships that took them from Lebanon to Algiers and later to Tunisia. Tensions remained high in Lebanon throughout the early fall, though a multilateral peacekeeping force comprised of U.S. marines as well as French and Italian troops had arrived in the country ostensibly to keep the peace between the warring Lebanon factions.

Israel's Defense Minister Ariel Sharon, who had initiated and directed Israeli operations in Lebanon, pinned his hopes for an Israeli-Lebanese peace treaty on Bashir Gemayel, the head of the Israel-backed Christian Phalangists. Gemayel had become president of Lebanon chiefly through force of arms. When he was assassinated on September 14, Sharon seized on the event to order Israeli troops into West Beirut.

Two days later, the gates of hell were unhinged when Lebanese Christian forces entered two refugee camps in West Beirut and slaughtered hundreds of innocent Palestinians. The sickening pictures of victims of all ages strewn over the ground in different poses of death reached Jews in the United States (and elsewhere) when they returned home from Rosh Hashonah services. I knew I must look at the televised pictures to confirm the evil that had been done, but I wanted to close my eyes as if darkness would revert the ghastly event into something that did not happen.

What did the Israeli commanders in the field know about the onset of the slaughter? What precautionary measure could they—and should they—have taken to forestall it? These questions dominated the deeply troubled conversations among Jews wherever they met. All the pride associated with the history of Israeli military successes suddenly seemed to be tarnished. The moral authority of Israel as a "light among nations" was further compromised in the way Prime Minister Begin tried by means of a wisecrack to deflect world criticism of Israel's bystanding role in the massacre—"Goys kill goys, and Jews are blamed."

When an Israeli board of inquiry was convened, dominated by members drawn from the highly respected and independent Israeli judiciary, it was hoped that the traditional Jewish respect for a rule of law—Torah—would prevail over political attempts at obfuscation. Eventually the panel cited Defense Minister Ariel Sharon for neglect of duty during the massacre, thus forcing his resignation on February 11, 1983.

About the time the work of the board first got under way, I received a telephone message from Dr. Isam Sartawi, an American-trained Palestinian physician who had given up his medical practice to head the PLO's political office, first in Beirut and then in Paris. I knew Sartawi to be a brave and honest man who, at the risk of his life, worked tirelessly for a Middle East peace based on security for Israel, a homeland for the Palestinians, and friendly American relations with the governments and people of the area.

Sartawi said he had an important message from Yassir Arafat, but as he was barred from entering the United States because of his PLO role, he hoped I could meet him at a relative's home in Toronto. If so, we could discuss the implications of what Arafat had in mind.

I later met Sartawi in Toronto. He told me, in essence, that Arafat was prepared to go before the General Assembly of the United Nations and announce his willingness to enter into peace negotiations with Israel as a state, provided Israel in turn recognized the PLO as the representative of the Palestinian people and their aspirations. He wanted my help in drafting a statement which would make his purposes plain. I told Sartawi that I would be willing to discuss with Arafat how he could best promote his goal of mutual recognition, but I believed the statement he had in mind should be made before the U.N. Security Council, not the General Assembly. Sartawi, in welcoming my reaction, said he would transmit the substance of our conversation to Arafat, and he assured me that I would presently be contacted directly by his chief.

[IV]

Meanwhile, I had other things on my mind. I believed I owed it to the memory of Nahum Goldmann and Mendès-France, my partners in drafting the Paris Declaration, to urge Israel's leaders to complete the second part of the Camp David accords. This part called for a five-year period of "autonomy" for the West Bank and Gaza, at the end of which the issue of sovereignty would be settled by the parties at interest. I also thought it was important to accept a renewed invitation I had received from President Mubarak to visit him in Egypt.

I was due to be in Israel at the end of November and early December 1982 for meetings with the board of regents for the University Teaching of Jewish Civilization, and for the International Friends of Beth Hatefusoth. The timing was right for President Mubarak, and it was agreed that when my work in Israel was over, I would head for Egypt.

In Israel I found that most of the political leaders with whom I spoke were either defensive about their personal role in the invasion of Lebanon and its grim sequel, or complained because Diaspora Jews had not automatically rallied as before in defense of Israel's conduct. My own devotion to the well-being of Israel was as strong as ever. But I maintained that states, like individuals, can profit from their mistakes when it is friends, not enemies, who call attention to their errors. To be of maximum help to Israel, Diaspora Jews must take care to maintain their credibility among their own neighbors. They could more effectively support Israel when its cause was just, if they had not compromised their credibility beforehand by lapsing into silence when they profoundly disagreed with a major action by Israel's government. One might challenge the timing, tone and substance of the criticism voiced, but the right to question a course of action was always in order.

In Egypt, Mubarak was still haunted by the posthumous shadow cast by Sadat. He voiced his dismay over the Israeli invasion of Lebanon, its bombardment of Beirut, and the slaughter of the Palestinians in the refugee camps. These events added to the difficulties he faced in Egypt and complicated his efforts to prod the Arab world toward a settlement with Israel. He asked for my help in impressing on both Israeli and American officials the need to break the cycle of violence in Arab-Israeli relations; on my part, I expressed the hope that despite all obstacles, he would continue actively to promote a peaceful settlement of the conflict.

In his own way, Mubarak did try from time to time to promote such a settlement. The wonder is that he did this even though his proposals seemed to be rejected out of hand by the leaders of Likud, and despite the manner in which he was treated when he met in the United States with the Presidents of Major Jewish Organizations. I had seen that body grow from around sixteen to more than sixty president-members, displacing the Zionist organization as the instrument of American Jewry in matters related to Israel. But I was made uneasy by two aspects of that development. One was the tendency among some president-members to compete with one another as if to prove their superior devotion to Israel. The other was the way some chairmen of the organization viewed their place as a platform for unilateral pronouncements on American-Israeli relations. At a meeting with President Mubarak, some of the members sought to lecture him in graceless fashion. I would not have blamed Mubarak if he had walked out of the meeting in a blaze of anger. As an embarrassed witness to the event, my main reaction was to regret anew the lead I had taken three decades earlier in the creation of the Presidents of Major Jewish Organizations.

Upon my return to Chicago from Israel and Egypt in early January 1983, a letter from Arafat was waiting for me. I had been encouraged to believe that it would deal specifically with ways to promote mutual recognition between Israel and the PLO. Instead it dealt only in generalities. Arafat remarked that the "general situation in the Middle East was critical enough to warrant active concern and intervention by all forces and personalities committed to the ideal of a just and honorable peace in the region." He then went on to say:

> The American Jewish community in particular and Jewish Diaspora in general are particularly qualified to play a decisive role in such a

process. This was amply demonstrated by the universal interest generated around the Paris declaration jointly signed by you and the late Dr. Nahum Goldmann and President Mendès-France. My only regret is that Dr. Goldmann and President Mendès-France passed, lamentably, away, before I was able to meet them, as I publicly affirmed in my welcome of the Paris declaration. The death of these two great Jewish personalities, while representing a setback to the peace efforts, should stimulate us to work harder to fulfill the vision they died before materializing.

In this spirit, I would like to renew the invitation I extended to you then, in order to discuss the ways and means which may enable us to do so.

Before I could reply, there was a telephone call from Isam Sartawi in Paris. He wanted to know if I had received a letter from Arafat. Yes, I said, but the text dealt only with generalities and carefully avoided specific possibilities. Under the circumstances, I could not accept the invitation to meet with Arafat in what was now his Tunis headquarters. I reminded Isam that when we were together in Toronto, we had an important discussion about a possible historic statement which Chairman Arafat would make before the U.N. Security Council. Although the desired statement was not forthcoming, I still wished to work with Isam to see what the next step might be after he conveyed the substance of our conversation to Arafat.

In a letter I then wrote to Arafat, I explained why I could not come to see him, but I avoided slamming the door in his face. Part of my letter read:

> As I am sure Isam has informed you, I have been convinced for some time that a negotiated peace is the only way for Israel to secure its future and for the Palestinian people to achieve self-determination, possibly in association with Jordan as I know you have been discussing with King Hussein. Rather than recognition of the other being a political weapon or a card to be played at the right time in the negotiations, I have come to see recognition more as a prerequisite to any meaningful progress. I firmly believe that there is considerable understanding and sympathy for the Palestinian desire to achieve a homeland, but until the Palestinian cause is articulated in a Western idiom and in a clear manner, it will be all but impossible to achieve the kind of American, Jewish and international support that is needed and to finally end the suffering to which your people and the people of Israel have been subjected.
>
> I am sure that a conversation between us on these topics would be of

great value to me. But I am also convinced that with time so precious, for such a meeting to be most worthwhile for you, we should know what goal should be discussed and how each of us might make our contribution.

It is a great loss to me to be without the collaboration and friendship of Dr. Goldmann and President Pierre Mendès-France. They were both extraordinary people with whom I shared a great confidence in the hope for a humanity at peace.

I was soon reminded that it was one thing to exhort Israel to negotiate a settlement for peace with the Arabs. It was another thing to have an Arab with whom to negotiate. The reminder took the form of Isam Sartawi's tragic fate. Aside from his dealings with me, Sartawi had been working with Pierre Schori of the Swedish foreign office in trying to open contacts between the PLO and American Jews. To that same end, he had issued a brave statement which appeared in the *Wall Street Journal*. He said, in effect, that had he been permitted to speak at the PLO's national council meeting in Algiers, he would have called for a recognition of Israel's right to exist, support for U.N. Resolutions 242 and 338, and the elimination of the inflammatory provision of the PLO covenant which called for the destruction of Israel and of the Zionist movement.

When I read Sartawi's statement, I telephoned him in Paris from my Chicago office, and my first words to him were: "Isam, I have called to find out if you were still alive." I complimented him on his courage. Soon after, in April 1983, Sartawi was murdered by Palestinian extremists while attending a Socialist International meeting in Albufeira, Portugal. According to Pierre Schori, he had been gunned down for trying to open contacts with Jews at a time when official PLO policy still called for the destruction of Israel.

[V]

In the years that followed, I remained deeply committed to the search for peace between Arabs and Israelis. This entailed many trips to Israel, speeches in the United States, meetings with Palestinian Arabs when they visited Chicago, appearances before American Jewish organizations, and constant contact with Israeli figures such as Abba Eban and a group of retired Israeli generals who believed it was self-destructive for the Israeli government to try to hang on to the occupied territories. I was also in fairly close touch with the U.S. State Department and aware of the brave attempts by my friend Secretary of State George Schultz to safeguard the security of Israel and yet try to resolve the Arab-Israeli conflict. Israel had no wiser or more steadfast friend in the world of diplomacy than Secretary Schultz. I tried to the limit of my ability to see that he was both understood and supported by the leadership of American Jewish organizations.

As my eightieth birthday drew near, I was honored in celebratory dinners arranged by organizations in which I had been a member in years past—everything from the B'nai B'rith to the Committee on Economic Development. But the only celebration which I permitted to be used for the usual fund-raising purposes was emblematic of my concern for the survival and growth of Jewish culture. It was a celebration in Chicago, with several thousand "close friends" in attendance, which raised funds for the Weizmann Institute in Israel. Not the least source of pleasure I found in the event was that my lifelong friends from AZA days in Kansas City—Abe Margolin, William Horowitz, and Lew Sutin—were on hand.

A point was reached where the health of Ethel, my devoted helpmate for more than fifty-eight years of married life, demanded a reduction in my travel. I relinquished my formal leadership of the Israeli-based cultural organizations and the presidency of the Memorial Foundation, where I was succeeded by Lord Immanuel Jakobovits, chief rabbi of Great Britain and a noted scholar.

I am not decidedly emotional, at least not in judging myself. Yet as I bring this memoir to a close, I seem to be enveloped in an elegiac mood. The more so when I ask myself what it was that motivated me from boyhood onward to participate in so many different commitments on so many different fronts over so many years.

I think of my mother and father—of my constant desire to please them by fulfilling their ambitions for me. I think of the members of my immediate family—my wife and children who, along with many friends, stimulated my attempts to venture what I have reported in this memoir. I also think of the people I never personally knew by name, but whom I had a sense of representing in some degree—when I tried to speak the common meaning of their common voice.

It would be a false "humbleness" if I said I did not enjoy the admiration of others. But the pleasure I find in this pales in comparison with the excitement I have known in the thick of battles which were, in my view, worth fighting. I know that one man supported by his family and friends is but a slender reed against the challenges that face humankind; yet a cluster of such slender reeds, bound together, may form a bridge over which people can move from that which "is" to that which "ought to be."

In any case, I am grateful for the opportunities to have served others. It is, in a fundamental sense, a form of self-service. Ben Sira, in his *Book of Wisdom*, wrote: "Let not thy hand be stretched out to take and closed in time of giving." To this I would add a truth about self-service: that we rise by raising others, that he who bends over to aid the fallen, stands erect; that the help due others entails—in addition to material things—a smile, a word of encouragement, a sympathetic ear.

I remind myself that every man has his unique being as a gift from God, and it is his responsibility to realize it in its wholeness. "In the world to come," so runs a celebrated saying of the Hasidic Rabbi Zusya, they will not ask me, 'Why were you not Moses?' They will ask me, 'Why were you not Zusya?'" If I were engaged as a lawyer arguing my own case, I would submit that I tried to realize, at least in the public realm, the "wholeness" of whatever was in my being as a Jew and as an American.

Index

anti-Semitism, 44–45; genesis of Aleph Zadik Aleph, 46–49; first AZA convention, 50–51; at Kansas University, 51–53, elected Grand Aleph Godol, 53–55; at Creighton University, 57–58; relationship with Dean TePoel at law school, 58–61; start in the law, 63–65; marriage to Ethel Riekes, 66–67.

Early civic activities: drawn into Omaha reform movement, 69–71; and public housing, 72–77; appointed special assistant to U.S. attorney general, 77–78; becomes president of Omaha lodge, B'nai B'rith, 79; and rise of Nazism in Germany, 80–85; impact of Kaplan's *Judaism as a Civilization*, 87–88; deepening involvement in public housing, 87–94; appraisal of New Deal, 95–96.

Early years in Washington (1940–1946): housing for defense, 98–101; moves to Washington with family, 102; works with Palmer, 103–105; Pearl Harbor attack, 105; Ethel's miscarriage, 106; works with Blandford, 107–111; search for Jewish unity during war years, 112–116; appointed commissioner of Federal Public Housing Authority and administrator of U.S. Housing Authority, 117–126; asked by Truman to stay on, 128–129; conversion of wartime housing for returning veterans, 19–20; proposed "GI town," 23–25.

Work as a developer: forms American Community Builders, 136; construction of Park Forest, 138–145; provisions for schooling, 145–146; provisions for religious worship, 147–148; sale of water system, 148; industrial development of Park Forest, 167; association with Marshall Field's, 168; planning and building of Ashdod (Israel), 186–189, 216–219; Old Orchard Shopping Center, 188–191; Oak Brook Shopping Center, 219–221, 233–234; forms KLC, 276–277; forms Urban Investment and Development Company, 280–284; merger with Aetna Life and Casualty Company, 307–309; building of Water Tower Place, 309–314.

President of International Order of B'nai B'rith: election as president, 163; creation of Conference of Presidents, 164–165; visits to lodges, 166–170; response to school desegregation, 170–173; and security of Israel, 175–182; meeting with Adenauer, 182–184; first visit to Israel, 184–189; secures freedom for Moroccan Jews, 196–201; trip to Latin America, 201–202; consequences of Suez war,